The Neuropsychology of High-level Vision

Collected Tutorial Essays

Carnegie Mellon Symposia on Cognition

Anderson: Cognitive Skills and Their Acquisition

Carroll/Payne: Cognition and Social Behavior

Clark/Fiske: Affect and Cognition

Cole: Perception and Production of Fluent Speech

Farah/Ratcliff: The Neuropsychology of High-Level Vision: Collected Tutorial Essays

Granrud: Visual Perception and Cognition in Infancy

Gregg: Knowledge and Cognition

Just/Carpenter: Cognitive Processes in Comprehension

Klahr: Cognition and Instruction

Klahr/Kotovsky: Complex Information Processing: The Impact of Herbert A. Simon

Lau/Sears: Political Cognition

MacWhinney: Mechanisms of Language Acquistion

Siegler: Children's Thinking: What Develops?

Sophian: Origins of Cognitive Skills

VanLehn: Architectures for Intelligence

THE NEUROPSYCHOLOGY OF HIGH-LEVEL VISION

Collected Tutorial Essays

Edited by

Martha J. Farah
University of Pennsylvania

Graham Ratcliff
Harmarville Rehabilitation Center, Pittsburgh

LEA LAWRENCE ERLBAUM ASSOCIATES, PUBLISHERS
1994 Hillsdale, New Jersey   Hove, UK

Lawrence Erlbaum Associates, Inc. Publishers
365 Broadway
Hillsdale, New Jersey 07642

Library of Congress Cataloging-in-Publication Data

The Neuropsychology of high-level vision : collected tutorial essays /
    edited by Martha J. Farah, Graham Ratcliff.
        p.   cm. — (Carnegie Mellon symposia on cognition)
    Includes bibliographical references and index.
    ISBN 0-8058-0910-4 (cloth : acid-free paper). — ISBN
0-8058-0911-2 (paper : acid-free paper)
    1. Visual perception—Congresses. 2. Cognition—Congresses.
3. Visual agnosia—Congresses. I. Farah, Martha J. II. Ratcliff,
Graham. III. Series.
QP441.N46 1994
152.14—dc20   93-50127
                                                       CIP

Printed in the United States of America

10 9 8 7 6 5 4 3 2 1

Contents

Preface   vii

PART I.   Object Representation and Recognition

1. **Cortical Visual Areas and the Neurobiology of Higher
   Visual Processes**   3
   Alan Cowey

2. **Issues of Representation in Object Vision**   33
   *D. I. Perrett, M.W, Oram, J. K. Hietanen, and
   P. J. Benson*

3. **Intermediate Visual Processing and Visual Agnosia**   63
   *Glyn W. Humphreys, M. Jane Riddoch, Nick Donnelly,
   Tom Freeman, Muriel Boucart, and
   Hermann M. Muller*

4. **Category Specificity in Visual Recognition**   103
   Freda Newcombe, Ziyah Mehta, and Edward H.F. de Haan

5. **Specialization within Visual Object Recognition:
   Clues from Prosopagnosia and Alexia**   133
   Martha J. Farah

PART II.   Visual Word Recognition

6. **Functional Mechanisms in Pure Alexia: Evidence from
    Letter Processing**   149
    Martin Arguin and Daniel N. Bub

7. **Neglect Dyslexia: Attention and Word Recognition**   173
    Marlene Behrmann

**PART III.   Top-Down Processes in Vision: Attention
              and Imagery**

8. **Visual Attention**   217
    *Michael I. Posner, Peter G. Grossenbacher, and
    Paul E. Compton*

9. **Dissociating Components of Visual Attention:
    A Neurodevelopmental Approach**   241
    Mark H. Johnson

10. **Visual Mental Images in the Brain: Current Issues**   269
    Stephen M. Kosslyn and Lisa M. Shin

PART IV.   High-level Vision With and Without Awareness

11. **Mechanisms of Implicit Reading in Alexia**   299
    H. Branch Coslett and Eleanor M. Saffran

12. **Covert Recognition**   331
    Andrew W. Young

13. **Implicit Perception in Visual Neglect: Implications for
    Theories of Attention**   359
    Marcie A. Wallace

Author Index   371
Subject Index

Preface

Many book prefaces begin with the story of how two colleagues were talking and decided that they would write a book together. In this case, such a discussion also took place. The time had come, we agreed, for a comprehensive, theoretically-oriented treatment of the neuropsychology of vision and visual cognition. We would write it!

Some days later, and in a more sober state, we reconsidered. To cover the range of topics that belonged in such a volume would be a stretch, even for the two of us writing together, and each of us was already committed to other writing projects. With some sadness, we abandoned the project.

Around the same time, the Carnegie Mellon Psychology Department made its annual call for proposals for the Carnegie Symposium on Cognition. Carnegie Symposia are small meetings on some aspect of cognition, in which invited speakers gather for a few days of presentations and discussion with CMU students and faculty. Each speaker also writes a book chapter, and Lawrence Erlbaum Associates publishes the book. This seemed an ideal way to create the book we had envisioned. We could have leading researchers from each of the different subtopics of visual neuropsychology contribute chapters on their specialty.

The symposium itself took place in May 1991, and was a great success, thanks to many individuals and organizations who helped in various ways. The speakers themselves were, of course, the principle contributors to the scientific life of the meeting. They included the authors of the chapters in this volume, as well as other distinguished scientists who presented commentaries at the meeting: Susan Carey, Patricia Carpenter, Jim Hoffman, Marcel Just, Jay McClelland, and Tim Shallice. We were fortunate to have Betty Boal of CMU providing administrative support for the meeting, with help from numerous other CMU staff and students, and Susan Chase and Laurie Ford from the Harmarville Rehabilitation Center. Financial support for the meeting was generously provided by the Harmarville Rehabilitation Center, the Office of Naval Research, and the American Psychological Association.

In planning this book, we tried to meet the goals of the book we had contemplated writing ourselves. Specifically, we wanted to provide a balanced and theory-oriented review of the state of the art in the neuropsychology of high-level vision. We were particularly concerned with avoiding two common failings of edited books—a lack of coherence among chapters, and a tendency for authors to focus on narrow projects. We therefore adopted a more directive, some might say bossy, approach to editing this book than is normally taken. We assigned topics to authors, as opposed to inviting them to write on anything relevant to the neuropsychology of high-level vision. We also asked each author to incorporate into their chapter a "tutorial overview" of their assigned topic.

As a result of the authors' very gracious cooperation with this plan, and Judi Amsel's knowledgeable editorial support, we believe the book provides broad and balanced coverage of current knowledge in the neuropsychology of high-level vision. Most chapters combine a general overview of the chapter topic with a set of recent studies exemplifying state-of-the-art research on the topic. Some chapters are exclusively tutorial overviews. We have certainly learned from the chapters presented here. We hope that others familiar with this area will enjoy the combination of up-to-date review with new findings and ideas, and that readers from other areas of vision, cognitive psychology, and neuroscience will find the book a helpful introduction to visual neuropsychology.

Martha J. Farah
Graham Ratcliff

I OBJECT REPRESENTATION AND RECOGNITION

1 Cortical Visual Areas and the Neurobiology of Higher Visual Processes

Alan Cowey
University of Oxford

"But the Emperor has nothing on at all." In the crowd assembled to admire the Emperor's splendid but invisible new clothes, the little child who uttered Hans Christian Andersen's immortal words could do so precisely because he was a child, an innocent unrestrained by an adult's reluctance to offend. For a few pages let us look childlike at some common beliefs about the neural basis of higher level vision and ask whether they are all built on granite or some are on shifting sands. The issue is important because to use an equally memorable tautology, "If we are not right, we are wrong." I think we shall find that our ideas are not about to collapse but that some rebuilding and shoring-up are needed.

WHAT IS HIGHER-LEVEL VISION?

A higher level implies a lower level. What is the measure of level, the cognitive altimeter? Those who teach vision to students soon learn that higher level refers to the bits of visual perception that are complicated, in some sense more interesting, and poorly understood. Faces, objects, words, and consciousness are high level; edges, acuity, flow fields, detection thresholds, and visual reflexes are low level. Is it ever possible truly to understand higher levels before understanding the lower levels on which they depend? Those who take the existence of different levels of explanation for granted may find this a curious question but its self-evidence is not ubiquitous. Thirty years ago, in an invited lecture in Cambridge, England, David Hubel described his experiments with Torsten Wiesel on the receptive field properties of visual cortical neurons. Two Cambridge physiologists were overheard to comment on the futility of studying the visual cortex before we had understood the retina. We still do not fully understand the retina, nor how simple and complex cortical cells acquire their properties, but the leap from lower to higher was surely worthwhile. As T. H. Huxley said, "It's only by going beyond the truth that one gets anywhere near the truth." Let there be no apology for studying higher level vision before the eye surrenders its secrets.

CORTICAL VISUAL AREAS IN PRIMATES

The representation of the central few degrees of the retina on to the lateral surface of the striate cortex, Area 17, of monkeys was first demonstrated by Talbot and Marshall in 1941. It took another 20 years before Daniel and Whitteridge (1961) plotted the representation of the entire retina on to striate cortex. Striate cortex was not referred to then as primary visual cortex or by its handy modern label V1 because no other visual areas were then charted in monkeys. It was another 3 years before V2 and its topography were described (Cowey, 1964), and the end of that decade before V3, V4, and what is now known as MT or V5 (depending on which side of the Atlantic one prefers) were first described. By the end of the 1970s there were about a dozen well-established visual areas in the macaque monkey's brain and at that delicious but brief period, which lasted perhaps 5 years, it seemed possible to relate each secondary or tertiary area to predominantly one aspect of visual information processing, and to selective disturbances of vision that sometimes occur following brain damage in neurological patients (Cowey, 1979, 1981, 1985).

As occasionally happens, the discovery of yet more visual areas has, as Chesterton's Father Brown said of clues to crime, thrown darkness rather than light on the problem. Figure 1.1 shows a lateral view of the right cerebral hemisphere of a macaque monkey with several of the sulci opened out to reveal their depths. The instant impression is that it resembles a relief map of complicated and mountainous terrain. Visual areas, in most of which the retina is topographically represented to greater or lesser extent, abound and the pattern continues on the medial and ventral surfaces. Figure 1.2 shows the increasingly popular box and lines version of the same thing (Goldberg & Colby, 1989), which yearly grows more like the subway map of a major city without offering the same help in finding our way about. Indeed, it is already out of date because about 30 visual areas have now been identified in both Old- and New-World monkeys (Felleman & van Essen, 1991). Who would be bold enough to deny that our brains are not even more complex?

What can be made of this multiplicity of visual areas in relation to higher order visual processing? There is evidence from anatomical studies, from neurophysiological properties of neurons in these areas, from the effects of focal ablation or damage in monkeys and neurological patients, and more recently from neuroimaging.

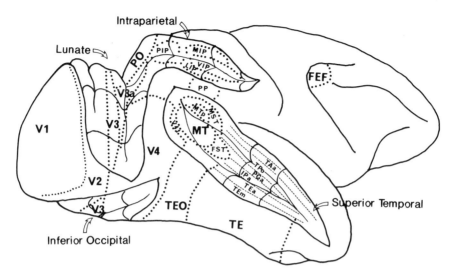

FIG. 1.1. Surrealistic view of the lateral surface of the right cerebral hemisphere of a macaque monkey. The lunate, intraparietal, inferior occipital and superior temporal sulci have been opened to reveal their interior. Various visual areas are outlined. The difference in size of lettering has no significance and was done to minimize clutter. Further areas are present medially and ventrally. It is important to remember that the size and position of areas are approximate, and almost certainly vary among different brains.

Figures 1.1 and 1.2, which portray only cortical visual areas, conceal an uncomfortable fact: There are many "parallel" pathways from the eye into the brain. Relative to the geniculo-striate pathway we know little about their properties in primates and the contribution they may make to vision. We do not even know which of the well-known classes of retinal ganglion cells (Pα, Pβ, and Pγ) provide the innervation for most of them. Although their importance to what are sometimes referred to as reflexive and purely subcortical visual functions such as circadian and other rhythms, the pupillary reflex, and postural adjustments to optic flow fields (see Simpson, 1984, for review) is undoubted, anatomical studies show that they could influence cortical visual areas. For instance, the retino-recipient region of the inferior pulvinar projects to extrastriate visual areas. The ventral lateral geniculate nucleus has projections to dLGN, as does the superior colliculus. Some of these pathways could well be involved in the phenomenon of blindsight (see later discussion).

Figure 1.3 is also a reminder that the overwhelming majority of optic axons terminate in the dLGN and that there are two metaphorically parallel pathways, whose contrasting contribution to vision has been intensively studied in the last decade. The retinal Pα cells innervate the two magnocellular layers of the dLGN,

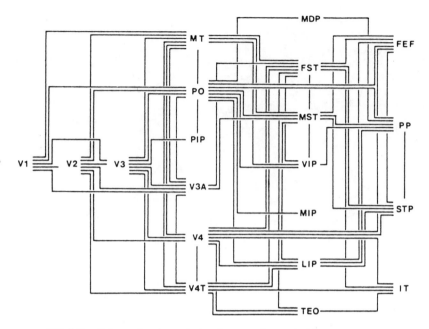

FIG. 1.2. Schematic view of visual areas shown in Fig. 1.1, and arranged in hierarchical order from left to right. Each of the lines represents both a forward and a back projection. From Goldberg and Colby, 1989. Copyright 1989. Reprinted by permission.

whose projection neurons provide the M pathway to predominantly layer 4C of Area V1. The Pβ cells innervate the parvocellular dLGN, whose projection neurons form the P pathway innervating predominantly layer 4CB of V1.[1] From here the segregation is continued (although imperfectly) with the M pathway continuing to layer 4B, and from there both directly and sequentially to the thick cytochrome oxidase stripes of V2, to V3, and to Area MT. The P pathway bifurcates to innervate the cytochrome oxidase (CO) blobs of V1, which provide the major input to the thin CO stripes of V2, and the interblobs of V1, which innervate the pale CO stripes of V2. In a manner not yet understood, both P compartments of V2 project to V4 and thence to Area TE.

---

[1]The decision to refer to these two pathways as P and M was not felicitous. Physiologically the chief (perhaps only) input to the magnocellular and parvocellular layers is from primate α and β cells, whose morphological counterparts are Polyak's *P*arasol and *M*idget ganglion cells. This means that *m*idgets innervate the P pathway and *p*arasols innervate the M pathway, a discordance that would be difficult to surpass. Worse still, there is a long and distinguished tradition of using the abbreviation P to refer to all projection neurons in dLGN, whether from parvo- or magnocellular layers. Unfortunately it is probably too late to eradicate this unfortunate solecism.

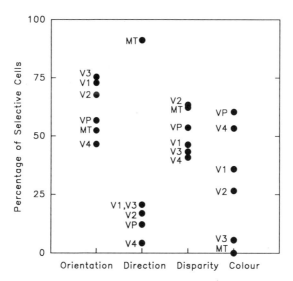

FIG. 1.3. The percentage of cells in six different visual areas that are tuned to orientation, direction, disparity, and color. Each point is the mean of from 1 to 10 different investigations and the substantial variation in estimates among different studies is not shown. The major, and perhaps only, impressive difference is that neurons in Area MT are highly selective for direction of motion and unselective for colour whereas the opposite pattern occurs for V4. The points were calculated from the data presented by Felleman and Van Essen, 1987.

It might be thought that the clear anatomical segregation of the P and M pathways should be reflected in their physiological properties and role in behavior. For example, Pα cells and neurons in the M channel have broadband spectral responses, high contrast gain, are relatively transient, are more likely to be nonlinear, and respond well to high temporal modulation. They seem well equipped to detect achromatic contrast and moving or brief or flickering stimuli. The P channel seems better equipped to deal with color contrast and color change. Some of these predictions about P and M pathways, principally their role in color and depth, and discrimination of flicker and movement have been amply confirmed by ingenious experiments in which one pathway has been selectively damaged at the level of the dLGN (for reviews, see Merigan & Maunsell, 1990; Schiller, Logothetis, & Charles, 1990). However, as soon as these two major pathways are damaged at an early extrastriate cortical level—for example, Area V4 versus Area MT, the contrasting deficits are much less clear. For example, removing all or part of V4 has relatively slight effect on wavelength discrimination in the corresponding part of the visual field (Heywood & Cowey, 1987, 1992; Schiller & Logothetis, 1990). Nor are other important distinctions between the P and M channels uncontested, even at the level of the dLGN, notably those involving acuity and adaptation level. Although the P channel is often said to respond to higher spatial frequencies than does the M channel and the discrimination of fine detail is imparied by parvocellular lesions (Schiller et al., 1990), there is evidence from single-cell recordings that resolution in the two channels may not be significantly different (Crook, Lange-Malecki, Lee, & Valberg, 1988). With respect to adaptation level, it has been argued that at scotopic levels only the M channel is active (Purpura, Kaplan, & Shapley, 1988), yet even earlier it was shown that some parvocellular cells changed their characteristic photopic color-opponent organization to a rod-based scotopic sensitivity with dark adaptation (Wiesel & Hubel, 1966), implying that they are not night-blind. Lastly, even the anatomical and physiological apartheid of the two channels has been challenged (Martin, 1992), although this may not be as damaging as some believe because interactions between the two channels are almost a sine qua non of selectively attending to one at the expense of the other or conjoining their separate signals in the creation of percepts.

For once, the clearest evidence of a reasonably sharp distinction between P and M channels comes from psychophysical examination of patients with cerebral achromatopsia, where much if not all of the disorder can be interpreted in terms of selective destruction of a major extrastriate part of the P channel (Heywood, Cowey, & Newcombe, 1991). Cerebral achromatopsia is a rare disorder caused by cortical damage to the lingual and fusiform gyri on the ventro-medial surface of the occipito-temporal region (see Damasio, Yamada, Damasio, Corbett, & McKee, 1980; Zeki, 1990 for reviews). It is usually but not invariably conjoined with prosopagnosia. The patient describes the visual world as gray where it used to be colored and is unable to sort insoluminant colors (the Farnsworth–Munsell 100-hue test) into their proper spectral order, arranging them instead at random. Yet the patient may be able to tell whether two insoluminant and contiguous hues are identical or different, even with small differences in hue (Heywood et al., 1991). How is this accomplished? Many neurons in the magnocellular dLGN and its Pα cell retinal input, and in its cortical representation, have no null point at which the chromatic border between isoluminant colors becomes undetectable (Derrington, Krauskopf, & Lennie, 1984; Hubel & Livingstone, 1990; Lee, Martin, & Valburg, 1989; Saito, Tanaka, Isono, Yasuda, & Mikami, 1989). These neurons are excellently equipped to signal borders, but cannot indicate whether they are chromatic or luminance borders. The achromatopsic patient may therefore use chromatic differences to detect borders and to perceive their orientation but has no information about the sign of the color. This interpretation of the deficit as a selective lesion in the extrastriate representation is consistent with a conspicuous reduction in contrast sensitivity at high spatial frequencies. However, the increment threshold spectral sensitivity curve has the normal form, indicative of color-opponent (P channel) activity, and cerebral achromatopsia may therefore be the result of destroying one arm of the cortical outputs of the P channel and implying that others, although still intact, make no contribution to the conscious appreciation of color. In recent experiments Heywood and I have found compelling evidence for this view. A high resolution color monitor was filled with an array of 38×38 small gray squares of different and consistently varying intensity. When a group of the squares, forming a cross, had either red or green light added while keeping mean luminance the same as the grays, the subject rapidly detected the position and shape of the hidden chromatic target. But no color was reported and red and green figures looked identical.

If part of the P channel can be selectively disrupted by a cortical lesion, what of the M channel? Although still incompletely described, there are patients whose visual impairment is the inverse of achromatopsia (Milner & Heywood, 1989; Rovamo, Hyvarinen, & Hari, 1982). For example, patient DF could arrange Munsell hues with only slight increase in errors whereas her error scores with gray stimuli were grossly abnormal. Unfortunately the locus of the damage in such patients is unknown.

If the roles of the P and M channels are still imperfectly understood, our ignorance of the function of their many cortical way stations is, by comparison, deep. Perhaps this should not surprise us because it is easier to demonstrate an area than to elucidate its role in vision. Nonetheless, in recent years it had been argued by several authors, including me, that the receptive field properties of cells in different visual areas differ substantially and in a manner that conveniently signposts their role in behavior and reinforces our views about the modular arrangement of the human brain and the probable cause of selective visual disorders such as achromatopsia, prosopagnosia, object agnosia, visual neglect, and impaired perception of movement and depth and position. This attractive but simple-minded view is increasingly difficult to sustain. For example, although there is evidence that the proportion of cells tuned to a particular category of stimulus was highest for disparity in V2, for movement and directional sensitivity in Area MT, for wavelength and color in V4, and for orientation in V2 and V3 (e.g., Cowey, 1985; Zeki, 1978), the conspicuous differences described in earlier reports have not stood the test of time. Figure 1.3, based on the survey by Felleman and Van Essen (1987), shows that the only striking and consistent difference among these visual areas is that in Area MT directional sensitivity is high whereas color sensitivity is low. What it does not show is the likely explanation for earlier mistakes, namely the huge variance in the results of different investigators, which in turn almost certainly reflects the absence of uniform criteria for classifying receptive fields and the presence of contrasting physiologically and neurochemically defined subcompartments within some visual areas, for example, the thick, thin and pale cytochrome oxidase stripes in V2.

There is a further, and more interesting explanation for what is sometimes seen as the disappointing similarity between the receptive field properties of cortical visual areas. Stimuli such as bars, spots, and pure colors may be too simple to uncover differences among areas because they are all components of

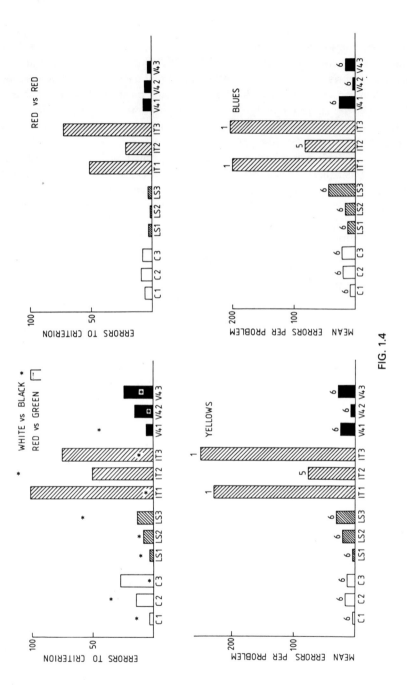

FIG. 1.4

more complex and more appropriate stimuli. For example, it is possible to find cells tuned to wavelength in V1, V2, V3, VP, V4, Area TEO, Area TE, and in the rostral superior temporal sulcus. If one asks instead whether there are more complex stimuli to which the cells in a particular visual area may be tuned, the differences between some areas are more impressive. For example, many cells in V2 respond to cognitive or illusory contours that are not perceived by cells in V1 (von der Heydt & Peterhans, 1989); cells in V4 respond to color as opposed to wavelength (i.e., they have properties that equip them to mediate color constancy; Zeki, 1983b); only in Area MT are cells known to respond to the global motion of a pattern rather than to the direction of motion of its component elements (Movshon, Adelson, Gizzi, & Newsome, 1985), or to the relative motion of a stimulus and its background (Allman, Miezin, & McGuinness, 1985); only in parietal Area PO is the fovea less well represented than the peripheral retina to the extent that magnification factor actually falls with retinal eccentricity (Gattass, Sousa, & Covey, 1985). Finally, the entire temporal lobe from the superior temporal sulcus dorsally to the occipito-temporal sulcus ventrally (see Fig. 1.1) is studded with as-yet poorly mapped subregions in which cells are predominantly tuned to complex biological stimuli such as faces and paws, or to aspects of them such as identity, expression, gaze and posture, the commonest feature varying according to the subarea (Desimone, Albright, Gross & Bruce, 1984; Desimone & Ungerleider, 1980; Gross, 1992 for review).

FIG. 1.4.   Top left shows the number of errors made by four groups of monkeys to reach a criterion of 90% correct on a discrimination of black versus white (asterisks) followed by red versus green Munsell colours that are equiluminant for the average young human observer. There were no statistically significant differences among the groups for black vesus white whereas the three monkeys with inferotemporal lesions were impaired at the color discrimination. This impairment was confirmed with other colors, as shown in the remaining histograms. In top right the animals had to discriminate between two different and isoluminant Munsell reds. In bottom left and right the animals were presented with six different color discriminations of increasing difficulty, in the yellow and then the blue range. If an animal failed to solve a problem, it was not presented with the next and even more difficult problem. The numbers above each bar indicate how many of the discriminations the animal solved and the bar indicates the mean number of errors for each problem that was attempted. Note that two of the three animals with inferotemporal lesions solved only the easiest discrimination in the yellow and in the blue ranges (which means that only two problems were attempted) and that all three animals were impaired. Note also that the three animals with V4 lesions were not impaired. The figures are drawn from data presented in tabular form by Heywood et al., 1988. Abbreviations: C, unoperated control; LS, lateral striate; IT, inferotemporal; V4, visual area V4.

As cells with such properties have not been described in earlier visual areas or in any point of the M-dominated dorsal pathway through the parietal lobes it is reasonable to say that the visual areas of the rostral temporal lobe are specialized, in a manner still poorly understood, for the perception of other animals or parts of animals, and their actions.

Nor are such cells restricted to primates, for very similar results have been reported in sheep (Kendrick & Baldwin, 1989). Comparable experiments to investigate whether there are cells that respond selectively to other classes of visual stimuli have not been carried out, or not nearly as extensively, but the possible relevance of what has already been demonstrated, to varieties of visual agnosia, is obvious.

GRANDMOTHER CELLS

The kind of neuron just described is sometimes referred to as a *grandmother cell* (although this is a corruption of the original term *mother cell*) because it may underlie the perception of a particular object, such as the owner's grandmother,· no matter what the viewing conditions, that is, size, orientation, colouring, expression, and so forth. Conceived of in this way the grandmother cell occupies the pinnacle of a particular processing hierarchy and underlies the object-centered representation of some object. The destruction of an area in which grandmother or mother cells for a particular class of stimulus, such as faces, were concentrated could then lead to and explain higher level visual disorders such as prosopagnosia. Although the idea, as opposed to the term, of grand-mother cells is often attributed to Lettvin, it was proposed even earlier by Konorski (Gnostic units) and by Sherrington (pontifical cells) and its evolution can be traced to the 19th-century doctrine of specific nerve energies (see Gross, 1992, for excellent brief account). In recent years the term has been increasingly used perjoratively, to pour scorn on an extreme and improbable example of hierarchical processing and as a straw man easily put to the torch. In truth it is difficult to find anyone who ever advocated the idea that only one cell underlay a particular percept and that any particular cell was involved in only one percept (Konorski may have been an exception), and the idea of hierarchical processing is not incompatible with the more fashionable neural nets and distributed process-ing. The well-known fact that grandmother cells are too broadly tuned to be Gnostic units is precisely what is needed for ensemble coding, where each cell is involved in many percepts. Grandmother cells are thus a compromise between coding by means of Gnostic units (which provide unambiguous signals but are poorly equipped to provide subtle changes in learning and memory and that would need to be present in impossibly high numbers to mediate all our percepts) and coding in which each cell is even more broadly tuned, which is ideal for minimizing numbers and representing changes associated with learning and memory but is prone to interference between stored representations. But as long as networks for different classes of stimuli, such as faces or colors, are regionally segregated, distributed coding is no better or worse than clustering of grandmother cells at explaining certain visual disorders caused by local brain damage. We might also note that the idea of ensemble coding is not new (Gross, 1992). In fact it is even older than Sherrington's pontifical cell. Examples are the Young–Helmholtz theory of color vision whereby the relative activity of large numbers of only three basic types of broadly tuned retinal receptors was used to explain how we could discriminate thousands of hues, and the place theory of the perception of pitch. What is new is a consideration of the minimum number of cortical cells in a neural network that would be required to provide an unambiguous representation of a particular stimulus such a face. If the cells in a network are broadly tuned to just a small number of what might be called canonical views of the head, rather like red, green, and blue in color vision, the answer is "not very many," certainly tens rather than thousands. However, in an examination of the best orientation of a face in a large number of face cells no bias was found; that is, all orientations were equally represented (see chapter 2 of this volume).

VISUAL AREAS AND SELECTIVE ATTENTION

Selective attention is one of our most striking perceptual abilities. It is also one of the most thoroughly investigated psychologically. Yet its neural basis at the single-cell level is barely understood, although there are numerous studies in which gross electrical activity is correlated with perceptual performance and attentional disturbances are correlated with localized brain damage. Why is this, given that we know so much about the receptive field properties of visual cortical neurons? The likely answer is that the latter are often studied in anesthetized animals whereas selective attention by definition requires consciousness and some behavioral response that reveals the attention. One paradigm for studying selective attention is the relative enhancement of a neuron's response when the stimulus presented within the receptive field is an important and expected signal for some learned response. First demonstrated in the superior colliculus (Goldberg & Wurtz, 1972), the phenomenon is present in several extrastriate visual areas. This is an example of attending to a particular region of space. Similar enhancement has been demonstrated according to the nature of the stimulus within the receptive field; for example, the response to a previously determined optimal stimulus, say red, could be attenuated if a stimulus to which the cell is indifferent, for instance, green, is simultaneously presented in the receptive field and is made the subject of the animal's attention (Moran & Desimone, 1985). Interestingly, the latter phenomenon was present in Areas V4 and TE but was not found earlier in the system in V1 and V2. Selective enhancement and selective inhibition almost certainly require extensive and exquisitely precise interconnections between different visual areas and between different physiological compartments within an area. Both have been demonstrated in abundance and the extensive back projections from higher to lower areas, which are much more widely dispersed than the forward projections (Shipp & Zeki, 1989a, 1989b), are at least anatomically appropriate for a role in selective attention. It has sometimes been regarded as puzzling that extensive interconnections exist between areas described as operating in parallel and dealing with different aspects of vision, for example, Area MT concerned with movement in the so-called dorsal pathway and Area V4 concerned with pattern in the so-called ventral pathway. One very good reason for their anatomical cross links is that it could enable each to influence the responsiveness of the other. How the attention is voluntarily instigated and then mediated at the cellular level is a mystery, but the fact that a lesion within the dorsal parietal region can produce a severe neglect affecting all classes of visual stimuli, including those thought to be processed chiefly by the ventral occipito-temporal pathways, supports the proposal by Posner, Grossenbacher, and Compton (see chapter 7 of this volume) of an anatomically discrete attentional system.

INFERRING FUNCTION FROM THE RECEPTIVE FIELD PROPERTIES OF NEURONS

Our understanding of the brain would be immeasurably poorer without the revelations of single-unit recording over the past 30 years. Nonetheless, the triumphs can blind us to the awkward fact that receptive field properties themselves do not unerringly indicate the role in behavior of neurons or visual areas. Although it is reasonable and sensible to suppose that an area in which the neurons are selective for some particular class of visual stimulus, such as wavelength or disparity or faces, is involved in an appropriate psychological category of perception, in this case color or depth or face recognition respectively, the supposition may prove to be wrong. To take a hypothetical example first, the behavioral role of neurons tuned to disparity may rest in vergence movements of the eyes, in accommodation linked to vergence, in extracting form from background, in deducing the curvature of a solid object, in detecting the direction in which an object is moving in depth. None of these computations requires that the viewer has a conscious experience of distance, whether it be absolute or relative, which might also be the principal function of the cells. Further experiments are required to elucidate the role in behavior and they have often not been done. As if life were not already difficult enough, a demonstration of a behavioral impairment following brain damage in a task that requires the discrimination of depth does not tell us why the impairment occurred. For example, removal of that part of Area V2 concerned with the central few degrees of the visual field in monkeys substantially impairs stereoacuity (Cowey & Wilkinson, 1991). But without further experiments it is unclear whether the elevation in the stereothresholds is caused by faulty vergence, or deletion of the cortical mechanisms for registering small disparities, or by disconnecting the latter from the process by which relative distance is perceptually experienced.

This dangerous gulf between perception and the receptive field properties of neurons is well illustrated by two topical examples. In the macaque monkey, Area V4 has understandably been implicated in the perception of wavelength and color on the basis of the receptive field properties of its cells and it has been proposed that it is homologous to the "color center" in the human lingual and fusiform gyri, whose destruction leads to cerebral achromatopsia (Zeki, 1990). These are wholly reasonable proposals but they might be incorrect. Removal of Area V4 in macaques has only slight effects on hue discrimination (Heywood & Cowey, 1987; Heywood, Gadotti, & Cowey, 1992; Schiller & Logothetis, 1990) but severely impairs form discrimination. This is about as close as one could get to a pattern of defects that is the inverse of that seen in a patient with a complete loss of cortical color vision following damage to the lingual and fusiform area (Heywood et al., 1991). Striking hue discrimination impairments occurred in monkeys following lesions in inferotemporal cortex, geographically much closer to the fusiform area of our brain (Heywood, Shields, & Cowey, 1988; see also Fig. 1.4), yet this region has not been implicated in color vision on the basis of receptive field properties, probably because the percentage of color selective cells is much lower here than in Area V4. The second example concerns proso-pagnosia—the perception and recognition of faces—which can be independently and severely impaired following damage to ventromedial cortex of the temporal lobe, probably just rostral to the damage that produces pure achromatopsia. Not surprisingly, it has been suggested that prosopagnosia is caused by destruction of a region related to the cortex of the rostral two thirds of the superior temporal sulcus of the macaque money. The latter is the region in which cells selectively sensitive to faces or parts of faces are most frequently encountered, particularly in the upper and lower banks of the sulcus in regions TPo, TEa, and TEm (see Fig. 1.1). However, when it is bilaterally and entirely removed in monkeys the animals show no impairment on tasks measuring discrimination between faces, or recognition of their recency, familiarity, or identity, despite the fact that prosopagnosic patients performed poorly on the same tasks (Heywood & Cowey, 1992). However the monkeys were impaired at discriminating the angle of regard in photographs of faces (Campbell, Heywood, Cowey, Regard, & Landis, 1990), suggesting that the face cells of the superior temporal sulcus are involved in the perception of important social signals and that face cells in other regions such as the lateroventral inferior temporal cortex may be better candidates for the recognition of faces. These different behavioral roles could not have been estab-lished simply by examining the receptive field properties of cells in the temporal lobe.

COVERT KNOWLEDGE

Brain damage often impairs higher cognitive functions such as memory, language, and visual identification. Yet by using techniques such as forced-choice guessing, or reaction times, or the measurement of autonomic responses, it has been shown that some patients have information about present or past stimuli of which they are not consciously aware and that they cannot use under normal circumstances. Examples of such covert knowledge are given in several other chapters of this book, but this section concentrates on visual detection and discrimination and asks whether the phenomenon tells us anything interesting about cortical visual areas and whether the latter in turn cast any light on the phenomenon.

Perhaps the first question to ask is: Why is it interesting? After all, we have no conscious awareness of many afferent signals in the central nervous system and it is important that we should not. For example, I am unaware of most of the signals from the musculature and inner ear that enable me to stand upright. So why be surprised by covert recognition of faces by prosopagnosic patients? One answer is that we do not even have covert knowledge of, for instance, neural events in the cerebellum that control balance and posture. However, this should be taken with a pinch of salt for it has not been satisfactorily investigated. A reason more relevant to the present discussion is that the kind of information that is being processed or accessed in covert recognition is usually thought of as the hallmark of cortical analysis and conscious cognitive awareness, for example, the identity of a face. If a patient is completely unable to distinguish overtly between familiar and unfamiliar faces but can do so covertly (reaction times, electrodermal response, heart rate), this suggests that the cortical machinery for the analysis of faces is intact. Covert recognition in relation to a particular pattern of brain damage may therefore indicate which areas and pathways suffice for analysis and which are additionally needed for awareness.

One of the best known examples of covert recognition is *blindsight,* the ability of some patients with absolute visual field defects (a scotoma) to detect and localize visual stimuli presented within the blind region when they are forced to guess (see Cowey & Stoerig, 1991; Weiskrantz, 1989, for reviews). Discrimination of movement, flicker, and orientation may also be present. Two patients who were asked to reach for objects they could not see adjusted their grasp in accordance with the shape and size of the objects (Marcel, 1983). These extensive abilities, some of which would certainly be classed as higher order perception in normal vision, are present despite consistent denials by the patients that they see anything in their field defects. It is hardly surprising that initial responses to reports of blindsight were skeptical, and it was suggested that the patients may have been detecting light scattered into their intact field, or were transmitting information from the defective part of the retina by a route to remaining striate cortex, or were using a lax criterion for discriminating faint signals, or were simply showing characteristics of normal vision close to threshold (Campion, Latto, & Smith, 1983). All these objections have proved to be groundless. When the targets are confined to the natural blind spot they cannot be detected, despite the fact that the optic disk actually scatters more light than the retina. A lax criterion is incompatible with a very low false-positive error rate. The absence of conscious awareness is present no matter what the intensity of the stimuli and even when discrimination is almost perfect, that is, by definition well above threshold. Even if blindsight is mediated by surviving striate cortex (as proposed, yet again, by Celesia, Bushnell, Toleikis, & Brigell, 1991 and by Fendrich, Wessinger, & Gazzaniga, 1992) it is not clear why it is not accompanied by overt recognition. And with respect to the last point it has been shown, using retrograde tracers in surviving striate cortex adjacent to a lesion in striate cortex, that there is no anatomical route by which information from the part of the retina corresponding to a field defect can reach the surviving striate cortex by direct but unusual routes through the dorsal lateral geniculate nucleus (Cowey & Stoerig, 1989).

What is the neuroanatomical basis of blindsight? It is commonly attributed to the retino-tectal pathway, although Fig. 1.1 is a reminder that there are several candidates. A particularly compelling demonstration of the role of the midbrain pathway was provided by Mohler and Wurtz (1977), who showed that although removal of part of the striate cortex still allowed a monkey to detect and localize stimuli within the field defect, the animal became totally insensitive to the stimuli when the retinotopically corresponding part of the superior colliculus was subsequently removed. However, it is still not known whether the same would be true of other types of target and, more important, the superior colliculus has ascending projections to both the dLGN and the pulvinar nucleus, which in turn project (the dLGN sparsely, the pulvinar heavily) to extrastriate visual areas (Fries, 1981; Kisvarday, Cowey, Stoerig, & Somogyi, 1991; see Cowey & Stoerig, 1991, for review). Some aspects of blindsight are present after hemispherectomy, which by definition precludes any role of cerebral cortex on that side, but others such as discrimination of wavelength (Stoerig & Cowey, 1992) and direction of movement may well involve or even require cortex and the survival of retinal axons that are thought to relay information only to cortex (Cowey, Stoerig, & Perry, 1989).

Electrophysiological evidence that visual information continues to reach extrastriate visual cortex in the absence or brief inactivation of striate cortex was presented by Rodman, Gross, and Albright (1989a,b). They found that about half of the neurons in Area MT of macaque monkeys retained their characteristic tuning for direction of movement after the retinotopically corresponding part of the striate cortex was removed or cooled. But subsequent destruction of the superior colliculus abolished their visual sensitivity. The demonstration that Area MT remains visually excitable without its customary input from striate cortex urgently needs to be investigated in patients with similar damage, for example by one of the neuroimaging methods discussed later, for it suggests that the primary visual cortex may be indispensible for visual awareness. If so, it should not be possible to provoke visual phosphenes by direct stimulation of the extrastriate cortex in a patient with hemianopia, and visual imagery should be likewise impaired. Other attempts to record from visual Areas V2 and V4 after cooling the striate cortex have not been successful (Girard & Bullier, 1989; Girard, Salin, & Bullier, 1991). However, the recordings were made under anesthesia and it is not yet known whether these areas are inactive in the alert monkey and at any other time than immediately following the cooling. Further experiments with V2 and V4 are needed because narrow wavelength tuning is common in both areas, is not present in the superior colliculus, and wavelength discrimination has now been demonstrated in blindsight (Stoerig & Cowey, 1992). Visually evoked potentials of cortical origin can certainly be recorded even in patients with total cortical blindness (Celesia et al., 1991), but blindsight has not yet been tested in these patients.

The fact that blindsight is absent, or limited to detection and localization, in some patients with cortical blindness has sometimes been used to question its authenticity. In fact its variability is to be expected if extrastriate visual area are involved, for damage to the latter and their underlying white matter is bound to vary widely. It will be surprising if modern neuroimaging methods do not soon throw light on this problem by correlating brain damage and regional metabolic activity with the quality of the residual visual abilities in blindsight. For example, when patients with blindsight correctly discriminate the direction or velocity of moving stimuli, does visual area MT show increased metabolic activity? Analogues of blindsight in other modalities are also to be expected but have been little investigated. "Unfeeling touch" in a patient with complete loss of conscious perception of touch following damage to the somatosensory cortex was reported by Paillard, Michel and Stelmach (1983) and "deaf hearing," which is necessarily rare because it requires a bilateral destruction of the primary auditory cortex, has been revealed by using forced-choice guessing with a patient who was cortically deaf (Michel, 1990).

Blindsight is an extreme form of covert knowledge where all consciousness of visual events in a field defect is abolished. Other examples, where vision remains but discrimination and recogniton are impaired, are no less interesting. Prosopagnosia has already been mentioned, and it would be informative to know whether the covert knowledge of faces could also be demonstrated by forced-choice guessing or by other methods than autonomic responses or reaction times or what Young (see chapter 11 of this volume) calls "indirect methods of testing recognition." Forced-choice guessing was used by Sergent and Ponceau (1990) with prosopagnosic patient PV by asking the patient which of two names was correct for each face. Although the patient failed to recognize any of the faces and insisted that she was only guessing, with 2AFC her performance was 40/48, suggesting that the method used so successfully in blindsight might reveal extensive covert knowledge in varieties of visual agnosia.

Other means of eliciting covert knowledge take advantage of the different voluntary motor responses that are made to objects of different size and orientation. A recent example, concerning severe object and shape agnosia, is given by Goodale, Milner, Jakobson, and Carey (1991). Patient DF was so severely impaired, despite having full visual fields, that she could not discriminate between a horizontal and vertical line, or a square and a grossly different rectangle. Nevertheless, she could orient her hand appropriately to "post" a card through a slot of variable orientation and correctly compose her grasp when reaching for objects she could not tell apart. Additionally, she vividly experienced the McCollough effect, that is, a color aftereffect where the perceived illusory aftercolor in a colorless grating depends on its orientation in relation to previously viewed colored gratings of different orientations (Humphrey, Goodale, & Gurnsey, in press). Both orientation and color must therefore be represented in her cortical visual pathways, but not in areas indispensible to the perception of shape and orientation.

VISUAL AGNOSIA AND THE RELATION BETWEEN HIGHER AND LOWER ORDER DEFECTS

The idea that object agnosia, including prosopagnosia, and especially agnosia of the apperceptive type, might be reducible to a collection of individually simple sensory losses has a long history, from Bay (1953) to Campion (1987), that has shrugged off experimental attempts to show that agnosia cannot be explained in this way (Ettlinger, 1956). Apart from the conceptual muddle that often accompanies the use of the terms *apperceptive* and *sensory,* and that is thoroughly discussed by Campion, the major problem in evaluating Bay's theory and its more recent variants is that it is only too easy to dismiss negative results by proposing that the appropriate sensory thresholds have not been examined. It is certainly true that a fully comprehensive range of visual sensory thresholds is rarely obtained with agnosic patients, for obvious reasons. However, in a recent attempt to reexamine this question (Young, DeHaan, Heywood, Edelstyn, Young, & Newcombe, in preparation), thresholds for the detection and discrimination of gratings, color, correlated movement, reflectance, shape from motion or from luminance contrast, relative position, texture, and orientation were all tested in a group of more than 50 patients with localized brain damage. Although there were substantial threshold elevations in some patients, there was no correlation between the pattern or severity of the impairments and the presence or absence of visual agnosia. When considered together with previous but more limited investigations of this problem it is difficult to see what else could be measured. Similar results have been obtained with monkeys in which either area V4 or the inferotemporal cortex was removed bilaterally (Cowey, Dean, & Weilkrants, in preparation). Following either of these ablations, monkeys are severely impaired at visual discrimination learning and retention and the disorder is often regarded as a likely model of visual object agnosia. However, their thresholds for acuity, contrast, contrast matching, spatial frequency discrimination, hyper-acuity, and size and shape were all normal. Yet several years after operation they remained deeply agnosic as assessed by pattern discrimination learning. It is difficult to avoid the conclusion that at least one principal form of agnosia in both patients and monkeys has nothing to do with low-level sensory processing and everything to do with registering the configural properties of visual stimuli, and that it is probably caused by destruction or disconnection of a region, like the inferior temporal cortex in monkeys, where cells respond chiefly to particular configurations of elements that are in isolation perceived normally.

The neurobiological underpinning for category specific agnosias is far less secure. Although the organization of the visual areas in the temporal lobe of monkeys provides a plausible basis for the various varieties of prosopagnosia—for example, identity versus expression—and even for the distinction between recognition of animate and inanimate objects (see especially chapter 4 of this volume), some of the more bizarre human dissociations have no ready-made neurobiological basis. For example, there are reports of agnosic patients who are particularly impaired at recognizing different food objects, or small manipulable objects, or whose knowledge of indoor objects is much poorer than that of outdoor objects. This is not the right venue for a discussion of this controversial topic, which at present has no parallel in behavioral work with monkeys with the possible exception of facial bearing (Heywood & Cowey, 1992). One of the best known category specific disorders, that is, poorer recognition of pictures of animate than inanimate objects, is even present in normal monkeys (Gaffan & Heywood, 1993), suggesting that the acquired disorder is simply an exaggeration of a normal characteristic for those patients. However, one view of category specificity is that the disorder lies in semantic knowledge (Warrington & McCarthy, 1987) and that different semantic categories of necessity have different weighting values from multiple sensory systems. On this basis it is just about possible to see how damage to one group of visual areas or to a subset of their outputs could lead to highly selective higher order disorders.

HOW MANY VARIETIES OF SELECTIVE VISUAL DISORDERS ARE THERE?

Although there may be as many as 30 different cortical visual areas in the macaque monkey, and it would be surprising if there were fewer in the human brain, there are only a handful of putative selective visual disorders. Damage to Area MT in monkeys impairs the discrimination of several types of movement in the corresponding part of the visual field (Newsome & Pare, 1988; Newsome & Wurtz, 1988). However, the disturbances are transient and the entire area together with adjacent areas like MST and FST may have to be removed before movement discrimination is permanently impaired (Cowey & Marcar, 1992; Marcar & Cowey, 1992). Even then, the monkeys show no gross symptoms of the kind reported in a "motion blind" patient by Zihl, Von Cramon, and Mai (1983), although their psychophysical performance does closely resemble that reported in other patients (Vaina, 1989; Vaina, LeMay, Bienfang, Choi, & Nakayama, 1990), whose damage as assessed by magnetic resonance imaging (MRI) scans embraces the region of the human brain tentatively identified as Area MT by positron-emission tomography (PET) scans. Although further fractionation of the disorder has barely begun, there is already evidence that, as with prosopagnosia, varieties of the disorder exist. For example, patient AF is grossly impaired at perceiving coherent movement within visual dynamic noise, at discriminating speed, and extracting form from relative motion. But he nevertheless perceives several types of higher order motion, apparently normally. For example, he readily perceives three-dimensional structure from motion and can identify biological actions such as shaking hands and riding a bicycle from the movement pattern of luminous dots on the joints of a human actor filmed in the dark, the Johansson illusion (Vaina et al., 1990). Such dissociations are only paradoxical until it is realized that even within the so-called movement channel there are several divergent outputs to different visual areas.

The first hints of regional variation in the extent to which visual neurons are tuned to retinal disparity between bolstered reports of selective impairments in the perception of depth based on disparity (for reviews, see Cowey, 1985; Ptito, Zatorre, Larson, & Tosoni, 1991). Alas it was probably a false dawn, for sensitivity to retinal disparity has proved to be an abundant characteristic of neurons in many visual areas (Goldberg & Colby, 1989) and with the benefit of hindsight this is only to be expected given that there are several forms of retinal disparity, namely; velocity, size, orientation, horizontal, vertical, spatial frequency, local, global, crossed, uncrossed. One might therefore expect each area to be sensitive to disparity in those features that it codes best—for example, movement—but the examination of patients with disorders of disparity-based depth perception in relation to fine-grained differences in the type of disparity has hardly begun. An exception may be the distinction between local and global stereopsis. For example, Ptito et al. reported a clear effect of anterior temporal lesions on the latter but not the former, a result that cannot be attributed to faulty vergence, which would be expected to affect both. Moreover, it echoes findings with monkeys with ablation of inferotemporal cortex (Cowey & Porter, 1979). However, tests of global stereopsis with random dot stereograms, where the subject has to identify the apparent depth of a hidden figure, may yield an impairment precisely because the target has a shape and temporal lobe damage also impairs the perception of shape. Impairments in local stereopsis have also been reported in patients (Danta, Hilton, & O'Boyle, 1978) and in monkeys with ablation of the foveal representation in Area V2 (Cowey & Wilkinson, 1991). But it is not yet clear whether the reason lies in faulty vergence or whether lesions in other visual areas would have similar effects.

One of the best known selective visual disorders is human cerebral achromatopsia following damage in the region of the lingual and fusiform gyri (see Zeki, 1990, for review). The fact that it is usually accompanied by prosopagnosia and spatial disorientation tells us about more about the role of adjacent regions of cortex rather than casting doubt on selectivity. However, the attractive hypothesis that it is caused by destruction of a region homologous to Area V4 in the monkey looks increasingly untenable. Not only are monkeys with V4 ablation only mildly impaired at any hue discrimination, including tasks where luminance is irrelevant and therefore cannot be used to solve color discrimination by other means, they are grossly impaired at form discrimination—which is not an invariable characteristic of achromatopsia (Heywood & Cowey, 1987; Heywood, Gadotti, & Cowey, 1992). If reports that the properties of many neurons in V4 render them particularly suitable for registering color rather than just wavelength are correct (Schein & Desimone, 1990; Zeki, 1983b), the proposed role of V4 in color constancy may be a better guide to evaluating the effects of damaging it. However, there are no reports of a selective disorder of color constancy in human subjects.

The controversy about the nature of prosopagnosia is as long as its history. When prosopagnosic patients are also tested with nonfacial visual stimuli from categories that, like faces, contain a large number of examples—for example, flowers and cars—they may be similarly impaired, even though the number of exemplars (e.g., models of car) falls well short of the number of faces a normal observer can identify, suggesting that the specificity is more apparent than real. However, it has recently been reported that impaired recognition of faces can exist without any associated impairment of the perception of members of other categories (see chapter 11 of this volume), and even that a prosopagnosic sheep farmer who could not recognize familiar friends and neighbors could nevertheless distinguish between photographs of familiar and unfamiliar sheep (McNeil & Warrington, 1993). A comparable disorder has not been described in monkeys, despite the extensive investigation of so-called face neurons discussed earlier in this chapter. One reason may be the great difficulty in demonstrating recognition of identity in monkeys. We use a name for each face we know, or some roundabout description amounting to biographical details. But what amounts to a name for a monkey? Heywood and Cowey (1992) attempted to substitute a particular reward value, which had to be indicated by the monkey, for the name of each of four faces and found no evidence of "prosopagnosia" after removal of the facecell area in the superior temporal sulcus. However, it is unrealistic to expect that monkeys could indicate the identity of more than a few faces this way (it would be like testing facial recognition in people with the restriction that only four or so names could be used) and the role of temporal lobe visual areas in face recognition in monkeys may have to be evaluated indirectly by other tests at which prosopagnosic patients perform poorly, for example, discriminating familiar from novel faces.

Visuospatial neglect and impaired perception of spatial position are well-known consequences of damage to the dorsal part of the occipito-parietal region (see chapter 7 of this volume) and have been related to what is often called the "dorsal system" in the macaque brain, which includes visual areas MT, PO, VIP, and so on. However, the complete removal of the inferior parietal lobule in macaques does not produce the florid visual neglect often seen in clinical patients and there is still no convincing evidence that the animals' perception of allocentric spatial relations resembles the spatial mislocation seen in patients. For example, although monkeys are impaired on the famous landmark task where they must indicate which of two identical plaques is closer to a landmark, their impairment could as easily reflect neglect of the landmark when the latter is progressively distanced from the plaques as an inability to appreciate the relative positions of the stimuli (Lawler & Cowey, 1987).

In summary, there is evidence of selective disorders of the perception and/or recognition of movement, color, faces, depth, and space in neurological patients. It is possible that fine-grained analysis will yield further distinctions, as it certainly has within the category of faces, where identity can be separately disturbed from qualities such as gender, age, and expression. Even fewer independent disorders have been uncovered in monkeys despite our knowledge of their visual areas. It is not clear whether this reflects the lack of sophistication of our perceptual tests and the fact that it is difficult and slow to make and evaluate lesions confined to one area, or whether clusters of visual areas function collectively in a manner that makes it an insuperable practical problem to assess their individual contribution, as some computational approaches to the brain would suggest.

NEUROIMAGING—MIRAGE, OR MIRROR ON THE MIND?

It is always exciting to see a field transformed by technological advance. It happened in the 1970s with experimental neuroanatomy, which was revitalized by the development of axoplasmic tracers and immunocytochemistry. There are signs of a similar resurgence in neuropsychological studies of functional localization as a result of modern neuroimaging methods, all of which have been mentioned in this book. But without decrying their triumphs, it may be wise to consider their limitations.

It has been possible for many years to record the electrical activity of the brain, for example, event-related potentials (ERP), from scalp electrodes. Why has it told us so little about localization of function? After all, the temporal resolution is excellent, far better than PET will ever achieve. The limitation is part technological, part physiological. It is only recently that a combination of miniaturization of electrodes and amplifiers together with the development of powerful computers allows us to record simultaneously from a large enough number of channels to pinpoint the source of the signals. The work of, for example, Jeffreys (1989) and Bötzel and Grüsser (1987), shows how one can localize activity associated with the perception of faces using ERPs. But these are events that can be associated with particular perceptual acts precisely because the two are time locked. Irrelevant activity can therefore be discarded by averaging. The latter is not so straightforward with neural events that cannot be time locked to a particular stimulus, hence the negligible contribution of electrical recording to higher level functions such as imagery or the lengthy perusal of visual displays. The physiological limitation is just as severe. Scalp recordings measure summed electrical activity. There is no a priori reason why overall activity in an area should change in a manner readily detectable by scalp electrodes when that area is engaged by visual stimulation or voluntary mental activity. Presumably the interplay of cortical microcircuits, measuring tens of microns, changes, but remains invisible at the scalp. Nevertheless, by analyzing the electroencephelograph (EEG) frequency bands in terms of mean amplitude, peak frequency, and power, Beaumont and Kenealy (1991) recently showed changes in the beta 2 and theta bands (but not in alpha or delta) in subjects performing semantic association and word generation tasks. Using tasks formally similar to those employed by Posner, Peterson, Fox, and Raichle (1988) in a PET scanning demonstration of regional changes of cerebral blood flow associated with mental events, they reported essentially similar findings with a less invasive and vastly cheaper technique.

Changes in cerebral blood flow, signaled by positron emission following injection or inhalation of radioactive molecules, can be independent of overall electrical activity in an area and can therefore do something that electrical measures cannot do. But it is instructive and salutary to bear in mind the practical and theoretical limitations of PET. Even assuming that PET becomes more widely affordable and that the ethical problems associated with the repeated use of radioactive tracers in normal subjects and in patients for nondiagnostic and nontherapeutic purposes are surmountable, other problems remain. The first is the theoretical limit of $2mm^3$ in spatial resolution. This is satisfactory for many purposes but means that PET may never reveal fine-grain localization such as cytochrome oxidase blobs or orientation columns in V1, or indeed many of the physiologically defined compartments in cortical visual areas. The second is the frankly unsatisfactory temporal resolution, at present about 40 s and predominantly a result of the fact that only about 1% of the radiation is currently detectable. Better cameras could in theory improve detection to an extent that temporal resolution becomes a few seconds. For some neural events this may still be far too long.

The third obstacle is that changes in blood flow do not indicate whether the associated neural events are excitatory or inhibitory, or both, yet this is precisely the kind of information one would like to have in relation to selective attention and mental gating. Of course metabolic PET (for example, the use of fluorodopa to reveal dopaminergic binding sites) may solve this problem as long as suitable radioligands can be found for other transmitter systems, notably GABA, acetylcholine, nor-adrenalin, and glutamate.

The fourth problem is that an absence of any substantial change in blood flow in a particular area does not necessarily mean that the area fails to participate in or is unimportant to some particular task. It may fail to change because it is involved in the control tasks too, or because its blood flow is already high, or, if not high, because whatever it does can be achieved without vascular changes, or because increases in subparts of an area are offset by decreases in others at a spatial resolution too small for PET to detect. To take a hypothetical example, if selectively attending to one or the other eye were accompanied by increases and decreases in blood flow within left- and right-eye columns in striate cortex, they would be invisible to the PET camera.

Detecting a change in cerebral blood flow must be distinguished from the additional problem of assigning that change to a particular cytoarchitectonic area of cortex. For example, PET scans are often superimposed on a "standard" brain using an atlas derived from many real brains. But if the natural variation in brain size and sulcal pattern is considerable, it would be easy to mislocalize by as much as the width of a gyrus. PET scanning is therefore at its best when the results from blood flow are superimposed on an MRI of the subject's own brain (e.g., Mora, Carman, & Allman, 1989; Sergent, Ohta, & Macdonald, 1992). But even here, accurate localization of activity indicated by changes in blood flow is not the same as localization to an anatomically defined region. If there is as much variation between human brains as there is between simian brains in the absolute and relative size of different regions (e.g., the area of the striate cortex varies by 100% in *Macaca fascicularis;* Van Essen, Newsome, & Maunsell, 1984), it could be easy to attach the wrong anatomical label to an accurately localized area delineated by blood-flow measurements.

Despite these limitations PET has revealed, or could reveal, much more than the classical study of dysfunction in patients with focal brain damage. First, the spatial resolution in PET is much finer than that of the great majority of brain lesions. For example, the demonstration by PET of a "color-area" on the medial surface of the occipital lobe (Zeki et al., 1991) within the much larger area that is customarily damaged in patients with cerebral achromatopsia (see Zeki, 1990, for review) is a real advance, as is the demonstration by Sergent et al. (1992) of heightened rCBF in a region of the right extrastriate cortex during categorization of the gender of a face, but in the fusiform gyri and rostral temporal cortex bilaterally during face identification, and in the left ventral temporal cortex during object recognition. Just as important, repeated PET on the same subject should be able to reveal changes over time, for example during learning or in rehabilitation from brain injury. The not infrequent jibe that PET is simply an elegant and expensive way of confirming the discoveries made in a century of clinical neurology and neuropsychology is certainly false, although its initial use in that way is understandable.

What of other imaging methods in relation to perception and cognition? As mentioned earlier, one outstanding advantage of evoked electrical activity is its superb temporal resolution, and brain electrical activity mapping (BEAM) is improving so fast that for some purposes it could rival PET. Magnetoen-cephalography (MEG) or magnetic source imaging (MSI) exploits the weak magnetic field generated by localized neuronal activity, which can be instan-taneously detected, measured, and localized. Unlike scalp-recorded VEPs, neu-romagnetic signals are not distorted by intervening tissue, and unlike PET the temporal resolution is superb and the spatial resolution not subject to the same theoretical limit. In combination with MRI it offers the hope of unsurpassed localization. Unfortunately, it is currently limited to a small region of the head and a depth of a few centimeters. It also requires an associated superconducting magnet.

Static MRI is unsurpassed for revealing anatomical details such as the borders between gray and white matter, or the location of damage, by recording the mobility of protons in tissue. Although MRI is best known as a means of reveal-ing the outlines of sulci and subcortical nuclei, spectroscopic MRI (SMRI) can in theory detect the distribution of almost any organic molecule (e.g., neuro-transmitters) and may yet become a means of following metabolic changes less invasively than PET. One needs a crystal ball to know which of all these meth-ods, or in which combination, will eventually prevail but there is a fair chance that they will revolutionize the study of higher nervous processes in the next few years, especially functional MRI.

CONCLUSIONS

The anatomical and neurophysiological demonstration that the posterior half of the cerebral cortex in monkeys is a patchwork of visual areas has transformed many of our ideas about visual processing. It is widely assumed, but still un-proved, that the human brain is similar. Localization of function, in a modular brain, is enjoying a renaissance and for the first time there are convincing computational reasons for regional and functional segmentation on a scale that not even the discredited phrenologists imagined. However, the particular role played by each area is far from certain and probably cannot be established solely by anatomical connectionist studies or single-cell recordings. Much of the evi-dence for the existence of selective visual disorders of a kind that would be expected in a modular brain, and that point to the function of particular modules, comes from the neuropsychological study of patients or monkeys with focal brain injury. It is ironic that this period of enormous and productive expansion of the study of such patients and monkeys coincided with attacks on the "lesion method." It is now clear that the lesion method is effective precisely because the cerebral cortex is so modular. Other methods than anatomy and single-cell electrophysiology are needed to demonstrate functional modularity in the human brain and the several forms of neuroimaging promise a rich harvest. But it is uncertain which neuroimaging methods will be most informative and there is a danger of worshipping the rising rather than the setting sun.

REFERENCES

Allman, J., Miezin, F., & McGuinness, E. (1985). Direction- and velocity-specific responses from beyond the classical receptive field in the middle temporal area (MT). *Perception, 14*, 105–126.

Bay, E. (1953). Disturbances of visual perception and their examination. *Brain, 76*, 516–550.

Beaumont, J. G., & Kenealy, P. (1991). Identification of cognitive operations in cerebral activity: A comparison of PET and EEG. *Experimental Psychology Society Abstracts (Sussex), July*, 26–27.

Bötzel, L., & Grüsser, O-J. (1987). Potentials evoked by face and nonface stimuli in the human electroencephalogram. *Perception, 16*, A21.

Campbell, R., Heywood, C.A., Cowey, A., Regard, M., & Landis, T. (1990). Sensitivity to eye gaze in prosopagnosic patients and monkeys with superior temporal sulcus ablation. *Neuropsychologia,28*(11), 1122–1142.

Campion, J. (1987). Apperceptive agnosia: The specification of description of constructs. In G. W. Humphreys & M. J. Riddoch (Eds.), *Visual object processing: A cognitive neuropsychological approach* (pp. 197–232). Hillsdale, NJ: Lawrence Erlbaum Associates.

Campion, J., Latto, R. M., & Smith, Y. M. (1983). Is blindsight an effect of scattered light, spared cortex, and near-threshold vision? *Behavioral and Brain Sciences, 6*, 423–448.

Celesia, C. G., Bushnell, D., Toleikis, S. C., & Brigell, M. G. (1991). Cortical blindness and residual vision. *Neurology, 41*, 862–869.

Cowey, A. (1964). Projection of the retina onto striate and prestriate cortex in the squirrel monkey, Saimiri sciureus. *Journal of Neurophysiology, 27*, 366–393.

Cowey, A. (1974). Atrophy of retinal ganglion cells after removal of striate cortex in a rhesus monkey. *Perception, 3*, 257–260.

Cowey, A. (1979). Cortical maps and visual perception. The Grindley Memorial Lecture. *Quarterly Journal of Experimental Psychology, 31*, 1–17.

Cowey, A. (1981). Why are there so many visual areas? In F. O. Schmitt, F. G. Worden, G. Adelman, & S. G. Dennis (Eds.), *The organisation of the cerebral cortex* (pp. 395–413). Cambridge, MA: M.I.T. Press.

Cowey, A. (1985). Disturbances of stereopsis by brain damage. In D. J. Ingle, M. Jeannerod, & D. N. Lee (Eds.), *Brain mechanisms and spatial vision* (pp. 259–278). Dordrecht, Netherlands: Martinus Nijhoff.

Cowey, A., Dean, P., & Weiskrantz, L. (in preparation). Normal visual thresholds in visually 'agnosic' monkeys.

Cowey, A., & Marcar, V. L. (1992). The effect of removing superior temporal cortical motion areas in the macaque monkey. I. Motion discrimination using simple dots. *European Journal of Neuroscience, 4*, 1219–1227.

Cowey, A., & Porter, J. (1979). Brain damage and global stereopsis. *Proceedings of the Royal Society of London, B*(204), 399–407.

Cowey, A., & Stoerig, P. (1989). Projection patterns of surviving neurons in the dorsal lateral geniculate nucleus following discrete lesions of striate cortex: Implications for residual vision. *Experimental Brain Research, 75,* 631–638.

Cowey, A., & Stoerig, P. (1991). The neurobiology of blindsight. *Trends in Neurosciences, 14*(4), 140–145.

Cowey, A., Stoerig, P., & Perry, V. H. (1989). Transneuronal retrograde degeneration of retinal ganglion cells after damage to striate cortex: Evidence for selective loss of PB cells. *Neuroscience, 29,* 65–80.

Cowey, A., & Wilkinson, F. (1991). The role of the corpus callosum and extrastriate visual areas in stereoacuity in macaque monkeys. *Neuropsychologia, 29,* 465–479.

Crook, J. M., Lange-Malecki, B., Lee, B. B., & Valberg, A. (1988). Visual resolution of macaque retinal ganglion cells. *Journal of Physiology (London), 396,* 205–224.

Damasio, A., Yamada, T., Damasio, H., Corbett, J., & McKee, J. (1980). Central achromatopsia: Behavioral, anatomical and physiologic aspects. *Neurology, 30,* 1064–1071.

Daniel, P. M., & Whitteridge, D. (1961). The representation of the visual field on the cerebral cortex in monkeys. *Journal of Physiology (London), 159,* 203–221.

Danta, G., Hilton, R. C., & O'Boyle, D. J. (1978). Hemisphere functions and binocular depth perception. *Brain, 101,* 569–589.

DeHaan, E., Heywood, C. A., Edelstyn, N., Newcombe, F., & Young, A. (in preparation). Ettlinger revisited: perceptual impairments and recognition disorders.

Derrington, A. M., Krauskopf, J., & Lennie, P. (1984). Chromatic mechanisms in the lateral geniculate nucleus of macaque. *Journal of Physiology (London), 357,* 241–265.

Desimone, R., Albright, T. D., Gross, C. G., & Bruce, C. (1984). Stimulus selective properties of inferior temporal regions in the macaque. *Journal of Neuroscience, 8,* 2051–2062.

Desimone, R., & Ungerleider, L. G. (1989). Neural mechanisms of visual processing in monkeys. In H. Goodglass & A. R. Damasio (Eds.), *Handbook of Neuropsychology* (Vol. 2, pp. 267–299). Amsterdam, Netherlands: Elsevier.

Ettlinger, G. (1956). Sensory deficits in visual agnosia. *Journal of Neurology, Neurosurgery and Psychiatry, 19,* 297–307.

Felleman, D. J., & Van Essen, D. C. (1987). Receptive field properties of neurons in area V3 of macaque monkey extrastriate cortex. *Journal of Neurophysiology, 57,* 889–920.

Felleman, D. J., & Van Essen, D. C. (1991). Distributed hierarchical processing in the primate cerebral cortex. *Cerebral Cortex, 1,* 1–47.

Fendrich, R., Wessinger, M., & Gazzaniga, M. S. (1992). Residual vision in a scotoma: Implications for blindsight. *Science, 258,* 1489–1491.

Fries, W. (1981). The projection from the lateral geniculate nucleus to the prestriate cortex of the macaque monkey. *Proceedings of the Royal Society of London, B*(213), 73–80.

Gaffan, D., & Heywood, C. A. (1993). A spureous category—specific visual agnosia for living things in normal human and non-human primates. *Journal of Cognitive Neuroscience, 5*(1), 118–128.

Gattass, R., Sousa, A. P. B., & Covey, E. (1985). Cortical visual areas of the macaque. Possible substrates for pattern recognition mechanisms. In C. Chagas, R. Gattass, & C. G. Gross (Eds.), *Pattern recognition mechanisms* (pp. 1–20). Vatican City: Pontifical Academy of Sciences.

Girard, P., & Bullier, J. (1989). Visual activity in area V2 during reversible inactivation of area 17 in the macaque monkey. *Journal of Neurophysiology, 62,* 1287–1302.

Girard, P., Salin, P. A., & Bullier, J. (1991). Visual activity in macacque area V4 depends on area 17 input. *Neuroreport, 2,* 81–84.

Goldberg, M. E., & Colby, C. L. (1989). The neurophysiology of spatial vision. In: *Handbook of Neuropsychology, 2,* 301–315.

Goldberg, M. E., & Wurtz, R. H. (1972). Activity of superior colliculus in behaving monkey: 2. The effect of attention on neuronal responses. *Journal of Neurophysiology, 35,* 560–574.

Goodale, M. A., Milner, A. D., Jakobson, L. S., & Carey, D. P. (1991). A neurological dissociation between perceiving objects and grasping them. *Nature, 349,* 154–155.

Gross, C. G. (1992). Representation of visual stimuli in inferior temporal cortex. *Philosophical Transactions of the Royal Society of London, B, 335,* 3–10.

Heywood, C. A., & Cowey, A. (1987). On the role of cortical area V4 in the discrimination of hue and pattern in macaque monkeys. *Journal of Neuroscience, 7,* 2601–2617.

Heywood, C. A., & Cowey, A. (1992). The role of the "face-cell" area in the discrimination and recognition of faces by monkeys. *Philosophical Transactions of the Royal Society of London, B. 335,* 31–38.

Heywood, C. A., Cowey, A., & Newcombe, F. (1991). Chromatic discrimination in a cortically blind observer. *European Journal of Neuroscience, 3,* 802–812.

Heywood, C. A., Gadotti, A., & Cowey, A. (1992). Cortical area V4 and its role in the perception of color. *Journal of Neuroscience, 12,* 4056–4065.

Heywood, C. A., Shields, C., & Cowey, A. (1988). The involvement of the temporal lobes in colour discrimination. *Experimental Brain Research, 71,* 437–441.

Hubel, D. H., & Livingstone, M. S. (1990). Color and contrast sensitivity in the lateral geniculate body and primary visual cortex of the macaque monkey. *Journal of Neuroscience, 10,* 2223–2237.

Humphrey, G. K., Goodale, M. A., & Gurnsey, R. (in press). Orientation discrimination in a visual form agnosic. *Psychological Science.*

Jeffreys, D. A. (1989). A face-responsive potential recorded from the human scalp. *Experimental Brain Research, 78,* 193–202.

Kendrick, K. M., & Baldwin, B. A. (1989). Visual responses of sheep temporal cortex cells to moving and stationary human images. *Neuroscience Letters, 100,* 193–197.

Kisvarday, Z. F., Cowey, A., Stoerig, P., & Somogyi, P. (1991). Direct and indirect retinal input into degenerated dorsal lateral geniculate nucleus after striate cortical removal in monkey: Implications for residual vision. *Experimental Brain Research. 86,* 271–292.

Lawler, K. A., & Cowey, A. (1987). On the role of posterior parietal and prefrontal cortex in visuospatial perception and attention. *Experimental Brain Research, 65,* 695–698.

Lee, B. B., Martin, P. R., & Valburg, A. (1989). Nonlinear summation of M- and L-cone inputs to phasic retinal ganglion cells of the macaque. *Journal of Neuroscience, 9,* 1433–1442.

Logothetis, N. K., Schiller, P. H., Charles, E. R., & Hurlbert, A. C. (1990). Perceptual deficits and the activity of the colour-opponent and broad-band pathways at isoluminance. *Science, 247,* 214–217.

Lueck, C. J., Zeki, S., Friston, K. J., Deiber, M. P., Cope, P., Cunningham, V. J., Lammertsma, A. A., Kennard, C., & Frackowiak, R. S. J. (1989). The colour centre in the cerebral cortex of man. *Nature, 340,* 386–389.

Marcar, V. L., & Cowey, A. (1992). The effect of removing superior temporal cortical motion areas in the macaque monkey: II. Motion discrimination using random dot displays. *European Journal of Neuroscience, 4,* 1228–1238.

Marcel, A. J. (1983). Conscious and unconscious perception; an approach to the relations between phenomenal experience and perceptual processes. *Cognitive Psychology, 15,* 238–300.

Martin, K. A. C. (1992). Parallel pathways converge. *Current Biology, 2,*(10), 555–557.

McNeil, J. E., & Warrington, E. K. Prosopagnosia: A face-specific disorder. *The Quarterly Journal of Experimental Psychology,* 46A,(1), 1–10.

Merigan, W. H., & Maunsell, J. H. R. (1990). Macaque vision after magnocellular lateral geniculate lesions. *Visual Neuroscience, 5,* 347–352.

Michel, F. (1990, September). Hemi-anacousia is usually unknown to the patient. Abstracts, Russell Trust/Wellcome Trust Symposium, Consciousness and Cognition. St. Andrews.

Milner, A. D., & Heywood, C. A. (1989). A disorder of lightness discrimination in a case of visual form agnosia. *Cortex, 25,* 489–494.

Mohler, C. W., & Wurtz, R. H. (1977). Role of striate cortex and superior colliculus in the guidance of saccadic eye movements in monkeys. *Journal of Neurophysiology, 40,* 74–94.

Mora, B. M., Carman, G. J., & Allman, J. M. (1989). In vivo functional localization of the human visual cortex using positron emission tomography and magnetic resonance imaging. *Trends in Neurosciences, 12,* 282–286.

Moran, J., & Desimone, R. (1985). Selective attention gates visual processing in the extrastriate cortex. *Science, 229,* 782–784.

Movshon, J. A., Adelson, E. H., Gizzi, M. S., & Newsome, W. T. (1985). The analysis of moving visual patterns. In C. Chagas, R. Gattass, & C. G. Gross (Eds.), *Pattern recognition mechanisms* (pp. 117–151). Vatican City: Pontifical Academy of Sciences.

Newsome, W. T., & Pare, E. B. (1988). A selective impairment of motion perception following lesion of the middle temporal visual area (MT). *Journal of Neuroscience, 8,* 2201–2211.

Newsome, W. T., & Wurtz, R. H. (1988). Probing visual cortical function with discrete chemical lesions. *Trends in Neurosciences, 11,* 394–400.

Paillard, J., Michel, F., & Stelmach, G. (1983). Localization without content: A tactile analogue of "blindsight." *Archives of Neurology, 40,* 548–551.

Posner, M. I., Peterson, S. E., Fox, P. T., & Raichle, M. E. (1988). Localization of cognitive operations in the human brain. *Science, 240,* 1627–1631.

Ptito, A., Zatorre, R. J., Larson, W. L., & Tosoni, C. (1991). Stereopsis after unilateral anterior temporal lobectomy. *Brain, 114,* 1323–1333.

Purpura, K., Kaplan, E., & Shapley, R. M. (1988). Background light and the contrast gain of primate P and M retinal ganglion cells. *Proceedings of the National Academy of Sciences of the USA, 85,* 4534–4537.

Rodman, H. R., Gross, C. G., & Albright, T. D. (1989a). Afferent basis of visual response properties in area MT of the macaque: 1. Effects of striate removal. *Journal of Neuroscience, 9,* 2033–2050.

Rodman, H. R., Gross, C. G., & Albright, T. D. (1989b). Afferent basis of visual response properties in area MT of the macaque: 2. Effects of superior colliculus removal. *Journal of Neuroscience, 10,* 1154–1164.

Rovamo, J., Hyvarinen, L., & Hari, R. (1982). Human vision without luminance contrast system: Selective recovery of the red-green colour-contrast system from acquired blindness. *Documenta Ophthalmologica Proceedings Series, 33,* 457–466.

Saito, H., Tanaka, K., Isono, H., Yasuda, M., & Mikami, A. (1989). Directionally selective response of cells in the middle temporal area (MT) of the macaque monkey to the movement of equiluminous opponent colour stimuli. *Experimental Brain Research, 75,* 1–14.

Schein, S. J., & Desimone, R. (1990). Spectral properties of V4 neurons in the macaque. *Journal of Neuroscience, 10,* 3369–3389.

Schein, S. J., Marrocco, R. T., & DeMonasterio, F. M. (1982). Is there a high concentration of color-selective cells in area V4 of monkey visual cortex? *Journal of Neurophysiology, 47,* 193–213.

Schiller, P. H., & Logothetis, N. K. (1990). The color-opponent and broad-band channels of the primate visual system. *Trends in Neurosciences, 13,* 392–398.

Schiller, P. H., Logothetis, N. K., & Charles, E. R. (1990a). Functions of the colour-opponent and broad-band channels of the visual system. *Nature, 343,* 68–70.

Schiller, P. H., Logothetis, N. K., & Charles, E. R. (1990b). Role of the color-oponent and broad-band channels in vision. *Visual Neuroscience, 5,* 321–346.

Sergent, J., Ohta, S., & Macdonald, B. (1992). Functional neuroanatomy of face and object processing. A positron emission tomography study. *Brain, 115*(1), 15–36.

Sergent, J., & Ponceau, M. (1990). From covert to overt recognition of faces in a prosopagnosic patient. *Brain, 113,* 989–1004.

Sergent, J., & Signoret, J-L. (1992). Functional and anatomical decomposition of face processing: evidence from prosopagnosia and PET study of normal subjects. *Philosophical Transactions of the Royal Society London B, 335*, 55–62.

Shipp, S., & Zeki, S. (1989a). The organization of connections between areas V1 and V1 in macaque monkey visual cortex. *European Journal of Neuroscience, 1*, 309–332.

Shipp, S., & Zeki, S. (1989b). The organization of connections between areas V5 and V2 in macaque monkey visual cortex. *European Journal of Neuroscience, 1*, 333–353.

Simpson, J. I. (1984). The accessory optic system. *Annual Review of Neuroscience, 7*, 13–41.

Stoerig, P., & Cowey, A. (1992). Wavelength discrimination in blindsight. *Brain. 115*, 425–444.

Talbot, S. A., & Marshall, W. H. (1941). Physiological studies on neural mechanisms of visual localization and discrimination. *American Journal of Opthalmology, 24*, 1255–1264.

Vaina, L. M. (1989). Selective deficits of visual motion interpretation in patients with right occipito-parietal lesions. *Biological Cybernetics 61*, 1–13.

Vaina, L. M., LeMay, M., Bienfang, D. C., Choi, A. Y., & Nakayama, K. (1990). Intact "biological motion" and "structure from motion" perception in a patient with impaired motion mechanisms: A case study. *Visual Neuroscience, 5*, 353–369.

Van Essen, D. C., Newsome, W. T., & Maunsell, J. H. R. (1984). The visual field representation in the striate cortex of the macaque monkey: Asymmetries, anisotropies and individual variation. *Vision Research, 24*, 429–448.

von der Heydt, R., & Peterhans, E. (1989). Mechanisms of contour perception in monkey visual cortex: 1. Lines of pattern discontinuity. *Journal of Neuroscience, 9*, 1731–1748.

Warrington, E. K., & McCarthy, R. A. (1987). Categories of knowledge. Further fractionations and an attempted integration. *Brain, 110*, 1273–1296.

Weiskrantz, L. (1989). Blindsight. In F. Boller & J. Grafman (Eds.), *Handbook of neuropsychology* (Vol. 2, pp. 375–385). Amsterdam, Netherlands: Elsevier.

Wiesel, T. N., & Hubel, D. H. (1966). Spatial and chromatic interactions in the lateral geniculate body of the rhesus monkey. *Journal of Neurophysiology, 29*, 1115–1156.

Zeki, S. (1990). A century of cerebral achromatopsia. *Brain, 113*, 1721–1777.

Zeki, S., Watson, J. D. G., Lueck, C. J., Friston, K. J., Kennard, C., & Frackowiak, R. S. J. (1991). A direct demonstration of functional specialization in human visual cortex. *Journal of Neuroscience, 11*, 641–649.

Zeki, S. M. (1978). Functional specialisation in the visual cortex of the rhesus monkey. *Nature, 274*, 423–428.

Zeki, S. M. (1983). Colour coding in the cerebral cortex: The reaction of cells in monkey visual cortex to wavelengths and colours. *Neuroscience, 9*(4), 741–765.

Zihl, J., von Cramon, D., & Mai, N. (1983). Selective disturbance of movement vision after bilateral brain damage. *Brain, 106*, 313–340.

2 Issues of Representation in Object Vision

D. I. Perrett
M. W. Oram
J. K. Hietanen
P. J. Benson
University of St. Andrews

OBJECT RECOGNITION AND ITS PROBLEMS

Visual recognition can be described as the matching of the retinal image of an object to a description or representation of the object stored in memory. Different views of an object generate different retinal images, yet recognition requires realization of the object's common identity across the distinct viewpoints. The ability to achieve such generalized recognition is termed *object constancy* and is the subject of this chapter.

It is implausible that we should hold in memory an exhaustive list of descriptions, one for each different view of an object experienced. Indeed, if this were so we would not be able to recognize familiar objects from novel viewpoints. Some ability to transform an object's image (in size, orientation, and perspective) would avoid the necessity to store separate descriptions of all possible views of an object. Such visual processing would thus require only a limited selection of views to be stored in memory to allow object recognition from even novel viewpoints.

Object- and Viewer-Centered Representations

The degree to which the visual system can transform an image differs among models of object recognition. On the one hand, an unlimited capacity to transform across views would mean that only one description of an object needs to be stored in memory to allow direct recognition of that object from any viewpoint (Lowe, 1985, 1987; Marr, 1982; Marr & Nishihara, 1978). The capacity to generalize across perspective view depends on the coordinate system used to describe an object. Marr proposed an object-centered coordinate system in which the object's parts were specified relative to the main axis of the object itself (Marr, 1982; Marr & Nishihara, 1978). For example, a head can be (very) approximately described as a cylinder with a protruding wedge (a nose) sticking out at 45°, halfway down the main axis of the cylinder. Such object-centered descriptions are economical because they are valid for all possible vantage points of the observer.

Marr (1982; Marr & Nishihara, 1978) noted that objects could also be described using a viewer-centered system of representation where an object's parts are described using a frame of reference or coordinate system based on the observer. For example, a head might be described as a cylinder with a wedge pointing to the left, if the head is seen in left profile. Obviously such representations depend on the vantage point of the observer. They provide a very limited ability to accommodate transformation across perspective view. Marr argued that viewer-centered systems of recognition were uneconomical because they would require a large number of view-specific "templates" of objects to be stored in memory. Baron (1981) proposed a viewer-centered system for recognizing people in which a different template was needed for every change in perspective view of 20°, for different lighting conditions and for different image sizes. With a more extensive capacity to generalize across viewpoint, recognition could be based on a small number (6–20) of descriptions of an object from particular "characteristic" views (e.g., Gray, 1986; Koenderink & van Doorn, 1976, 1979; Perrett, Smith, Potter et al., 1985).

Thus one of the major problems of recognition (coping with different views) can be solved in two different ways. It can either be solved by storing one representation of an object's appearance covering all vantage points or it can be solved by storing several representations of an object's appearance, each from a different vantage point. Before assessing which alternative is more appropriate in accounting for human vision, it is first appropriate to comment on the functions of different types of representations.

UTILITY OF DIFFERENT REPRESENTATIONS

To recognize what an object is (e.g., is it a lion or an elephant) ultimately requires a description that holds true for all vantage points of the viewer. For this function a frame of reference based on the object itself (an object-centered description) is appropriate. Viewer-centered representations may be used as an intermediate stage for the computation of view general descriptions but they are not the most appropriate descriptions for recognition. Marr (1982) noted that a single object-centered representation held in memory confers efficiency in the process of recalling information associated with the object's identity. If one learns that a particular type of insect gives a painful bite, it is important to be able to retrieve this information when the insect is encountered from any viewpoint. It would be inefficient (if not dangerous) to learn the association between the capacity to inflict pain and the insect's appearance from only one view. For example, we might have learned the association between a bite and the insect's front view but would not know how to react when the same insect lands on our skin presenting a profile view.

Different visual tasks may require different types of representations. Visual guidance of actions, for example, requires visual information about objects that is specified with the viewer as the frame of reference. For the viewer to reach out and grasp an object it is essential that the viewer knows where in the environment the object lies and what its orientation is with respect to him or herself. Essentially this utilization of visual information requires a viewer-centered reference.

The information about an object that is required for action could also be covered by the same series of viewer-centered representations used for recognition. In this case each representation would need to be specific for one example of the object's position and orientation relative to the viewer. Alternatively action and recognition could rely on separate representations. In one visual pathway or system, action could be guided by representation of position of the object and the three-dimensional orientation of major components relative to the observer. A second visual pathway subserving recognition could employ a smaller number of viewer-centered descriptions (generalizing across distance) or a single three-dimensional, object-centered representation (generalizing across all vantage points).

Keeping two types of representation in the nervous system appears problematic, particularly because the putative action and recognition systems would need to be linked so that the observer can know what he or she is picking up or interacting with. The advantage conferred, however, would be a reduction in specificity and number of separate representations required for action and recognition. Representations for actions could be based on simple volumetric primitives (cones, cylinders, etc.; Biederman, 1985; Marr, 1982), with no information about surface pattern or object identity, whereas representations for recognition might make explicit identity but lack specificity for position, distance, and orientation.

Neurophysiological studies of temporal and parietal cortex support the contention of separate representations for identification and visually guided action. Parietal cells are selective for the distance and orientation of objects that can be grasped (H. Sakata, personal communication, October, 1992), but not for object identity (Rolls et al., 1979). Conversely, cells in temporal cortex are selective for object identity but not for distance or orientation (Perrett, Rolls, & Caan, 1982).

It is interesting to note the neuropsychological dissociation between patients with agnosia (failing to recognize what an object is) and those with apraxia (having difficulty in interacting with objects). The agnosic patient DF described by Milner et al. (1991) has great difficulty recognizing the identity of objects (e.g., mistaking scissors for a screwdriver). Nonetheless she is able to interact with objects, guiding her hand in the appropriate shape to grasp objects of differing position, orientation, and size. DF's abilities again make the point that, to guide an action, representations do not have to make explicit what the object is. The representations need only specify information in terms of the affordances of the object for action (e.g., that it is large, has a graspable component extending horizontal to the left of object's bulk, and is .6 m away). Other patients have apraxia without agnosia. For some of these patients there may be evidence of a double dissociation of symptoms with those of DF.

In summary of this section, different cognitive operations require different types of representation. Recognition of what an object is requires a view-invariant representation, whereas realizing how to interact with an object requires view-specific representations. Consistent with these speculations, neurophysiological and neuropsychological studies suggest that the brain employs different types of representation for guiding action and object recognition in the brain.

THEORETICAL PREDICTIONS
FOR CHARACTERISTIC VIEWS

The main focus of this chapter is the nature of representations supporting object recognition. Recently, theoretical accounts and experimental data have increasingly supported an account of recognition based on viewer-centered representations. Although models based on a limited number of characteristic views are becoming more popular in theoretical and computational models of vision (e.g., Poggio & Edelman, 1990; Seibert & Waxman, 1990; Ullman, 1989), the number of characteristic views necessary to represent an object and the manner in which they can be defined is not yet clear. The following sections review different schemes for defining characteristic views.

Geometrically Faceted Objects (Widgets)

In the context of computer vision, several investigators have suggested schemes in which visual features (lines, edges, corners, vertices, surface faces) of the object that are visible from a set of neighboring views, could be used to classify these views as discrete from other views that share other features (Chakravarty & Freeman, 1982; Gray, 1986; Ikeuchi, 1987; Thorpe & Shafer, 1983).

Gray (1986) concentrated on an idealized machined tool part termed a *widget* (see Fig. 2.1). Gray divided up a hypothetical "viewing" sphere surrounding the widget into clusters of adjacent views and investigated the trade-off between the number of component features (e.g., T-junctions) shared by a cluster of adjacent views and the number of clusters. When the viewing sphere was divided into eight clusters, each member of a cluster was found to share at least nine features with all other members of that cluster. Splitting the viewing sphere into nine view clusters, Gray found that cluster members shared far more (17) features in

GRAY'S CHARACTERISTIC VIEWS

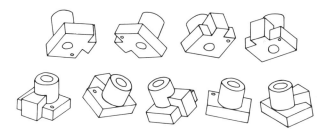

FIG. 2.1. Characteristic views of a "widget" revealed by feature analysis. Nine characteristic views of a widget defined by cluster analysis of the visibility of corner, edge, and other visual features (adapted from Gray, 1986).

common. With 10 clusters the number of common features was still 17. With such diminishing returns Gray speculated that nine view clusters might be sufficient for recognition. Thus the widget could be coded in an economical way by storing one list of features for each of the nine qualitatively different view clusters. Any arbitrary chosen view of the widget will share a large number (17) of features with one of the nine views. Figure 2.1 illustrates nine views at the center of the different view clusters Gray defined as characteristic.

Smooth Objects and Singularities

Most studies in computer vision have focused on regular geometrical objects for which features are fairly easy to define. Different features are needed to describe the appearance of smooth objects. Mathematical extension of singularity theory has been used to classify the shape of contours (or singularities) of smooth objects (Callahan & Weiss, 1985; Koenderink & van Doorn, 1976). Stable aspects or characteristic views have been defined as clusters of views across which singularities remain qualitatively unchanged (for a nonmathematical account, see Perrett & Harries, 1988). Figure 2.2 illustrates the different patterns of singularities that occur when a solid dumbbell shape is rotated through 180°. Classification of singularities may present a challenge to mathematics but their applicability to object recognition (particularly human recognition) has yet to be substantiated. For any moderately complex object the appearance of singularities defines far too many characteristic views.

Principal Axis

Models of recognition based on viewer- and object-centered descriptions both predict that a particular view or set of views of an object should be more easily recognizable than other views. For viewer-centered models of recognition, there

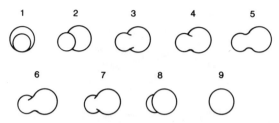

FIG. 2.2. Characteristic views of a smooth dumbbell defined by singularities. Rotation of a smooth and opaque dumbbell shape through
180°. Nine views predicted to be stable and characteristic from consideration of singularities (line contours separating visible and occluded
surfaces). Views are said to be stable because a slight rotation produces small changes in the shape of the singularities. In between each
aspect is a transitional state (not shown) where the line singularities
change qualitatively in configuration when a very small rotation is
made. From D. I. Perrett and M. H. Harries, 1988, *Perception, 17*, p. 707.
Copyright 1988 by Pion Press. Reprinted by permission.

will be some views of an object in which particular features are not clear and
these will be difficult to match to the relevant set of stored characteristic views of
the object. Similarly the object-centered model of recognition of Marr and
Nishihara (1978) requires definition of an object's principal axis to be used as a
reference for describing the disposition of the object's parts. According to this
model, views foreshortening the principal axis should be more difficult to recognize.

In Lowe's (1985, 1987) object-centered recognition model, the three-
dimensional relationships of simple object features (or parts) are defined in
relation to other parts (without reference to a principal axis). The process of
recognition takes place by comparing the two-dimensional relationship of very
simple features in the image (lines, corners, etc.) with the relative position of
object parts that would arise from all possible two-dimensional projections
(views) of a three-dimensional object model. If two image features have a relationship consistent with the projection of two object parts from one vantage
point, then one can predict the position of a third part of the object and a third
visual feature in the image. For example, while matching an image to a crude
model of a car, a pair of lines consistent with the front bumper and the driver's
door suggest the position of a third circular feature corresponding to the driver's
side headlight. If this prediction is confirmed, the "viewpoint consistency" constraint is satisfied and there is evidence that the interpretation of the view and
object under inspection is correct. In this scheme, too, some parts may have
particular salience and perhaps could be more easily used to assess the viewpoint
consistency constraint. Again one predicts that views in which these salient

features are occluded will be more difficult to recognize. According to this model, the views that are difficult to recognize will depend on the specific object in question rather than the general appearance of the principal axis.

Summarizing this section, all theoretical models predict that some views will be easier to recognize than others, however, the models differ in their predictions of which views will be easy to recognize. Marr and Nishihara's (1978) theory predicts that the visibility of the object's principal axis will be important for recognition. In Lowe's (1985, 1987) theory recognition is unrelated to the principle axis but depends on visibility of multiple (and salient) object parts. Other models predict that recognition will be facilitated at several characteristic views. These models differ in the choice of visual features used to define characteristic views.

PSYCHOLOGICAL EVIDENCE
FOR CHARACTERISTIC VIEWS

Before describing the relevant empirical assessments of these predictions it is important to note a subtle change in definition. So far, the term *characteristic view* has been reserved for special views defined theoretically as useful for matching images to stored descriptions of objects during recognition. Characteristic views can also be defined experimentally as views subjects find easier to recognize, or that are preferentially represented in neural circuits. Consistent with preceding literature both definitions are used interchangeably.

Previous Evidence Relevant to Characteristic Views

Warrington and Taylor (1973) reported that patients with right parietal cortex lesions were poorer than control subjects at recognizing objects from unusual views. They noted that the unusual views were often ones in which the principal axis (defined as the axis of elongation) was foreshortened by perspective (see Fig. 2.3).

Rather than assessing which views are difficult to recognize, Palmer, Rosch, and Chase (1981) investigated which views are "canonical," that is views that human subjects find easiest to recognize and regard as most typical. The authors found that the results of three different psychological assessments converged on the same canonical view; for most objects this was a view in which the object's principal axis (or surfaces) was 45° to the line of sight (see Fig. 2.4). In the first line of experiments subjects were asked to rate the typicality of different views of 12 familiar objects. For most of the items studied, a 45° view was judged by subjects as typifying an object more than views of the same object taken at right angles to the object's surfaces (i.e., front, side, back, or top sides). Second, the 45° degree (or $\frac{3}{4}$) view was most easily brought to mind in an imagery task.

FIG. 2.3. Foreshortening of the principal axis. Left: a view of a bucket that is easy to recognize perhaps because the principal or long axis is easy to detect. Right: an unusual view in which the long axis of the object is foreshortened. This may make the object difficult to recognize even for normal subjects. After right posterior brain lesions, this difficulty is further exaggerated. From Figure 6 of "The contribution of the right parietal lobe to object recognition" by E. K. Warrington and A. M. Taylor, 1973, *Cortex, 9,* 159. Copyright 1973. Adapted by permission.

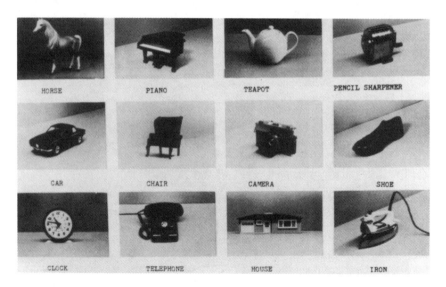

FIG. 2.4. Canonical views of objects. Examples of 12 experimental objects showing the views judged to be most canonical. Note that for several objects the principal axis is at 45° to the line of sight in the canonical view (from Palmer et al., 1981).

Finally, the canonical views defined with the first two methods tended to be recognized in a naming task faster than other views.

From the work of Warrington and Taylor (1973) and Palmer et al. (1981) it would seem that if an object's principal axis is drastically foreshortened then recognition is impaired, but if the principal axis is 45° to the line of sight then recognition may be enhanced. Both findings give credence to the model of Marr and Nishihara (1978), which relies on the relationship of parts to the principal axis (though one should perhaps note that in this 45° view the principle axis is actually foreshortened to quite an extent). Lowe's model (1985, 1987) does not predict any particular importance of the principal axis, because the viewpoint consistency constraint can be satisfied just as well from views where the principal axis is obscured.

One might have predicted from Marr and Nishihara's (1978) model that if recognition was tied to the principal axis, then the view that is regarded as canonical should always be one with the object's axis at right angles to the line of sight (i.e., a side view). This was the case for only two objects assessed by Palmer et al. (1981), the house and teapot (Fig. 2.4). Such an observation suggests that the canonical perspective is a compromise view maintaining both the principal axis and other features or surfaces.

Indeed, in a more recent study of object silhouettes, Warrington and James (1986) found no evidence for a systematic relationship between recognition and the visibility of the principal axes. Instead their results were more closely related to the visibility of salient features.

It is possible, however, that multiple systems of recognition are employed by the brain. Biederman (1985) suggested that recognition of an object might depend on the visibility of particularly salient components. Recognition abilities of different brain-damaged patients also suggest that structural encoding utilizing the principal axis can be dissociated from the processing of local salient features.

Perhaps the most salient feature of a pepper pot is the set of perforations at the top of the pot. Humphreys and Riddoch (1984) decreased the salience of such important features not by occluding them from view but by photographing the objects in an unusual orientation, for example, the pepper pot lying horizontal on a table surface, as if knocked over on its side. With such images the visibility of the object's principal axis is unaffected. Humphreys and Riddoch reported four patients who were impaired in matching images of objects when the principal axis was foreshortened in one image. These patients were able to match images despite changes in feature saliency. A fifth patient, however, showed the reverse pattern, impaired matching when the object's primary distinctive feature was made less salient but no impairment with modification to the principal axis.

Views Preferentially Inspected

Perrett and Harries (1988) measured the amount of time subjects spent inspecting different views of objects when attempting to learn their appearance. They found

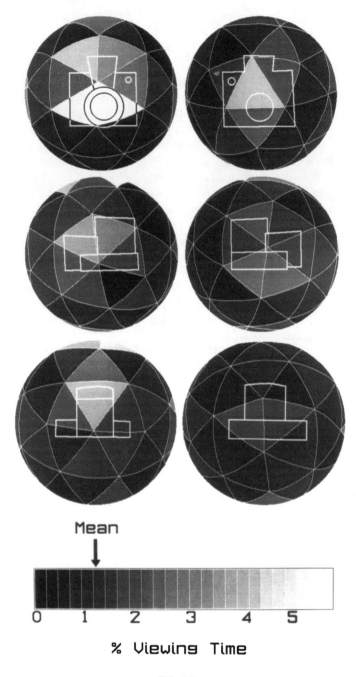

Mean

0   1   2   3   4   5
% Viewing Time

FIG. 2.5.

that subjects did not distribute their time randomly but instead focused on a small number of views. The same views were inspected whether subjects were encoding the object's appearance into memory, or were attempting to recognize the object having been previously exposed to all views evenly (Harries, Perrett, & Lavender, 1991). Measurement of inspection time thus presents a naturalistic index of which views subjects found important for recognition. The results of these preferential inspection studies fit a model of recognition based on a number of characteristic views or salient features, rather than a single object-centered description.

Perrett and Harries (1988) found that when instructed to learn the appearance of three-dimensional objects with a smooth but irregular shape (potatoes!), subjects preferentially inspected two types of view in which the principal axis was either parallel or perpendicular to the line of sight. These can be referred to simply as "end" and "side" views, respectively (Views 1 and 5 in Fig. 2.2). Subjects' view preferences did not therefore correspond to characteristic views predicted by singularity theory (see earlier discussion). Moreover, for end views the principal axis is foreshortened to the extent that it is no longer visible. Assuming that subjects preferentially inspect objects at views that facilitate recognition, these findings contradict the model of Marr and Nishihara (1978). Their model predicts that subjects should only prefer views where the principal axis is maximally visible, that is, side views.

A similar choice of side and end views has been found in inspection studies of a wide variety of objects (Harries et al., 1991; Perrett & Harries, 1988). Figure 2.5 illustrates the results of a study in which the subjects attempted to learn the appearance of a widget (equivalent to that in Fig. 2.1 and Fig. 2.6) inside a glass sphere. This allowed inspection strategies to be measured with the object free to rotate about any arbitrary chosen axis (Perrett, Looker, & Harries, 1992).

Again, subjects were found to focus on just a few views that could be described as side and end views. The preferentially inspected views were therefore unrelated to those predicted to be characteristic by cluster analysis (Gray, 1986; see previous discussion). For faceted objects such as a widget, the side and end views chosen by subjects are views in which one or more of the object's major

---

FIG. 2.5.   Viewing sphere for a widget. Reconstruction of the viewing sphere from six orthogonal views. Thick white and black lines trace the shape of a real three-dimensional widget from frame-grabbed images. Thin white lines trace the boundaries of 80 equilateral triangular tessellations covering the surface of the viewing sphere. Each tessellation was assigned a gray scale intensity proportional to the amount of time subjects spent looking through the tessellation at the widget below. Tessellations overlying views where the line of sight was approximately normal to the surfaces of widget received more inspection than other tessellations (from Perrett, Looker, & Harries, in press).

FIG. 2.6. View of a widget displaying maximum structural information. Computer graphic illustration of a perspective view frequently
chosen by subjects when instructed to choose one view that presented
maximal structural information.

surfaces lie normal to the line of sight. Subjects thus preferentially inspect a
series of "plan views," equivalent to those drawn by an architect or structural
engineer in representing an object. The benefit of these views and the reason that
they are used in an architect's plan is that the two-dimensional shape or cross-
section of components is not distorted by perspective in the third dimension.

    Our visual systems may use depth from stereopsis and motion parallax to
enable us to appreciate three-dimensional shape from any perspective view, but
to be sure of the exact proportions of three-dimensional objects it would appear
that we prefer to rely on two-dimensional shape recognition. Indeed, our stereopsis is unable to resolve depth differences within small objects at a distances
greater than 3 m. To learn an object's appearance we therefore orient objects to

minimize perspective distortion and standardize or stabilize the possible two-dimensional appearance.

Figure 2.7 illustrates views inspected by subjects while learning the appearance of a series of three-dimensional model heads (Harries et al., 1991). Again, subjects spent more time looking at views that could be labeled side views and end views (i.e., profile and face views) than views in between (e.g., the $\frac{1}{2}$ profile views). The same views were preferentially inspected in a different experiment where subjects first learned the appearance of heads from a video displaying the heads rotating evenly and then interacted with the models in an attempt to recognize them. This would indicate that subjects were selectively building up and utilizing stored structural descriptions of face and profile views of the heads.

The back and face views are both views in which the major axis is foreshortened (i.e., end views), yet only the front view receives high amounts of inspection. The face view contains far more salient features than the back of the head, so presumably importance assigned behaviorally to views (and to stored representations) reflects a combination of attributes (including orientation of major axes and feature information or salience).

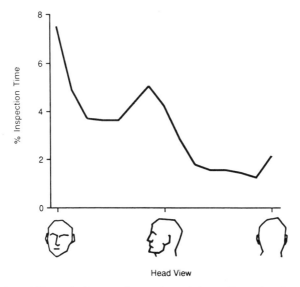

FIG. 2.7. Effect of view on inspection of three-dimensional model heads. Lower: schematic illustration of views inspected. Upper: time that subjects spent inspecting different views of three-dimensional model heads as they learned the heads' appearance. Duration of inspection is expressed as a percentage of the total viewing time; views are expressed as an angle of rotation from full face (90° = left or right profile). Subjects spent significantly more time inspecting views close to the full face and to the left and right profiles than to intermediate views (from Harries et al., in press).

Imagery and Recognition

Using an imagery paradigm, Thomas, Perrett, Davis, and Harries (1992) found that subjects were able to form a mental image of face and profile images of head models more easily than half-profile images. In this study they had first learned the appearance of the heads from all views evenly. Again the results suggest that face and profile representations (but not half-profile representations) were preferentially stored in memory.

Psychological measures are, however, not always so straightforward to interpret. In the study of Thomas et al. (1992) recognition of the same model heads (used in the imagery task) by the same subjects was found to be more efficient (judged by reaction times and accuracy) for half-profile views than for face and profile views (Fig. 2.8). Superior recognition of heads in the 45° or half profile has been reported in other studies (see Bruce, Valentine, & Baddely, 1987, for review) and is similar to the findings of increased ease of recognition of 45° views of other objects (Palmer et al., 1981).

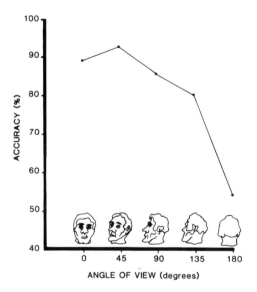

FIG. 2.8.   Effect of view on accuracy for recognition of model heads. Average accuracy of subjects' identification of six model heads whose appearance had first been learned from all views evenly. Views are expressed as an angle of rotation from full face (90° = left or right profile). Schematic illustration of views of one model head are shown at the base. Subjects were more accurate (and faster) In recognizing the half-profile view than other views of the head (from Thomas et al., 1992).

The recognition advantage can be interpreted as a consequence of the half-profile view activating both representations for the face and profile. In physiological terms (see later discussion) the half-profile would activate populations of neurons tuned to the full face and the profile face because of the broad tuning for perspective view displayed by cells. By contrast, images of the face and profile will activate only one type of representation or cell population. An analogous situation is found in color vision where wavelength discrimination is most efficient for yellow wavelengths even though there are no yellow cones. Yellow light activates both red and green cones because of their broad spectral tuning.

Views Maximizing Structural Information

When subjects are asked to imagine a single (canonical) perspective view that most typifies an object, the view they choose may be a compromise between two or three characteristic views. Indeed, when subjects were asked to imagine a view of a widget (equivalent to that in Fig. 2.1) that presented the most structural information, they tended to choose a view in between views defined as characteristic from preferential inspection (Perrett, Looker, & Harries, 1992 and Fig. 2.6).

In the study of Palmer et al. (1981) the choice of canonical view varied across objects. Such variation can be explained by acknowledging an influence of salient features (see previous discussion). For objects such as a clock, teapot, and house the most salient features are visible from a single surface, so the view chosen as canonical is orthogonal to this surface. For the horse, car, and other objects, salient features exist on at least two surfaces and the view chosen as canonical reflects a compromise between these surfaces.

Additional Frames of Reference in Object Recognition

The first two sections distinguished between viewer- and object-centered representations that utilize, respectively, the observer and the object's principal axis as frames of reference for describing the disposition of object parts. The psychological evidence presented earlier suggests that recognition frequently relies on the viewer-centered descriptions, but the brain mechanisms underlying recognition may well employ additional frames of reference. Specifying the view of an object with respect to the observer does not uniquely specify an object's three-dimensional orientation in space. Thus an upright face, a horizontal face, and an inverted face are all the instances of the same view if the observer is taken as the only frame of reference. An object's orientation may need to be specified with greater precision before it can be matched to stored internal (viewer-centered) representations.

Rock (1973) argued that objects are often recognized on the basis of a gravitational reference frame. Humphreys and Riddoch (1984) further suggested that descriptions of objects can be based on an extrinsic frame of reference, which is either the gravitational axis or some prominent surface of the scene (e.g., a table-top surface on which the object sits). Thus an object whose principal axis is foreshortened by perspective becomes easier to recognize when cues are provided from the scene as to the axis of foreshortening (see Fig. 2.9). A similar inference about the use of an extrinsic scene-based axis can be drawn from the work of Hinton and Parson (1988) and Humphrey (1988). The choice of intrinsic or extrinsic axes depends on the geometry of the object and the visibility of scene-based axes.

Measures of preferential inspection also indicated that subjects align the component axes of objects with gravity or to a scene-based axis aligned with gravity (Perrett, Looker, & Harries, 1992). This suggests that the coding of the plan views into memory is orientation specific. If plan views were stored in a manner where orientation did not matter, then alignment of plan views during inspection should have been random with respect to extrinsic axes.

The conclusion that recognition is orientation specific and related to external axes is in keeping with other psychological studies (Hinton & Parsons, 1988; Humphrey, 1988; Jolicoeur, 1985; Parsons, 1987; Rock, 1973; Rock & di Vita, 1987). Langdon, Mayhew, and Frisby (1991) also found that for the widget object (equivalent to that studied by Gray, 1986), changing the retinal orientation decreased the perceived similarity between different views. The findings of most studies thus converge on the conclusion that there are descriptions of objects held in memory that are vantage-point dependent and do not show perfect generalization over orientation. In other words, descriptions used in many forms of object recognition are viewer centered and orientation specific.

In summary of this section, the psychological studies indicate that recognition depends on representations of multiple views of each object. Subjects prefer to inspect the appearance of end and side views when learning the appearance of an object or attempting to recognize it. Views defined as characteristic with this inspection technique are not predicted from an analysis of singularities (e.g., bounding contours) or simple geometric features (e.g., edges and corners). Marr and Nishihara's (1978) theory predicts side views but not end views to be characteristic because the principal axis is foreshortened in end views. For many objects recognition appears to be most efficient for a view 45° to the object's principal axis. The recognition advantage of this canonical view may reflect that it can be matched to stored viewer-centered representations of both sides and end views of the object. Psychological evidence also suggests that the representations employed at some stage in object recognition are not only view specific but also have a specific orientation with respect to gravity or a scene-based axis.

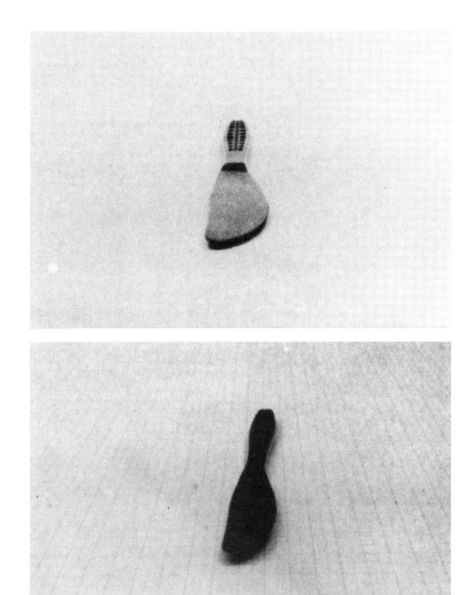

FIG. 2.9. Effect of perspective cues on recognition. The object depicted is difficult to recognize when the principal axis is foreshortened.
When the image includes a scene-based axis aligned with the object's
principal axis, recognition of the object's orientation and identity is
facilitated (from Humphreys & Riddoch, 1984).

PHYSIOLOGICAL EVIDENCE
FOR CHARACTERISTIC VIEWS

Cells Selectively Responsive to Heads

Cells in the temporal cortex (particularly the superior temporal sulcus) of monkeys have been found that respond selectively to hands, faces, and other classes of biologically significant objects. These cells provide an opportunity to investigate directly the manner in which objects are represented in the nervous system.

Early studies showed that the majority of cells responsive to the head were selective for perspective view: some cells responding to the face, other cells responding to the profile (Desimone, Albright, Gross, & Bruce, 1984; Perrett, Smith, Potter et al., 1985). The same cells, though view-specific, have been found to generalize response to one view of the head across image position, size, and orientation, and across different lighting conditions (Hietanen, Perrett, Oram, Benson, & Dittrich, 1992; see Perrett, Harries, Bevan et al., 1989, for review). The properties fit high-level, viewer-centered representations and contradict the strict interpretation of Marr and Nishihara's (1978) model of recognition, which argued that a low-level representation of surfaces in the world (a 2.5-dimensional sketch) was mapped directly onto three-dimensional, object-centered representations of objects (Marr & Nishihara, 1978). In a similar way the cell properties do not fit Lowe's model (1985, 1987) where low-level features (oriented edges and corners, etc.) are mapped directly to three-dimensional, object-centered representations

Distribution of View Coding and Width of View Tuning

Because the cells in the temporal cortex displayed viewer-centered properties, responding selectively to a given view of the head, the question arose as to how many separate views of the head were represented by the cells in the cortex. Were all views represented evenly or were particular characteristic views preferentially coded (as suggested by some theoretical accounts of recognition)? If the latter was the case, which particular views were preferentially coded?

Initial studies (Perrett, Smith, Potter et al., 1985) suggested that only four views of the head (the face, two profiles, and back) were represented in the horizontal plane. No cells were found responding selectively to the half-profile view. Later studies demonstrated that there were more views coded than just four (Hasselmo, Rolls, Baylis, & Nalwa, 1989; Perrett, Harries, Bevan et al., 1989; Perrett, Harries, Mistlin & Chitty, 1989; Perrett, Mistlin & Harries, 1989; Perrett et al., 1991). Recent quantitative and extensive studies have, however, confirmed the notion of preferential coding of particular views (Harries & Perrett, 1991; Perrett et al., 1991). Although cells are tuned to a whole range of views in the horizontal plane there is statistical preference for the face and profile (see Fig. 2.10).

What is quite remarkable is that the neurophysiological evidence for the importance of particular head views parallels the importance of different views in behavioral studies (compare Figs. 2.7 and 2.10). It would appear that not only the same views are important physiologically and psychologically but also the relative importance of views is comparable. The face and profile views appear more important than half-profile views, but all of these front views are more important than the rear views of the head.

. The tuning of an individual cell for perspective view shows a gradual decline in response as the head is turned away from the cell's optimal view (Fig. 2.11). If cells are preferentially coding only a few characteristic views, then cell tuning for perspective view needs to be broad to accommodate all nonoptimal views in between characteristic views. Measurements made on a sample of 73 cells indicated that, on average, responses declined to one-half maximal response for a rotation of the head 60° from the cells' optimal views (Perrett, Harries, Bevan et

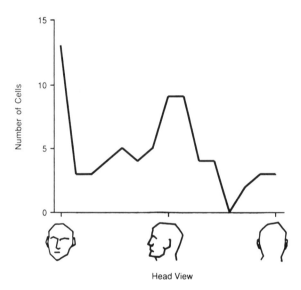

Head View

FIG. 2.10. Distribution of view tuning across a population of cells responsive to the head. Lower: schematic illustration of views coded. Responses were assessed to real three-dimensional heads or two-dimensional video images of heads. Upper: number of cells found with an optimal view sensitivity to different persepctive views expressed as an angle of rotation from full face (90° = left or right profile). Significantly more cells exhibit a preference for views within 22.5° of the face, profile, and the back views of the head than for intermediate views (Binomial Test, p = .0002) (adapted from Perrett et al., 1991).

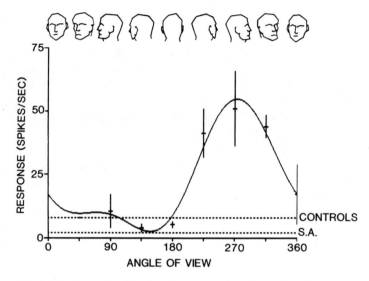

FIG. 2.11. Example of tuning for perspective view of a viewer-centered cell responsive to the sight of the head. The mean responses
(±1SE) are illustrated for one cell to eight views of the head. View,
expressed as the angle of rotation from face, is illustrated schemat-
ically at the top. The curve is the best fit second–order cardioid function, relating response to view. Dashed lines are the mean responses
to control stimuli and spontaneous activity (SA). Responses to the
views close to the right profile (270) were greater than response to
other views, controls, and spontaneous activity.

al., 1989; Perrett, Harries, Mistlin, & Chitty, 1989; Perrett, Mistlin, & Harries,
1989; Perrett et al., 1991). Thus cells tuned to the face will be one-half activated
by the sight of a view of the head rotated toward profile by 60°. With this broad-
view tuning, selective coding of the four characteristic views can cover the whole
range of perspective views in the horizontal plane. This would be analogous to
the situation in color vision where retinal cones cover the complete visible
spectrum of colors with only three broadly tuned color pigments.

Physiological evidence thus fits with the evidence obtained from the psychological studies, both suggesting that the visual appearance of the head is represented in the nervous system by high-level, viewer-centered descriptions of a
small number of characteristic views. Though these cell populations each cover
only a limited range of vantage points, their outputs could be combined to form
descriptions that generalize across multiple vantage points. Indeed a minority of
cells in the temporal cortex do respond to multiple views of the head and body
(see next section). These cells have properties equivalent to object-centered
representations (Hasselmo et al., 1989; Perrett, Harries, Mistlin, & Chitty, 1989;

Perrett, Mistlin, & Chitty, 1987; Perrett, Mistlin, & Harries, 1989; Perrett et al., 1991; Perrett et al., 1984; Perrett, Smith, Potter et al., 1985).

Coding of Other Objects

If such view tolerance is a general property of visual coding, then the appearance of objects other than heads could also be represented by a small number of high-level, viewer-centered representations. In this context it is relevant to note that physiological data indicate that the cellular coding of the entire body, hands, arms, and legs is similar to the coding of the head (Perrett, Harries, Mistlin, & Chitty, 1990; Perrett, Smith, Mistlin et al., 1985). For example, there are separate populations of cells selective for the sight of the static views of the hands. Like cells selective for the head, cells responsive to hands exhibit a high degree of selectivity and do not respond when tested with other stimuli (including two-dimensional grating patterns, arousing food items or general "junk" objects such as a clock). Of particular interest here are the observations that the cells tolerate relatively large changes in size and orientation of the hand (upright/horizontal; Desimone et al., 1984) but tolerate a limited range of perspective rotation ($\pm 50°$, Perrett and Chitty, unpublished studies, 1987).

Much less is known about the neural representation of arbitrary objects other than faces and body parts. From the work of Miyashita (1990) it would appear that nonbiological objects that acquire importance during the life of the individual are coded in the cortex that lies anterior and ventral in the temporal lobe. Miyashita trained monkeys to match complex radially symmetrical fractal patterns (similar to colored snowflakes) presented successively in a fixed series of 100 items. After extensive training, cells in the anterior temporal cortex were found to show a high degree of selectivity for particular patterns. Interestingly, the cells showed selectivity for a small number of patterns (typically 2 or 3 out of the 100) that were temporally associated (e.g., pattern numbers 91, 92, and 93). This learned association is analogous to the responses of object-centered cells selective for several different head views (patterns) of the same individual. The association between different head views can also be learned through temporal sequence of views during head rotation. The cells studied by Miyashita displayed high-level visual constancies tolerating changes in stimulus size, position, and orientation (in the picture plane). It was not possible to examine tolerance of change in perspective view using Miyashita's matching task.

Recent studies by Tanaka, Saito, Fukada, and Moriya (1991) suggest that coding of faces, hands, and arbitrary objects share an earlier stage of analysis in the inferior temporal (IT) cortex. At this stage cells are selective for complex combinations of features independent of their retinal position. Some cells in this area also exhibit selectivity for particular views of objects such as hands and faces. Unlike coding in the superior temporal sulcus (STS) and in anterior temporal cortex the coding in the inferior temporal cortex is mainly orientation specific and size specific. Thus some cells respond to the sight of faces but only faces of certain size and orientation (e.g., small and horizontal faces!). This suggests a model of cognition whereby different visual constancies are established successively. Cells in the STS exhibiting high-level, viewer-centered selectivity for one view of an object (generalizing over size and orientation with respect to gravity) may depend on the combined inputs from appropriate earlier viewer-centered descriptions in IT cortex that are size and orientation specific.

The physiological data and the psychological data from preferential inspection studies indicate that a wide variety of objects (including body parts and arbitrary objects) are represented in a very similar way to the head. It would appear that at one level of recognition processing, internal representations are high level (e.g., generalizing across size) but view specific. These may be constructed from more specific viewer-centered descriptions residing at an earlier stage of processing.

In summary of this section, the neurophysiological findings of the importance of different views parallel those of psychological studies. The brain appears to represent biologically significant objects (e.g., faces, hands) with multiple populations of nerve cells, each population tuned to one perspective view. Views found characteristic at the psychological level were found preferentially represented at the neural level. Thus for the head, more cells were tuned to the face and profile views than to intermediate views. Cell tuning for view was broad (tolerating 50°–60° of rotation). Therefore neural representation of a few characteristic views can cover recognition of all views in between those that are characteristic. Arbitrary objects appear to be represented at the neural level in a similar way to biologically significant objects although coding may involve different regions of the temporal cortex. Coding at an earlier level appears specific with respect to perspective view and orientation.

PHYSIOLOGICAL MECHANISMS OF IDENTITY CODING

Predictions from *Prosopagnosia*

One interesting representational issue concerns the specificity of representations and neural coding. From the description of cells responsive to the head, it is possible to imagine how a given type of object is discriminated from other types of object by populations of cells each representing one view of that object type. What is not clear is how the identity of an individual object or face is represented in the nervous system.

The clinical literature is relevant to this issue. It has been known for more than a century that face recognition can be impaired after brain damage (Wilbrand, 1892). The condition referred to as *prosopagnosia* (Greek for face-not-knowing) is particularly bizarre because patients may fail to recognize their spouses or even themselves when they look in the mirror and yet patients may recognize other types of object and may be able to recognize people from their clothing or voice (Bodamer, 1947; Ellis & Florence, 1990).

So far cells that respond to head have been described as if they respond equally to all individuals. Because prosopagnosia appears to be a deficit in recognizing identity, it might be predicted that particular cells would be sensitive to facial identity (Barlow, 1972; Konorski, 1967). Such a postulate appeared to contradict models of recognition dependent on neural population coding. Furthermore, the likelihood of confirming such a prediction was understandably doubted because searching for such cells would be like looking for a needle in a haystack (Hofstader, 1980).

Despite the improbability of finding such tuning at the cellular level, the 1980s saw several research groups report cells in the temporal lobe that responded differently to different faces (Baylis, Rolls, & Leonard, 1985; Desimone et al., 1984; Heit, Smith, & Halgren, 1988; Kendrick & Baldwin, 1987; Perrett, Harries, Bevan et al., 1989; Perrett, Harries, Mistlin, & Chitty, 1989; Perrett, Mistlin, & Harries, 1989; Perrett et al., 1991; Perrett et al., 1984, 1987; Yamane, Kaji, & Kawano, 1988). In these resports, about 10% of the cells responsive to faces were found to show sensitivity to identity.

Viewer-Centered and Object-Centered Coding of Identity

Within each of the populations of cells sensitive to different views of the head, a fraction of the cells again appear to be sensitive to the identity of familiar faces. Thus some cells that are selective for the right profile display additional selectivity for identity. These cells may respond to the right profile of one individual but not to the left profile of the same individual or to any view of a second individual (e.g., Fig. 2.12). These data suggest that for each known individual there would be cell populations selectively tuned to four characteristic views of that person (in the horizontal plane). Although additional representations of the person at intermediate views might also exist, they would be less numerous.

As mentioned earlier, a minority of cells studied in the temporal cortex have been found to display object-centered properties (responding, e.g., to the sight of the head from any perspective view but not responding to other objects). Selectivity for identity can be found among cells exhibiting object-centered responses. Indeed if, as argued previously, object-centered descriptions are most useful for recognizing what an object is, then one would expect more identity sensitivity to be manifest among this class of cell. Preliminary data indicate that there may indeed be more object-centered cells displaying identity sensitivity than viewer-centered cells but so far very few object-centered cells have been studied (Perrett et al., 1991). An example of an object-centered cell displaying sensitivity to

MH

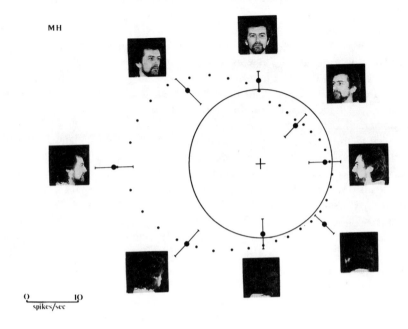

O———10
spikes/sec

PB

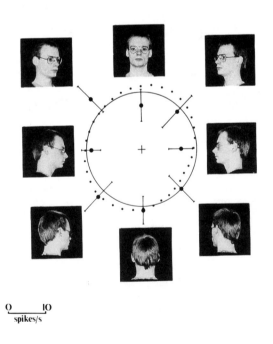

O———10
spikes/s

FIG. 2.12

56

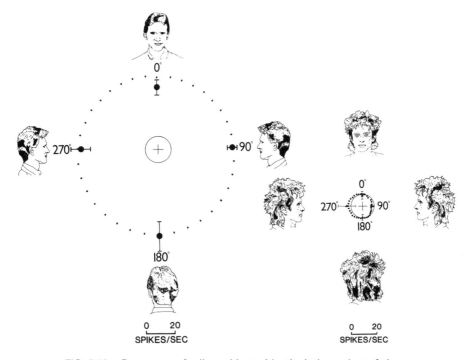

FIG. 2.13. Responses of cell sensitive to identity independent of view. Responses of one cell to four views of one experimenter (JH shown on the left) were significantly greater than responses to the same four views of a second experimenter (DP shown on the right). Calibration bars = 10 spikes/second (from Perrett, Harries, Bevan et al., 1989).

identity independent of view is shown in Fig. 2.13. The responses of this cell to four views of one experimenter (JH) were all significantly greater than responses to controls and spontaneous activity. The cell was, however, unresponsive to a second experimenter (DP).

The findings just described support the model of recognition whereby the outputs of populations of cells separately sensitive to the appearance of the

FIG. 2.12. Tuning for perspective view of a cell sensitive to identity. Upper: the mean and standard error of response from five trials are illustrated for eight views of one experimenter (MH). Response magnitude to each view is depicted as the distance of a large dot to the central cross. The dotted line is the best fit second-order cardioid function. The cell responded more to the right profile view of MH than the cell's spontaneous activity (central circle). Lower: the cell did not respond to any of the eight views of a second equally familiar individual (PB). All stimuli were tested in random order (from Perrett, Harries, Bevan et al., 1989).

person seen from face, left and right profile, and back views are pooled together to establish the responses of (object-centered) cells selective for an individual person seen across all perspective views. In line with this hierarchical model is the finding that object-centered responses occur at longer latencies than view-specific responses (Perrett, Hietanen, Oram, & Benson, 1992b).

To summarize this section, it was perhaps predictable from the neuropsychological studies of prosopagnosia that some neural mechanisms would be selective for faces. Nevertheless, the response selectivity exhibited by some cells to differences in between familiar faces has been found to be surprisingly high. The single-cell studies suggest that the appearance of each familiar face is represented by cell populations tuned to separate characteristic views of that individual's face, profile, and so forth. View-independent representation of individuals is formed by combining the outputs of view-specific cells.

ACKNOWLEDGMENTS

We acknowledge the contributions of M. H. Harries, R. Bevan, S. Thomas, and W. Dittrich to some of the experiments reported here. This research was funded by project grants from the SERC, ESRC, and NEDO (Japan). DP was supported by a Royal Society University Research Fellowship and JH by the Pirkanmaa Cultural Foundation, Kordelin Foundation, and Aaltonen Foundation.

REFERENCES

Barlow, H. B. (1972). Single units and sensation: A neuron doctrine for perceptual psychology. *Perception, 1,* 371–394.

Baron, R. J. (1981). Mechanisms of facial recognition. *International Journal of Man-Machine Studies, 15,* 137–178.

Baylis, G. C., Rolls, E. T., & Leonard, C. M. (1985). Selectivity between faces in the responses of a population of neurons in the cortex of the superior temporal sulcus of the macaque monkey. *Brain Research, 342,* 91–102.

Biederman, I. (1985). Recognition by components: A theory of human image understanding. *Psychological Review, 94,* 115–147.

Bodamer, J. (1947). Die Prosop-agnosie. *Archiv für psychiatrie und zeitschrift für Neurologie,* [Archive for Psychiatry and Journal for Neurology] *179,* 6–53.

Bruce, V., Valentine, T., & Baddely, A. (1987). The basis of the ¾ view advantage in face recognition. *Applied Cognitive Psychology, 1,* 109–120.

Callahan, J., & Weiss, R. (1985). A model for describing surface shape. In *Proceedings of the IEEE Conference on Computer Vision and Pattern Recognition* (pp. 240–245). New York: IEEE Computer Society.

Chakravarty, I., & Freeman, H. (1982). The use of characteristic views as a basis for recognition of three dimensional objects. *SPIE 336, Robot Vision,* 37–45.

Desimone, R., Albright, T. D., Gross, C. G., & Bruce, C. (1984). Stimulus-selective properties of inferior temporal neurons in the macaque. *Journal of Neuroscience, 8,* 2051–2062.

Ellis, H. D., & Florence, M. (1990). Bodamer's (1947) paper on prosopagnosia. *Cognitive Neuropsychology, 7,* 81–105.

Gray, M. (1986). Recognition planning from solid models. *Proceedings of the Alvey Computer Vision and Image Interpretation Meeting, Bristol, September 1986* (pp. 41–43). Sheffield, England: Sheffield University Press.

Harries, M. H., & Perrett, D. I. (1991). Visual processing of faces in temporal cortex: Physiological evidence for a modular organization and possible anatomical correlates. *Journal of Cognitive Neuroscience, 3,* 9–24.

Harries, M. H., Perrett, D. I., & Lavender, A. (1991). Visual inspection during encoding and recognition of 3-D heads. *Perception, 20,* 669–680.

Hasselmo, M. E., Rolls, E. T., Baylis, G. C., & Nalwa, V. (1989). Object-centered encoding by face-selective neurons in the cortex in the superior temporal sulcus of the monkey. *Experimental Brain Research, 75,* 417–429.

Heit, G., Smith, M. E., & Halgren, E. (1988). Neural encoding of individual words and faces by the human hippocampus and amygdala. *Nature, 333,* 773–775.

Hietanen, J. K., Perrett, D. I., Oram, M. W., Benson, P. J., & Dittrich, W. H. (1992). The effects of lighting conditons on responses of cells selective for face views in the macaque temporal cortex. *Experimental Brain Research, 89,* 157–171.

Hinton, D., & Parsons, L. M. (1988). Scene-based and viewer-centered representations for comparing shapes. *Cognition, 30,* 1–35.

Hofstader, D. R. (1980). *Gödel, Escher, Bach: An eternal golden braid.* Harmondsworth, England: Penguin.

Humphrey, G. K. (1988). Visual object identification: Some effects of image foreshortening and monocular depth cues. In Z. Pylyshyn (Ed.), *Computational processes in human vision: An interdisciplinary perspective* (pp. 429–442).

Humphreys, G. W., & Riddoch, M. J. (1984). Routes to object constancy: Implications from neurological impairments of object constancy. *Quarterly Journal of Experimental Psychology, 36A,* 385–415.

Ikeuchi, K. (1987). Generating an interpretation tree from a CAD model for 3D-object recognition in bin-picking tasks. *International Journal of Computer Vision, 1,* 145–165.

Jolicoeur, P. (1985). The time to name disoriented natural objects. *Memory and Cognition, 13,* 289–303.

Kendrick, K. M., & Baldwin, B. A. (1987). Cells in temporal cortex of conscious sheep can respond preferentially to the sight of faces. *Science, 236,* 448–450.

Koenderink, J. J., & van Doorn, A. J. (1976). The singularities of the visual mapping. *Biological Cybernetics, 24,* 51–59.

Koenderink, J. J., & van Doorn, A. J. (1979). The internal representation of solid shape with respect to vision. *Biological Cybernetics, 32,* 211–216.

Konorski, J. (1967). *Integrative activity of the brain.* Chicago: University of Chicago Press.

Langdon, P. M., Mayhew, J. E. W., & Frisby, J. P. (1991). In search of characteristic view 3-D object representations in human vision using ratings of perceived differences between views. In J. E. W. Mayhew & J. P. Frisby (Eds.), *Model recognition from stereoscopic cues* (pp. 243–248). Cambridge, MA: MIT Press.

Lowe, D. (1985). *Perceptual organization and visual recognition.* Boston: Kluwer.

Lowe, D. (1987). Three-dimensional object recognition from single two-dimensional images. *Artificial Intelligence, 31,* 355–395.

Marr, D. (1982). *Vision.* San Francisco: Freeman.

Marr, D., & Nishihara, H. K. (1978). Representation and recognition of the spatial organization of 3-dimensional shapes. *Proceedings of the Royal Society of London, B*(200), 269–294.

Milner, A. D., Perrett, D. I., Johnston, R., Benson, P. J., Jordan, T. R., Heeley, D. W., Bettucci,

D., Mortara, F., Mutani, R., Terazzi, E., & Davidson, D. L. W. (1991). Perception and action in "visual form agnosia." *Brain, 114,* 405–428.

Miyashita, Y. (1990). Associative representation of visual long term memory in the neurons of the primate temporal cortex. In E. Iwai & M. Mishkin (Eds.), *Vision, memory and the temporal lobe* (pp. 75–87). New York: Elsevier.

Palmer, S., Rosch, E., & Chase, P. (1981). Canonical perspective and the perception of objects. In J. Long & A. Baddeley (Eds.), *Attention and performance IX* (pp. 135–151). Hillsdale, NJ: Lawrence Erlbaum Associates.

Parsons, L. M. (1987). Visual discrimination of abstract mirror-reflected three-dimensional objects at many orientations. *Perception and Psychophysics, 42,* 49–59.

Perrett, D. I., & Harries, M. H. (1988). Characteristic views and the visual inspection of simple faceted and smooth objects: "Tetrahedra and potatoes." *Perception, 17,* 703–720.

Perrett, D. I., Harries, M. H., Bevan, R., Thomas, S., Benson, P. J., Mistlin, A. J., Chitty, A. J., Hietanen, J. K., & Ortega, J. E. (1989). Frameworks of analysis for the neural representation of animate objects and actions. *Journal of Experimental Biology, 146,* 87–114.

Perrett, D. I., Harries, M. H., Mistlin, A. J., & Chitty, A. J. (1989). Recognizing objects and actions: Frameworks for neuronal computation and perceptual experience. In D. M. Guthrie (Ed.), *Higher order sensory processing. Studies in neuroscience series* (pp. 155–173). Manchester, England: Manchester University Press.

Perrett, D. I., Harries, M. H., Mistlin, A. J., & Chitty, A. J. (1990). Three stages in the classification of body movements by visual neurons. In H. B. Barlow, C. Blakemore, & M. Weston-Smith (Eds.), *Images and understanding* (pp. 94–108). Cambridge, England: Cambridge University Press.

Perrett, D. I., Hietanen, J. K., Oram, M. W., & Benson, P. J.(1992b). Organization and functions of cells responsive to faces in the temporal cortex. *Philosophical Transactions of the Royal Society of London, 335,* 23–30.

Perrett, D. I., Looker, S., & Harries, M. H. (in press). Using preferential inspection to define the viewing sphere and characteristic views of an arbitrary machined object. *Perception, 21,* 497–515.

Perrett, D. I., Mistlin, A. J., & Chitty, A. J. (1987). Visual cells responsive to faces. *Trends in Neuroscience, 10,* 358–364.

Perrett, D. I., Mistlin, A. J., & Harries, M. H. (1989). Seeing faces: The representation of facial information in temporal cortex. In J. J. Kulikowski, C. M. Dickinson, & I. J. Murray (Eds.), *Seeing contour and colour* (pp. 770–754). Oxford, England: Pergamon.

Perrett, D. I., Oram, M. W., Harries, M. H., Bevan, R., Hietanen, J. K., Benson, P. J., & Thomas, S. (1991). Viewer-centered and object-centered encoding of heads by cells in the superior temporal sulcus of the rhesus monkey. *Experimental Brain Research, 86,* 159–173.

Perrett, D. I., Rolls, E. T., & Caan, W. (1982). Visual neurones responsive to faces in the monkey temporal cortex. *Experimental Brain Research, 47,* 329–342.

Perrett, D. I., Smith, P. A. J., Mistlin, A. J., Chitty, A. J., Head, A. S., Potter, D. D., Broennimann, R., Milner, A. D., & Jeeves, M. A. (1985). Visual analysis of body movements by neurons in the temporal cortex of the macaque monkey: A preliminary report. *Behavioral Brain Research, 16,* 153–170.

Perrett, D. I., Smith, P. A. J., Potter, D. D., Mistlin, A. J., Head, A. S., Milner, A. D., & Jeeves, M. A. (1984). Neurons responsive to faces in the temporal cortex: Studies of functional organization, sensitivity to identity and relation to perception. *Human Neurobiology, 3,* 197–208.

Perrett, D. I., Smith, P. A. J., Potter, D. D., Mistlin, A. J., Head, A. S., Milner, A. D., & Jeeves, M. A. (1985). Visual cells in the temporal cortex sensitive to face view and gaze direction. *Proceedings of the Royal Society of London, B, 3,* 293–317.

Poggio, T., & Edelman, S. (1990). A network that learns to recognize three-dimensional objects. *Nature, 343,* 263–266.

Rock, I. (1973). *Orientation and forms*. New York: Academic.

Rock, I., & di Vita, J. (1987). A case of viewer-centered object perception. *Cognitive Psychology, 19*, 280–293.

Rolls, E. T., Perrett, D. I., Thorpe, S. J., Puerto, A., Roper-Hall, A., & Maddison, S. (1979). Responses of neurons in area 7 of the parietal cortex to objects of different significance. *Brain Research, 169*, 194–198.

Seibert, M., & Waxman, A. M. (1990). Learning aspect graph representations from view sequences. In D. S. Touretzky (Ed.), *Advances in neural network information processing systems* (Vol. 2) (pp. 258–265). San Mateo, CA: Morgan Kaufman.

Tanaka, K., Saito, H-A., Fukada, Y., & Moriya, M. (1991). Coding visual images of objects in the inferotemporal cortex of the macaque monkey. *Journal of Neurophysiology, 66*, 170–189.

Thomas, S., Perrett, D. I., Davis, D. N., & Harries, M. H. (1992). *Effect of perspective view on recognition of faces*. Manuscript submitted for publication.

Thorpe, C., & Shafer, S. (1983). Correspondence in line-drawings of multiple views of objects. In *Proceedings of the 8th International Conference on Artificial Intelligence* (Vol. 2, pp. 959–965). Los Altos: William Kaufman Publishers, Inc.

Ullman, S. (1989). Aligning pictorial descriptions: An approach to object recognition. *Cognition, 32*, 193–254.

Warrington, E. K., & James, M. (1986). Visual object recognition in patients with right hemisphere lesions: Axes or features? *Perception, 15*, 355–366.

Warrington, E. K., & Taylor, A. M. (1973). The contribution of the right parietal lobe to object recognition. *Cortex, 9*, 152–164.

Wilbrand, H. (1892). Ein fall von seelenblindheit und hemianopsie mit sectionsbefund [German Journal for Neural Medicine]. *Deutche Zeitschrift für Nervenheilkunde, 2*, 361–87.

Yamane, S., Kaji, S., & Kawano, K. (1988). What facial features activate face neurons in the inferotemporal cortex. *Experimental Brain Research, 73*, 209–214.

3 Intermediate Visual Processing and Visual Agnosia

Glyn W. Humphreys,
M. Jane Riddoch
University of Birmingham

Nick Donnelly
University of Kent

Tom Freeman,
Muriel Boucart
Universite Paris V

Hermann M. Müller
Birkbeck College

Despite having a history as long as that involving any cognitive disorder, neurological impairments of visual perception—the impairments underlying the syndrome of visual agnosia—remain poorly understood. This is likely due to several factors. One is that frank disorders of visual perception, unaccounted for by, for example, loss of acuity or generalized dementia, remain clinically rare. For this reason alone, some writers have even doubted their existence. For instance, writing in only 1972, Bender and Feldman claimed that visual agnosia did not exist, independent of problems in basic perceptual functions or in general cognitive function. Today, the case for the existence of visual agnosia as a clinical phenomenon is more secure. There exist several good single-case and group studies of patients with selective problems in particular perceptual processes mediating visual object recognition, which cannot be attributed to impaired basic perceptual or general cognitive functions (e.g., Grailet, Seron, Bruyer, Coyette, & Frederix, 1990; Humphreys & Riddoch, 1987b; Ratcliff & Newcombe, 1982; Riddoch & Humphreys, 1987a, 1987b; Warrington & Shallice, 1984; Warrington & Taylor, 1978). Perhaps even more serious as far as understanding visual agnosia is concerned is that, even when patients can be shown to have normal acuity and to be intellectually intact, attempts to link disorders to explicit models of visual perception have made only slow progress. Our thesis is that there needs to be close interlinking of neuropsychological studies with detailed computation-

al models of normal cognitive function, in order to understand a given neuropsychological disorder and in order to use neuropsychological evidence to evaluate
particular models. We illustrate this by a discussion of both prior and current
theoretical accounts of agnosia. We then attempt to go some way beyond this
with reference to three single cases we have worked on, each of which (we
argue) has a selective disturbance of a particular perceptual process. To account
for such patients, the nature of these different processes must be articulated.

Lissauer's Classification

Lissauer (1890) made a general distinction between patients that has dominated
conceptual thought on agnosia over the past century. He distinguished between
patients with impaired *apperceptive* and those with impaired *associative* processes. Lissauer argued that apperceptive processes are involved in establishing a
stable perceptual representation of the visual world whereas associative processes are involved with linking perceptual representations to stored knowledge
about objects. The relations between apperceptive and associative visual processes were not articulated, though it may be presumed that apperceptive processes precede those involved in association. To be termed an *apperceptive
agnosic*, patients should have an impairment of visual perception, but not one
that is simply due to poor acuity or to a visual field defect. To be termed an
associative agnosic, patients should have intact perceptual processes, and yet
still be poor at accessing stored object knowledge—at recognizing objects.

Many studies of agnosia have been content to classify patients in terms of
Lissauer's (1890) broad distinction, not attempting to go further to explore the
nature of the apperceptive or associative disorder. In addition, very often the
clinical boundaries between these two classes of patients may be crudely drawn,
and may simply come down to whether patients can copy the objects they fail to
recognize and whether they can discriminate simple visual shapes—two clinical
tests used to establish whether visual perception is intact or impaired. However,
copying performance is often difficult to evaluate. For instance, patients may fail
to copy because of a constructional deficit or because of a problem in scanning
attention and/or in marking the location of inspection in between eye movements
to the model and the copy; thus a problem in copying does not necessarily
indicate a problem in on-line visual object recognition. To the contrary, patients
may be able to produce an acceptable end copy even with severely impaired
perceptual processing. This last point is illustrated by the case of HJA, described
by Humphreys and Riddoch (1987b) (this same patient is discussed in more
detail in Case 1 later). HJA showed clear effects of perceptual variables on his
visual object recognition (e.g., there were marked effects of the stimulus exposure duration, and of whether or not figures were overlapping). Nevertheless, he
was able to produce accurate copies of items he failed to recognize (see Fig. 3.1
for one example). Humphreys and Riddoch suggested that patients with percep-

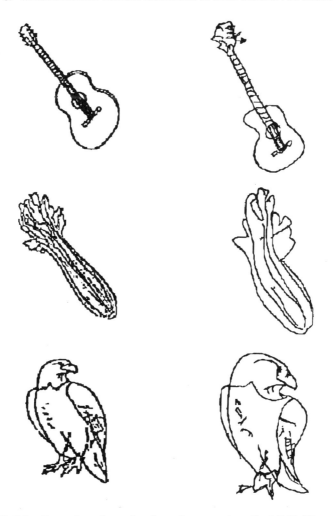

FIG. 3.1. Examples of copying from the agnosic patient HJA (Humphreys & Riddoch, 1987a). He was unable to identify any of the stimuli shown (copy on the right).

tual impairments can produce accurate copies by adopting a piecemeal, line-by-line copying strategy. This strategy can be successfully adopted even if patients are unable to (for instance) group perceptual information appropriately, just so long as the patients can perform a controlled attentional scan across a display.

A similar argument can be made about the problems involved in interpreting the data from shape discrimination tasks. As we discuss later, we do not always know how shape discrimination tasks are performed. Patients may succeed at shape discrimination when given simple stimuli under no time pressures, and yet have compromised processing of multiple shapes (see Case 1). In over a century of study, few questions have been raised about whether the apperception-association divide is the best way to slice the visual perception cake, or whether differences between patients within each category are just as great as those across the two categories.

More Recent Classifications

In the past 10 years or so, attempts have begun to be made to develop a fuller conceptual account of visual perceptual disorders. Investigators have separated several processes that fall within the general apperception-association umbrella. To illustrate, Warrington (Kartsounis & Warrington, 1991; Warrington, 1982, 1985) distinguished between the processes involved in shape coding, figure-ground segmentation, and perceptual and semantic classification. Humphreys and Riddoch (1987a) distinguished between the coding of visual features at different spatial scales, the integration and grouping of these features, the mapping of these features to stored representations of objects, access to stored knowledge about the structural properties of objects, access to stored semantic knowledge about object function and interobject associations. Farah (1990) distinguished between patients with impaired grouping of elementary features, those with problems disengaging attention from selected groups, those with problems representing structural descriptions of objects with complex parts, and those with problems representing structural descriptions of objects with multiple parts (see chapter 5). The distinctions made by Warrington and by Humphreys and Riddoch are characterized by the view that visual object recognition proceeds from the coding of simple features (e.g., edges at particular orientations, or even primitive shapes), to the grouping and description of those features, to a process of mapping input descriptions to stored knowledge, to the retrieval of particular types of stored knowledge. These distinctions preserve Lissauer's (1890) basic classification, but split both the apperceptive and the associative stages down into a number of separable components. Figure 3.2 indicates the relations between these more elaborated accounts and Lissauer's original apperception-association dichotomy. Within each framework, each putative process can be assessed by particular tests, as described in the next section.

The Fractionation of Apperception

Warrington's (Kartsounis & Warrington, 1991; Warrington, 1982, 1985) framework distinguishes between three separate apperceptive processes: shape coding, figure-ground segmentation, and perceptual classification (the ability to judge that objects are the same across transformations in viewpoint). Humphreys and Riddoch (1987a) additionally distinguished feature grouping and image segmentation, and the process of mapping input descriptions onto stored structural

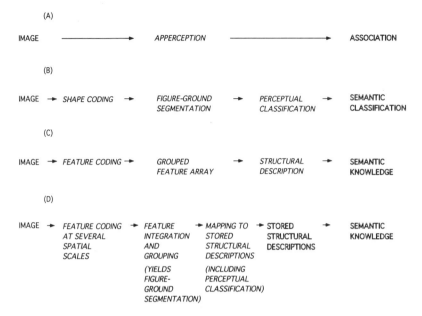

FIG. 3.2.   Relations between Lissauer's (1890) distinction between apperceptive and associative agnosia and more recent accounts of agnosia following Warrington (1985) (B); Farah (1990) (C); Humphreys & Riddoch, 1987a (D).

representations. These distinctions are based on findings showing that selective patients can have problems with tests thought to tap each putative process.

Shape coding is standardly assessed using the "Efron shape-matching" test, in which patients have to match shapes equated for total flux (after Efron, 1968). To perform this task, it is insufficient to encode image intensity or only the orientation of the edges of the shapes. Figure-ground segmentation may be assessed by requiring patients to find a target figure against a background of varying degrees of random visual noise or by having the patient identify sets of overlapping figures (relative to control conditions, where the same figures are nonoverlapping; see Riddoch & Humphreys, 1987a). Perceptual classification is typically assessed by tasks requiring patients to match objects seen from different viewpoints. Examples of each test are shown in Fig. 3.3.

Patients with diffuse bilateral brain damage, often following carbon monoxide poisoning, have been shown to be impaired at the Efron shape-matching test; patients with unilateral right posterior lesions have been shown to be impaired at detecting figures in visual noise and in matching objects seen from different views (e.g., Benson & Greenberg, 1969; Warrington, 1985; Warrington & James, 1986; Warrington & Taylor, 1973, 1978). Patients can be poor at match-

(A)

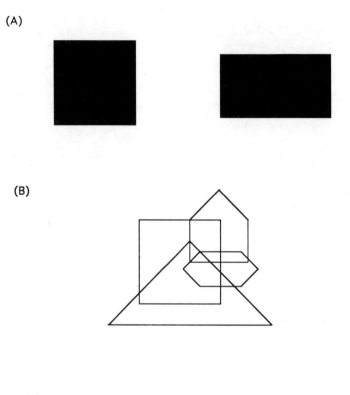

(B)

(C)

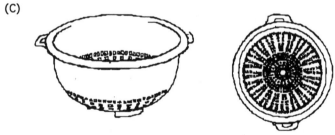

FIG. 3.3. Example tests used to assess various subprocesses within visual object recognition. (A) stimuli from the Efron shape-matching test; (B) overlapping figures; (C) stimuli for a different-view matching test. In the Efron test, subjects are asked to judge whether the two stimuli have the same shape. In the overlapping figures test, subjects may be asked to name the individual overlapping figures. In the different-view matching test, subjects are asked whether the items shown are the same object, irrespective of any differences in viewpoint.

ing across viewpoints even when their ability to discriminate simple visual attributes of stimuli is intact (Humphreys & Riddoch, 1984).

Humphreys and Riddoch (1987a) attempted to be more explicit about the processes involved in figure-ground segmentation, stating that it typically involves cooperative interactions between grouping processes at different levels of resolution. Such interactions may break down in a number of ways, one of which is that global information might override information about more local perceptual groups, leaving patients with undifferentiated global representations of objects. We attempt to expand upon this account within this chapter.

The Fractionation of Association

It is also possible to distinguish between some of the processes involved in mapping visual input representations to stored object knowledge so that objects are recognized and not merely perceived (i.e., so that some selective item-specific action be applied). Riddoch and Humphreys (1987b) argued that stored knowledge about the perceptual structure of objects can be distinguished from stored semantic knowledge concerned with object function and associative relations between objects. Their argument was based on a case study of a patient, JB, with a marked problem in naming visually presented objects. In addition, he performed poorly on a visual association test in which he was given triplets of objects and had to judge which two of the three were used together (e.g., a hammer, a nail, and a screw). When he was given the names of the objects he performed perfectly, so it was not the case that he misunderstood the nature of the task. In contrast to his performance on visual naming and visual association tasks, which Riddoch and Humphreys judged to require access to stored semantic knowledge, JB was good at discriminating between line drawings of real objects and drawings of "nonobjects" that were created by interchanging the parts of real objects (an *object decision* task; see Fig. 3.4). This pattern of performance—good object decision but poor visual association—was interpreted as showing good visual access to stored structural knowledge about objects along with poor visual access to semantic knowledge (note that auditory access to semantic knowledge seemed intact in this case, given JB's ability to perform the association task with auditory input).

Arguments have been raised concerning Riddoch and Humphreys' (1987b) interpretation. In particular, it has been suggested that the visual association test required verbal mediation, perhaps because the items used were related verbally rather than functionally (e.g., Farah, 1990). A patient with poor retrieval of object names from vision would then have difficulty with the task, even if visual access to associative semantic knowledge is intact. It might then also follow that object decision performance reflected access to semantic knowledge, rather than access to a structural knowledge system functionally separable from the semantic system.

FIG. 3.4. Example stimuli from an object decision test. Real objects are depicted on the left and their partner nonobjects are shown on the right (after Riddoch & Humphreys, 1987b).

Recently, Chertkow, Bub, and Caplan (1992) observed a similar dissociation to that reported by Riddoch and Humphreys (1987b) in patients suffering Alzheimer's disease—namely, good object decision being demonstrated alongside poor matching of functionally similar objects. We also recently observed the same dissociation in a patient with poor performance on a range of tasks seeming to depend on access to semantic (functional/associative) knowledge (Riddoch, Bateman, & Humphreys, in preparation). This patient, EH, was poor at picture-word matching when there were semantically related picture distractors (e.g., choosing a hose rather than a bucket), she made semantic errors when asked to gesture to visually presented objects (e.g., using a hammer as a saw), and she was close to chance at the pictorial version of Howard and Orchard-Lisle's (1984) "pyramids and palm trees" task (in this task the patient might be asked to choose whether a picture of a palm tree or that of a deciduous tree goes with a picture of a pyramid, a task requiring visual access to associative knowledge about the items). These results support the distinction between different types of stored knowledge mediating visual object recognition. Chertkow et al. suggested that the dissociation is due to the patients being able to carry out a basic "visual identification procedure" while failing to retrieve full semantic knowledge. This identification procedure would normally subserve on-line object recognition, which does not require full retrieval of all our factual knowledge about a given object. However, were that the case, patients would be expected to interact normally with objects in everyday life, which is certainly not the case. Both the patients we have observed, JB and EH, were markedly impaired in everyday tasks and would use objects inappropriately on occasions. Our alternative distinction separates stored perceptual knowledge about the structure of objects from stored semantic knowledge. Patients showing good object decision alongside poor visual association matching have visual access to the former but not the latter knowledge store. Whichever the case, the data clearly indicate that the association process, as first discussed by Lissauer (1890), can be fractionated into a number of subprocesses.

In other patients, the recognition problem seems to be one in which stored perceptual knowledge about objects can be selectively impaired. Sartori and Job (1988) reported a patient with object recognition problems following herpes simplex encephalitis infection. This patient, Michelangelo, was impaired at object decision, despite appearing to have otherwise intact visual perception. In another similar case reported by Silveri and Gainotti (1988), the patient was poor at answering definitions that emphasized the visual properties of objects although she was good with definitions emphasizing functional properties. Such cases suggest that patients can have impaired perceptual knowledge about the structural characteristics of objects along with relatively intact verbal semantic knowledge. Figure 3.2 illustrates a simple framework for these patterns of dissociations.

Models of Object Processing

The other side of the problem of providing fully articulated accounts of visual object recognition disorders is the lack of well-specified theories of object processing. Similar to the finer grained frameworks derived from neuropsychological studies, a form of hierarchical processing model may be generally agreed upon for normal object recognition. A prototypical model would separate (a) "early" stages of visual processing, concerned with the registration of primitive visual features, (b) intermediate processes involved in grouping these features and in segmenting figure from ground, and (c) "late" processes involved in activating stored object knowledge. This framework characterizes many current theories (e.g., Biederman, 1987; Marr, 1982). Much less well developed are accounts of how these different processing stages interact, or how processes leading to visual object recognition relate to processes traditionally labeled as *attentional*—by which we mean processes involved in selecting between competing visual descriptions in order that one such description should determine action. However, accounts concerned with interactions between processes, and with the interaction between object processing and visual attention, are needed in order to understand the complex ways in which visual object recognition may break down.

On the Relations Between Patients

One other difficulty in the field is in understanding the relations between different patients. Relatively few patients have been investigated in detail, and in many instances the cases have been examined within the context of rather different approaches to object recognition. Hence the relations between different patients are difficult to specify. This holds even for the attempts to develop finer grained accounts of visual perceptual impairments. For instance, Humphreys and Riddoch (1987a) distinguished patients with problems in basic shape processing, in perceptual classification, and in shape integration, all of whom may coarsely be described as having apperceptive problems. Warrington (1985; see also Warrington & James, 1988) distinguished between *pseudo-agnosics* with poor shape perception and apperceptive agnosics with problems only in perceptual classification. Kartsounis and Warrington (1991) additionally argued for figure-ground segmentation processes being impaired while shape perception (e.g., judged from performance on the Efron shape-matching test) remains relatively intact. Farah (1990) distinguished patients with impaired grouping of local image features, those with problems disengaging attention from selected groups (*dorsal simultanagnosics*) those with problems representing objects with many parts (*ventral simultanagnosics*), and those with problems representing objects with complex parts (the latter two constituting two forms of associative agnosia). As we noted earlier, some of these distinctions can be made by assessing performance on specific tasks—the Efron test, tests with overlapping figures, tests of matching objects depicted in different views. However, some of the distinctions between patients are not closely tied to performance on any single diagnostic task (e.g., problems due to reduced visual processing capacity vs. problems in representing objects with multiple parts). Moreover, as we have noted, the procedures involved in performing some of the diagnostic tests may not be well specified in processing terms (i.e., in terms of an explicit model). For instance, it is by no means clear how the Efron shape-matching test is usually performed. Is matching based on the length of single sides of the shapes? Does it depend on the orientation of low spatial frequency components in the image? Does it require computation of the relations between the sides (we take it that computation of the relationship between two or more component features, such as edges at particular orientations, is the hallmark of shape processing)? What is needed here is converging evidence concerning the procedures normally involved in a given task. As it is, it is conceivable that patients could have problems with the test for any of several reasons. There is a consequent danger that one person's shape agnosic is another person's pseudoagnosic or even dorsal simultanagnosic—each so labeled because of performance on a range of tasks not well worked through in processing terms.

We believe such problems can only be overcome by a two-pronged attack, in which more detailed and theoretically informed tests are carried out on patients, and in which testing is coupled to the development of more detailed theoretical accounts (based on studies of normal visual perception, and/or on computational modeling). These different aspects of research are mutually relevant. Neuropsychological assessment should be theoretically informed, but the results can also be used to develop theory further.

This chapter is confined to a discussion of what we term *intermediate visual processing* problems, involved in coding the relations between visual attributes prior to accessing stored object knowledge (though we argue that it is difficult to keep stored object knowledge separate from visual encoding processes). Disorders in the registration of primitive visual information (e.g., lines and edges at particular orientations, of particular colors, or containing particular spatial frequencies), or disorders due to impairments of stored object knowledge, are not considered. We outline our argument for the close coupling of detailed empirical tests and explicit models with respect to three cases.

CASE 1: NOISY PARALLEL GROUPING

The first case is HJA, a patient we have documented in a number of studies (e.g., Humphreys & Riddoch, 1987b; Riddoch & Humphreys, 1987a).

Case Details

HJA suffered a stroke peri-operatively in 1981, producing a bilateral lesion of the occipital cortex, extending anteriorly toward the temporal cortex. This left him with a bilateral superior altitudinal field defect, but with intact lower visual fields. Acuity was normal. After the stroke, HJA was unable to recognize many common objects by sight, though tactile object recognition was preserved. He was prosopagnosic, had considerable difficulty finding his way, and had difficulty on color discrimination tests (see Humphreys, Troscianko et al., 1992, for a more detailed discussion of HJA's color processing). His reading was reduced to operating in a letter-by-letter fashion. In tests performed over the 10 years since his stroke, HJA's perceptual performance has essentially remained stable (Humphreys & Riddoch, in press, c).

Summary of Object Recognition Performance

When initially tested in 1981, HJA named about 60% of common household objects correctly, and this reduced to around 40% when line drawings of the same objects were presented. In a retest in 1990 he named 80% of the real objects correctly, but still only about 40% of the line drawings. When unable to name an object, he was unable to demonstrate recognition by any other means (e.g., circumlocution, gesturing), and he scored poorly on matching tests that require access to semantic or functional knowledge about objects from vision (Riddoch & Humphreys, 1987a). Tactile object identification was normal. His visual identification was characterized by visual naming errors (e.g., drawing of an onion → necklace). Such errors never involved HJA identifying the whole object as a part (e.g., identifying a deer as an antler; see Case 2), but always indicate some awareness of the whole shape of the object.

HJA can match photographs of objects shown from some unusual viewpoints (in particular, if the distinctive features of objects are salient in both views; Humphreys & Riddoch, 1984), and he is able to copy objects he cannot recognize (see Riddoch & Humphreys, 1987a). He is also able to perform the Efron shape-matching test, when simultaneously presented with two shapes to match and given unlimited viewing time (Humphreys, Riddoch, Quinlan, Price, & Donnelly, 1992). On the basis of these test results, it might be argued that HJA is an associative agnosic, having intact perceptual processes.

Against this is the difference between his identification of real objects and line drawings, which suggests some underlying perceptual deficit. This is corroborated by evidence showing that HJA's object identification is strongly affected by exposure duration and he is poor both at identifying overlapping figures and at object decision tasks with line drawings relative to silhouettes (i.e., at deciding whether a picture is of a meaningful or a meaningless object; Riddoch & Humphreys, 1987a). In each of these instances, manipulation of a perceptual variable (exposure time, overlap of line contours, the presence of internal contours in line drawings) exerts an abnormal effect on his object processing. The perceptual deficit is simply not shown by tests such as copying, (some forms of) unusual view matching, and shape matching. What is characteristic of these perceptual tasks that HJA can do is that they can be performed in a serial, piecemeal fashion. He performs poorly when stimuli must be perceived "at a glance" (under reduced exposure conditions), and when stimuli contain multiple segmentation cues (with overlapping figures, and with line drawings as opposed to silhouettes). Indeed, one reason why his identification of real objects is superior to that of line drawings may be because in real objects, surface details constrain segmentation.

Some More Specific Tests

The difficulty HJA experiences when visual stimuli are presented briefly and when they contain multiple cues for segmentation suggested to us that there may be a deficit in grouping visual features in parallel across visual forms. From the Gestalt psychologists on, it has long been recognized that grouping between local features of visual stimuli is· important for normal visual perception. Grouping processes normally operate in parallel across visual forms. For instance, Donnelly, Humphreys, and Riddoch (1991) had normal subjects perform a task in which they were presented with varying numbers of *vertex* stimuli, the task being to decide whether all of the vertices faced "in" toward fixation or whether one faced out (see Fig. 3.5). There was no effect of the number of vertices on performance. However, changing the task in a very simple way produced a dramatic effect. When all the vertices were reversed so that they either all faced away from fixation or one faced in (subjects had to decide whether one faced in), reaction times (RTs) increased at a rate of about 30 ms per vertex. Reversing the vertices changes some of the relationships that the Gestalt psychologists thought important for visual recognition: namely, continuation between the terminators of the junctions and whether the junctions form a single closed shape. The presence of such relationships enables visual elements to be grouped into a single perceptual object. In the absence of such relationships, performance is inefficient and each junction treated as a separate perceptual object—producing effects of the number of junctions present.

The ability to group form information in this way is fundamental to our ability to identify briefly presented objects, when there is insufficient time for serial scrutiny. It is also likely to be important for our ability to encode the relations between parts of complex objects, and to segment objects apart in complex

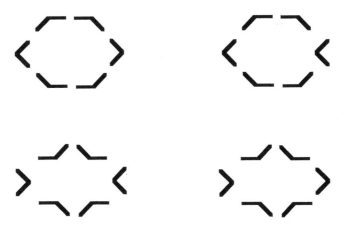

FIG. 3.5. Example stimuli from Donnelly et al. (1991).

displays. Indeed, computational models of object coding and segmentation typically depend on the relations between image features being simultaneously available for comparison (e.g., Lowe, 1987). An impairment that hinders parallel grouping should make identification particularly difficult with short exposures and when there are multiple segmentation cues available.

We have also tried to go beyond this by examining HJA's performance on tasks more specifically designed to tap parallel grouping processes.

Grouping via Collinearity. Boucart and Humphreys (1992) used a task in which HJA (and normal subjects) had to judge whether pairs of stimuli were in the same orientation or whether they were mirror reversed. One attribute of this task is that, on both "same" and "different" trials, stimuli can have the same identity; hence matching is forced to operate on the basis of visual representations of the stimuli rather than (for example) on their names (cf. Posner & Keele, 1967). There were three kinds of stimuli: outline drawings, fragmented forms in which the fragments corresponding to the outline of the forms were collinear and grouped to form a closed figure ("well-structured forms"), and fragmented forms in which the fragments corresponding to the outline were rotated so as to eliminate local collinearity ("poorly structured forms"). The global outlines of the well- and poorly structured forms were the same, as were their low spatial frequency components (Boucart & Bonnet, 1991). Thus the stimuli can be used to test whether specific grouping processes, namely those dependent on computing collinearity between local elements of form, are operative in agnosic patients. Example stimuli are shown in Fig. 3.6.

Normal subjects are faster at matching outline drawings and well-structured forms than they are at matching poorly structured forms (particularly when the forms have the same *global* orientation on different trials; in this case, matching is facilitated by segmenting the stimuli into their parts and judging the location of the parts in each item; see Fig. 3.6). Apparently, the presence of local structure (in this case, collinearity) aids object segmentation.

In contrast to normal subjects, HJA showed no difference between the three types of stimuli. Using stimuli with appropriate local structure did not facilitate his performance. Interestingly, HJA was relatively good at the task when the forms differed in their global orientation. Despite being poor at grouping based on collinearity, HJA remains sensitive to global orientation. We return to this point when we summarise HJA's case.

Grouping Shape Conjunctions. The procedure used by Donnelly et al. (1991) to assess spatially parallel grouping is based on visual search studies in which the number of distractor items in visual displays is manipulated. Search is presumed to be based on parallel coding of displays when there are few (or at least nonlinear) effects of the number of distractors present (e.g., Treisman & Gelade, 1980). Hence visual search procedures can provide another technique of assessing whether parallel grouping processes are intact in patients.

Over the past 10 years or so, a good deal has been made of the distinction between search for a predesignated target defined by the process of a simple disjunctive feature relative to the background, and search for a target defined by a conjunction of features (Treisman, 1988; Treisman & Gormican, 1988). Search for a disjunctive target can be relatively independent of the number of distractors present; search for a conjunction target can be strongly affected by the number of distractors. Indeed, search for conjunction targets can be a linear function of the number of distractors, with the slope on target-present trials being about half that

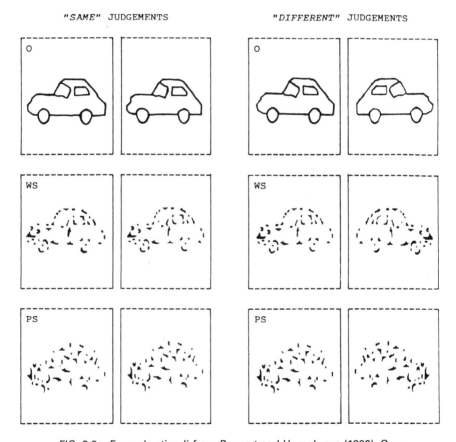

FIG. 3.6. Example stimuli from Boucart and Humphreys (1992). O = outline drawings; WS = well-structured fragmented forms; PS = poorly structured fragmented forms. These stimuli all have the same global orientation, and matching of the fragmented forms is facilitated by segmenting each object into its parts and judging the relative positions of the parts. In other conditions in the same experiment, different shapes could differ in their global orientation.

on target-absent trials. This pattern, of linear search functions and 1:2 present:absent slope ratios, has been taken as indicative of an underlying serial search process, that is self-terminating on target-present trials. In contrast, disjunctive targets may be detected by means of a parallel search process. The apparent serial search for conjunction targets has been taken to indicate that conjunctions can only be encoded in a spatially serial fashion (Treisman, 1991; Treisman & Gelade, 1980).

More recently, though, several pieces of evidence have emerged showing that at least some conjunctions are coded in parallel across visual displays. For instance, this is suggested by Donnelly et al.'s (1991) findings, because target and distractor vertices differed only in the arrangement of their component orientations, not in the presence of a disjunctive feature. Duncan and Humphreys (1989) and Humphreys, Quinlan, and Riddoch (1989) reported similar evidence. For instance, Humphreys et al. had subjects search for ⊥ stimuli presented among ⊤ and ⊣ distractors (i.e., containing horizontal and vertical line components but placed in a different arrangement to those present in targets). When the background contained homogeneous distractors, there were minimal effects of the number of distractors on search time. When there were heterogeneous distractors, there were marked linear effects and a 1:2 present:absent slope ratio. The effects of the heterogeneity of the distractors indicates that search for simple form conjunctions is determined by grouping between the items in displays. Homogeneous distractors are more similar to one another than they are to targets; by being more similar homogeneous distractors form a group separate from targets, making search efficient. Heterogeneous distractors do not group strongly, and may be as likely to group with the target as they are to group with each other; search is then inefficient. Such results indicate that simple form conjunctions are encoded in parallel, and furthermore, they serve as important components for grouping processes.

The idea that simple form conjunctions are important for grouping meshes with computational work on *blocks world*, which attempts to recover scene properties such as surface orientation and location from scenes made up of polyhedral objects containing only trihedral corners (i.e., corners derived from three polyhedral faces; Clowes, 1971). In the blocks world, no information is available about the structure of the blocks from shading; the only information available consists of straight line segments connecting various types of line junctions. Correct interpretation depends on appropriate labeling of the lines as corresponding to convex, concave, or object boundary edges, with the labeling being consistent across the scene. Algorithms for line labeling involve coding the particular form of junction present, and computing the relations between junctions at different locations in the image. Providing it is assumed that the corners of the blocks are orthogonal, the three-dimensional orientations of all the surfaces and edges of the blocks can be computed from the arrow and Y-junctions present (e.g., Mulder & Dawson, 1990; Perkins, 1968). Efficient computation of the relations between the parts of objects, and between the objects in a scene, relies upon junctions being represented in parallel (e.g., see Enns & Rensink, 1990). That is, grouping between simple form conjunctions (such as corners) may be crucial for normal visual object recognition.

We have investigated HJA's ability to group form conjunctions in parallel using search tasks that require the detection of conjunction targets presented among homogeneous or heterogeneous distractors (Humphreys, Riddoch, Quinlan, et al., 1992). The experiments were based on those reported by Humphreys et al. (1989), in which subjects with normal vision had to detect a ⊥ target among either homogeneous T-distractors or heterogeneous T, ⊣, and ⊢ distractors. Sample data from HJA and from young and age-matched controls are shown in Figs. 3.7 and 3.8 (with homogeneous and heterogeneous distractors, respectively). Figures 3.7 and 3.8 also contain data from patient L, a prosopagnosic patient originally reported by Bauer (1984).

Asked to find a simple form conjunction amongst homogeneous distractors, HJA produces an abnormal performance pattern. His RTs are slow, he makes numerous errors, there are substantial effects of the number of distractors, and absent responses are slower than present responses. In young control subjects and in L, there are minimal effects of the number of distractors in the field; in older control subjects (age-matched to HJA) some effects of the number of distractors are present are apparent. Nevertheless, RTs and error rates for HJA are outside the control range. In addition, all the control subjects show a pattern of search performance in which RTs on target-absent trials tend to be faster than those on target-present trials. Such "fast absent" responses suggest that, with homogeneous distractors, responses can be based on a representation of the whole display as a single group (on absent but not on target-present trials). L's data show that this pattern of performance can be found even when overall RTs are slow. HJA shows no sign of fast responding on absent trials. HJA's performance is not changed by giving him extended practice, though his response latencies can then decrease to be at least as fast as those of L (Fig. 3.7).

We can contrast HJA's abnormal search pattern with homogeneous distractors with his normal pattern of performance with heterogeneous distractors (Fig. 3.8). With heterogeneous distractors, all control subjects show reliable effects of the number of distractors, and the slope of the search function for present responses is about half that for absent responses. HJA performs similarly, and in this case his RTs and error rates are comfortably within the control range. (In fact, HJA can perform better than age-matched control subjects, and better than L, who shows overall slow response latencies. HJA has had considerable experience at these and similar tasks, leading to his fast RTs. This emphasizes that the abnormal RTs and errors found with homogeneous displays are specific to the task; they are not a general characteristic of HJA's performance.)

HJA manifests a selective deficit in visual search for form conjunctions presented with homogeneous distractors; that is, he is impaired with displays in

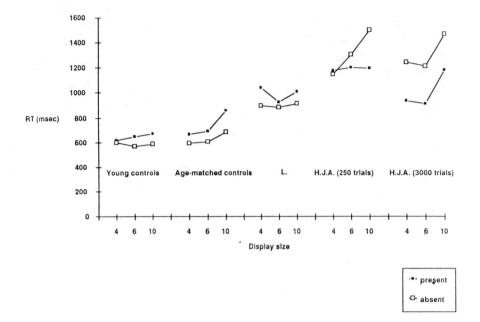

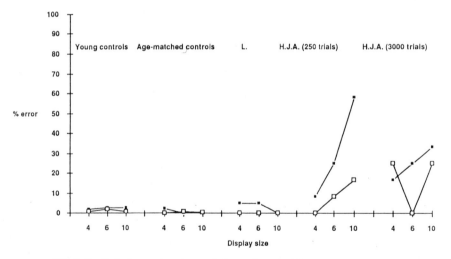

FIG. 3.7. Data from visual search for an inverted T-target among upright T-distractors (for young controls, controls age-matched to HJA, the agnosic L, and HJA). Data are presented for HJA after two levels of practice (500 trials and 3,000 trials).

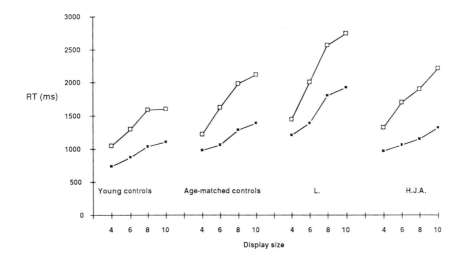

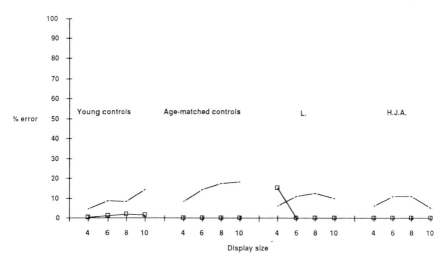

FIG. 3.8.   Data from visual search for an inverted T-target among heterogeneous T, ⊣, and ⊢ distractors (for young controls, controls age-
matched to HJA, the agnosic L, and HJA).

which, normally, parallel grouping can be used to segment targets from distractors. With heterogeneous displays, where parallel grouping is normally inefficient because of the existence of multiple distractor groups and the likely grouping of targets and distractors, HJA performs relatively well. This pattern is not characteristic of all patients with problems in visual object or face recognition (e.g., patient L shows a normal pattern of performance, despite his overall slow response latencies, suggesting normal visual processing of simple form conjunctions). We take these results to support the argument that HJA has a deficit in the parallel grouping of form conjunctions. Note that this deficit does not necessarily mean that HJA searches the displays serially. Indeed, if this were the case, we would expect his performance to be comparable with homogeneous and heterogeneous distractors. HJA was generally faster with homogeneous displays, and the effects of display size were considerably less, even after little practice (cf. Figs. 3.7 and 3.8). HJA processes homogeneous displays in parallel, but his processing is inefficient and error-prone.

A Simulation

One positive attribute of using tasks such as visual search is that performance can be related to explicit computational models. One such model is SERR (standing for SEarch via Recursive Rejection), developed by Humphreys and Müller (1993). SERR attempts to model the way in which visual search is influenced by grouping between distractors, and between targets and distractors (see previous discussion). SERR is a hierarchically organized connectionist model, containing separate, retinotopically organized "maps" for single line orientations (e.g., horizontal and vertical edges), line terminators, and simple junctions (e.g., L-junctions at particular orientations). The model groups junctions in parallel across its visual field by means of within-map excitatory connections. Units corresponding to different interpretations of junctions at particular orientations in an image are inhibitory. The model uses a Boltzmann-machine activation function (Hinton & Sejnowski, 1986), and so operates stochastically—units can be placed into an "on" state even if there is no bottom-up support from input on the model's "retina"; similarly, units may not be placed into an on state on occasions even when there is good bottom-up support. Hence there is a degree of noise in the model's activation functions, and the level of noise can be manipulated by means of a "temperature" parameter (see Hinton & Sejnowski for the analogy with a real physical system). Because of the noise within the system, grouping can induce instability into the system, because groups may sometimes be formed between units that are not well-supported by bottom-up activation. To introduce stability in SERR, grouping between junction units is gated by activity within a set of *location units,* which are activated by the presence of stimuli at given locations, but which are indifferent to the nature of the stimuli (i.e., they encode where stimuli are, but not what they are). For instance, in order to be placed into an on state, location units must be activated by correlated firing of units corresponding to several image features at a given location (e.g., edges of one orientation, terminators, and so forth), because correlated firing is unlikely to be produced simply by noise. The activation of location units is used to gate grouping between junction units (this is implemented by replicating the junction units in a set of *match maps,* in which within-map and across-map links are enabled), so that grouping only operates when there is reasonable evidence for the presence of some stimulus at a given location in the field. It turns out that location units provide the model with some other, interesting properties; we return to this point in due course.

When a stimulus display containing a number of junction elements is presented to SERR, units are placed into on or off states at different representational levels as activation is passed through the system. Like junctions support one another to form stable groups; disparate junctions compete. Decisions are made by activating a set of *decision templates,* set according to the targets and distractors in the experiment. Templates pool activity across their input match maps, so that the template receiving most activation will usually be that corresponding to the largest group. If the template for the predesignated target reaches threshold, a "present" response can be made. However, because in search tasks there are typically more distractors than targets, the template for a distractor group will usually reach threshold first. Search then proceeds recursively by rejecting that distractor group and continuing search through the remaining stimuli that are not yet rejected. That is, search can proceed via recursive rejection of distractors. Figure 3.9 illustrates SERR's hierarchical architecture.

SERR simulates human search for simple form conjunctions, with there being little effect of the number of distractors with homogeneous distractors, but linear effects of the number of heterogeneous distractors. This is because homogeneous distractors form a single stable group that can be rapidly rejected; indeed "absent" responses can be faster than present (because the distractors are typically rejected before the target's template reaches threshold), conforming to the data we have observed with normal subjects. With heterogeneous distractors, there is competition between groups, slowing performance. In addition, there is a high likelihood that targets are "missed" (because they can be inhibited by competing distractor groups); misses are corrected by rerunning search, introducing serial effects on performance. SERR demonstrates that linear search functions can be generated by a spatially parallel search mechanism operating with internal noise (cf. Townsend, 1972).

Lesioning the Model

Given the fit of the model to normal data, we have gone on to investigate whether pathological visual search performance, of the type we have observed in HJA, can be generated by the model when *lesioned.* Previous attempts have been made

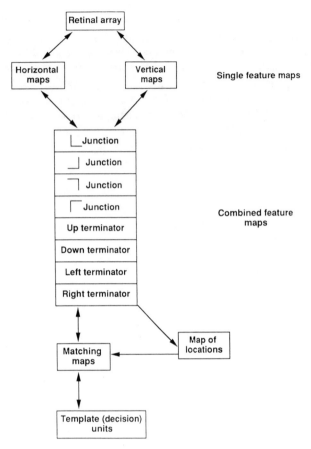

FIG. 3.9.   The architecture of the SERR model of visual search (from Humphreys & Müller, 1993).

to lesion connectionist models to test whether the lesioned model generates data matching those of brain-damaged human subjects, with mixed success (e.g., see Patterson, Seidenberg, & McClelland, 1989, for one example). In such attempts, lesions have been simulated by (for example) adding random noise to the weights between units or by setting to zero units at particular levels of representation.

In one set of simulations, we (Humphreys, Freeman, & Müller, 1992) simulated the effects of brain damage by running SERR at a higher temperature, so that there is increased noise in its activation functions. Figure 3.10 gives sample search functions generated by SERR when run under "low" and when run under "high" temperature conditions. Somewhat to our surprise, increasing the noise within the model (i.e., by introducing a higher temperature) selectively affected performance with homogeneous distractors. With homogeneous distrac-

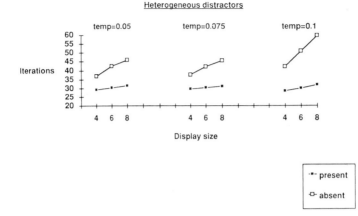

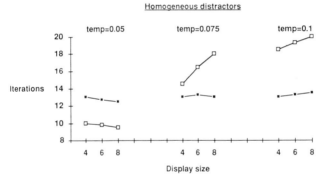

FIG. 3.10. Search functions for a form conjunction target generated by SERR when run under three different temperature conditions. With the temperature parameter set to .05, the model simulates normal visual search performance (Humphreys & Müller, 1993). With this parameter set to .075 and .1, there is increased noise within the activation function. An abnormal search pattern is then generated. There is little effect of the temperature parameter on the detection of a form conjunction amongst heterogeneous distractors. However, with homogeneous distractors there are now positive effects on the display size on performance, with the effect most pronounced on absent responses—with the temperatures set to .05, there are no effects of display size and fast absent responses. The functions generated by the model under the high temperature settings are similar to the abnormal search functions generated by the agnosic patient HJA (Figs. 3.7 and 3.8).

tors, decision times at the higher temperature were overall slower and there were some effects of the number of distractors in the field. There was relatively little effect of increasing the temperature on search with heterogeneous distractors.

We were surprised with this result, because our intuition suggested that increasing the noise within the activation function should harm performance most in the condition that was initially most difficult (i.e., with heterogeneous displays). However, one effect of increasing the noise in the activation functions was to make it more likely that junction stimuli activated inappropriate junction representations (e.g., an L-junction in the input might activate a $\lrcorner$ junction representation of a $\lrcorner$ junction). With heterogeneous displays this did not exert a drastic effect on performance because the chance of the target junction activating an inappropriate junction unit, harming performance, was offset by this occurring between distractors; in the latter case, this could have the effect of reducing competition between distractor groups, facilitating search. In contrast, because search with homogeneous displays depends on grouping between distractors, inappropriate coding of distractors generated competition within what should have been stable distractor groups, impeding search.

Thus the effects of increasing the noise in SERR's activation functions is to produce a selective impairment on search with homogeneous relative to heterogeneous distractor junctions. This, of course, is the same pattern of disturbance we have observed in HJA. Accordingly we may propose that, far from having an associative agnosia, HJA has a fundamental impairment due to increased noise in the processes that normally group together computationally important properties of forms—such as corner junctions. An effect of this noise is to impair image segmentation via parallel grouping; elements in the field that ought to group instead form competing subgroups, leading to inappropriate segmentation of images, and consequently impaired object identification. It is interesting in this respect that a characteristic identification error made by HJA is to *oversegment* objects. For example, when shown a paintbrush on one occasion he stated that it was "two separate objects," and continued to maintain that this was so even when told otherwise (Humphreys & Riddoch, 1987b). Introducing multiple segmentation cues, by using line drawings rather than silhouettes and overlapping rather than single figures, exacerbates the problem.

One further point to note from this simulation is that, simply by adding to noise to the activation functions, we have been able to introduce slopes into search functions that are flat under low noise conditions. This confirms earlier theoretical arguments that apparently serial search functions can be generated by parallel processes operating with certain constraints (e.g., limited resources; see, e.g., Townsend, 1972). Our simulation extends this by operationalizing the constraints in terms of noise within an activation function. The simulation is also consistent with our argument that, despite being poor at detecting junction targets among homogeneous distractors, HJA is nevertheless carrying out spatially parallel (though in his case, noisy and inefficient) visual search. Indeed, as we observed with HJA, search with homogeneous distractors remains more efficient than that with heterogeneous distractors (in terms of overall response times and the effects of the display size), even when high noise levels are introduced (and only search with homogeneous distractors is strongly affected). Under high noise conditions parallel search becomes inefficient, but search does not necessarily become serial.

Knowing Where but Not What

A behavioral characteristic of HJA, and of a number of other agnosics in the literature, is that even though they fail to identify objects, they may nevertheless reach and navigate around objects, and they have no difficulties locating the objects in space. In addition, as we noted earlier, even when they misidentify objects they can show appreciation of their general form (e.g., they do not identify a part as the whole object). Within SERR, this dissociation between knowing where but not what objects are is captured by the difference in activating location units (activation in location units is preserved when the model is lesioned by increasing its internal noise) and in activating units corresponding to particular types of form information (e.g., representations of junctions show strong effects of the noise level). Thus, even when the model has a high degree of internal noise it is possible to recover accurate location information, and also to identify the general form of the objects, according to the activity in the location units. The global description of a form conveyed by the location units corresponds to what Pomerantz (1983) described as a Type P representation, in which only the positions of the local elements are described, as opposed to a Type N representation, in which the nature of the local elements are specified. Type P representations may be used to identify the general nature of an object (e.g., that it is an animal), including its global orientation (see earlier discussion). However, it may not be sufficient to identify the specific object (e.g., that it is a cow).

Summary of Case 1

HJA is impaired at tasks that are normally achieved by efficient parallel grouping. For instance, he is unable to use local structure (e.g., collinearity between line segments) to help segment and match fragmented figures; he is unable to group figures so as to avoid display size effects in search for form conjunctions. In addition, we have been able to simulate the selective pattern of performance produced by HJA in visual search for form conjunctions, by increasing the noise level within the activation functions of a connectionist model of visual search. The convergence between the neuropsychological and the simulation data supports our argument that, in this patient, there is a problem in intermediate visual processing that disrupts object recognition. This impairment can be conceptualized in terms of there being increased noise in the coding of form information, which particularly hinders parallel grouping and segmentation based on junctions of line elements.

CASE 2: ATTENTIONAL CAPTURE BY LOCAL CLOSURE

The second patient, GK, may also be described as agnosic in that he is impaired at visually identifying objects, his misidentification errors are visually related to the target object, and, on such occasions, he demonstrates no knowledge of what the objects are (e.g., he cannot gesture appropriately to objects he fails to identify). It might also be argued that GK has a problem in early shape perception because he can perform poorly on the Efron shape-matching test (Fig. 3.3). However, we argue that finer grained analysis reveals a problem due to GK's attending inappropriately to the parts of objects, and that this impairment can be understood in terms of the interplay between visual-perceptual and attentional processes. Detailed models of this interplay are needed to account for such disorders.

Case Details

GK (born August 11, 1939) suffered two cerebrovascular accidents (CVAs) in 1986, resulting in separate lesions to the left and right parietal lobes. He was initially cortically blind, but sight recovered over a period of 3 months. When tested in 1989, there was no visual field defect and Snellen acuity was normal. GK has several problems in everyday life. Most notable is a visual disorientation and optic ataxia (see Holmes, 1918); GK finds it difficult to negotiate his visual environment, he will bump into and misreach to objects. Under proprioceptive guidance (e.g., reaching to a part of his own, as opposed to the examiner's body), performance is considerably improved. In addition to this, he is dysnomic, and produces frequent phonemic paraphrasias; he has a reduced auditory digit span (3), and makes both visual and phonemic paraphrasia errors in reading single words. Color identification is relatively normal.

Tests of GK's object recognition in 1988 revealed the following pattern of performance. In naming photographs and line drawings of common objects he made two types of error: Either he visually misidentified an object (e.g., cellotape → hose), or he made a phonemic paraphrasia (e.g., kangaroo → kana, kanagral, kanagroo). When he made a phonemic paraphrasia, he was able to provide accurate semantic information about the object ("lives in Australia, Joey, jumps along"). When he made visual misidentifications, his semantic descriptions conformed to his misidentification ("use it in the garden to water flowers in the summer"). He was more accurate at identifying photographs than line drawings and he tended to make proportionally more visual errors with line drawings

TABLE 3.1
GK's Identification of Line Drawings and Photographs Drawn
from Biological Categories (e.g., Animals)
and from Categories of Artifacts (e.g., Vehicles)

	Correct	Visual Errors	Naming Errors
Photographs	168/200	8	24
Line drawings	155/300	102	43
Biological categories	140/250	41	49
Artifacts	144/250	66	20

than with photographs. Visual errors also tended to be more frequent with artifacts (e.g., clothing, items of furniture, vehicles) than with objects from biological categories (e.g., animals, fruits, and vegetables). Illustrative data are given in Table 3.1. Many visual errors corresponded to identifying a part of an object as if it were the whole object (e.g., deer → antler; fire engine → ladder). Like HJA, GK was strongly affected by the exposure duration (e.g., he named correctly 69 from a set of 76 line drawings presented for an unlimited viewing time, but only 37 when the drawings were presented for 2 s each). Presenting drawings for shorter durations induced visual naming errors.

Considered in absolute terms, GK's ability to retrieve appropriate semantic information from line drawings of objects is better than that of HJA (e.g., tested under unlimited viewing conditions in 1990, HJA identified 30 out of the set of 76 line drawings also given to GK). In addition to the phonemic paraphrasias GK makes, which are unaffected by the nature of the stimulus, there is a visual component to his recognition impairment: GK makes visual misidentifications; he is abnormally affected by photographic detail and by exposure duration. However, unlike HJA, he makes errors by identifying parts as whole objects.

Tests of Shape Perception

GK was very poor at simple tests of line orientation discrimination and shape perception. He scored 49/90 when required to decide whether single lines were horizontal or vertical, and performed at chance when required to decide if pairs of horizontal, vertical, or horizontal and vertical lines were the same or different. He scored 50/96 and 45/88 on two versions of the Efron shape-matching task (the two versions used different length ratios for the sides of the shapes, and they used squares that were respectively 5cm × 5cm and 4cm × 4cm in area). Using the set of shapes based around the 5cm × 5cm square, he scored 62/96 when asked to decide whether a single shape was a square or a rectangle.

Despite his poor performance at judging line orientation, GK was nevertheless able to identify different junctions composed of two or three line orientations. Asked to identify T, L, +, Y, →, and Ψ junctions, GK scored 58/60. In a further test, GK was asked to identify the presence of two junctions in composite figures (e.g., to identify ↔ as two arrows, U as two Ls). On some "double junctions" GK performed well (e.g., 14/16 on ↔ and U), but not on others (e.g., 3/16 on H and >—<). Our suspicion was that GK discriminated double junctions on the basis of one area of local closure between the parts. For instance, if local closure was computed within the top U-region in the H double junction figures, then the figure might be identified incorrectly as the U ("two L") double junction (indeed, this was the identification response GK made). Discriminations based on local closure within just one part of the stimulus may similarly render the >—< double junction difficult to identify.

In order to assess GK's tendency to attend to the presence of local closure, and to ignore global shape, he was given compound forms, in which global shapes were constructed from the appropriate arrangement of local shapes (cf. Navon, 1977). In one case he was asked to decide whether the global shape was a square or a triangle. The global shape itself could be composed of open (Xs) or closed shapes (Os). When the local shapes were closed, GK performed above chance but at an impaired level; when the local shapes were open, he performed well (Fig. 3.11). When there is closure at the local level GK is impaired at discriminating global shape—indeed, he typically complained that he failed to see any global shape when the local elements were closed.

Studies of normal subjects indicate that closure is computed as a graded property of shape (e.g., Donnelly et al., 1991; Treisman & Souther, 1985), and that, as the degree of closure across a shape increases, so it becomes more likely that the shape is attended as a single perceptual object. In GK's case, the presence of local closure dominates his parsing of displays, so that a closed part is judged inappropriately as the whole object. Normally, object recognition may depend on encoding the relations between descriptions computed both locally and more globally, across the whole object. Whether local or global descriptions

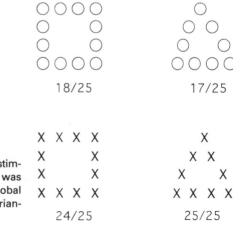

FIG. 3.11. The compound stimuli used with GK. The task was to decide whether the global shape was a square or a triangle.

are selected for action (e.g., for object identification) will depend on a number of factors, including whether either description is familiar, whether they form a good gestalt, and where attention is focused (cf. Humphreys & Riddoch, 1993a). GK appears to attend to local grouping cues, such as local closure, and then finds it difficult to attend to more global groups, even when they are familiar. This may occur because local groups now attract his attention more strongly than normal or because global groups fail to attract attention. For instance, there may be a deficit in his attending to form information computed across relatively wide areas of field.

A failure to attend to global shape descriptions may help explain GK's poor performance on the Efron shape-matching test, and on its identification variant (requiring single shapes to be identified as squares or rectangles), if such tasks require attention to global shapes covering broad areas of field. Consistent with this, GK performed well on the shape identification variant of the Efron test using small shapes (based around a 4 cm $\times$ 4 cm square). He may fail on the matching version of the test with small shapes because both shapes present need to be attended.

In sum, we propose that GK tends to identify parts as wholes because his attention is captured by local closure. This may occur more with line drawings than with photographs because the texture information, available in photographs, may overrule local closure based on contour information. It may occur more with artifacts than with objects from biological categories because artifacts are more likely to be composed of functionally separate (and separately nameable) parts. The familiarity of the part as a perceptual whole in its own right can determine whether attention is focused on the part when it is a component of a larger perceptual whole.

In addition to problems due to capture by local closure, two other problems are apparent. One is that, once he attends to a local part of an object, he has difficulty disengaging attention. This is indicated by (a) his problem with the shape-matching variant of the Efron test, even when he can perform the identification variant (with small shapes), and (b) his lack of explicit knowledge of whether he is presented with a whole object or a part (from which the whole can be identified). In the shape-matching task, performance could be improved if GK could switch attention from one shape to the other. Similarly, knowledge of whether a whole object or just a part was presented could be gained if, after attending to the part, GK scanned the complete stimulus.

The second additional problem is that GK lacks access to explicit information about line orientation. Nevertheless, he can discriminate junctions composed of single line orientations. At the very least, this suggests that access to line orientation information can be impaired even when outputs from processes computing line orientation can be used for coding junctions (see also Milner et al., 1991, for further evidence on dissociations between the use of orientation information for perceptual judgments and for action). More speculatively, the result may suggest that line junctions are computed independently of single line orientations. This last issue is tangental to the main concern of this chapter, and we do not discuss it further. In the General Discussion section, we consider the relations between the apparent attentional capture by local closure and the problem in disengaging attention.

CASE 3: SERIAL PROCESSING OF CONTRAST INFORMATION

The two cases we have discussed have highlighted the importance of grouping processes in intermediate vision, and the ways in which impairments of grouping and inappropriate attention to local perceptual groups can disrupt object recognition. In this third case, we show a third way in which problems in grouping can arise in agnosia.

Case Details

The third case is an intelligent adolescent boy, AS (born June 5, 1977), with marked deficits in visual object and face recognition. AS's development until age 6 years was normal. However, he then suffered brain damage after having gone into coma, due to infection by a rare renal disease. Subsequently his ability to identify many common objects and to recognize familiar faces was severely compromised. Although able to trace around pictures, AS shows chance performance at the Efron shape-matching and identification tasks across a range of stimulus sizes. He also fails at unusual view-matching tests. His visual object identification is characterized by visual naming errors (e.g., asparagus → screwdriver). The vast majority of the errors suggest an awareness of the whole object, and do not involve identifying a part of the whole. When unable to identify an object appropriately, AS does not have access to appropriate semantic information. He performs poorly at semantic matching tests; he cannot gesture in the absence of correct naming. Like both HJA and GK, the identification of real objects is better than that of photographs or line drawings. Color naming is generally good.

Tests of Spatially Parallel Visual Processing

As with HJA, we have assessed AS's performance on a range of visual search tests in order to elucidate the kinds of processing he can carry out in a spatially parallel manner. Given the task of finding a target defined by a color difference relative to the background (red target, green distractors), AS performs well; his RTs are relatively fast and he is unaffected by the number of distractors present (Fig. 3.12). These data indicate that AS is able to detect stimuli across his visual

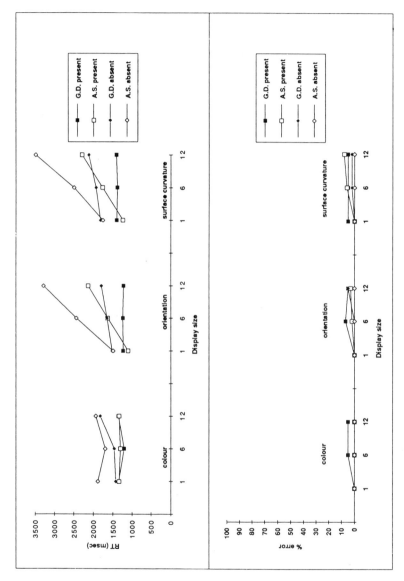

FIG. 3.12.   Search functions for AS and a control with a matched contrast sensitivity function, in tasks requiring detection of targets defined by color, orientation, and sur- face curvature from shading.

93

fields in a spatially parallel fashion when the target is defined within the color domain. In contrast, when given the task of detecting a target such as a line orientation differing by 45° relative to its background, there are marked costs on performance. Although RTs with a single target are close to those found in the color-search task, there are marked effects of the number of distractors (Fig. 3.12). AS's visual search performance in Fig. 3.12 is shown alongside that of an age-matched control subject chosen to have a similar contrast sensitivity function to AS. The control, unlike AS, can detect the orientation target from spatially parallel search, showing minimal effects of the number of distractors.

We have observed similar results in a range of visual search tasks, all of which involved search for a target defined by a feature in the form domain that is normally able to sustain parallel search functions (e.g., size, the presence of a hollow vs. a complete figure, etc.). Such results suggest that AS is unable to process form information in parallel. Note that the problem is not simply one of how well AS can discriminate stimuli within the form domain, because his ability to discriminate single oriented lines differing by 45° is just as efficient as his ability to discriminate red and green squares (Fig. 3.12). The problem is that he fails to sustain this discrimination when presented with multiple items.

In fact, the situation is to some extent more general than a problem in dealing with form information, because AS seems unable to process contrast differences in parallel across his visual field. We had AS search displays of "Ramachandran" figures, comprised of circles in which a concave or convex surface was created by top- or bottom-lit shading (see Ramachandran, 1988). AS is able to detect single targets as efficiently as the control subject; his accuracy is also good. However, whereas the control shows no effects of display size, AS shows effects of the order of 35 ms per item (Fig. 3.12). These figures do not contain edge information; rather surface descriptions are derived by the continuous contrasts present. That such contrast differences do not "pop out" for AS suggests a severe impairment in parallel visual processing within the whole contrast domain.

GENERAL DISCUSSION

We have discussed the cases of three patients, each of whom (a) has problems in visual object recognition, (b) makes visually related misidentification errors, (c) shows better identification of real objects than photographs or line drawings, and (d) does not show access to appropriate semantic information when visual misidentifications occur. These four characteristics point to the patients having problems gaining access to stored knowledge about objects, due to a problem in early or intermediate visual processing. Indeed, other tests with each patient have shown that each has generally good stored knowledge about visual objects— each patient is able to describe both the function and the visual appearance of known objects; their agnosias are not due to an impairment of stored knowledge. Nevertheless, the precise problems in each case seem subtly different.

HJA

We have proposed that HJA has abnormally noisy parallel grouping of form conjunctions such that local junctions that should be grouped together tend to segment apart. The result is that visual descriptions of objects are often parsed incorrectly, leading to failures of object identification. Nevertheless, processing continues to be spatially parallel, and he remains able to localize objects and to derive information about their coarse global shapes. We have been able to simulate this pattern of performance in an explicit computational model of visual search, SERR. The main characteristics of SERR that are important for capturing the data are: (a) There is parallel grouping of simple form conjunctions; (b) search is based on the selection of groups of items rather than particular regions of field; and (c) a location map registers where stimuli are even when there is inaccurate encoding of what the stimuli are. Disruption of the grouping mechanism leads to segmentation of regions of field where grouping should take place, and to competition within perceptual groups. It is not implausible to extend this suggestion from the currently limited world of SERR (which deals only with right angular junctions), to more general two-dimensional grouping processes. An impairment to such processes could then lead to the kind of oversegmentation errors that characterize HJA's everyday object recognition. Note that we do not extend our argument to other types of grouping, such as grouping local patterns of movement. It is likely that different grouping mechanisms exist for different visual inputs (e.g., for movement, for static form), so that selective impairment of one but not all types of grouping may be expected. Consistent with this, HJA seems able to group a moving pattern of light dots on a face in order to judge the facial expression; this occurs even though he is severely impaired at judging the emotional expression of static photographs of faces (Humphreys, Donnelly, & Riddoch, 1993). Also, even when grouping processes in SERR are disrupted by lesioning, location encoding and the description of coarse global shape remain accurate within the map of locations. The model shows how problems in grouping in the form domain can coexist with intact localization and global shape processing.

GK

Case 2, GK, requires us to consider the relations between visual processing and attention. We propose that, normally, attention enhances the processing of attended visual information (Downing, 1988; Müller & Humphreys, 1991) and inhibits the processing of stimuli at nonattended regions (e.g., Moran & Desimone, 1985). This facilitates the computation of a figure against the contextual ground. Attention may be set voluntarily to a region of field, or it may be set by stimulus-driven information (e.g., if a figure is closed, or if it is familiar; see Donnelly et al., 1991; La Berge, 1983, for supporting evidence of these two kinds of effects). In GK's case, the fixing of attention by stimulus properties seems dominated by the presence of local closure, perhaps due in the first place to more global groups failing to attract attention; locally closed shapes capture GK's attention. When this occurs, GK identifies the attended part of the object as the whole.

In addition to locally closed areas capturing GK's visual attention, they also seem to exert an abnormal hold once attended. GK cannot judge whether he is presented with a whole object or a part, even when the whole object is identifiable from the part, and he is also additionally impaired by tasks requiring the judgement of one relative to two shapes (e.g., the Efron shape-matching task with small figures). This may represent a second problem; that is, GK has deficits both because local closure captures his attention, and because, once captured, his attention is fixed. However, we prefer to think that the two problems are linked. Elsewhere (Humphreys & Riddoch, 1993a, 1993b) we have argued that the ability to disengage attention from objects is based on an interaction between two separate mechanisms: an orienting mechanism that responds to salient differences between stimuli within the visual field, and a maintenance mechanism that acts to hold attention to objects. These two mechanisms interact in a mutually inhibitory fashion. Inhibition of the orienting mechanism by the maintenance mechanism helps prevent distraction. Inhibition of the maintenance mechanism by the orienting mechanism leads to attention being switched to new locations. It is possible that GK's deficits reflect a disorder of the orienting mechanism, perhaps because it is not activated by global shape information. Consequently, GK orients to a property such as local closure. Also, he may then fail to have information concerning the location of the overall shape (allowing the misidentification of wholes as parts). Once his attention is engaged on the locally closed area, inhibition of the orienting mechanism (a normal process) then leads to his attention becoming fixed. Humphreys and Riddoch (1993a) argued that a bilateral problem in orienting can be involved in at least some cases of visual disorientation. We propose this for GK here, but extend our previous work by showing how an attentional deficit may interact with processes in object recognition, and how orienting is influenced by object properties such as local closure.

GK has bilateral parietal lesions. Neurophysiological evidence points to a distinction between ventral (occipital-temporal) and dorsal (occipital-parietal) visual systems, which seem characterized respectively for processing what and where a stimulus is (e.g., Ungerleider & Mishkin, 1982). The dorsal visual system is also strongly implicated in visual attentional operations. For instance, some parietal cells show enhanced firing to attended visual signals independent of the response involved (Wurtz, Goldberg, & Robinson, 1982). Such response-independent effects suggest that the cells mediate central attentional processing (Wurtz, 1985). The dorsal system also selectively receives input from so-called *magno-cellular* cells, which themselves show properties such as sensitivity to rapid visual onsets and low spatial frequencies (Livingstone, 1988; Livingstone & Hubel, 1988). The roles of the dorsal visual system may thus involve (a) providing a spatial map of occupied regions of the visual field in order that attention is oriented to correctly spatial locations (this map may itself be based on relatively coarse global descriptions of objects—something like the map of locations in SERR); and (b) orienting attention to occupied locations within the map. In addition, magno-cellular cells may also play a role in linking local visual information into global perceptual groups (Kartsounis & Warrington, 1991; Livingstone & Hubel, 1988). Lesions of this cortical area may thus disrupt a patient's ability to localize visual information and their ability to attend to global visual descriptions. A consequence may be that the patient's attention is drawn to local perceptual groups—as we have observed with GK.

AS

The third case, AS, presents with a further differentiable disorder of intermediate visual processing, an inability to process contrast information in a spatially parallel manner. Because of this, performance is disrupted whenever tasks require the integration of form information from separate regions of field. For example, in the Efron task AS may be unable to encode the square and rectangular shapes accurately because he processes the horizontal and vertical edge components independently and serially. We consider AS's problem one of intermediate vision because his ability to discriminate contrast, spatial frequency, and edge orientation per se is not dramatically impaired (at least relative to other subjects who do not have the clinical problems apparent in AS), as evidenced by his visual search performance when there are single stimuli in the field. The problem is that he seems unable to assimilate form (and more generally contrast) across the visual field. Of course, without parallel processing and grouping of visual information, visual object recognition is very impaired.

Comparing the Patients

HJA, GK, and AS have different impairments in intermediate vision. HJA and AS seem to have primary problems with processes involved in grouping visual information—though in HJA's case the problem seems to be abnormally noisy grouping processes (producing incorrect segmentations), whereas in AS's case the problem is in forming any perceptual groups within the form domain. Both of these problems can be related to lesions of the ventral system mediating object perception. The problems go along with a relatively intact ability to switch attention across space (e.g., see Figs. 3.8 and 3.12 for evidence of this). Because the ability to switch attention remains intact, the patients do not misidentify parts of objects as perceptual wholes. In GK's case, we suggest a problem within his dorsal visual system such that attention is drawn inappropriately to local perceptual groups; there may be no primary problem within the ventral object perception system. Nevertheless, attentional capture by local perceptual groups interacts with object encoding, precipitating visual misidentifications on occasions. These contrasting impairments of intermediate visual processing may only be revealed by relatively fine-grained analyses using tests sensitive to the different perceptual processes involved.

In the future, we look to an increasing number of studies in which patients are subject to tests of particular visual processes, for which well-articulated theories of normal processing exist. To illustrate this point, consider the report made by Stevens (1983). He noted that the agnosic patient JR (previously documented by Wapner, Judd, & Gardner, 1978) was unable to describe the presence of subjective contours in two-dimensional Kanisza-type figures. What is particularly interesting about this report is that JR could describe the presence of illusory contours when given stereogram versions of the stimuli. Thus the problem was particular to the interpretation of two-dimensional form cues. Recent computational work suggests how illusory contours may be formed by local interactions between form elements, based on properties such as continuation and collinearity (e.g., Grossberg & Mingolla, 1985). Joint work that parametrically assesses the effects of variables such as the spacing between elements, and their spatial scale, in normal subjects, patients such as JR, and computational models, should provide telling evidence on the subtle way(s) in which visual processing can break down after brain damage.

ACKNOWLEDGMENTS

This work was supported by grants from the Medical and the Science and Engineering Research Councils of Great Britain to the first and second authors. Our thanks to Derrick Watson who helped collect some of the data reported with AS.

REFERENCES

Bauer, R. M. (1984). Autonomic recognition of names and faces in prosopagnosia: A neuropsychological application of the guilty knowledge test. *Neuropsychologia, 22,* 457–469.

Bender, M. B., & Feldman, M. (1972). The so-called "visual agnosias." *Brain, 95,* 173–186.

Benson, D. F., & Greenberg, J. P. (1969). Visual form agnosia. *Archives of Neurology, 20,* 82–89.

Biederman, I. (1987). Recognition-by-components: A theory of human image understanding. *Psychological Review, 94,* 115–147.

Boucart, M., & Bonnet, C. (1991). A study of the effect of structural information and familiarity in form perception. *Quarterly Journal of Experimental Psychology, 43A,* 223–248.

Boucart, M., & Humphreys, G. W. (1992). The computation of perceptual structure from collinearity and closure: Normality and pathology. *Neuropsychologia, 30,* 527–546.

Chertkow, H., Bub, D., & Caplan, D. (1992). Constraining theories of semantic memory: Evidence from dementia. *Cognitive Neuropsychology, 9,* 327–365.

Clowes, M. (1971). On seeing things. *Artificial Intelligence, 2,* 79–116.

Donnelly, N., Humphreys, G. W., & Riddoch, M. J. (1991). The parallel computation of primitive shape descriptions. *Journal of Experimental Psychology: Human Perception and Performance, 17,* 561–570.

Downing, C. J. (1988). Expectancy and visual-spatial attention: Effects on perceptual quality. *Journal of Experimental Psychology: Human Perception and Performance, 14,* 188–202.

Duncan, J., & Humphreys, G. W. (1989). Visual search and stimulus similarity. *Psychological Review, 96,* 433–458.

Efron, R. (1968). What is perception? *Boston Studies in Philosophy of Science, 4,* 137–173.

Enns, J., & Rensink, R. A. (1990). Influence of scene-based properties on visual search. *Science, 247,* 721–723.

Farah, M. J. (1990). *Visual agnosia.* Cambridge, MA: MIT Press.

Grailet, J. M., Seron, X., Bruyer, R., Coyette, F., & Frederix, M. (1990). Case report of a visual integrative agnosia. *Cognitive Neuropsychology, 7,* 275–309.

Grossberg, S., & Mingolla, E. (1985). Natural dynamics of perceptual grouping: Texture boundaries and emergent segmentations. *Perception & Psychophysics, 38,* 141–161.

Hinton, G. E., & Sejnowski, T. J. (1986). Learning and relearning in Boltzmann machines. In D. E. Rumelhart & J. L. McClelland (Eds.), *Parallel distributed processing: Explorations of the microstructure of cognition* (pp. 282–317). Cambridge, MA: MIT Press.

Holmes, G. (1918). Disturbances of visual orientation. *British Journal of Ophthalmology, 2,* 449–468, 506–518.

Howard, D., & Orchard-Lisle, V. (1984). On the origin of semantic errors in naming: Evidence from a case of global aphasia. *Cognitive Neuropsychology, 1,* 163–190.

Humphreys, G. W., Donnelly, N., & Riddoch, M. J. (1993). Expression is computed separately from facial identity, and it is computed separately for moving and static faces: Neuropsychological evidence. *Neuropsychologia, 31,* 173–181.

Humphreys, G. W., Freeman, T., & Müller, H. M. (1992). Lesioning a connectionist model of visual search: Selective effects on distractor grouping. *Canadian Journal of Psychology, 46,* 417–460.

Humphreys, G. W., & Müller, H. M. (1993). SEarch via Recursive Rejection (SERR): A connectionist model of visual search. *Cognitive Psychology, 25,* 43–110.

Humphreys, G. W., Quinlan, P. T., & Riddoch, M. J. (1989). Grouping effects in visual search: Effects with single- and combined-feature targets. *Journal of Experimental Psychology: General, 118,* 258–279.

Humphreys, G. W., & Riddoch, M. J. (1984). Routes to object constancy: Implications from neurological impairments of object constancy. *Quarterly Journal of Experimental Psychology, 36A,* 385–415.

Humphreys, G. W., & Riddoch, M. J. (1987a). The fractionation of visual agnosia. In G. W. Humphreys & M. J. Riddoch (Eds.), *Visual object processing: A cognitive neuropsychological approach* (pp. 281–306). London: Lawrence Erlbaum Associates.

Humphreys, G. W., & Riddoch, M. J. (1987b). *To see but not to see: A case study of visual agnosia.* London: Lawrence Erlbaum Associates.

Humphreys, G. W., & Riddoch, M. J. (1993a). Interactions between object- and space-processing systems revealed through neuropsychology. In D. E. Meyer & S. Kornblum (Eds.), *Attention and performance XIV* (pp. 84–110). Cambridge, MA: MIT Press.

Humphreys, G. W., & Riddoch, M. J. (1993b). Interactive processes in unilateral visual neglect.

In I. Robertson & J. C. Marshall (Eds.), *Unilateral neglect* (pp. 139–168). London: Lawrence Erlbaum Associates.

Humphreys, G. W., & Riddoch, M. J. (in press). Neurological disturbances of vision: Approaches to assessment and treatment. In M.J. Riddoch & G. W. Humphreys (Eds.), *Cognitive neuropsychology and cognitive rehabilitation* (pp. –). London: Lawrence Erlbaum Associates.

Humphreys, G. W., Riddoch, M. J., Quinlan, P. T., Price, C. J., & Donnelly, N. (1992). Parallel pattern processing in visual agnosia. *Canadian Journal of Psychology, 46,* 377–416.

Humphreys, G. W., Troscianko, T., Boucart, M., Donnelly, N., & Harding, G. (1992). Covert processing in different visual recognition systems. In D. Milner & M. Rugg (Eds.), *The neuropsychology of consciousness* (pp. 39–68). London: Academic.

Kartsounis, L. & Warrington, E. K. (1991). Failure of object recognition due to a breakdown of figure-ground discrimination in a patient with normal acuity. *Neuropsychologia, 29,* 969–980.

LaBerge, D. (1983). Spatial extent of attention to letters and words. *Journal of Experimental Psychology: Human Perception and Performance, 9,* 371–379.

Lissauer, H. (1890). Ein fall von seelenblindheit nebst einem Beitrage zur Theori derselben [A case of visual agnosia with a contribution to theory]. *Archiv für Psychiatrie und Nervenkrankheiten, 21,* 222–270.

Livingstone, M. S. (1988). Art, illusion and the visual system. *Scientific American, 258,* 68–75.

Livingstone, M. S., & Hubel, D. H. (1988). Segregation of form, color, movement, and depth: Anatomy, physiology, and perception. *Science, 240,* 740–749.

Lowe, D. G. (1987). Three-dimensional object recognition from single two-dimensional images. *Artificial Intelligence, 31,* 355–395.

Marr, D. (1982). *Vision.* San Francisco: Freeman.

Milner, A. D., Perrett, D. I., Johnson, R. S., Benson, P. J., Jordan, T. R., Heeley, D. W., Bettucci, D., Mortara, F., Mutani, R., Terazzi, E., & Davidson, D. L. W. (1991). Perception and action in visual form agnosia. *Brain, 114,* 405–428.

Moran, J., & Desimone, R. (1985). Selective attention gates visual processing in the extrastriate cortex. *Science, 229,* 782–784.

Mulder, J. A., & Dawson, R. J. M. (1990). Reconstructing polyhedral scenes from single two-dimensional images: The orthogonality hypothesis. In P. K. Patel-Schneider (Ed.), *Proceedings of the 8th biennial conference of the CSCSI* (pp. 238–244). Palo Alto, CA: Morgan-Kaufman.

Müller, H. M., & Humphreys, G. W. (1991). Is luminance-increment detection capacity limited or not? *Journal of Experimental Psychology: Human Perception and Performance, 17,* 107–124.

Navon, D. (1977). Forest before trees: The precedence of global features in visual perception. *Cognitive Psychology, 9,* 353–383.

Patterson, K. E., Seidenberg, M. S., & McClelland, J. L. (1989). Connections and disconnections: Cognitive and neuropsychological studies of phonological reading. In R. G. M. Morris (Ed.), *Parallel distributed processing: Implications for psychology and neurobiology* (pp. 131–181). Oxford, England: Oxford University Press.

Perkins, D. N. (1968). Cubic corners. *MIT Research Laboratory of Electronics Quarterly Progress Report, 89,* 207–214.

Pomerantz, J. R. (1983). Global and local precedence: Selective attention in form and motion perception. *Journal of Experimental Psychology: General, 112,* 516–540.

Posner, M. I., & Keele, S. W. (1967). Decay of visual information from a single letter. *Science, 158,* 137–139.

Ramachandran, V. S. (1988). Perception of shape from shading. *Nature, 331,* 163–166.

Ratcliff, G., & Newcombe, F. (1982). Object recognition: Some deductions from the clinical evidence. In A. W. Ellis (Ed.), *Normality and pathology in cognitive function* (pp. 147–171). New York: Academic.

Riddoch, M. J., Bateman, A., & Humphreys, G. W. (in preparation). *Semantic agnosia.* Manuscript in preparation.

Riddoch, M. J., & Humphreys, G. W. (1987a). A case of integrative visual agnosia. *Brain, 110,* 1431–1462.

Riddoch, M. J., & Humphreys, G. W. (1987b). Visual object processing in optic aphasia: A case of semantic access agnosia. *Cognitive Neuropsychology, 4,* 131–185.

Sartori, G., & Job, R. (1988). The oyster with four legs: A neuropsychological study on the interaction of visual and semantic information. *Cognitive Neuropsychology, 5,* 105–132.

Silveri, M. C., & Gainotti, G. (1988). Interaction between vision and language in category-specific semantic impairment. *Cognitive Neuropsychology, 3,* 677–709.

Stevens, K. A. (1983). Evidence relating subjective contours and interpretations involving interposition. *Perception, 12,* 491–500.

Townsend, J. (1972). Some results on the identifiability of parallel and serial processes. *British Journal of Mathematical and Statistical Psychology, 25,* 168–169.

Treisman, A. (1988). Features and objects: The fourteenth Bartlett lecture. *Quarterly Journal of Experimental Psychology, 40A,* 201–237.

Treisman, A. (1991). Search, similarity, and integration of features between and within dimensions. *Journal of Experimental Psychology: Human Perception and Performance, 17,* 652–676.

Treisman, A., & Gelade, G. (1980). A feature-integration theory of attention. *Cognitive Psychology, 12,* 97–136.

Treisman, A., & Gormican, S. (1988). Feature analysis in early vision: Evidence from search asymmetries. *Psychological Review, 95,* 15–48.

Treisman, A., & Souther, J. (1985). Search asymmetry: A diagnostic for preattentive processing of separable features. *Journal of Experimental Psychology: General, 114,* 285–310.

Ungerleider, L. G., & Mishkin, M. (1982). Two cortical visual systems. In D. J. Ingle, M. A. Goodale, & R. J. W. Mansfield (Eds.), *Analysis of visual behavior* (pp. 549–586). Cambridge, MA: MIT Press.

Wapner, W., Judd, T., & Gardner, H. (1978). Visual agnosia in an artist. *Cortex, 14,* 343–364.

Warrington, E. K. (1982). Neuropsychological studies of object recognition. *Philosophical Transactions of the Royal Society of London, B*(298), 15–33.

Warrington, E. K. (1985). Agnosia: The impairment of object recognition. In P. J. Vinken, G. W. Bruyn, & H. L. Klawans (Eds.), *Handbook of clinical neurology* (pp. 333–349). Amsterdam, Netherlands: Elsevier Science.

Warrington, E. K., & James, M. (1986). Visual object recognition in patients with right hemisphere lesions: Axes or features? *Perception, 15,* 355–366.

Warrington, E. K., & James, M. (1988). Visual apperceptive agnosia: A clinico-anatomical study of three cases. *Cortex, 24,* 13–32.

Warrington, E. K., & Shallice, T. (1984). Category-specific semantic impairments. *Brain, 107,* 829–854.

Warrington, E. K., & Taylor, A. M. (1973). The contribution of the right parietal lobe to visual object recognition. *Cortex, 9,* 152–164.

Warrington, E. K., & Taylor, A. M. (1978). Two categorical stages of object recognition. *Perception, 7,* 695–705.

Wurtz, R. H. (1985). Stimulus selection and conditionial response mechanisms in the basal ganglia of the monkey. In M. I. Posner & O. S. M. Marin (Eds.), *Attention & performance XI* (pp. 441–455). Hillsdale, NJ: Lawrence Erlbaum Associates.

Wurtz, R. H., Goldberg, M. E., & Robinson, D. L. (1982). Brain mechanisms of visual attention. *Scientific American, 246,* 124–135.

4 Category Specificity in Visual Recognition

Freda Newcombe and Ziyah Mehta
Department of Neurosurgery
The Radcliffe Infirmary
Oxford, England

Edward H. F. de Haan
Utrecht University, The Netherlands

The issue of category specificity and its relevance for the study of brain-behavior relationships is not new. Indeed, it is well embedded in 19th-century and early 20th-century neurology. Consider Broadbent's (1884) introduction to a fascinating paper "On a Particular Form of Amnesia: Loss of Nouns." In his first sentence, he is clear about the neuropsychological objective that continues to inform our current approach: "On two previous occasions I have brought before the Society cases of affection of speech with post-mortem examinations, and have endeavoured by their means to elucidate the mechanism of speech and thought" (p. 249). He went on to describe the case histories of three patients who behaved rationally and cooperatively and who were able to produce fluent and appropriate phrases (e.g., "I am very much better today, thank you" (p. 250) and "I hope you will be able to do me good . . . to take this away (p. 253)) but were "scarcely if ever known to utter a noun substantive" (p. 250). He considered the anatomical lesions in these cases and suggested that the loss of nouns may be due to a disconnection—"cutting off the naming centre from the motor speech apparatus" (p. 259). He also considered the functional implications of this particular naming problem:

> The extraordinary analysis of language made by disease of the brain in cases such as these will strike anyone who gives the subject a moment's thought. A single "part of speech," the noun substantive, is separated from all the others, and while they can be spoken fluently and appropriately, utterance of nouns of all kinds fails entirely; they do not come for the expression of thoughts or wants, they are not suggested by objects presented to the sight, and they cannot be repeated imitatively. This analysis by disease is all the more remarkable, in as much as it corresponds with the analysis of language arrived at by logicians and grammarians. (p. 254)

Nearly a century later, Damasio and Damasio (1990b) refined this observation. On the basis of modern neuroimaging and detailed behavioral observation, they proposed that systems in the anterior sector of the left temporal cortices "probably constitute the neural basis for the reference lexicon (the collection of words that denotes concrete entities and actions"). They further specified that "damage to the left anterotemporal sector including the temporal pole (area 38) and the anterior part of the inferotemporal region (areas 21, 20, 37), causes a severe defect for naming of concrete entities" (p. 281). Patients possess the generic information about a given animal or object. They are aware of its visual and functional properties. But they cannot access the unique name label. The nominal problem can be further fractionated. With a lesion confined to area 38, the Damasios reported that "the defect is restricted to the retrieval of proper nouns, e.g., the names of persons or places" (p. 282). This intriguing hypothesis has received some experimental support (Semenza & Zettin, 1988) and presumably raises interesting questions for psycholinguists in relation to the organisation of the mental lexicon.

Could the same flow pattern of information processing characterize nonverbal, visual object recognition? Do the right occipito-temporal pathways, identified in clinical (e.g., Milner, 1968; Newcombe & Russell, 1969) and primate (Desimone, Albright, Gross, & Bruce, 1984; Desimone, Schein, Moran, & Ungerleider, 1985; Gross, Rocha-Miranda, & Bender, 1972; Livingstone, 1988; Ungerleider & Mishkin, 1982) research as crucial for shape recognition, carry and trigger information of increasing specificity until the uniqueness, the quiddity of the object, is identified. If so, are some categories more vulnerable to disruption because of differences in number, ambiguity, and uniqueness of their exemplars? Cups and saucers, for example, are perhaps more obviously discriminable than lions and tigers.

The brief in this chapter is to consider the evidence for category specificity in visual recognition, perhaps arbitrarily setting aside disorders of word recognition, whether in the visual (*alexia*) or auditory (*auditory agnosia*) modalities. Part of the task is to consider whether there is good evidence for category specificity and, if so, what light this may throw on the functional and/or the anatomical architecture of visual recognition. Neuropsychological studies of dyslexic patients, according to Allport (1979), have provided "the single most important contribution to our knowledge of the separable subsystems involved in word recognition" (p. 228). To what extent can studies of failures of visual recognition generate, inform, and constrain our understanding of the functional (and anatomical) architecture of object recognition?

Before broaching these issues, we should perhaps consider the status of the visual recognition disorders (the *agnosias*) as primary syndromes. Whereas disorders of language (*aphasia*), memory (*amnesia*), and motor programming (*apraxia*) have been regarded as syndromes in their own right (i.e., not invariably reduced to "lower level" sensory failure), the relationship between agnosic (recognition) defects and early visual sensory disorders remains contentious. The widely quoted and opposing views of Bay (1950a, 1950b, 1953) and Ettlinger (1956) do not call for extensive discussion. Briefly, Bay considered that recognition disorders could be reduced to intellectual confusion and/or (sometimes subtle) sensory impairment (see also Bender & Feldman, 1972). The reductionist case has gained some strength from the fact that visual sensory processing is seldom adequately examined in a routine clinical examination. In contrast, Ettlinger reported a lack of concordance between sensory defects and recognition impairments in a series of 30 patients with brain lesions, including subgroups with and without visual field defects and perceptual disorder (agnosia). In this seminal study, a variety of psychophysical tests were used, comprising brightness discrimination, flicker fusion, acuity, local adaptation, tachistoscopic acuity, and apparent movement perception. Performance was compared with that of 48 normal control subjects. Among the patients, there were 12 without visual field defect or perceptual loss, 10 with field defects but without perceptual loss, and 8 with both field defects and perceptual loss. Moreover, there was no significant increase in sensory deficit in the latter group where field defect and perceptual loss co-occurred. Subsequently, there have been remarkably few comprehensive studies that have addressed this issue. Campion (1987), however, raised a caveat to the strong claim that agnosia can occur in the absence of visual sensory loss: Precise definitions have not been allocated to the terms *sensory* and *apperceptive* function; and studies of perception have failed to distinguish between descriptions that are based on task and those that refer to function. The possibility, therefore, that a particular *constellation* of sensory deficits may provide a necessary, if not sufficient, cause of recognition disorders remains to be explored. Alternatively, the crude dichotomies (e.g., early sensory processing versus perceptual loss) lend a superficial clarity to the argument that, although convenient, may not reflect the complexity of information processing and its neural support. Suffice it to say that, within the boundaries of the present topic, striking recognition disorders certainly exist in the absence of generalized intellectual deterioration and significant sensory loss (e.g., Humphreys & Riddoch, 1987; Levine, 1978; Newcombe & Ratcliff, 1975; Rubens & Benson, 1971; Taylor & Warrington, 1971). Likewise, there are well-studied cases of prosopagnosia in whom visual sensory processing appears to be largely intact (Bruyer et al., 1983; Rizzo, Corbett, Stanley, Thompson, & Damasio, 1986), but none of these patients is entirely free from sensory impairment. There are also many patients with relatively pure memory disorders who do not display any difficulty in the recognition of common objects or familiar faces.

Consider now the clinical varieties of agnosia and the problem of their functional independence. The term agnosia (from the Greek "without knowledge") has been included in the labeling of disorders affecting the perception/recognition of faces (*prosopagnosia*), body parts (*autotopagnosia*), objects (agnosia, often with the qualifier visual), spatial relationships (*visuospatial ag-*

nosia), and topographical schemata (*topographical agnosia*). The term has also been extended to include a failure to perceive or a denial of disability (*anosognosia*). How independent are these syndromes and can each one in turn be further dissected, according to *sensory modality* and *category* of stimulus? Before narrowing down our inquiry to the recognition of faces and objects it may be worth noting that even the label of anosognosia, which apparently covers gross symptoms of denial, can be fractionated. A domain-specific impairment has been reported in a patient who acknowledges her impaired memory, left hemiplegia, and left hemianopic field defect, but lacks any insight into her total inability to recognize familiar faces, even when consistently failing recognition tests (Young, de Haan, & Newcombe, 1990). Likewise, a domain-specific form of unilateral neglect has been reported (Young, de Haan, Newcombe, & Hay, 1990): The patient was unable to recognize the left half of faces (or half-faces presented in isolation), even when stimuli were presented in his intact right visual field. He did not experience comparable difficulty in recognizing the left side of everyday objects or car fronts (another stimulus class demanding within-category discrimination between visually similar items). Anosognosia for one limb rather than one side of the body has also been described. The reader is referred to two cogent reviews of the anosognosic syndromes and their theoretical interpretation (Bisiach, Vallar, Perani, Papagno, & Berti, 1986; McGlynn & Schacter, 1989). Not only is there strong evidence for the independence of the various agnosic syndromes, but also dissociations can be found that argue in favor of the fine-grain modularity of brain organization and the categorization that appears to be its characteristic feature, whether at a neuronal (Phillips, Zeki, & Barlow, 1984) or cognitive (Rosch, Mervis, & Gray, 1976) level.

We now focus exclusively on disorders of face and object recognition, and address three questions: (a) Can face and object recognition disorders be confidently dissociated?; (b) do faces represent a special category?; and (c) what type of category-specific effects have been elicited in disorders of object recognition?

THE DISSOCIATION OF FACE AND OBJECT RECOGNITION

Clinical Evidence

The classical literature contains several well-studied clinical accounts of dissociation. The spectrum has been tabulated by Farah (1990) as a basis for a functional and anatomical interpretation of the concordance and the diversity of clinical manifestations. The existence of a severe disorder of face recognition with no corresponding impairment of object recognition is irrefutable. Thus Bodamer (1947) described patients with circumscribed and disproportionately severe difficulty in recognizing famous and familiar people by visual inspection of the face. Case 1, asked to look at himself in a mirror, "explored the mirror as if it was a picture, corrected himself, stared in the mirror for a long time as if he had a completely unknown object in front of him and subsequently stated that he did see a face, including all the features which he described. He also knew it was his own face, but he did not recognize it as his own. It could just as well be someone else's, or even a woman" (pp. 95–96). In similar circumstances, the patient studied by MacRae and Trolle (1956) grimaced or stuck his tongue out, "just to make sure" (p. 96). A patient studied by Pallis (1955) was unable to recognize his wife and doctors and failed to identify pictures of Hitler and Marilyn Monroe but "promptly recognized, named, and demonstrated the use of a wide variety of test objects . . . the significance of line drawings was immediately apparent to him, and he could accurately describe the content of various pictures he was shown" (p. 220). When analyzing his difficulties, he added the gloss: "I can see the eyes, nose, and mouth quite clearly, but they just don't add up" (p. 219). A similar account is given in the case of prosopagnosia studied by Cole and Perez-Cruet (1964), who "could not put it all together" (p. 238).

It is more difficult to find convincing cases of severe object agnosia without prosopagnosia; it is not always clear that face recognition has been comprehensively tested. An early descriptive study by Nielsen (1936) suggests that this dissociation occurs. He described an 85-year-old patient, CHC, who had been extremely fit prior to the onset, in December 1937, of a series of cardiovascular accidents from which he made remarkable partial recoveries until his death in November 1939. In January 1939, "when fully rested," he recognized familiar people (his attorney, an old friend, and his adopted son) "but never any inanimate object" (p. 178)—apart from a set of artificial teeth. He could not recognize food, a bottle of milk, a drinking glass, a derby hat, or cars. Nielsen was impressed by his patient's good, albeit circumscribed, powers of visualization "With all this visual disability relative to inanimate objects he recognized and revisualized all living things" (p. 179). For example, he recognized his six nurses "by sight alone" (p. 179; an important qualification as prosopagnosic patients can become very astute in using other clues, such as voices and footsteps, to guide recognition), daffodils, and other flowers. By contrast, another of Nielsen's patients, Flora D, age 46 years, who suffered from cerebral anoxia following inhalation of pus during treatment of a lung abscess, was able to recognize some objects (a pen-knife, a watch dangling from a chain, a pen, and a pencil—but not a key or a coin) but aroused the suspicions of her examiners when she failed to recognize her hands. They then discovered that she could not recognize body parts, artificial teeth, a doll, or a person's face as a face. Nevertheless, "revisualisation as well as recognition of inanimate objects was good" (p. 184). She could describe the topography of the city. Death supervened, however, before she could be tested for the revisualization of animate objects. At postmortem, the brain showed cortical destruction of the left occipital lobe and a focal area of softening in each parietal lobe. According to Nielsen, the lesions were similar to those shown after carbon monoxide poisoning. The postmortem study of CHC's brain also showed bilateral lesions. In the left hemisphere, there was a subcortical lesion in the angular gyrus (to which his dysgraphia was attributed), a small lesion in the left lingual gyrus (to which a transient upper right quadrantanopia was attributed), and a severe left temporal-lobe lesion (to which his language impairments were attributed). In the right hemisphere, there were two lesions: One had destroyed visual cortex and visual association areas (Brodman's areas 18 and 19) and the other lesion involved the right uncus (with extensive oedema), to which his transient left hemiplegia was attributed. Neither of these patients had "pure" agnosic syndromes but the recognition disorders were disproportionately severe.

Developmental Prosopagnosia

The independence of prosopagnosia from disorders of visual object recognition is further supported by unequivocal evidence of childhood prosopagnosia, in both developmental and acquired forms. A 12-year-old girl, AB, could recognize only the most familiar faces (McConachie, 1976). She had no difficulty in recognizing objects or in reading. Her mother was reported to have a similar problem in recognizing faces. Examined two decades later (de Haan & Campbell, 1992), she displayed the same difficulty in recognizing faces, whether of close colleagues whom she met on a day-to-day basis or well-known public figures. The problem existed in the absence of visual object agnosia or reading difficulty. On the contrary, her performance on verbal intelligence tests has consistently been in the superior range (most recent Wechsler Adult Intelligence Scale [WAIS] IQ, 140). There is no evidence of a primary visual memory problem. Performance abilities, although average, have never reached the same high level and, at one time, subtle perceptual difficulties were observed, reflected in increased recognition thresholds for tachistoscopically presented pictorial material. The matching of visual material (overlapping figures and line drawings) was reported to be slow and laborious.

We are currently examining a retired mathematician who contacted our laboratory on the basis of a published article to express his appreciation for the label—prosopagnosic—that he had finally achieved. He had not been fully aware of his condition until adolescence. At the age of 16 years, while on holiday, he stood in a queue for 30 min next to a family friend whom he had known all his life, without any experience of familiarity. The friend complained—mildly—to his parents and his father reacted strongly to this apparent discourtesy. Soon after, cycling from the village to his home, he saw a man walking toward him. In his own words: "Mindful of my father's recent forceful comments, I decided to play it safe. As we passed, I said "Good morning, Sir." My father said later that I had never addressed him as politely before or since."

This gentleman does not recognize his relatives. Presented with 45 photographs of celebrities, he recognized only 3, all politicians, and then only by idiosyncratic features (e.g., Churchill—"a spotted bow-tie and there is that quirk to the mouth"; Margaret Thatcher—"that look of permanent indigestion"). This is a man of high intelligence and rich vocabulary, who reads fast and accurately, and writes with great elegance. On screening tests, we have not as yet detected problems with topographical orientation or color discrimination, but our examination is far from complete.

Prosopagnosia has also been described after injury in childhood. A key study by Young and Ellis (1989) established a clear dissociation between face and word recognition. A young girl, KD, contracted meningitis with hydrocephalus and shunt complications in the first years of life. She had suffered from transient blindness immediately after the cerebral infection. She was comprehensively examined between the ages of 8 and 11 years. At that time, she was completely unable to recognize familiar people in everyday life or from photographs. Family members, including her mother, were easily identified by their voices. Her difficulty in recognizing faces was disproportionately severe but other perceptual problems were elicited. She could recognize many everyday objects but photographs and line drawings (especially in atypical views) presented a problem. Nevertheless, it was clear that her severe prosopagnosic problems were not due to semantic memory impairment (she gave appropriate verbal descriptions of animals that she could not recognize), inability to retrieve names, or gross sensory loss. She was able to match pictures of faces (although using a laborious feature-by-feature strategy) and correctly reported facial features (e.g., length of hair, orientation of the head, and how many teeth were showing).

Thus, the clinical evidence has established prosopagnosia as a syndrome in its own right. It is frequently but not invariably accompanied by achromatopsia and topographical disorientation. It exists in developmental and acquired forms. It is usually associated with bilateral occipito-temporal lesions (Damasio, Damasio, & van Hoesen, 1982). There have been reports of prosopagnosia associated with unilateral right-hemisphere lesions (e.g., Landis, Cummings, Christen, Bogen, & Imhof, 1986), but a definitive view requires a combination of refined behavioral studies and postmortem evidence.

FACE SPECIFICITY

Can Visual Disorders Be Restricted to Face Recognition?

Again, this is an open question that requires empirical evidence. From a theoretical standpoint, Hay and Young (1982) made an important distinction between *uniqueness* and *specificity*. Uniqueness is posited when some or all of the perceptual and cognitive processes used for faces are different in nature. In contrast, the notion of specificity suggests that it is not the processes themselves but their organization into a separate functional system dealing only with facial stimuli that could produce a face-specific system. Physiological research (e.g., Perrett et al., 1984, 1985; Rolls, 1984; Rolls & Baylis, 1986) lends substantial support to this viewpoint. Moreover, it suggests an astonishing specificity of neuronal tuning, such that different groups of cells respond selectively to specific faces, face orientation, direction of gaze, and emotional expression.

Phylogenetic evidence is indeed interesting in that human beings, unlike primates (Desimone, Albright, Gross, & Bruce, 1984), show a marked *inversion* effect. The recognition of faces, compared with other visual stimuli, is disproportionately less accurate if the face is presented upside down in a learning experiment (Scapinello & Yarmey, 1970; Yin, 1969). The effects of inversion are even stronger for photographs of real faces, even when the stimuli consist of schematic line drawings of faces (Raskin & Tweedy, 1987). These findings lend further support to the notion that face processing is in some way special.

In discussing these findings, Farah (1990) drew attention to an interesting ecological effect: Whereas the face-sensitive cells of the macaque monkey respond comparably to upright and inverted faces, those of men and sheep (Kendrick & Baldwin, 1987) respond selectively only to upright faces. Arboreal creatures need to identify faces in rapidly changing orientations that often include an inverted view. Human beings and sheep rarely stand on their heads to recognize their conspecifics.

None of these findings can be used as evidence for absolute specificity, as is apparent from a corpus of single-unit recording data compiled since the first classical account of the specific visual properties of inferotemporal cortical neurons in the monkey (Gross et al., 1972). More plausibly, there are specialized areas of visual cortex that lend themselves to the perception and coding of complex visual patterns. Faces are among the most biologically important visual stimuli to which human beings must respond on a day-to-day basis. Such stimuli warrant a highly specialized neuronal network, as in the case of word perception and recognition. The same system can nevertheless adapt itself to the learning of new patterns that are not necessarily biologically useful. For other species, other stimuli will be preferentially treated perhaps by an analogous region. Bees, for example, need to recognize more than the spatial frequency and line orientation of their food sources: They learn to distinguish between different flowers and are reported to store flower patterns as a low-resolution eidetic image or photograph (Gould, 1985). They also learn complex meaningless patterns.

Developmental evidence, based on infants under the age of 1 year, suggests that there are measurable differences in the processing of information about faces compared with geometrical shapes, suggesting a (possibly innate) hemispheric asymmetry for face processing: Discrimination between mother and stranger occurs faster in the LVF-RH (left visual field presentation-right-hemisphere initial reception) than in the reverse combination. A comparable asymmetry was not observed for shape recognition (de Schonen, Gil de Diaz, & Mathivet, 1986).

How specific, then, is the disorder of face recognition in patients? Most of the reported cases describe visual recognition difficulties that include other categories of stimuli, including chairs (Faust, 1955), buildings (Pallis, 1955), animals (Bornstein, 1963), and cars (Lhermitte, Chain, Escourolle, Ducarne, & Pillon, 1972). One relatively pure case of prosopagnosia (Newcombe, 1979) spontaneously commented that he could no longer identify flowers; he was aware that a plant on the window sill in the laboratory was a common pink flower (in fact a geranium) but could not identify it. Although a keen driver, who had owned several makes of car, he was no longer able to recognize more than a few unusually shaped vehicles (e.g., the old VW beetle). Prior to his illness, he had enjoyed watching horse racing to the tune of modest financial investment. Subsequently, he was no longer able to identify the individual horses.

Does prosopagnosia ever exist in the pure form? This might be so, according to De Renzi's (1986) intriguing report of a 72-year-old public notary who remained profoundly prosopagnosic 16 months after a stroke that had also caused a transient topographical memory loss and a persistent left hemianopia. He was able to resume work but could no longer identify old clients or even close family members, unless he could hear their voices. Unlike many other cases of prosopagnosia, he did not show any significant perceptual impairment, other than a very poor score (18) on Benton's face-matching test. Because of his relatively good performance on other tasks (e.g., object recognition, figure recognition, Ghent's overlapping figures, and Street's completion test), he was considered a good subject to test the hypothesis of a specific impairment of the experience of familiarity. In fact, he could identify his own electric razor, wallet, glasses, and neckties, when each of them was presented together with 6 to 10 objects of the same category, chosen to resemble physically the target. He was also able to identify his own handwriting from that of nine other people who wrote the same sentence. He identified a Siamese cat from photographs of other cats and sorted 20 Italian coins from 20 foreign coins. He easily recognized his car on parking lots. "On all of these tasks," the author reported "he performed unhesitatingly and correctly" (p. 249). Both he and his wife denied that he had any problem in identifying personal objects, in daily life. This is an intriguing claim from a highly experienced neuroscientist. It does, however, provoke questions that we should be prepared to examine. What would other prosopagnosic patients do in a similar situation? Apart from obvious features such as size and color, what subtle clues might an intelligent patient (with full insight into his difficulties) use—familiar signs of wear and tear, surface markings, idiosyncratic calligraphy? In other words, the distinguishing features of the target and the nature and number of the foils have to be considered. This is not to repudiate the case; it provides a fascinating hypothesis that warrants investigation. Farah pursues the issue of the specificity of face recognition mechanisms further in chapter 5.

CATEGORY SPECIFICITY:
THE LIVING/NONLIVING DICHOTOMY

Category-specific dissociations have been well established in studies of language, in the domains of auditory comprehension, speech production, naming, and reading (Goodglass & Budin, 1988; Goodglass, Klein, Carey, & Jones, 1966; Wapner & Gardner, 1979; Yamadori & Albert, 1973). Goodglass and Budin concluded that category-specific and modality-specific lexical dissociations are only observed in relation to the auditory input of language. They suggested that their 60-year-old aphasic patient with a marked and selective auditory comprehension deficit limited to body parts, colors, numbers, and letters "highlights a distinction brought to light by Warrington and her collaborators and the dissociations involving letters, colours, body parts, or numbers which are specific to a subset of aphasics" (p. 76).

One of the four cases reported by Warrington and Shallice (1984), who showed category-specific semantic impairment after recovery from herpes simplex encephalitis, case JBR, is particularly relevant for the present topic. Although all four patients had shown significantly more difficulty in identifying living things and foodstuffs than inanimate objects, this dissociation was particularly striking in JBR. Whereas he could identify 90% of inanimate objects from pictures and 79% from definitions, he could identify only 6% of living things from pictures and 9% from definitions. He was sometimes able to extract superordinate information from words (e.g., snail—"an insect animal"); he was nevertheless more impaired even at this level when attempting to access information about living things compared with objects.

Temple (1986) described an anomia in a 12-year-old boy, which reflected the same dissociation. This is a particularly well-studied case in that his performance was compared in detail with that of his twin sister, as well as with a control group of younger children whose mean naming age on a locally standardized test was comparable to that of the anomic boy. Naming performance was studied on a set of 144 object-pictures taken from the standardized set of Snodgrass and Vanderwart (1980). Stimuli were drawn from four categories: living creatures (48), indoor objects (48), food (24), and clothing (24). Unlike his twin sister and the control group, this boy showed a highly significant failure to name animals as compared with items drawn from the three other categories. His difficulty could not be explained in terms of either frequency or familiarity. In fact, the average familiarity rating for the animal stimuli (3.84) was higher than that for clothes (2.67), foods (2.56), and indoor objects (2.56). Retesting a year later revealed the same pattern of difficulty. Moreover, the same dissociation was observed in responsive naming. Likewise, he was able to describe indoor objects (e.g., ashtray—"It's glass . . . it's got a big round in it. You can put your ash in it.", p. 1235), in such a way that they could be deduced by a listener. His description of animals, however, were largely unrecognizable (e.g., lion—"fat and eyes and ears and he's brown and black lines and eats apples," p. 1263). It is interesting, nevertheless, that his descriptions of objects tended to relate to function rather than their visual appearance.

Clinical Evidence

The dissociations in recognizing animate and inanimate objects were first made explicit by Nielsen (1936), who speculated cautiously that "there is a little evidence that one occipital lobe may be the major for animate, the other for inanimate objects" (p. 81), and suggested that "from the standpoint of cerebral localization, it is necessary to distinguish between recognition of animate and inanimate objects because one function is not infrequently lost without the other" (p. 251). He concluded that, in cases of visual agnosia for inanimate objects and pictures, "the lesion affects either both occipital lobes or the major one plus the splenium of the corpus callosum. In most cases the lesions have been subcortical" (p. 240).

Selective Loss in Visual Recognition and Mental Imagery

Bauer and Rubens (1985) provided a helpful analysis of the spectrum of the visual recognition disorders and their clinical manifestation. Cases of visual agnosia with intact verbal intelligence and the ability to read normally are rare. We have had the opportunity to study just such a case of visual agnosia at varying intervals since 1971, and are still hesitant about the taxonomic label. The clinical picture has been remarkably stable, and the patient himself, MS, has been an impeccable subject: cooperative, patient, and hard-working, with no expectation other than that of providing information that may be helpful to others in the future. The remarkable consistency of his test performance over the years testifies not only to the stability of his condition, but to the sustained effort that he invests in all our investigations.

The case has been described in detail elsewhere (Heywood, Cowey, & Newcombe, 1991; Newcombe & Ratcliff, 1975; Newcombe, Young, & de Haan, 1989; Ratcliff & Newcombe, 1982; Young, Newcombe, Hellawell & de Haan, 1989), and is only briefly summarized here. MS, born on October 7, 1948, was one of five children, all of whom developed normally. He is the only left-handed member of a family in which there is no known history of sinistrality. On leaving school, he joined the police force and was selected as a young cadet driver in the London area. In January 1970, he contracted a febrile illness, with frontal headaches and vomiting, subsequently diagnosed as encephalitis. The permanent sequelae have included a left homonymous hemianopia, amnesia (he cannot remember after an hour's delay the content of stories or the structure of designs presented in standard memory tests), visual agnosia, prosopagnosia, central achromatopsia, topographical disorientation, and topographical memory loss. No sensory motor deficits have been detected (even in the acute state of his illness) and he is now exceptionally fit physically. Apart from his full-time job in a REMPLOY factory, he swims long distances on a regular weekly basis in order to achieve sponsored targets for a charity for the disabled.

When we first examined MS, we were struck by the severity of the visual object agnosia in daily life where he can misrecognize common objects on the basis of visual similarity. Thus, peas can be mistaken for beans, a washbasin for a urinal, and a camera tripod for a stool. His ability to recognize Snodgrass pictures depends on the selection. In recent years he has correctly identified 7 out of 72 and on another occasion 25 out of 80. Of the 36 line drawings of the Oldfield picture-naming test (Newcombe, Oldfield, Ratcliff, & Wingfield, 1971) he has recognized only 7 to 11, when tested in 1972, 1975, 1985, 1988, and 1990. On this test, he has consistently recognized six objects (watch, scissors, screw, clock, book, and chair). In contrast, he has failed to recognize line drawings of other equally familiar objects (e.g., bed, tap, boat, comb, pencil, and key). But in watching his efforts to identify a larger range of pictures, we observed a remarkable failure to identify animals. Two sets, comprising 45 pictures of animals, were shown to him on several occasions during the past 18 years. He has only reliably identified a cow, explicitly because of the udders. He does not recognize pictures of cows that do not include this visual/functional cue. Occasionally, he recognizes a dog, but his capacity to do so is item-specific. Less familiar animals (giraffe, camel, elephant) could neither be described verbally nor identified pictorially. He could not reliably classify pictures or names of animals as domestic or wild. Although nonhuman animals were usually recognized as such, certain pictures tended to confuse him. Thus, two polar bears, standing on their hind legs, were described as a human couple, and an ape sitting on a rock with arms folded was identified as a man in his 30s. He seemed unable to access information about animals, whether at a lexical or pictorial level.

Within the broad group of living creatures, MS has difficulty in judging subcategories. Asked to sort 80 printed words (20 from each of the four classes) under the printed headings "Animals," "Birds," "Fish," and "Insects," he made 25 (31.3%) errors. This task was carried out without a single error by our 46-year-old hospital car-park attendant, as well as by all the clerical staff in our department. Indeed, MS's explicit notions of the categories of "Fish" and "Insect" were vague and ill-formed. Asked to explain the concepts (as for a visitor from outer space who had never seen them before and needed to recognize them) he gave the following descriptions: (a) Birds—"A flying animal with wings and a tail. A pointed head. An animal that flies in the air . . .”; and (b) Insects—“A wild small animal . . . I think of flies or insects just on the ground.”

We then sought more experimental evidence of his disproportionate difficulty in recognizing and accessing information about animals, and asked whether it could be demonstrated in other types of cognitive activity. There are three areas in which we have explored the animate/inanimate distinction further: category judgment, category fluency, and imagery.

CATEGORY JUDGMENT

The first question concerned the extent to which MS's ability to retrieve knowledge of living things was influenced by an item's typicality or familiarity. He was asked to match nouns to category labels, a task that requires explicit knowledge of the categories to which items belong. The effects of typicality and familiarity on access to semantic categories in normal subjects have been well investigated (Shoben, 1982). Would the pattern of MS's performance correspond?

Typicality

In the typicality experiment (Young, Newcombe, Hellawell, & de Haan, 1989), names were selected from the category-structure norms standardized in Britain by Hampton and Gardiner (1983). Twenty items—10 of high typicality (mean weighting less than 2.0) and 10 of low typicality (mean weighting more than 2.0)—were selected for each of 10 semantic categories. The 10 categories comprised 5 living (birds, fish, flowers, fruit, and insects) and 5 nonliving (clothing, furniture, sports, vehicles, and weapons). MS was presented with a category label (in uppercase lettering) and simultaneously one of the nouns (in lowercase lettering). In judging whether the noun was a member of the specified category, MS moved a vertically mounted lever toward his body for a "yes" response and away from his body for a "no" response. There were sets of 40 trials for each semantic category and the sequence of presentation for each block was arranged in random order. Control subjects followed the expected pattern: Responses were faster to high- than to low-typicality items, there was no difference between reaction times from the living and nonliving categories, and no interaction effect between typicality and category. There were very few errors and no evidence of a speed-accuracy trade-off.

MS also showed faster responses to items of high typicality than to low-typicality items. But he responded faster to items from nonliving than from living categories. More important, there was an interaction effect such that this difference was more striking for the low-typicality items. At the same time, he showed a high error rate for low-typicality members of living semantic categories.

Familiarity

A similar experiment (Young et al. 1989) was carried out to explore the influence of familiarity when typicality was controlled (e.g., a penguin is a bird of high familiarity but low typicality). The experimental procedure was similar and the findings were comparable. As with normal subjects, his responses were faster to high-familiarity than low-familiarity items. But MS was faster to make category judgments for items from nonliving than from living categories. Again, the main effects were subject to an interaction: MS's reaction times were markedly slower for low-familiarity items in the living category. And once again his error responses reflected this pattern of difficulty.

Thus, MS's responses were very slow and also inaccurate when category judgments were explicitly required for items within the living category, of either low typicality or low familiarity.

Priming

Young and co-workers (1989) further explored MS's implicit knowledge of category membership, adopting Becker's (1980) priming paradigm. We were therefore measuring the facilitating effect of a previously presented stimulus on response to a subsequent item. In this experiment, category labels appeared as primes when MS was engaged in a lexical decision task, in which nouns and nonwords were the targets. The effect of related, neutral, and unrelated category primes was investigated. The neutral prime consisted of the label; *Blank.* In the case of related prime, the label *Fish,* for example, would precede the word *haddock.* As an example of an unrelated prime, the label *Sport* might precede the word *table.* There was an equal number of word targets and nonword targets. Nonwords were also preceded by a category label. For MS, primes were presented for 500 ms followed by a target exposed for 1.5 s. Again he operated a response lever, moved toward his body to signal "word" and away from his body to signal "nonword."

Control subjects showed the expected pattern: Their responses were faster for nouns preceded by related than by neutral primes and also faster for nouns preceded by neutral than by unrelated primes. They therefore exhibited the two predictable priming effects (Posner & Snyder, 1975): *facilitatory* (a faster response after a related than after a neutral prime) and *inhibitory* (a faster response after a neutral than after an unrelated prime). In contrast, MS showed a significant facilitatory effect but no inhibitory component. This form of priming, according to Posner and Snyder, is characteristic of *automatic priming.* Such an interpretation is in accord with the typicality/familiarity experiments. MS appears to be impaired at getting access to the explicit information that would be required to exploit the primes as predictors of targets. In the priming experiment, however, there was no interaction effect between category and typicality: Priming effects of a related category label were no less for low-typicality living items than from any other item.

From these experiments, we concluded that the living/nonliving distinction provided a useful notional framework for analysing MS's recognition disorder. We were not convinced, however, that MS's performance on tests of explicit as compared with implicit knowledge is measuring the same abilities. We tentatively concluded that different memory systems are involved in the performance of explicit and implicit tasks and that knowledge without awareness may reflect the associative aspect of lexical organisation, a useful if limited system.

Category Word Fluency

Category fluency tasks have not been widely used until comparatively recently, although the original Binet Children's Intelligence Test included a task in which subjects were asked to name as many objects as possible in 60 s. Subsequent studies of word association went so far as to claim that the "meaningfulness" of a word is often defined by the number of associations it evokes under time pressure (Spreen & Schulz, 1966). Written measures of initial letter fluency, developed by Thurstone, (1944) for the measurement of "primary mental abilities," were then adapted for clinical purposes (e.g., how many words beginning with a given initial letter—F, A, and S—could a subject produce orally in 60 s.). Letter fluency was incorporated in several aphasia batteries and has been used specifically for studies of frontal-lobe dysfunction (Benton, 1968; Borkowski, Benton, & Spreen, 1967; Jones-Gotman & Milner, 1977; Ramier & Hécaen, 1970). In contrast, impairments of category fluency have been associated with left-hemisphere damage and, more specifically, with the presence of dysphasic symptomatology. In a study of the long-term consequences of focal wartime missile injury to the brain, Newcombe (1969) gave category fluency tasks: Veterans were asked first to name as many objects as possible in a minute, then as many animals as possible within the same time limit, and then finally to name alternately exemplars from the categories of birds and colors. The latter version of the task was the most sensitive to dysphasia. As far as we can ascertain, no studies have been carried out that systematically compare the performance of the same subjects on both initial letter and category fluency tasks, but we are currently investigating the possibility of dissociated deficits, related to frontal-lobe and left temporal-lobe lesions respectively. There is some anecdotal evidence to support the dissociation: Jones-Gotman and Milner remarked that frontal patients with initial letter fluency deficits do not show a comparable problem with category fluency.

In the case of MS, we assumed that category fluency tasks would provide another source of information regarding MS's semantic impairments and their category-related nature. In a previous publication (Young et al., 1989) we reported fluency data collected in 1980, 1985, 1986, and 1988. We analyzed data for eight semantic categories, of which half referred to living classes (animals,

TABLE 4.1
Word Fluency: Number of category
exemplars generated in one minute
by the patient, M.S., and control subjects

Categories	MS	Controls
Occupations	20.3	12.6
Clothes	16.7	14.5
Sports	15.0	13.6
Crime	13.3	8.3
Drinks	12.7	12.9
Furniture	10.0	10.1
Colors	9.7	13.2
Diseases	9.0	7.5
Animals	7.7	15.7
Vegetables	7.0	10.8
Fruit	6.7	10.9
Tools	6.3	10.9
Birds	4.0	13.7

fruits, birds, and vegetables) and the remainder to nonliving classes (occupations, clothes, sports, and furniture). Compared with Brown's (1978) control data, MS's average performance tallies with that of control subjects, as far as the nonliving categories are concerned. In contrast, he is significantly worse than the controls at producing exemplars from all four living categories. We have further data on fluency tasks and these merely confirm the finding that he is significantly impaired when living exemplars are required. Not unexpectedly, taking a broader spectrum of responses (for a 1 min period for each of 13 categories), and rating each category according to the number of responses given, we found that there was no relationship ($\rho = .001$) between MS's performance and that of the young male control subjects (see Table 4.1), where the numbers represent the mean number of responses given for each category. The data for MS represent an average for four different test sessions over an 8-year period.

On inspection, MS's responses are remarkably consistent over the years. Access to some of the living categories is very limited. Thus, he has never been able to cite more than four fish (cod, haddock, mackerel, and salmon), four flowers (rose, chrysanthemum, daffodil, and carnation), and four insects (fly, ant, wasp, and bee).

Imagery

In the early clinical literature there was a difference of opinion as to whether or not agnosic disorders were due to the loss of visual memory images. Lange (1936) concluded that this was not necessarily so, and commented on the wide variety of agnosic cases, with different degrees of impairment of recognition on the one hand and capacity to evoke visual images on the other. One of the first cases of loss of visual imagery was described by Charcot (1883). The onset of the disorder was sudden. The perceived world of the patient changed, together with a loss of visualization. Everything appeared strange, even well-known places, the faces of his wife and children, and his own image in the mirror. Wilbrand's (1892) agnosic patient was interesting in that her visual imagery was said to be good. She could visualize with closed eyes her home and the town in which she lived. Strong visual images often intruded into her perception. Visual imagery was said to be intact in one of Nielsen's (1936) patients (Flora D) previously described. Lange noted that some agnosic patients dream; others do not.

The phenomenological approach has now been complemented by experimental studies of imagery and the deficits in mental imaging that may be associated with brain lesions. Farah, Levine, and Calvanio (1988) used a sentence verification task to study the loss of visual imagery in a 64-year-old male patient (RM) who had difficulty with reading and color naming but was not agnosic. The task material included statements that needed visual imagery for their verification (e.g., "a grapefruit is larger than an orange") and those not requiring imagery (e.g., "the U.S. government functions under a two-party system"). The sentences were originally devised by Eddy and Glass (1981) to study the effects of visual imagery on verification and the influence of visual interference (i.e., presenting the sentences visually rather than auditorily) on speed and accuracy of response. For auditory presentation, normal subjects responded comparably to the high- and low-imagery sentences. Visual presentation impaired performance on the high-imagery sentences. There was therefore some experimental support for the use of this material in studying an imagery deficit in a patient. In fact, RM performed well on the task provided that the verification questions did not require imagery for their solution.

This paradigm was then extended by Farah, Hammond, Mehta, and Ratcliff (1989) to explore the breakdown of semantic memory in a 36-year-old prosopagnosic patient who had sustained a severe closed-head injury in a traffic accident, at the age of 18 years. The patient, LH, made a good recovery and obtained a master's degree at college. Seven years after the accident, his verbal IQ on the WAIS was 132; the performance IQ (interestingly) was only 93. No impairments of language or memory were detected. Visual field loss was found in the upper left and lower right quadrants. He was unable to recognize live or photographed faces. He reported that he had great difficulty in recognizing animals, plants, and some foods. He recognized only 8 of 26 line drawings of animals compared with 24 out of 32 drawings of common objects.

Farah and her colleagues (1989) then carried out a study of this dissociation using the 48 living and 48 nonliving items selected by Warrington and Shallice (1984) for their previous study of category-specific semantic impairment. Questions were devised regarding the visual and nonvisual properties of both the living and nonliving items. Compared with the control subjects, LH had a selective and significant deficit in accessing visual information about living things (e.g., "are the hind legs of a kangaroo longer than the front legs?"). Control data made it clear that the selective impairment of the prosopagnosic patient was not a trivial effect of task difficulty.

Their study prompted us to devise further sentence verification tasks, with the expectation that the agnosic patient, MS, would be significantly impaired on imagery tasks concerned with living things—in particular, animals. In general, we were concerned to know more about MS's capacity to visualize. From informal testing, he did not appear to have any difficulty in visualizing letter shapes. For example, on an imagery task he could visualize tracking round an uppercase block letter *F*, giving the correct left/right directions. Also, he was able to identify words spelled backward, a task that intuitively at least, involves visualization of a letter sequence. Our experimental tasks were designed to compare his ability to visualize living things and inanimate objects. As a control, he was required to visualize word shapes.

There were six experimental tasks, of which four involved objects and two the shape of words. For all tasks, the three stimuli were presented in a vertical alignment. In all but one of the tasks, the subject was asked which two of the three items were more similar with respect to a given characteristic. In the remaining task, a named item had to be matched with one of the three drawings. All the stimuli were taken from Snodgrass and Vanderwart's (1980) pictures. There were 12 triples of organic items (animals, fruit, and vegetables), and 12 triples of inanimate objects (tools, kitchen utensils, furniture, parts of a building, and weapons). The items were chosen on the basis of overall visual similarity. Pilot trials were run with control subjects to establish which two of the three items in a triple were consistently judged to be more similar visually.

In the object imagery task, the written names of the three stimuli were presented simultaneously. The subject was asked to visualize the typical objects represented by those names and to say which two of the three were more similar visually. They were asked to consider only the outline shape of the object and not its size, color, or individual distinctive features. In the case of animals, subjects were asked to focus on the outline shape of the head only. In a control task, the subject was given a written question about each triple. For example, a question related to living items was: "Which two are found working together more often: pig, dog, or sheep?" For nonliving items, one of the questions was: "Which two can operate on a larger variety of items: scissors, spanner, or pliers?"

On a forced-choice recognition task, the subject was asked to identify the named object (e.g., "Which of these is a camel? and "Which of these is a saw?").

The control tasks tested imagery for word shape. Lowercase letters of the standard minimum height (e.g., *a, c,* and *e*) constituted the basic flat block shape. Ascender (e.g., *b, d,* and *h*) and descender (e.g., *g, p,* and *j*) letters introduced an upward or downward extension of the block shape. The exact shape of individual letters was not relevant. The subject was asked to consider only the shape generated by the word outline. On the word imagery task, the three word stimuli were presented vertically, typed in uppercase Roman script. The subject was required to imagine the words in lowercase and then to say which two were more similar in shape. Three practice trials were given to make sure that the notion of outline shape was well understood. As a control task, the same word stimuli were presented in lowercase and the subject was asked which two were more similar in shape.

Control data for these experimental tasks were obtained from nine policemen, of the same age group as MS. They had volunteered to take part in the experiments in their free time, knowing that MS was a former colleague. Their performance was used to establish the "correct" responses. Ambiguous trials, where the controls had not given a consistent response, were discarded.

Details of the experimental procedure and results are reported elsewhere (Mehta, Newcombe, & de Haan, 1992). The results can be summed up as follows. There was a clear-cut difference in MS's ability to visualize word shapes as compared with objects. Despite a significant impairment of object imagery, his ability to visualize word shapes was apparently intact. A dissociation between word and object recognition has been well documented in the clinical literature (e.g., Holmes, 1979), but we have not been able to discover any experimental studies of differences in the ability to image words and objects.

Second, these studies provided additional evidence of a category-related difference in processing visual information: MS displayed a disproportionately severe difficulty in visualizing living as compared with nonliving objects. Regarding the visualization of nonliving objects, MS performed at the same level as the control subjects. But the number of errors that he made in visualizing living items far exceeded that of the controls. We are not, incidentally, claiming that his capacity to visualize all nonliving objects is normal; just as, at first glance, his adequate copies of black-and-white line drawings do not imply that his ability to perceive these objects normally is intact. On the contrary, according to his own account, he does not appear to see the object as a whole, but rather describes some component parts and their two-dimensional spatial orientation, one to another. In much the same way, he copies object drawings on a slavish, line-by-line basis (Newcombe & Ratcliff, 1975). Named objects may evoke images of their distinctive features, based often on a knowledge of their functional properties. Thus, a cup and a jug might be judged to be visually similar on the basis of his knowledge that they are both held in the hand and therefore must have handles. From his drawings, he would appear to have access to images of some inanimate objects but virtually none to images of animals, other than the knowledge that they usually have a head, a horizontally elongated trunk, four legs, and a tail. In fact, his free drawings of animals are remarkably similar, and indeed

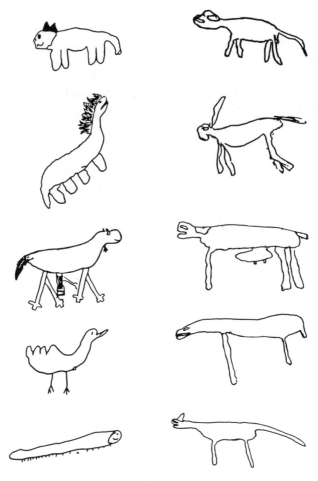

FIG. 4.1.

indistinguishable to "blind" judges who have only ever been able to recognize consistently his drawings of one animal—a cow—on the basis of its udders. A few specimens of his animal drawings are illustrated in Fig. 4.1 for comparison with those of a normal 8-year-old boy, the nephew of one of the authors, who has no pretensions to artistic talent and who seldom has the opportunity to watch a variety of animals in the environs of Brooklyn, New York. The drawings are supposed to represent (from top to bottom) a dog, a horse, a cow, a chicken, and a caterpillar.

In summary, MS has shown disproportionate difficulty in processing information about living as compared with nonliving items in a variety of contexts, including visual recognition, the retrieval of factual information, and the use of mental imagery.

REFLECTIONS

As a first approximation, the dichotomy—animate/inanimate—serves as a useful notational approach to MS's difficulties in identifying objects. We appear to be looking at one of the "natural" dissections produced by disease (Teuber, 1968), rather than one of those chance findings decried by the opponents of single-case studies. Our evidence, we claim, is robust. In the case of fluency, it has been replicated several times; and it has been consistently demonstrated in other experimental paradigms, including naming, priming, lexical decision, and imagery tasks.

The concept of category specificity is now well entrenched in studies of language and recognition disorders. But what is the veridical structure of these categories? Are they an intrinsic feature of the organization of the mental lexicon and/or of a visual image data bank, instantiated in nervous tissue? Are they a rational way of classifying/coding our knowledge of the world? Do they reflect formal properties of the visual stimuli in our environment? Are they shaped and constrained by neurobiology and by the motor and sensory systems involved in the processing of visual input?

Theoretical insights may emerge from several sources: artificial intelligence, cognitive theory, and the hypotheses generated by the study of behavioral and neuroanatomical correlations. Massively parallel processing provides a plausible framework for the multichanneling of visual input that has been demonstrated in the primate brain. Computational networks could, in principle, account for dissociations of the visual recognition disorders (McClelland & Farah, 1991).

In general, computer vision theorists tackle problems at the perceptual level where the dimensions of early visual sensory processing are reconciled and integrated to give an initial pictorial representation of the object. These entry-level representations are thought by cognitive theorists to take a canonical form (Palmer, Rosch & Chase, 1981). At this early level, MS may experience difficulty (i.e., in failing to match unfamiliar views of objects), although he does not experience the same difficulty when asked to categorize a stimulus as an object or nonobject (Kroll & Potter, 1984). He rejects all nonobjects but only a small percentage of objects.

Prototypes at this basic level representation vary in generality or specificity. They are in turn referred to stable and abstract representations. Important dissociations occur at this level of processing. Martin's (1987) patient, an amateur artist, made an impressive copy of a greeting card, complete with a village church and birds in a tree (adding rabbits frolicking in the field—a touch of poetic licence, perhaps), presumably because he identified the key objects and was able to draw on a rich gallery of their mental representations. In contrast, he could not copy adequately a meaningless geometric design (Rey Osterreith). This contrast perhaps illustrates the difference between data-driven (the latter) and representation-driven (the former) performance, also displayed by Goldstein's

(1940) patient who could not copy a square but could draw a church window "from memory." By contrast, MS can copy, slowly and in slavish fashion, but does not seem to be helped by mental representations of all but the most common objects (e.g., a cup, a table, and an apple). His drawings of animals, for example, suggest that he can draw only on a crude prototype with a rectangular body, a reptilian head, four legs, and a tail.

Theories regarding the organization of semantic memory provide a fruitful source of hypotheses (Warrington & McCarthy, 1987) rather than a universally agreed classificatory system. The hierarchical system, advocated by Collins and Quillian (1969) among others, appears both rational and consistent with pathophysiological data. On the whole, agnosic patients produce more information about superordinates than exemplars. Duensing (1952) focused on this point in a beautiful single-case study of an intelligent patient who suffered a partial occlusion of both posterior cerebral arteries. This patient could easily distinguish small differences in meaningless patterns; he described verbally the botanical differences between the leaves of plants such as rose and lilac, but he could not visually identify either of them. Categories of stimuli—furniture, faces, trees, fruit, and flowers—were recognized, but not their exemplars. This finding, however, does not necessarily explicate the animate/inanimate distinction. How then are concepts defined: as a summary description typically cast in features, a probabilistic account, or the exemplar hypothesis? In a cogent analysis of the power of these conceptual approaches to account for a number of the difficulties in satisfactory categorization (e.g., disjunctive concepts, unclear cases, simple typicality effects), Smith and Medin (1981) concluded that "the facts about object categorisation fit the probabilistic and exemplar views better than they do the classical view" (p. 175). Their caveat stems from the difficulty in incorporating, for example, Keil's (1979) work on ontological concepts. In his approach, the fundamental categories are taken to be "thing," "event," "physical object," "organism," "functional artifact," "animal," "plant," and "human." And the claim is that either two concepts have an identical set of features (predicates), or one is a proper subset of the other, or they share no features at all. Prototype theory nevertheless continues to offer a plausible background for continuous negotiation about the organization of representations (e.g., stacks versus fuzzy sets).

To what extent, if at all, could an analysis of patients' errors contribute to this modeling of object recognition? Shallice and Jackson (1988) pointed out that this cognitive approach is rare in modern case descriptions of associative agnosia. This is not only true but, at first glance, surprising. Consider the import of error analysis on theories of word recognition (Allport & Funnell, 1981; Coltheart, Patterson, & Marshall, 1980; Marshall & Newcombe, 1973). Lissauer (cited in Shallice and Jackson, 1988), however, provided a venerable exception to clinical practice in this respect. But his patient's, Gottlieb L's, protocol is of limited value given the perseveration that pervades his responses. Indeed the lack of purity in agnosic syndromes calls for a ruthless selection of rare cases to trace the functional architecture of the recognition disorders. In the same vein, was Gottleib L an associative agnosic or alternatively a classic example of a modality-specific anatomical disconnection similar (in many respects) to Case 1 of Newcombe and Ratcliff (1975)? His apparently well-preserved ability to recognize tactually presented objects together with the pattern of alexia without agraphia might suggest so. Remarkably few patients, purportedly with visual agnosia, are thoroughly examined in other modalities. If the recognition disorder is modality-specific, then the degradation of visual input may impose its own constraints, cutting across conventional category boundaries and thus confounding an analysis of error based on a universal conceptual grammar.

Are we then, at this stage, taking a bridge too far in seeking to impose a tight theoretical framework on disorders of object recognition? If that is the case, we continue to rely on pathophysiological evidence and the light it may shed on object recognition. Here models will be shaped by the increasing convergence of neuropsychological data, neurophysiological research, and modern neuroimaging. Neurological literature presents some useful leads. For example, Konorski's (1967) speculations about the nine *gnostic fields* (see Fig. 4.2) clearly distinguished between animate and inanimate objects and introduced subcategories that vary according to material (buildings vs. tools; faces vs. animals). In a similar vein, Damasio and his group (Damasio, 1989a, 1989b; Damasio, 1990a, 1990b; Damasio, Damasio, & Tranel, 1990; Damasio, 1990) made a major contribution to the modeling of category specificity in agnosia. Briefly, the theory interprets recall in terms of the synchronous reactivation (in the relevant sensory cortices) of modality-specific information, a notion reminiscent of Penfield and Roberts' (1959) *abiding facilitations*. The Damasio model sets in functional and physiological terms Lissauer's conceptions (cited in Shallice & Jackson, 1988): certain fundamental ideas invariably come to mind when an object is perceived, which usually relate to the object's name and those events that have been experienced most frequently and vividly in association with it. Memories laid down via different sensory modalities contribute to these associations. But it is only when they are brought into awareness and linked with the percept that the recognition of an object becomes complete. Damasio extended this concept to include amodal convergence zones that instantiate the combinatorial codes required to evoke these featured inscriptions. Objects can be classified according to their sensorimotor characteristics. Thus, manipulable tools will fall into a category that has different processing demands from those incorporating musical instruments, other man-made articles, animals, and other natural phenomena. A number of factors are proposed that may influence the neural mapping of different entities. They include physical structure, operation, sensory modality, frequency in the environment, and value to the observer. An individualized weighting of these factors might account for the varied patterns of recognition loss found in agnosia.

Finally, what is so special about animals? Or rather, what factors might

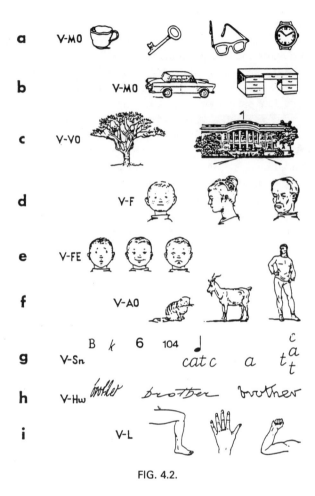

FIG. 4.2.

contribute to MS's difficulty in assessing information about animals? Clearly, age of acquisition would not provide a useful explanation. Elephants and giraffes are nursery familiars for many young children. Is the recognition of animals disproportionately dependent on visual imagery? If we say elephant or butterfly, do you not see these creatures in your mind's eye? If we mention horse, donkey, zebra, antelope, do you not have immediate images that, in their totality rather than in their separate features, are readily distinguishable? In contrast, the knowledge and imagery of tools requires a more deliberate, cognitively mediated appreciation of their functional use. Many animals are visually similar. Outside the domestic range, we handle or listen to very few of them. MS has not lost the capacity to visualize per se. He can, in his mind's eye, evoke the symbols of language as well as the form of some objects. But he may, in the case of objects, be even more restricted to canonical prototypes than the rest of us. Is it the specificity, the uniqueness of animals that is so difficult to represent and retrieve? We are not usually asked to identify and name 50 different chairs, unless operating within the higher flights of the antique business. Many objects, of different shape and design, are all accorded a common name. The name *elephant* applies uniquely to one distinctive form. In addition to his higher level visual perceptual loss—or perhaps because of it—has MS lost the ability to specify and identify this visually determined uniqueness?

REFERENCES

Allport, A. (1979). Word recognition in reading. In P. A. Kolers, M. E. Wrolstad, & H. Bouma (Eds.), *Processing of visible language* (Vol. 1, pp. 227–257). New York & London: Plenum.

Allport, D. A., & Funnell, E. (1981). Components of the mental lexicon. *Philosophical Transactions of the Royal Society of London, B*(295), 397–410.

Bauer, R. M., & Rubens, A. B. (1985). Agnosia. In K. M. Heilman & E. Valenstein (Eds.), *Clinical neuropsychology* (2nd ed., pp. 187–241). New York: Oxford University Press.

Bay, E. (1950a). *Agnosie und Funktionswandel: Monographien aus dem Gesamtgebiet der Neurologie und Psychiatrie* [Agnosia and change of function: monographs from neurology and psychiatry] (Vol. 73, pp. 1–94). Heidelberg, Germany: Springer.

Bay, E. (1950b). *Agnosie und Funktionswandel: Eine hirnpathologische Studie* [Agnosia and change of function: a brain pathology study]. Berlin: Springer.

Bay, E. (1953). Disturbances of visual perception and their examination. *Brain, 76,* 515–550.

Becker, C. A. (1980). Semantic context effects in visual word recognition: An analysis of semantic strategies. *Memory & Cognition, 8,* 493–512.

Bender, M. B., & Feldman, M. (1972). The so-called "visual agnosias." *Brain, 95,* 173–186.

Benton, A. L. (1968). Differential behavioral effects in frontal lobe disease. *Neuropsychologia, 6,* 53–60.

Bisiach, E., Vallar, G., Perani, D., Papagno, C., & Berti, A. (1986). Unawareness of disease following lesions of the right hemisphere: Anosognosia for hemiplegia and anosognosia for hemianopia. *Neuropsychologia, 24,* 471–482.

Bodamer, J. (1947). Die prosop-agnosie [Prosopagnosia]. *Archiv für Psychiatrie und Nervenkrankheiten, 179,* 6–53.

Borkowski, J. G., Benton, A. L., & Spreen, O. (1967). Word fluency and brain damage. *Neuropsychologia, 5,* 135–140.

Bornstein, B. (1963). Prosopagnosia. In L. Halpern (Ed.), *Problems of dynamic neurology* (pp. 283–318). Jerusalem: Hadassah Medical Organisation.

Broadbent, W. H. (1884). On a particular form of amnesia. Loss of nouns. *Medico-Chirurgical Transactions (1907), 67,* 249–264.

Brown, W. P. (1978). *Belfast category norms, 1971–1977.* Belfast: Queens University.

Bruyer, R., Laterre, C., Seron, X., Feyereisen, P., Strypstein, E., Pierrard, E., & Rectem, D. (1983). A case of prosopagnosia with some preserved covert remembrance of familiar faces. *Brain and Cognition, 2,* 257–284.

Campion, J. (1987). Apperceptive agnosia: The specification and description of constructs. In G. W. Humphreys & M. J. Riddoch (Eds.), *Visual object processing: A cognitive neuropsychological approach* (pp. 197–232). London: Lawrence Erlbaum Associates.

Charcot, J. M. (1883). Un cas de suppression brusque et isolée de la vision mentale des signes et des objets (formes et couleurs) [A case of the sudden and isolated loss of the mental vision of signs and objects (Shapes and colours)]. *Progrès Médical, 11*, 568.

Cole, M., & Perez-Cruet, J. (1964). Prosopagnosia. *Neuropsychologia, 2*, 237–246.

Collins, A. M., & Quillian, M. R. (1969). Retrieval time from semantic memory. *Journal of Verbal Learning and Verbal Behavior, 8*, 240–247.

Coltheart, M., Patterson, K. E., & Marshall, J. C. (Eds.). (1980). *Deep dyslexia*. London: Routledge & Kegan Paul.

Damasio, A. R. (1989a). The brain binds entities and events by multiregional activation from convergence zones. *Neural Computation, 1*, 123–132.

Damasio, A. R. (1989b). Time-locked multiregional retroactivation: A systems-level proposal for the neural substrates of recall and recognition. *Cognition, 33*, 25–62.

Damasio, A. R. (1990a). Category related recognition deficits as a clue to the neural substrates of knowledge. *Trends in Neuroscience, 13*, 95–98.

Damasio, A. R. (1990b). Synchronous activation in multiple cortical regions: A mechanism for recall. *Seminars in the Neurosciences, 2*, 287–296.

Damasio, A. R., Damasio, H., & Tranel, D. (1990). Impairments of visual recognition as clues to the processes of memory. In G. Edelman, E. Gall, & M. Cowan (Eds.), *Signal sense: Local and global order in perceptual maps* (pp. 451–473). New York: Wiley-Liss.

Damasio, A. R., Damasio, H., Tranel, D., & Brandt, J. P. (1990). Neural regionalization of knowledge access: Preliminary evidence. *Cold Spring Harbor Symposia on Quantitative Biology, 55*, 1039–1047.

Damasio, A. R., Damasio, H., & van Hoesen, G. W. (1982). Prospagnosia: Anatomic basis and behavioral mechanisms. *Neurology, 32*, 331–341.

Damasio, H., & Damasio, A. R. (1989). *Lesion analysis in neuropsychology*. New York: Oxford University Press.

Damasio, H., & Damasio, A. R. (1990). The neural basis of memory, language and behavioral guidance: advances with the lesion method in humans. *Seminars in The Neurosciences, 2*, 277–286.

de Haan, E. H. F., & Campbell, R. (1992). A fifteen-year follow up of a case of developmental prosopagnosia. *Cortex. 27*, 489–509.

De Renzi, E. (1986). Current issues in prosopagnosia. In H. D.Ellis, M. A. Jeeves, F. G. Newcombe, & A. Young (Eds.), *Aspects of face processing* (pp. 243–252). Dordrecht, Netherlands: Martinus Nijhoff.

de Schonen, S., Gil de Diaz, M., & Mathivet, E. (1986). Hemispheric asymmetry in face processing in infancy. In H. D. Ellis, M. A. Jeeves, F. G. Newcombe, & A. Young (Eds.), *Aspects of face processing* (pp. 199–209). Dordrecht, Netherlands: Martinus Nijhoff.

Desimone, R., Albright, T. D., Gross, C. D., & Bruce, C. (1984). Stimulus-selective responses of inferior temporal neurons in the macaque. *Journal of Neuroscience, 4*, 2051–2062.

Desimone, R., Schein, S. J., Moran, J., & Ungerleider, L. G. (1985). Contour, color and shape analysis beyond the striate cortex. *Vision Research, 25*, 441–452.

Duensing, F. (1952). Beitrag zur Frage der optischen Agnosie [Contribution to the question of optical agnosia]. *Archiv für Psychiatrie und Nerven Krankheiten, 188*, 131–161.

Eddy, J. K., & Glass, A. L. (1981). Reading and listening to high and low imagery sentences. *Journal of Verbal Learning and Verbal Behavior, 20*, 333–345.

Ettlinger, G. (1956). Sensory deficits in visual agnosia. *Journal of Neurology, Neurosurgery and Psychiatry, 19*, 297–307.

Farah, M. J. (1990). *Visual agnosia: Disorders of object recognition and what they tell us about normal vision*. Cambridge, MA: MIT Press.

Farah, M. J., Hammond, K. H., Mehta, Z., & Ratcliff, G. (1989). Category-specificity and modality-specificity in semantic memory. *Neuropsychologia, 27*, 193–200.

Farah, M. J., Levine, D. N., & Calvanio, R. (1988). A case study of mental imagery deficity. *Brain and Cognition, 8,* 147–164.

Faust, C. (1955). *Die zerebralen Herdstörungen bei hinterhaupt verletzungen und Beurteilung* [Focal cerebral dysfunction after injuries to the back of the head and assessment thereof]. Stuttgart, Germany: Thièrie.

Goldstein, K. (1940). *Human nature in the light of psychopathology.* Cambridge, MA: Harvard University Press.

Goodglass, H., & Budin, C. (1988). Category and modality specific dissociations in word comprehension and concurrent phonological dyslexia. *Neuropsychologia, 26,* 67–78.

Goodglass, H., Klein, B., Carey, P., & Jones, K. (1966). Specific semantic word categories in aphasia. *Cortex, 2,* 78–89.

Gould, J. L. (1985). How bees remember flower shapes. *Science, 227,* 1492–1494.

Gross, C. G., Rocha-Miranda, C. E., & Bender, D. B. (1972). Visual properties of neurons in inferotemporal cortex of the macaque. *Journal of Neuropsychology, 35,* 96–111.

Hampton, J. A., & Gardiner, M. M. (1983). Measures of internal category structure: A correlational analysis of normative data. *British Journal of Psychology, 74,* 491–516.

Hay, D. C., & Young, A. W. (1982). The human face. In A. W. Ellis (Ed.), *Normality and pathology in cognitive functions* (pp. 173–202). New York: Academic.

Heywood, C. A., Cowey, A., & Newcombe, F. (1991). Chromatic discrimination in a cortically colour blind observer. *European Journal of Neuroscience, 3,* 802–812.

Holmes, G. (1979). Pure word blindness. In C. G. Phillips (Ed.), *Selected papers of Gordon Holmes* (pp. 452–463). New York: Oxford University Press.

Humphreys, G. W., & Riddoch, M. J. (1987). *To see but not to see—A case study of visual agnosia.* Hillsdale, NJ: Lawrence Erlbaum Associates.

Jones-Gotman, M., & Milner, B. (1977). Design fluency: The invention of nonsense drawings after focal cortical lesions. *Neuropsychologia, 15,* 653–674.

Keil, F. C. (1979). *Semantic and conceptual development.* Cambridge, MA: Harvard University Press.

Kendrick, K. M., & Baldwin, B. A. (1987). Cells in temporal cortex of conscious sheep can respond preferentially to faces. *Science, 236,* 448–450.

Konorski, J. (1967). *Integrative activity of the brain.* Chicago: University of Chicago Press.

Kroll, J. F., & Potter, M. C. (1984). Recognizing words, pictures, and concepts: A comparison of lexial, object, and reality decisions. *Journal of Verbal Learning and Verbal Behavior, 23,* 39–66.

Landis, T., Cummings, J. L., Christen, L., Bogen, J. E., & Imhof, H. G. (1986). Are unilateral right posterior cerebral lesions sufficient to cause prosopagnosia? Clinical and radiological findings in six additional patients. *Cortex, 22,* 243–252.

Lange, J. (1936). Agnosien und Apraxien [Agnosias and Apraxias]. In O. Bumke & O. Foerster (Eds.), *Handbuch der Neurologie* (Vol. 11, pp. 807–960). Berlin: Springer.

Levine, D. (1978). Prosopagnosia and visual object agnosia: A behavioral study. *Brain and Language, 5,* 341–365.

Lhermitte, F., Chain, F., Escourolle, R., Ducarne, B., & Pillon, B. (1972). Etude anatomoclinique d'un cas de prosopagnosie [an anatomoclinical study of a case of prosopagnosia]. *Revue Neurologique, 126,* 329–346.

Livingstone, M. S. (1988). Art, illusion and the visual system. *Scientific American, 258,* 68–75.

MacRae, D., & Trolle, E. (1956). The defect of function in visual agnosia. *Brain, 79,* 94–110.

Marshall, J. C., & Newcombe, F. (1973). Patterns of paralexia: A psycholinguistic approach. *Journal of Psycholinguistic Research, 2,* 175–199.

Martin, A. (1987). Representations of semantic and spatial knowledge in Alzheimer's patients: Implications for models of preserved learning in amnesia. *Journal of Clinical and Experimental Neuropsychology, 9,* 191–224.

McClelland, J. L., & Farah, M. J. (1991). A computational model of semantic memory impairment: Modality-specificity and emergent category-specificity. *Journal of Experimental Psychology*.

McConachie, H. R. (1976). Developmental prosopagnosia: A single case report. *Cortex, 12*, 76–82.

McGlynn, S. M., & Schacter, D. L. (1989). Unawareness of deficits in neuropsychological syndromes. *Journal of Clinical and Experimental Neuropsychology, 2*, 143–205.

Mehta, Z., Newcombe, F., & de Haan, E. H. F. (1992). Selective loss of imagery in a case of visual agnosia. *Neuropsychologia, 30*, 645–655.

Milner, B. (1968). Visual recognition and recall after right temporal-lobe excision in man. *Neuropsychologia, 6*, 191–209.

Milner, B., Teuber, H-L. (1968). Alteration of perception and memory in man: Reflections on methods. In L. Weiskrantz (Ed.), *Analysis of behavioral change* (pp. 268–375). New York: Harper & Row.

Newcombe, F. (1969). *Missile wounds of the brain: A study of psychological deficits*. London: Oxford University Press.

Newcombe, F. (1979). The processing of visual information in prosopagnosia and acquired dyslexia: Functional versus physiological interpretation. In D. J. Osborne, M. M. Gruneberg, & J. E. Eiser (Ed.), *Research in psychology and medicine* (pp. 315–322). London: Academic.

Newcombe, F., Oldfield, R. C., Ratcliff, G. G., & Wingfield, A. (1971). Recognition and naming of object-drawings by men with focal brain wounds. *Journal of Neurology, Neurosurgery and Psychiatry, 34*, 329–340.

Newcombe, F., & Ratcliff, G. (1975). Agnosia: A disorder of object recognition. In F. Michel & B. Schott (Eds.), *Les syndromes de disconnexion calleuse chez l'homme* [Colloque International de Lyon, 1974]. Lyon, France: Hôpital Neurologique de Lyon.

Newcombe, F., & Russell, W. (1969). Dissociated visual perceptual and spatial deficits in focal lesions of the right hemisphere. *Journal of Neurology, Neurosurgery and Psychiatry, 32*, 73–81.

Newcombe, F., Young, A. W., & de Haan, E. H. F. (1989). Prosopagnosia without covert recognition. *Neuropsychologia, 27*, 179–191.

Nielsen, J. M. (1936). *Agnosia, apraxia, and aphasia: Their value in cerebral localization*. New York: Hoeber.

Pallis, C. A. (1955). Impaired identification of faces and places with agnosia for colours. *Journal of Neurology, Neurosurgery and Psychiatry, 18*, 218–224.

Palmer, S., Rosch, E., & Chase, P. (1981). Canonical perspective and the perception of objects. In J. B. Long & A. D. Baddeley (Eds.), *Attention and performance IX* (pp. 135–151). Hillsdale, NJ: Lawrence Erlbaum Associates.

Penfield, W., & Roberts, L. (1959). *Speech and brain mechanisms*. Princeton, NJ: Princeton University Press.

Perret, D. I., Smith, P. A. J., Potter, D. D., Mistlin, A. J., Head, A. S., Milner, A. D., & Jeeves, M. A. (1984). Neurones responsive to faces in temporal cortex: Studies of functional organization, sensitivity to identity and relation to perception. *Human Neurobiology, 3*, 197–208.

Perret, D. I., Smith, P. A. J., Potter, D. D., Mistlin, A. J., Head, A. S., Milner, A. D., & Jeeves, M. A. (1985). Visual cells in the temporal cortex sensitive to face view and gaze direction. *Proceedings of the Royal Society of London, B*(223), 293–317.

Phillips, C. G., Zeki, S., & Barlow, H. B. (1984). Localization of function in the cerebral cortex: Past, present and future. *Brain, 107*, 327–361.

Posner, M. I., & Snyder, C. R. R. (1975). Facilitation and inhibition in the processing of signals. In P. M. A. Rabbitt & S. Dornic (Eds.), *Attention and performance V* (pp. 668–682). London: Academic.

Ramier, A-M., & Hécaen, H. (1970). Rôle respectif des atteintes frontales et de la latéralisation lésionelle dans les déficits de la "fluence verbale" [The respective roles of frontal lesions and of laterality of lesion in deficits of verbal fluency]. *Revue Neurologique, 123*, 17–22.

Raskin, S. A., & Tweedy, J. (1987). Recognition of faces: Inversion effect. *Journal of Clinical and Experimental Psychology, 9,* 260.

Ratcliff, G., & Newcombe, F. (1982). Object recognition: Some deductions from the clinical evidence. In A. W. Ellis (Ed.), *Normality and pathology in cognitive functions* (pp. 147–172). New York: Academic.

Rizzo, M., Corbett, J. J., Stanley Thompson, H., & Damasio, A. R. (1986). Spatial contrast sensitivity in facial recognition. *Neurology, 36,* 1254–1256.

Rolls, E. T. (1984). Neurons in the cortex of the temporal lobe and in the amygdala of the monkey with responses selective for faces. *Human Neurobiology, 3,* 209–222.

Rolls, E. T., & Baylis, G. C. (1986). Size and contrast have only small effects on the responses to faces of neurons in the cortex of the superior temporal sulcus of the monkey. *Experimental Brain Research, 65,* 38–48.

Rosch, E., Mervis, C. B., Gray, W., Johnson, D., & Boyes-Braem, P. (1976). Basic objects in natural categories. *Cognitive Psychology, 8,* 382–439.

Rubens, A. B., & Benson, D. F. (1971). Associative visual agnosia. *Archives of Neurology, 24,* 305–316.

Scapinello, K. E., & Yarmey, A. D. (1970). The role of familiarity and orientation in immediate and delayed recognition of pictorial stimuli. *Psychonomic Science, 21,* 329–331.

Semenza, C., & Zettin, M. (1988). Generating proper names: A case of selective inability. *Cognitive Neuropsychology, 5*(6) 711–721.

Shallice, T., & Jackson, M. (1988). Lissauer on agnosia. *Cognitive Neuropsychology, 5,* 153–192.

Shoben, E. J. (1982). Semantic and lexical decisions. In C. R. Puff (Ed.), *Handbook of research methods in human memory and cognition* (pp. 287–314). New York: Academic.

Smith, E. E., & Medin, D. L. (1981). *Categories and concepts.* Cambridge, MA: Harvard University Press.

Snodgrass, J. G., & Vanderwart, M. (1980). A standardized set of 260 pictures: Norms for name agreement, image agreement, familiarity and visual complexity. *Journal of Experimental Psychology: Human Learning and Memory, 6,* 174–215.

Spreen, O., & Schultz, R. W. (1966). Parameters of abstractness, meaningfulness, and pronounceability of 329 nouns. *Journal of Verbal Learning and Verbal Behavior, 5,* 459–468.

Taylor, A. M., & Warrington, E. K. (1971). Visual agnosia: A single case report. *Cortex, 7,* 152–161.

Temple, C. M. (1988). Anomia for animals in a child. *Brain, 109,* 1225–1242.

Thurstone, L. L. (1944). A factorial study of perception. *Psychometric Monograph* (Vol. 4, pp. 1–150). Chicago: University of Chicago Press.

Ungerleider, L. G., & Mishkin, M. (1982). Two cortical visual systems. In D. J. Ingle, R. J. W. Mansfield, & M. A. Goodale (Eds.), *The analysis of visual behavior* (pp. 549–586). Cambridge, MA: MIT Press.

Wapner, W., & Gardner, H. (1979). A note on patterns of comprehension and recovery in global aphasia. *Journal of Speech and Hearing Research, 29,* 765–771.

Warrington, E. K., & McCarthy, R. (1987). Categories of knowledge: Further fractionation and an attempted integration. *Brain, 110,* 1273–1296.

Warrington, E. K., & Shallice, T. (1984). Category specific semantic impairments. *Brain, 107,* 829–854.

Wilbrand, H. (1892). Ein Fall von Seelenblindheit und Hemianopsie mit Sectons-befund [A case of visual imperception and hemianopia with post-mortem findings]. *Deutsche Zeitschrift fur Nervenheilkunde, 2,* 361–387.

Yamadori, A., & Albert, M. L. (1973). Word category aphasia. *Cortex, 9,* 112–115.

Yin, R. K. (1969). Looking at upside down faces. *Journal of Experimental Psychology, 81,* 141–145.

Young, A. W., de Haan, E. H. F., & Newcombe, F. (1990). Unawareness of impaired face recognition. *Brain and Cognition, 14,* 1–18.

Young, A. W., de Haan, E. H. F., Newcombe, F., & Hay, D. C. (1990). Facial neglect. *Neuropsychologia, 28,* 391–415.

Young, A. W., & Ellis, H. D. (1989). Childhood prosopagnosia. *Brain and Cognition, 9,* 16–47.

Young, A. W., Newcombe, F., Hellawell, D., & de Haan, E. H. F. (1989). Implicit access to semantic information. *Brain and Cognition, 11,* 186–209.

5

Specialization within Visual Object Recognition: Clues from Prosopagnosia and Alexia

Martha J. Farah
Carnegie Mellon University

The previous chapter posed a basic question about visual object recognition: Are all types of objects recognized in the same way, or are different kinds of visual object recognition systems used to recognize different types of object? Most current work on object recognition in cognitive science has assumed, explicitly or implicitly, that all visual stimuli are recognized by a common set of mechanisms. Cognitive scientists such as Marr (1982) and Biederman (1987), who proposed comprehensive theories of object recognition, did not specify different types of representations or processes for different types of stimulus. Rather, they described a single type of system capable of recognizing as wide a range of stimuli as possible.

In contrast, neuropsychological data of the kind presented by Newcombe, Mehta, and De Haan suggests a very different view of object recognition. They noted that brain damage can sometimes impair the recognition of certain categories of stimuli relative to others, consistent with some degree of specialization for different kinds of stimuli within high-level vision. They focused on perhaps the most surprising and counterintuitive dissociation, impaired recognition of "living things" relative to "non-living things," and reviewed a series of studies with case MS that strongly support the selectivity of this impairment. In the present chapter, I focus on two other forms of selectively impaired visual recognition, and discuss their implications for theories of normal vision. These are impairments of face recognition and printed word recognition.

NEUROPSYCHOLOGICAL EVIDENCE
FOR SPECIALIZATION WITHIN THE VISUAL
OBJECT RECOGNITION SYSTEM

As Humphreys et al. have described in chapter 3, damage to the visual areas of the brain can sometimes impair visual recognition ability, while leaving intact a person's general intellectual abilities as well as their perception of many of the basic elements of vision such as local contour, color, depth, motion, and so on. People with this condition, known as *visual agnosia,* retain full knowledge of the nonvisual aspects of the object, enabling them to recognize it by touching it, hearing any characteristic sound it might make, or identifying it from a verbal description. In the *associative agnosias* (a term coined in the 19th century, based on the belief that an inability to associate visual input with stored knowledge was the underlying cause), there is considerable residual perceptual ability, such that the person may be able to see an object well enough to draw a recognizable copy of it.

Associative visual agnosia does not always affect the recognition of all types of stimuli equally. The selectivity observed in some cases of agnosia suggests that there may be some division of labor within the visual recognition system, and provides us with clues as to the way in which visual recognition can be subdivided. The best known example of this is *prosopagnosia,* the inability to recognize faces after brain damage.

Dissociations Between Face Recognition
and the Recognition of Other Objects

Prosopagnosics cannot recognize familiar people by their faces alone, and must rely on other cues for recognition such as a person's voice, or distinctive clothing or hairstyles. The disorder can be so severe that even close friends and family members will not be recognized. One prosopagnosic recounted sitting in his club and wondering why another member was staring so intently at him. When he asked one of the waiters to investigate, he learned that he had been looking at himself in a mirror (Pallis, 1955)!

Although many prosopagnosics have some degree of difficulty recognizing objects other than faces, in some cases the deficit appears strikingly selective for faces. DeRenzi (1986) described a man who was sufficiently prosopagnosic that "the identification of relatives and close friends posed an insurmountable problem if he could not rely on their voices" (p. 246). He was able to identify all nonface objects with which he was presented, including persona items such as his own razor, wallet, eyeglasses, and so on, when presented along with several similar objects of the same type.

The most straightforward interpretation of prosopagnosia, with respect to the question posed at the outset, is that there is a specialized subsystem for recognizing faces, not necessary or less necessary for recognizing other types of object, and that this subsystem has been damaged in prosopagnosia. However, it is possible that faces and common objects are recognized using a single recognition system, and that faces are simply the most difficult type of object to recognize. Prosopagnosia could then be explained as a mild form of agnosia, in which the impairment is detectable only on the most taxing form of recognition task. This account has the appeal of parsimony, in that it requires only one, single type of visual recognition system, and perhaps for this reason has gained considerable popularity (Damasio, Damasio, & Van Hoesen, 1982; Humphreys & Riddoch, 1987). As Newcombe et al. point out in the previous chapter, it is difficult to assess the selectivity of prosopagnosia under naturalistic conditions. Even the apparently pure case described by DeRenzi (1986) could have relied on compensatory strategies for recognizing his own possessions.

To determine whether prosopagnosia is truly selective for faces, and hence whether the human brain has specialized mechanisms for recognizing faces, we must therefore assess the prosopagnosic performance on faces and nonface objects relative to the difficulty of these stimuli for normal subjects. One technical difficulty encountered in such a project is that normal subjects will invariably perform nearly perfectly on both face and nonface recognition tasks. The resultant ceiling effect will mask any differences in difficulty that might exist between tasks, making it pointless to test normal subjects in the kinds of recognition tasks that have traditionally been administered to patients.

With this problem in mind, Karen Klein, Karen Levinson, and I sought a visual recognition task that would allow manipulation of task difficulty for normal subjects, with the goal of setting normal performance at a moderate level (Farah, Klein, & Levinson, 1994). The performance of LH, a prosopagnosic patient (see Calvanio & Levine, 1989), on face and nonface stimuli could then be assessed relative to normal performance with these same stimuli, and the question of whether he is disproportionately impaired at faces could then be answered. We employed a recognition memory paradigm, in which subjects first studied a set of photographs of faces and nonface objects, and then performed an "old/new" judgment on a larger set of photographs, half of which were old. In a first experiment, we compared the recognition of faces to the recognition of a variety of nonface objects, which were paired with highly similar foils, as shown in Fig. 5.1. In this experiment, we succeeded in equating the difficulty levels of the two sets of stimuli for 10 normal subjects, at approximately 85% correct. For the same two stimulus sets, LH showed a significant performance disparity, achieving only 62% correct for faces and 92% correct for objects.

In a second experiment, we attempted to test a particular version of the hypothesis that face recognition is just harder than object recognition, which was promoted recently by Damasio and colleagues (e.g., 1982). According to this

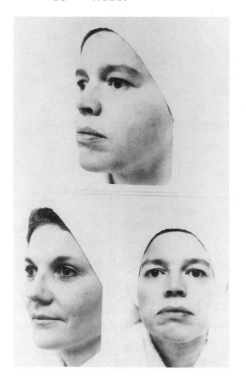

FIG. 5.1. Examples of face and nonface stimuli used to test recognition memory in normal subjects and a prosopagnosic subject.

account, it is the fact that faces are highly similar exemplars, all belonging to the same category (namely "face") that makes them particularly taxing. This hypothesis was tested by comparing recognition of exemplars of the category "face" and an equivalent number of exemplars all drawn from a single nonface category, namely eyeglass frames. Examples of the stimuli are shown in Fig. 5.2. The faces and eyeglass frames were divided evenly into sets of old items, which would appear in the study and test phases of the experiment, and sets of new items, which would appear only at test. Similar-looking eyeglass frames were separated into old and new sets to make the task more challenging (e.g., there were both old and new horn-rims, and old and new aviator-style frames). As before, LH was disproportionately impaired at face recognition relative to nonface recognition, when his performance is considered relative to normal subjects. In this experiment, 10 normal subjects found face recognition considerably easier than eyeglass frame recognition, achieving on average 87% faces correct and 67% eyeglass frames correct. LH showed significantly less face superiority in

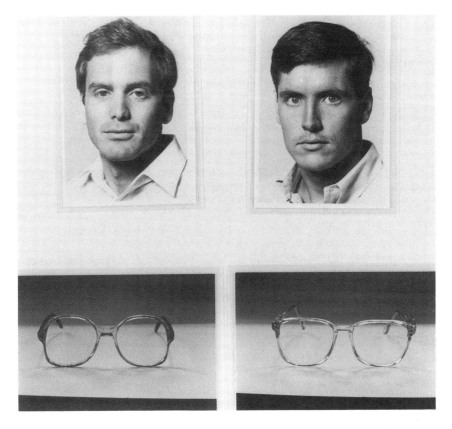

FIG. 5.2. Examples of face and eyeglass stimuli used to test recognition memory in normal subjects and a prosopagnosic subject.

this task than normal subjects, achieving 64% faces correct and 63% eyeglass frames correct. We conclude that LH's impairment in face recognition cannot be attributed to a more general problem with object recognition, or with the recognition of specific exemplars from any visually homogeneous category.

The conclusion that prosopagnosia is not merely a mild agnosia, manifesting itself on the hardest form of recognition, is further supported by the existence of the opposite dissociation, namely impaired recognition of common objects with preserved face recognition. For example, McCarthy and Warrington (1986) described a patient who was unable to recognize a single picture from a long series of pictures of common objects, but performed satisfactorily with pictures of the faces of famous people. The human neuropsychological data therefore suggest that the recognition of faces and common objects is carried out by at least partially distinct subsystems of the visual system. This conclusion is further bolstered by findings of the kind described by Perrett et al. in chapter 2. They and their colleagues have gathered evidence, from single-unit recordings, of a population of cells in the temporal cortex of monkeys that respond selectively to faces, including some that distinguish among faces (e.g., Perrett, Rolls, & Caan, 1982). Although other cells show selectivity for other kinds of objects, nonface cells show less selectivity and less overall response to their optimal stimuli than do face cells (Baylis, Rolls, & Leonard, 1985).

Dissociations Between Printed Word Recognition and the Recognition of Other Objects

As is described in detail by Bub and Arguin in chapter 6, people with *pure alexia* are impaired at reading, despite the preserved ability to recognize spoken words and the preserved ability to write. (This leads to the almost paradoxical situation in which people may be unable to read what they themselves have just written.) Although some pure alexics are entirely unable to read, the more usual form of the disorder involves extremely slow, letter-by-letter reading. If such patients are required to recognize even a short word in less than a few seconds, they may then fail entirely. Most people with pure alexia are not agnosic for objects other than printed words. This suggests that printed word recognition depends on at least some mechanisms that are not shared with other forms of visual recognition.

Before accepting this conclusion, we must consider an alternative hypothesis: Word recognition involves the same system that serves for the recognition of other kinds of objects, but word recognition taxes this system more heavily, perhaps because word recognition is learned later than other forms of visual recognition, or because different words resemble one another more than different nonword objects. According to this alternative hypothesis, the selective impairment in word recognition does not imply that different subsystems of visual object recognition are required for recognizing words and nonword objects.

The existence of the opposite dissociation, namely associative agnosia for objects without pure alexia, helps to rule out this alternative explanation. There are a number of associative agnosics who are not alexic. For example, a man described by Gomori and Hawryluk (1984) was impaired at recognizing a variety of common objects, as well as the faces of his family and friends. Nevertheless, he was able to read easily, even when interfering lines had been drawn across the printed words.

The dissociations among the agnosias for faces, common objects, and printed words cannot be explained, in any straightforward way, by the hypothesis that all three stimulus domains are recognized by a single, general-purpose object recognition system. Instead, they suggest that we have evolved different types of specialized recognition systems for different types of stimuli. This raises the question: How many specialized subsystems are there?

PATTERNS OF CO-OCCURRENCE AMONG THE ASSOCIATIVE AGNOSIAS: DELINEATING THE SUBSYSTEMS OF VISUAL OBJECT RECOGNITION

At first glance, the pairwise dissociability of face, common object, and printed word recognition would seem to imply that there are at least three different subsystems of visual recognition, each specialized for one of these categories of stimuli. If this were true, then we should observe all combinations of spared and impaired face, common object, and printed word recognition, provided we look at a large enough number of cases. With the goal of testing this prediction, I recently reviewed 99 cases of associative agnosia, and for each case noted the available information on the patient's face, common object, and printed word recognition (Farah, 1991). Table 5.1 shows the distribution of different patterns of ability and deficit, for those cases in which information was given about the recognition of all three categories of stimuli. For two of the possible patterns, there was only one case each that appeared to instantiate the pattern. Furthermore, in each of those case reports there was an inconsistency in the way the case was described, such that a description of the patient in one part of the case report conforms to the unusual pattern, whereas a description in a different part of the same case report would place the patient elsewhere in the table.

The distribution of cases across the different patterns of associative agnosia shown in Table 5.1 are consistent with two, rather than three, underlying types of visual recognition ability. As depicted by the diagram in Fig. 5.3, one subsystem

TABLE 5.1
The Number of Cases Found in the Literature for
Each Possible Combination of Impaired and Spared Face,
Common Object, and Printed Word Recognition

Impaired and Spared Classes of Stimuli	Number of Cases
Face recognition impaired; common object and word recognition spared	27
Face and common object recognition impaired; word recognition spared	15
Face, common object, and word recognition impaired	22
Word recognition impaired; face and common object recognition spared	not included in search
Common object and word recognition impaired; face recognition spared	16
Common object recognition impaired; face and word recognition spared	1?
Face and word recognition impaired; common object recognition spared	1?

FIG. 5.3. Graphical representation of the roles of two hypothetical types of visual recognition ability in the recognition of faces, common objects, and words.

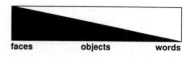

faces   objects   words

is essential for face recognition, useful for common object recognition, and not at all needed for printed word recognition, whereas the other subsystem is essential for printed word recognition, useful for common object recognition, and not at all needed for face recognition. According to this idea, one should never observe impaired recognition of common objects with intact recognition of faces and printed words, and rarely or never observe impaired recognition of faces and printed words with intact recognition of common objects. These are, in fact, the two patterns for which no clear cases have yet been reported.

TWO TYPES OF STRUCTURAL DESCRIPTION?

In the remainder of this chapter, I present a conjecture concerning the functions of the two types of visual recognition system, and some attempts that my collaborators and I have made to test this conjecture. As a starting point, recall that many current theories of object recognition hypothesize some form of *structural description*, that is, a representation of an object's shape in terms of parts, which are explicitly represented as shapes in their own right, along with the relations among parts. The more extensive the part decomposition, the more parts there will be in the object's representation, but the simpler those parts will be. The less the part decomposition, the fewer parts there will be in an object's representation, but the more complex those parts will be. The conjecture being put forth here is that word recognition involves extensive part decomposition, and hence requires the ability to represent a large number of parts, whereas face recognition involves virtually no part decomposition, and hence requires the ability to represent complex parts.

Reading and the Ability to Represent Multiple Parts

It would not surprise most nonpsychologists to learn that printed words are recognized by first recognizing their letters! In fact, experimental data and untutored intuitions agree on this issue: For example, Johnston and McClelland (1980) found that tachistoscopic word recognition was significantly more disrupted by a mask made up of letters than by one made up of letter fragments, consistent with the idea that a necessary stage in word recognition is the explicit recognition of the component letters. This suggests that words are a paradigm case of a type of object that must be decompósed into multiple parts in order to be recognized. (The word superiority effect, by which letters embedded in words are perceived better than words presented in nonwords or alone, might appear to imply that words are perceived holistically, without decomposition into letters. However, its implications are weaker than this. It implies only that, in addition to individual letter representations, word or letter-cluster representations are also activated, and that the activation states of the latter representations influence those of the former.)

There is also evidence that the underlying impairment in pure alexia consists of an inability to recognize multiple shapes, either simultaneously or in rapid sequence, resulting in the laborious letter-by-letter reading that is the hallmark of this syndrome. Such evidence was first noted by Kinsbourne and Warrington (1962) using both orthographic and nonorthographic stimuli, and has since been confirmed in different ways by other researchers. In all of these cases, however, the evidence has been associational: Subjects who have pure alexia are also found to have an impairment in the recognition of multiple items. Marcie Wallace and I recently attempted to find out whether the latter was a causal factor in the word recogniton impairment of pure alexia, or whether it was associated for some other reason (e.g., neighboring parts of the brain involved in the two abilities, such that a single lesion would be likely to impair both). We used additive factors logic to test the hypothesis that letter-by-letter reading results from difficulty with specifically visual processing of the multiple letters of a word. Because pure alexics read (if at all) letter by letter, the time it takes them to read a word is directly proportional to the number of letters in the word. If the slow, length-dependent reading times of these patients result from impairment at a visual stage of processing, then a manipulation known to affect the difficulty of visual encoding should exacerbate the word-length effects. By varying word length and visual quality, we should observe an interaction between their effects. As shown in Fig. 5.4, we found just this pattern of results in a pure alexic subject, but not in control subjects who were instructed to read letter by letter.

Face Recognition and the Ability to Represent Complex Wholes Without Part Decomposition

Just as words seem to have a natural decomposition into letters, so faces seem decomposable into such facial features as eyes, noses, and mouths. However, this alone does not tell us whether such features play the role of psychologically real parts in the visual representations that underlie face recognition. A recent series of experiments in collaboration with Jim Tanaka suggests that they do not, or that they do so to a lesser extent than the features of other, nonface, objects (Tanaka & Farah, 1993).

We reasoned as follows: To the extent that some portion of a pattern is explicitly represented as a part for purposes of recognition, then when that

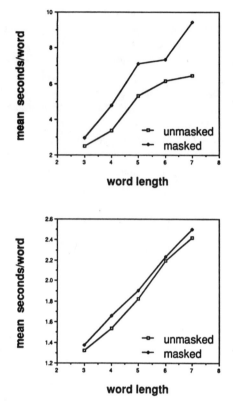

FIG. 5.4. The effects of word length and visual quality on the amount of time needed to read the letters of words aloud for a pure alexic subject (top) and normal subjects (bottom).

portion is presented later in isolation, subjects should be able to identify it as a portion of a familiar pattern. In contrast, if a portion of a pattern does not correspond to the way the subject's visual system parses the whole pattern, then that portion presented in isolation is less likely to be recognized. Tanaka and I taught subjects to identify a set of faces, along with a set of nonface objects, and then assessed their ability to recognize both the whole patterns and their parts. Examples of test stimuli are shown in Fig. 5.5. Relative to the recognition of such nonface objects as houses, inverted faces, and scrambled faces, the recognition of intact upright faces showed a greater disadvantage for parts relative to wholes. Figure 5.6 shows the results of the experiment comparing face and house recognition.

Recent experiments using a variant of the Johnson and McClelland (1980) masking paradigm mentioned earlier, provide converging evidence for these conclusions. Kevin Wilson, Maxwell Drain, and I found that, whereas word recognition is about equally disrupted by part (letter) masks and whole (word) masks, face recognition is more disrupted by whole (face) masks than part (scrambled feature) masks. Inverted faces do not show this difference between parts and wholes.

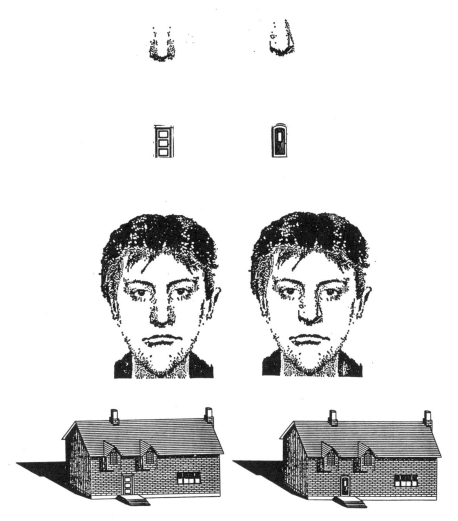

FIG. 5.5.   Examples of part and whole test items for faces and houses.

Given that normal subjects employ relatively less part decomposition in recognizing faces than in recognizing other objects, this suggests that prosopagnosics' impairment in face recognition might be due to an inability to encode faces as complex, undecomposed wholes. To test this hypothesis directly, Jim Tanaka, Maxwell Drain, and I compared the relative advantage of whole faces over face parts for normal subjects and for the prosopagnosic LH. Our initial plan was to administer the same task that Tanaka and I used with the normal subjects to LH, but despite intensive effort, LH could not learn to recognize a set of faces. We therefore switched to a short-term memory paradigm, in which a face was

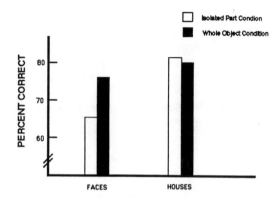

FIG. 5.6.   Results from the experiment contrasting recognition of part and whole versions of faces and houses.

presented for study, followed by a blank interval, followed by a second presentation of a face. The subject's task was to say whether the first and second faces were the same or different. There were two different conditions for the presentation of the first face: either "exploded" into four separate frames containing the head, eyes, nose, and mouth (in their proper relative spatial position within each frame), or intact. The second face was always presented in the normal format, so that the two conditions can be called "parts-to-whole" and "whole-to-whole." Normal subjects performed better in the whole-to-whole condition, thus providing further evidence that their perception of a whole face is not equivalent to the perception of its parts. In contrast, LH performed equally well in the two conditions, despite an overall accuracy comparable to the normal subjects', consistent with the hypothesis that he is impaired in the ability to see faces as wholes.

CONCLUSIONS

We are now in a position to draw some tentative conclusions regarding specialization within the visual recognition system. First, it seems clear that there is specialization. The double dissociations that exist between disorders of face and nonface object recognition, and between disorders of word and nonword object recognition, are inconsistent with the operation of a single, general-purpose object recognition system. Instead, they suggest that there is a division of labor within the object recognition system, with different subsystems needed for different types of visual stimulus.

Second, although the pairwise dissociability of faces, common objects and printed words might seem to imply the existence of three distinct subsystems, a closer look at the patterns of co-occurrence suggest that we need postulate only two subsystems: one that is essential for word recognition, useful for common object recognition, and not needed for face recognition, and another that is essential for face recognition, useful for object recognition, and not needed for word recognition.

Third, a tentative interpretation of these subsystems, in terms of the types of visual information processing they carry out, is the following: The first subsystem is needed to recognize objects by extensive part decomposition, in which numerous parts must be encoded. The second subsystem is needed to recognize objects with little or no part decomposition, in which relatively complex parts must be encoded. The evidence discussed in the section, Two Types of Structural Description?, is consistent with this interpretation. Further work is needed to test the empirical truth of this interpretation. In addition, work is needed to clarify the reasons why different types of objects come to be recognized by these different subsystems. For example, what aspects of the statistics of similarity and difference among individual objects make extensive part decomposition useful for words, less so for common objects, and relatively useless for faces?

Finally, these data put a lower limit on the degree of specialization within the object recognition system. Other dissociations may well reveal further dimensions of specialization, either at the level of visual shape representation (like those discussed here) or at later, more semantic levels of object representation. Case MS, described by Newcombe et al. in the previous chapter, shows a striking dissociation between recognition of living and nonliving things. As the authors demonstrate, this impairment with living things extends to nonvisual knowledge in verbal tasks, suggesting specialization of object knowledge at postperceptual, semantic levels of representation. In fact, in addition to his prosopagnosia, LH has a similar impairment in knowledge of living things (Farah, McMullen, & Meyer, 1991). Although the relation between these two kinds of impairment needs further investigation, the existence of at least a few cases over which they are doubly dissociated suggests that they may well be distinct problems.

ACKNOWLEDGMENTS

The author is now at the University of Pennsylvania. This chapter is an expanded version of an article written for *Current Directions in Psychological Science*. Preparation of the chapter, and much of the work described herein, was supported by ONR grant N00014-91-J1546, NIMH grant R01 MH48274, NIH career development award K04-NS01405, and a grant from the McDonnell–Pew Program in Cognitive Neuroscience. I gratefully acknowledge Jim Tanaka's collaboration in developing the ideas about face recognition that are presented here.

REFERENCES

Baylis, G. C., Rolls, E. T., & Leonard, C. M. (1985). Selectivity between faces in the responses of a population of neurons in the cortex in the superior temporal sulcus of the monkey. *Brain research, 342,* 91–102.

Biederman, I. (1987). Recogniton-by-components: A theory of human image understanding. *Psychological Review, 94,* 115–147.

Calvanio, R., & Levine, D. (1989). Prosopagnosia: A defect in visual configural processing. *Brain and Cognition, 10,* 149–170.

Damasio, A. R., Damasio, H., & Van Hoesen, G. W. (1982). Prosopagnosia: Anatomic basis and behavioral mechanisms. *Neurology, 32,* 331–341.

DeRenzi, E. (1986). Current issues in prosopagnosia. In H. D. Ellis, M. A. Jeeves, F. Newcome, & A. Young, (Eds.), *Aspects of face processing.* Dordrecht, Netherlands: Martinus Nijhoff.

Farah, M. J. (1991). Patterns of co-occurrence among the associative agnosias: Implications for visual object representation. *Cognitive Neuropsychology, 8,* 1–19.

Farah, M. J., Klein, K. L., & Levinson, K. (1994). *Is prosopagnosia selective for faces?* Manuscript submitted for publication.

Farah, M. J., McMullen, P. A., & Meyer, M. M. (1991). Can recognition of living things be selectively impaired? *Neuropsychologia, 29,* 185–193.

Gomori, A. J., & Hawryluk, G. A. (1984). Visual agnosia without alexia. *Neurology, 34,* 947–950.

Humphreys, G. W., & Riddoch, M. J. (1987). *To see but not to see.* Hillsdale, NJ: Lawrence Erlbaum Associates.

Johnston, J. C., & McClelland, J. L. (1980). Experimental tests of a hierarchical model of word identification. *Journal of Verbal Learning and Verbal Behavior, 19,* 503–524.

Kinsbourne, M., & Warrington, E. K. (1962). A disorder of simultaneous form perception. *Brain, 85,* 461–486.

Konorski, J. (1967). *Integrative activity of the brain.* Chicago: University of Chicago Press.

Marr, D. (1982). *Vision.* San Francisco: Freeman.

McCarthy, R. A., & Warrington, E. K. (1986). Visual associative agnosia: A clinical-anatomical study of a single case. *Journal of Neurology, Neurosurgery and Psychiatry, 49,* 1233–1240.

Pallis, C. A. (1955). Impaired identification of faces and places with agnosia for colors. *Journal of Neurology, Neurosurgery and Psychiatry, 18,* 218–224.

Perrett, D., Rolls, E. T., & Caan, W. (1982). Visual neurones responsive to faces in the monkey temporal cortex. *Experimental Brain Research, 47,* 329–342.

Tanaka, J. W., & Farah, M. J. (1993). Parts and wholes in face recognition. *Quarterly Journal of Experimental Psychology, 50,* 367–372.

VISUAL WORD
RECOGNITION

6 Functional Mechanisms in Pure Alexia: Evidence from Letter Processing

Martin Arguin
Daniel N. Bub
Montreal Neurological Institute

The characteristic features of pure alexia include very slow but on the whole accurate reading and massive effects of word length on performance. Patients appear to decode words as a sequence of isolated letters, without any access to the holistic process that is observed in the normal reader (Henderson, 1987; Schiepers, 1980). Published results indicate that the effect of word length on reading times varies greatly from one alexic patient to the other, but that, with very few exceptions, it is above—and sometimes far above—a 1-s increase for every additional letter (Bub, Black, & Howell, 1989; Coslett & Saffran, 1989; Farah & Wallace, 1991; Kay & Hanley, 1991; Patterson & Kay, 1982; Rapp & Caramazza, 1991; Reuter-Lorenz & Brunn, 1990; Shallice & Saffran, 1986; Warrington & Shallice, 1980).

Dejerine (1892), who gave the first description of letter-by-letter reading, interpreted it as a disconnection between the two occipital cortices and the mechanism representing the visual form of words in the left hemisphere. The damage may be cortical or subcortical, but the overall effect, according to him, would block the transfer of letter codes extracted from sensory features onto word units. The word-form system—the permanent description of the word's orthographic pattern—remains intact, however, and can be accessed from the language mechanism to recover the spelling of a word spontaneously or to dictation. Following are the attempts of a French patient documented nearly 100 years ago by Dejerine and Pélissier (1914) to decipher the phrase "Le siège d'Andrinople": "Le . . . . oui! C'est bien ça . . . L . . E . . . le. . . . après c'est un S . . . . E . . . . siècle, j'ai deviné le siè-cle . . . . D . . . . E . . . c'est bien ça . . . . . dEn . . . . . d'En-dri . . . . d'Endrino . . . . d' Andrinople . . . . . le siècle d'Andrinople . . . ça

ne doit pas être ça . . . . ça doit être plutot 'le siège d'Andrinople'." The characteristic strategy of laboriously concatenating individual letters to finally arrive at
the word is obvious in this example.

Current Accounts of Pure Alexia

Dejerine's (1892) explanation of pure alexia, though still widely referenced in
neurology textbooks, does not explain the letter-by-letter reading that is so characteristic of the syndrome and thus has not satisfied modern experimental psychologists. We may divide the contemporary accounts of the pure alexia syndrome into three general categories. First are those that assume a deficit affecting
the low-level perceptual processes responsible for the construction of a structural
description of the input (Rapp & Caramazza, 1991). Others interpret the syndrome in terms of a deficit at the stage of pattern identification (Farah & Wallace,
1991; Friedman & Alexander, 1984; Kinsbourne & Warrington, 1962, 1963;
Levine & Calvanio, 1978; Reuter-Lorenz & Brunn, 1990). Finally, another viewpoint maintains that a word-specific processing deficit is responsible for the
reading difficulties in pure alexia (Patterson & Kay, 1982; Shallice & Saffran,
1986; Warrington & Shallice, 1980). We summarize each of these accounts.

Low-Level Perceptual Deficit.   Rapp and Caramazza (1991) argued that
faulty perceptual analysis at the levels of putative retino-centric and stimulus-
centered feature representations is responsible for the reading deficits observed in
pure alexia. More specifically, they claimed that letter-by-letter reading may be
the result of decreasing left to right gradients in the accuracy of feature representations across each of these spatial reference frames. In support of this, they
reported impaired performance in partial report, letter detection, and feature
search (horizontal vs. vertical bars) tasks with items located to the right of
fixation—retino-centric representation—and with items to the rightmost part of
horizontal stimulus strings—stimulus-centered representation. We later describe
evidence against the notion that defective feature representations can provide a
general explanation of pure alexia.

Pattern Recognition Deficit.   The slowness of reading by pure alexics as well
as their propensity for morphically based identification errors has been widely
noted (Bub et al., 1989; Caplan & Hedley-White, 1974; Coltheart, 1981; Coslett
& Saffran, 1989; Farah & Wallace, 1991; Friedman & Alexander, 1984; Grossi,
Fragassi, Orsini, DeFalco, & Sepe, 1984; Kay & Hanley, 1991; Kinsbourne &
Warrington, 1962, 1963; Landis, Regard, & Serrant, 1980; Patterson & Kay,
1982; Rapp & Caramazza, 1991; Reuter-Lorenz & Brunn, 1990; Shallice &
Saffran, 1986; Stachowiack & Poeck, 1976; Staller, Buchanon, Signer, Lappin,
& Webb, 1978; Warrington & Shallice, 1980). The time required to decipher a
word is much higher than the duration expected from normal individuals who are

forced to read in a letter-by-letter manner. For example, it has been reported previously that subjects who read inverted text show word-length effects on reading times that are only about 200 ms per letter, considerably faster than the usual rates for normally oriented text in pure alexia (Koriat & Norman, 1985). Although the abnormal slowness of letter processing is not a necessary feature of letter-by-letter reading in principle, it nevertheless has been observed in nearly all pure alexics when this function has been examined. Furthermore, the argument has been made that the failure to find such a deficit in other cases may be due to the use of inappropriate methodology (Reuter-Lorenz & Brunn, 1990).

On the assumption that letters must be identified before words can be read, several authors have proposed that the systematic association between letter processing difficulties and the word reading disorder in pure alexia is, in fact, a reflection of a causal relationship (Farah & Wallace, 1991; Friedman & Alexander, 1984; Kinsbourne & Warrington, 1962, 1963; Levine & Calvanio, 1978; Reuter-Lorenz & Brunn, 1990).

According to Kinsbourne and Warrington (1962, 1963; see also Levine & Calvanio, 1978), the reading disorder seen in pure alexia arises from a difficulty in encoding many separate visual forms simultaneously, a disorder they called *simultanagnosia*. The main feature of this disorder is a reduced visual span; that is, the maximum number of items that may be reported from a briefly exposed array of items is one or two, even though perceptual thresholds for a single form appear to be within normal limits. Although Kinsbourne and Warrington (1962) acknowledged that their experiments could not "permit a decision about the exact stage in visual perception at which the pathological limitation is acting" (page 481), they argued that simultanagnosia is the underlying cause of the pure alexia that co-occurs with the perceptual disorder they observed in the patients. Thus: "Only one letter can be read at a time, and the interval before the visual system is ready for perception of the next is so long that reading must be a laborious hardship" (page 481).

The hypothesis that a disturbance in the simultaneous perception of multiple forms is the cause of pure alexia was later challenged when Warrington and Rabin (1971) showed that some of the simultanagnosic patients they studied did not exhibit the diagnostic behavioral features of pure alexia. In addition, Warrington and Shallice (1980) described a pure alexic patient who only showed a mild reduction of visual span, incommensurate with the severity of his reading disorder (although, as argued by Farah [1990], the reading impairment showed by this patient was unusually mild). This suggestion of a double dissociation between simultanagnosia and pure alexia appears as incompatible with an account of the latter disorder on the basis of the former.

More recently, Friedman and Alexander (1984), Reuter-Lorenz and Brunn (1990), and Farah and Wallace (1991) suggested that pure alexic patients suffer from a disturbance in the identification of letters that prevents the efficient perception of visual words. Thus, Reuter-Lorenz and Brunn showed an increased difference between the latency required to perform a name match and that necessary to do a structural match between pairs of letters. In a similar vein, Friedman and Alexander reported an increased identification threshold for single letters but normal thresholds on tasks requiring structural discriminations. These authors also presented evidence that their patient's identification disorder was not limited to letters but also extended to visual objects. Finally, some evidence reported by Farah and Wallace indicated that the recognition impairment in their patient extended to stimuli other than letters, such as geometric figures. They also showed that the effect of word length on reading time was increased by superimposing a visual mask over the stimulus. They argued that this multiplicative effect of masking, which was not observed in normal controls, implied that their patient's reading deficit originated from an impaired identification of individual letters.

Although the hypothesis of faulty letter identification might eventually offer a complete explanation of pure alexia, we believe that, at present, it has not been made sufficiently explicit to be entirely convincing. We emphasize that a consistent association between letter-processing deficits and a reading disorder in no way establishes a causal relationship between them. We require a theoretical account of how letter processing and normal word reading are constituted, and of how a deficit confined to letter processing actually predicts the type of reading performance that is characteristic of pure alexia.

Word-specific Deficit.   Warrington and Shallice (1980) argued that pure alexics have sustained damage to the word-form system, which makes impossible the use of visual lexical representations for word recognition. The word-form system is defined as a functional module responsible for the parsing of letter strings into familiar units and the visual categorization of these units. Furthermore, they suggested that the compensatory letter-by-letter reading strategy used by pure alexics involves a process labeled *reverse spelling,* which demands access to a spelling system that can be reached only through an abstract letter name code.

Another account that can also be viewed as an interpretation of the deficit at the level of whole-word processing was proposed by Patterson and Kay (1982) and later advanced by Kay and Hanley (1991). These authors claimed that letter-by-letter reading arises from a disconnection between peripheral letter analyzers and whole-word representations. This disconnection is assumed to prevent the normal spatially parallel mapping of abstract letter identities onto word-level representations, such that access becomes slow and sequential.

Both of these explanations are, in their current form, challenged by recent data. Shallice and Saffran (1986), Bub et al. (1989), Coslett and Saffran (1989), and Reuter-Lorenz and Brunn (1990) all presented evidence that at least some pure alexics can gain access to whole-word representations via a spatially parallel mapping procedure despite the superficial (and therefore misleading) aspects of their letter-by-letter reading performance.

Synopsis

In view of the multiplicity of accounts that have been provided for the pure alexia syndrome, one possibility that springs to mind is that the locus of functional damage responsible for the disorder varies from patient to patient and that no coherent account of the syndrome will ultimately be forthcoming (cf. Kay & Hanley, 1991). Although we cannot dismiss this eventuality, we cling to the view that generalization should remain an important theoretical goal for cognitive neuropsychology and therefore are unwilling, without strong proof, to interpret qualitative behavioral differences between patients as a simple indication of different underlying deficits.

It is conceivable that apparently qualitative behavioral differences between a subset of brain-damaged patients, in this case pure alexics, may be accounted for by variations of a single operation within an impaired functional module. Farah and Wallace (1991) recently defended such a view of pure alexia. The plausibility of this general notion was adequately demonstrated by Cave and Wolfe (1990), who showed that slight quantitative parameter variations in a model of visual search can account for qualitative performance differences observed between normal individuals. We assume then, unless faced with compelling evidence to the contrary which, we believe, has not yet been obtained in the analysis of pure alexia, that we should not automatically consider behavioral differences between patients as a necessary indication of different underlying deficits.

Arguably the most consistent observation in pure alexic cases, besides the fact that they read in a letter-by-letter fashion, is the slowness with which they process single characters. Assuming that a low-level perceptual deficit cannot account for all the observations gathered so far on pure alexia, a promising starting point is to propose that pure alexia may stem from a disorder affecting the mechanisms involved in the identification of alphanumeric stimulation.

There are two ways in which such a deficit may be manifest. First, it is possible that only the identification of single-characters is impaired, and that deficits at the level of word identification are primarily due to faulty input from some hypothetical "letter analyzer" module, the function of which is to provide identity codes to the word-form system (e.g. Farah & Wallace, 1991; Friedman & Alexander, 1984; Reuter-Lorenz & Brunn, 1990). This position holds that all word-level processing impairments in pure alexia may be predicted on the basis of the letter identification deficit. A second, more complex possibility, is that the deficit responsible for the slowness of letter processing similarly applies to the activation of word-level units. On this hypothesis, a common orthographic mechanism, involved in both letter and word identification, is defective. Assuming that the nature of the activation leading to identification is not equivalent between letters (either in isolation or in a random sequence) and words (which comprise patterns of interdependent letters and are much more numerous than letters), we may expect that the behavioral manifestations of a unitary orthographic deficit will have nonequivalent effects on the processing of these perceptual forms.

These contrasting positions are hard to disentangle empirically and it is not our main objective to do so. Whatever the situation, it appears that a necessary first step in testing the hypothesis of a deficit affecting the identification of alphanumeric stimulation in pure alexia is to carry out a detailed analysis of the constraints on single-character processing. Our aim thus is to identify the processing level that may be considered responsible for the general slowness of letter-by-letter reading in a patient, DM, whom we take as representative of the syndrome. The general discussion considers the possible relationship between the single-character processing deficit that is confirmed here, and word processing in pure alexia.

CASE REPORT

DM was an undergraduate student in engineering at the time he suffered from a ruptured arterio-venous malformation of the left-posterior cerebral artery in February 1990. Neurosurgery was performed in March 1990. Clinical testing revealed letter-by-letter reading, with an average increase in reading times of about 500 ms per additional letter in a word. It should be pointed out that this reading rate is somewhat faster than that of most other pure alexics reported in the literature. Warrington and Shallice's (1980) patient RAV, who appears to be the quickest letter-by-letter reader so far reported, also showed increases in reading times of about 500 ms per additional letter in a word. No other language deficits besides the processing of visual words was observed in DM. The experiments reported here were performed between July 1990 and December 1990. He was 23 years of age at the time of testing.

EXPERIMENTAL INVESTIGATIONS

The experiments reported here were aimed at specifying the processing level at which the impairment responsible for DM's very slow letter-by-letter reading performance is located. Particularly, two hypotheses are contrasted. One is that his poor reading is the result of defective low-level perceptual processes preventing the construction of an adequate structural representation of the stimulus. The second is that these low-level perceptual processes are intact in DM but that he suffers from a deficit affecting the operations involved in identification per se, that is, in matching a structural representation of the input with its corresponding memory representation.

EXPERIMENT 1

A first hypothesis that must be considered as a potential account of a reading disorder is that of defective encoding of visual features. This was previously suggested by Rapp and Caramazza (1991) and although there are reasons why such an explanation may not be satisfactory, empirical evidence must be the ultimate criterion by which to evaluate this claim. Experiment 1 assessed visual feature encoding in DM and a normal control subject with the use of a visual search task that was performed under normal or degraded exposure conditions.

The literature on visual feature search in normal individuals (Arguin & Cavanagh, 1988; Bergen & Julesz, 1983; Pashler & Badgio, 1985; Treisman, 1988) indicates a spatially parallel search process (Snodgrass & Townsend, 1980). Thus, target detection time in this task is not affected by the number of distractors presented with it and a degraded exposure condition has an additive effect on reaction times (RTs). A deviation from this pattern of results in DM should lead to the conclusion that he suffers from defective feature encoding.

Subjects in this experiment as well as in all the others that are reported in the first part of the chapter were DM and a normal control matched to DM for age, gender, handedness, and education. Also, in all experiments reported, stimuli were presented to the left of a fixation point that remained visible for 1,500 ms before the beginning of each trial. The task in Experiment 1 required to indicate verbally (yes/no) on each trial whether a prespecified target was present. The target, which was present on half the trials, was a horizontal bar and the distractors presented with it were vertical bars. The number of stimuli presented on each trial was either 2, 4, 6, or 8. On half the trials, the stimulus array was degraded by a mask of random dots of about 30% density. The stimulus display was not masked on the other half of the trials. The experiment was run in six blocks of 64 trials within which an equal number of trials were distributed randomly for each condition.

Trials on which subjects made an error (1.3% of the trials for DM and .7% for the normal control) or on which their response failed to trigger the voice key (1.3% of the trials for DM and 1.0% of the trials for the control subject) were eliminated from data analysis. Except where stated otherwise, all the effects reported in this chapter were significant beyond the .05 level on statistical analyses.

Average correct RTs observed in each condition and each subject are presented in Fig. 6.1. Analysis of these results in the normal control showed main effects of masking (unmasked = 550 ms; masked = 591 ms) and of target presence (absent = 585 ms; present = 556 ms) and an interaction of target presence × number of items. Simple effects of this interaction revealed an effect of number of items on target-absent trials (slope of 6.2 ms/item; $r = .91$) but none on target-present (slope of -4.2 ms/item; $r = .80$). DM's results were quite similar to those of the normal control. Thus, he showed main effects of masking

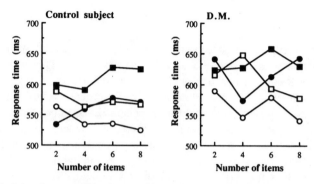

FIG. 6.1. Average RTs observed in each subject and each condition of Experiment 1–feature search. The panel on the left shows results of the normal control and that on the right the results of DM. Circles = unmasked displays. Squares = masked displays. Empty symbols = target-present trials. Filled symbols = target-absent trials.

(unmasked = 590 ms; masked = 621 ms) and of target presence (absent = 626 ms; present = 586 ms), and interactions of masking × number of items and of target presence × number of items. Simple effects of the two-way interactions indicated that no effect of number of items was present for either target-absent (slope of 2.4 ms/item; r = .36), target-present (slope of -7.1 ms/item; r = .94), unmasked (slope of -1.7 ms/item; r = .2), or masked (slope of -3.0 ms/item; r = .55) trials.

As can be seen, the results observed in DM closely match those shown by the normal control. Of main interest, neither subject showed any significant increase of RTs with the number of items on target-present trials and the effect of masking was additive in both cases. These results fail to provide support for the hypothesis of defective feature encoding in DM. This is in sharp contrast with the performance exhibited by the alexic subject studied by Rapp and Caramazza (1991) who showed a marked increase of RTs with number of items in a feature search task in which no masking of the stimulus array was used. DM's performance in Experiment 1 indicates that a feature-encoding deficit is not a necessary condition for pure alexia. If it is assumed that all pure alexic cases suffer from the same basic defect, evidence of a feature-processing deficit in some of them may be considered as an incidental event that cannot provide a reasonable account for the syndrome.

EXPERIMENT 2

In terms of low-level perceptual processes, another impairment that could potentially account for pure alexia is a difficulty in integrating the visual features that constitute written material. Research led by Treisman and others has shown that the feature integration process is required for normal perception and, if not performed, may lead to illusory conjunctions (Briand & Klein, 1987; Prinzmetal, 1981; Treisman & Paterson, 1984; Treisman & Schmidt, 1982). Another viable possibility is that the slowness of letter-by-letter reading in alexic patients is simply the result of a deficit in the processing of sequences of multiple elements.

To assess these possibilities, a second visual search experiment was conducted, this one requiring subjects to integrate feature combinations for target detection (conjunction search: Treisman, Sykes, & Gelade, 1977). In such a task, normal individuals typically show increasing RTs with the number of items displayed, and this increase is twice as high on target-absent trials as it is on target-present trials (Quinlan & Humphreys, 1987; Treisman, 1988; Treisman & Gelade, 1980; Treisman & Sato, 1990; Treisman et al., 1977; Wolfe, Cave, & Franzel, 1989), which is indicative of a serial self-terminating search (Snodgrass & Townsend, 1980). The hypothesis that DM suffers from a deficit in either integrating visual features or in processing a sequence of items predicts a larger effect of the number of items on RTs in this subject than in the normal control.

As was the case in Experiment 1, the task required to indicate verbally (yes/no) on each trial whether a prespecified target was present. The target stimulus was a black X that was present on half the trials. Distractors were white Xs and black Os and were present in equal numbers in each display. All stimuli were presented on a gray background. On each trial, either 2, 4, 6, 8, 10, or 12 items were presented. The experiment was run in five blocks of 60 trials within which an equal number of trials were distributed randomly for each condition.

Trials on which an error was made (2.0% of the trials for DM and 0.0% for the normal control) or on which the response failed to trigger the voice key (1.0% of the trials for DM and .7% of the trials for the control subject) were eliminated from data analysis.

Average correct RTs are shown in Fig. 6.2. Analysis of the normal control's data indicated main effects of target presence and of number of items and an interaction of those two factors. Analysis of this interaction showed a significant effect of the number of items that was about twice as high on target-absent trials (slope of 25.1 ms/item; $r = .98$) as it was on target-present trials (slope of 9.6 ms/item; $r = .90$). DM's results also revealed main effects of target presence and of number of items but the target $\times$ number interaction was not significant, thus indicating that the effect of number of items was similar on target-absent (slope of 14.7 ms/item; $r = .96$) and target-present trials (slope of 13.4 ms/item; $r = .95$).

A main aspect of the results of Experiment 2 was that although the slope of RTs as a function of the number of items was about twice as high on target-absent as it was on target-present trials in the normal control, the effect of the number of stimuli on RTs did not vary as a function of target presence in DM. These

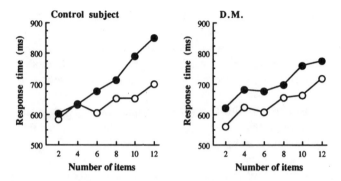

FIG. 6.2. Average RTs observed in each subject and each condition of Experiment 2—conjunction search. The panel on the left shows results of the normal control and that on the right the results of DM. Empty symbols = target-present trials. Filled symbols = target-absent trials.

patterns of effects indicate that the normal control searched the displays for a conjunction target through a serial self-terminating process whereas DM used a serial exhaustive search process. Patterns of results similar to that shown by DM have previously been reported in normal subjects during the search for a conjunction target under conditions that either precluded (Arguin, Joanette, & Cavanagh, 1990) or did not encourage (Houck & Hoffman, 1986; Pashler & Badgio, 1985) eye movements during the search task. Congruent with this, when asked, DM indicated that he attempted not to shift his eye fixation when searching for the target so that stimuli did not fall in his blind field.

With knowledge of the search process used by each subject, it is possible to calculate estimates of the average time taken to process a single item during the search for a conjunction target. For the control subject, this estimate is obtained by averaging twice the slope on target-present trials and the slope on target-absent trials because search was serial and self-terminating. In DM, the search being serial and exhaustive, the estimate of single-item processing time is calculated by averaging slopes on target-absent and target-present trials. The estimates obtained with these calculations indicate that the normal control required 22 ms to process a single item whereas DM took 14 ms to do so! Surprisingly, the speed of serial processing in DM is higher than in the control subject. This result clearly indicates that DM does not suffer from any deficit in integrating shape and color features or in processing multiple items in sequence. Unless one would argue that the integration of shape features is functionally different from the integration of color and shape, the observations from Experiment 2 may be taken as an indication that defective feature integration or impaired processing of sequences of items cannot be used as an account of DM's reading disorder.

EXPERIMENT 3

The previous two experiments have failed to provide support for a low-level perceptual deficit in DM. However, one specific aspect that we have not yet examined in this patient is the processing of horizontal arrays of items. According to Rapp and Caramazza (1991), this is a main factor in the origin of the reading disorder suffered by the patient they studied. One striking demonstration of this was obtained through the use of the partial-report paradigm (Sperling, 1960). In this task, their patient's accuracy in reporting the identity of a single letter in a three-item string was at 100% for the leftmost item but steeply declined to reach a low of about 30% for the rightmost item in the string. The power of the partial-report paradigm appears as very apt at demonstrating the presence of a low-level perceptual deficit in DM if he suffers from any.

In Experiment 3, two rows of three letters each were displayed one above the other for a duration of 150 ms. All the letters presented were consonants and no repeats were allowed. Subjects were asked for a full report of all the letters presented in one block of 20 trials. In another block of 60 trials, subjects had to report a single letter in the array. This letter was indicated by a 50-ms bar probe shown either above (for an upper row target) or below (for a lower row target) the target letter, immediately after the offset of the array of items.

Results of each subject in the full- and partial-report tasks are presented in Fig. 6.3. The normal control showed a uniformly high level of accuracy and no effect of task or lateral stimulus location was observed. In contrast, analysis of DM's results revealed a main effect of task and of lateral stimulus location, and a significant task × location interaction. Simple effects of this interaction showed

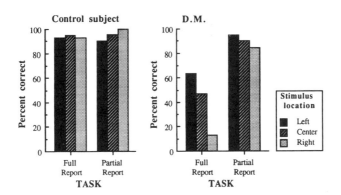

FIG. 6.3. Percentage of correct target identification as a function of the horizontal location of the target for each subject in Experiment 3—full and partial report.

that the more an item was to the right of the array the lower was the accuracy in the full-report task, but indicated a uniformly high performance level in the partial-report task.

Partial-report performance in DM does not support the hypothesis that a defective feature representation for the rightmost items in a letter string is a necessary characteristic of pure alexia. Indeed, support for this hypothesis would have required decreased performance with stimuli to the right of the array in both the full-report and partial-report tasks. We cannot conceive of any reason why defective feature representation for the rightmost stimuli could have sustained DM's high accuracy for these items in the partial-report task but failed to do so in full report. Rather, we suggest that the performance gradient exhibited by DM in full report may be the result of a slow sequential readout of letter identities that begins with the leftmost items. Because a single letter has to be reported in the partial-report task, this slow readout is not required, which allows the subject to reach a high level of accuracy. Support for this hypothesis of defective character identification in DM is provided by the next experiments.

EXPERIMENT 4

The previous three experiments, which were based on stringent tests of low-level perceptual functions, failed to provide any evidence that might support the notion that DM's reading disorder stems from an impairment at this level of processing. Thus, these experiments indicated normal feature encoding and feature integration, and a normal speed of processing of a sequence of items when identification of each of them was not required. From this, we may conclude that DM is quite able to obtain an adequate structural representation of the stimulation to which he is exposed and therefore that his poor reading performance must be due to a deficit that lies further in the visual processing stream. One possibility is that the processes involved in the identification of written characters—that is, in contacting memory representations of known characters from an intact structural description—may be at the origin of his slow letter-by-letter reading. A letter search task that required the identification of the characters presented for correct performance was designed to test this hypothesis.

Immediately before the start of each trial, the target to search for was presented auditorily and subjects were asked for a verbal (yes/no) response as to the presence of the target in the subsequent search array. A new target letter was used on each trial and the target was present on half the trials. When present, the target was uppercase in half the trials and lowercase in the other half. The stimulus set consisted in the letters A, B, E, G, N, and R, in both their uppercase and lowercase versions. Note that each of these letters is structurally very different between cases. Distractor items were chosen randomly from among the set of nontarget letters and half of them were uppercase and half lowercase. The stimulus array could be made of either two, four, six, or eight letters. The experiment was run in two blocks of 96 trials each within which an equal number of trials in each condition were distributed randomly.

The control subject made very few errors in this task (.5% of the trials), whereas DM committed many more errors than in Experiments 1 and 2 (7.3% of the trials). Only .5% of the responses emitted by the normal control failed to trigger the voice key whereas this happened on none of the trials for DM. Trials on which either an error or a voice-key failure occurred were eliminated from data analysis.

Correct RTs observed in the control subject and DM are presented in Fig. 6.4. Analysis of the normal control's data indicated main effects of target presence and of number of items, and an interaction of target $\times$ number. The effect of number of items displayed was significant in both target-absent and target-present trials, but this effect was about twice as high when no target was shown (slope of 140.5 ms/item; $r = 1.00$) as when one was present (slope of 55.5 ms/item; $r = .97$). The analysis of DM's results revealed the same significant effects as in the control subject, with an effect of number of items that was twice as high on target-absent trials (slope of 306.5 ms/item; $r = 1.00$) as it was on target-present trials (slope of 148.6 ms/item; $r = .97$).

It is clear from the results of Experiment 4 that search for the target letter was performed by both subjects through a serial self-terminating process, as indicated by the effect of number of items on target-absent trials, which was about twice that observed on target-present trials. We can now ask the critical question about these data: Does DM identify the letters at a slower rate than the normal control? Using the same method as that described in the discussion of Experiment 2, estimates of the time required to process a single letter were derived for both the normal control and DM. These estimates show that the control subject needed an

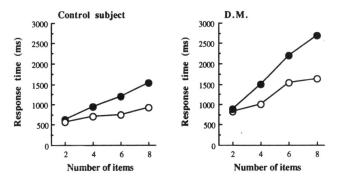

FIG. 6.4.   Average RTs observed in each subject and each condition of Experiment 4—letter search. Empty symbols = target-present trials. Filled symbols = target-absent trials.

average of 126 ms to process a single letter whereas it required DM an average of 302 ms to perform the same operation.

The slowness of single-letter processing exhibited by DM in Experiment 4 contrasts markedly with the results of the previous experiments in which his performance indicated normal low-level perceptual processes. From the results of the previous experiments, it was concluded that DM does not suffer from any deficit affecting the construction of a structural description of the input. If this conclusion is correct, the large difference between the time required by our two subjects to identify a single letter must be interpreted as an indication that DM's disorder occurs at the level at which an intact structural representation of the stimulation is matched to its corresponding memory representation for identification to take place.

The next experiments attempt to further specify the nature of this identification disorder. Thus, Experiment 5 uses the paradigm developed by LaBerge (1973) in order to determine whether the deficit suffered by DM prevents the automatic identification of known characters. Finally, Experiment 6 tests the hypothesis according to which the slowed identification of single characters in DM reflects a disorder in the selective processes—activation or inhibition—that may be required for the achievement of an appropriate match between an intact structural representation of the stimulation and its memory representation.

EXPERIMENT 5

LaBerge and Samuels (1974) put forward a model that holds that the identification of known alphanumeric characters in normal adults is an automatic process; that is, it does not require attention. The corollary of this hypothesis is that the processing of unknown characters does require attention. These authors presented an experiment conducted by LaBerge (1973) as support for their model. In that experiment, the main task observers had to perform was one of consecutive matching of letters. On some trials, however (switch trials), instead of being presented with the second letter for the main task, subjects were shown either two real letters or two fake characters and had to decide whether they were identical or different. Results on switch trials indicated that RTs were longer with fake characters than with real letters.

According to LaBerge and Samuels (1974), when subjects were shown the first letter for the consecutive matching task, they focused their attention on its representation in order to decide if it was identical or not with the one to follow. On switch trials, however, attention had to be shifted away from this representation and to the new stimuli displayed for simultaneous matching. If it is assumed that this attention shift requires time, it is possible to account for the results on switch trials by stating that identification of known characters is automatic and therefore does not suffer from attention being focused elsewhere. In contrast, under the hypothesis that the processing of unknown characters requires attention, this processing was delayed by the necessity of an attention shift away from the representation of the first letter displayed on each trial to that of the fake character. In support of this interpretation, LaBerge and Samuels reported that the RT advantage of real letters over fake characters is not observed if the simultaneous matching task is run without any preceding letter that could divert the subjects' attention.

Experiment 5 was run in order to determine whether DM's letter identification disorder implies that this process cannot be performed in an automatic fashion anymore. The method used is similar to that developed by LaBerge (1973). The stimuli used for the consecutive matching task were the letters a, g, n, and s. On switch—simultaneous matching—trials, the letters used were b, d, p, and q, and the fake characters were: ⌐, ⌐, ⌐, and ⌐. On each trial, subjects were required to indicate whether the two letters shown one after the other were identical or different (consecutive matching) or whether the pair of characters that followed the first letter, which was always presented at the beginning of a trial, were identical or different (simultaneous matching; switch task). One third of the trials were of the switch type. Only the results on those trials were analyzed.

DM showed an overall error rate of 11.5% whereas the control subject made an error in 4.2% of the trials. These trials were excluded from the data analysis. The correct RTs observed in each subject as a function of character type (real or fake) are presented in Fig. 6.5. Analysis of these results showed, in the normal control, that RTs were longer with fake characters (mean of 707 ms) than with real letters (mean of 647 ms). In contrast, DM's results did not indicate any significant RT difference between fake characters and real letters.

These observations support the hypothesis of a deficit in the automatic processing of letters in DM. Indeed, whereas the normal control shows a processing

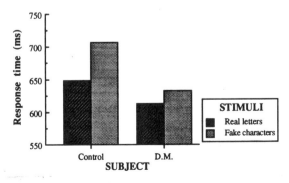

FIG. 6.5.   Average RTs observed in each subject as a function of character type on switch trials in Experiment 5.

advantage for real letters over fake characters, as LaBerge's (1973) subjects did, no such advantage for known characters was apparent in DM's data. The demonstration that automatic letter identification does not occur in DM, although important, still remains insufficient to provide a clear account of his deficit in the identification of alphanumeric stimulation. A more detailed examination of the processes that may be involved in identification is required.

EXPERIMENT 6

A common assumption in models of visual identification is that this process requires the occurrence of a match between a structural representation of a perceptual object and a memory representation the subject has of that particular object. Presumably, during this process, the constructed structural representation of the stimulation does not activate solely its own memory representation, but also neighboring representations that are structurally close to that of the target. Also, we may assume that lateral inhibition between the activated memory representations must occur so that the signal-to-noise ratio of the activation of the representations held in memory exceeds some identification threshold.

Given the conclusions reached on the basis of the previous experiments, one possible account of DM's character identification deficit is that the selection processes—activation or inhibition—that are required for the matching operation described previously are defective. Such a deficit implies that the achievement of a signal-to-noise ratio of activation of memory representations that overcomes the identification threshold would be delayed, therefore leading to slowed identification performance despite intact low-level—that is, structural—perceptual processes. Experiment 6 tests the hypothesis of defective selection processes in the identification operation as an account of DM's impaired character identification through a similarity priming paradigm.

Given that a letter prime shown before a single target letter mostly activates its own memory representation but also activates, to a lesser degree, representations of structurally close items, the hypothesis of impaired selection processes in DM predicts that the time required to identify the target will be much higher if it is preceded by a prime that is structurally similar to it than by a prime identical to or structurally different from the target. That is, given a prime that is similar to the target, the activation of the prime's memory representation will largely decrease the signal-to-noise ratio that may be obtained from the target, relative to other priming conditions. Indeed, those other priming conditions should mostly activate either the target representation (identical prime) or a representation that is not a structural neighbor of the target (structurally different) prime. If selection processes required for identification are impaired in DM, a similar prime should therefore increase RTs relative to the other priming conditions.

Subjects were required to verbally identify a single target letter on each trial.

Preceding target onset by a variable delay (stimulus onset asynchrony SOA: 0, 100, 200, or 300 ms), a letter prime was displayed above and below the location subsequently occupied by the target. Primes were either identical, structurally similar to, or structurally different from the target letter. Structural similarity was operationally defined as the confusability between a given pair of letters, which was determined on the basis of the confusion matrices published by Gilmore, Hersh, Caramazza, and Griffin (1979), Loomis (1982), Townsend (1971), and Van Der Heijden, Malhas, and Van Den Roovaart (1984). The stimuli used were the uppercase letters *O, Q, H,* and *M.* The experiment was run in three blocks of 120 trials within which an equal number of trials were distributed randomly for each condition.

Trials on which subjects either made an error (control: 0.0%; DM: .8%) or on which their response failed to trigger the voice key (control: 1.4%; DM: 0.0%) were not considered in the data analysis. Mean correct RTs for each type of prime are shown separately for each subject in Fig. 6.6. The effect of the SOA factor is not illustrated because, as is shown later, it did not interact with the effect of priming.

Analysis of the normal control's data revealed main effects of prime and SOA. This latter effect indicated decreasing RTs with increasing SOA. Pairwise comparisons performed on the priming factor showed shorter RTs with an "identical" prime than with either "similar" or "different" primes, with no difference between these latter conditions. This result is consistent with previous observations gathered in normal subjects (Eriksen & Hoffman, 1973; Taylor, 1977) and may be interpreted as a response competition effect, with RTs higher with any prime that is not identical to the target.

As was the case with the control subject, DM's results showed main effects of priming condition and of SOA. Again, the SOA effect reflected decreasing RTs with increasing SOA. However, the pattern of priming effect seen in DM is in

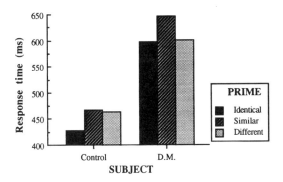

FIG. 6.6. Average RTs observed in each subject as a function of priming condition in Experiment 6—similarity priming.

marked contrast to that observed in the normal control. Thus, RTs with a prime similar to the target resulted in longer RTs than with either identical or different primes. RTs in these latter conditions did not differ.

On the basis of the observations reported in Experiments 1, 2, and 3, it appears that the abnormal priming pattern exhibited by DM cannot be accounted for on the basis of defective low-level perceptual processes. Rather, the conclusion emerging from the previous experiments is that DM's defective letter processing stems from an impairment at the level where an intact structural description of the input is matched to its corresponding memory representation, an operation that we deem is necessary for identification. The hypothesis tested by Experiment 6 is that DM's single-character identification disorder originates from an impairment of the selection processes involved in the identification operation, leading to an increase in the time required to reach a signal-to-noise ratio that exceeds the identification threshold. In support for this hypothesis, DM's results indicate that exposure to a prime physically similar to the target creates enough noise among representations that are structural neighbors to the target that follows that it markedly lengthens the time required for target identification relative to other priming conditions.

GENERAL DISCUSSION

Let us first briefly summarize the main observations. The first four experiments provided results indicating a character identification deficit in an alexic patient (DM), without any evidence for a disturbance affecting the processes responsible for the elaboration of a structural representation. The next two experiments described observations that clarified the nature of this identification disorder. These experiments indicated a loss of automatic identification of familiar characters in DM and provided evidence supporting the hypothesis of an impaired selection process—mediated by activation and inhibition—necessary for character identification.

What is the relationship between such a disorder in letter identification and the word-reading difficulties observed in DM and, possibly, in other alexic cases? This question should be addressed on two different levels. First, considering the nature of the deficit demonstrated here, it is fairly obvious that a reading strategy based on the explicit identification of each letter in a word will be abnormally slow and, therefore, give rise to massive length effects on reading times. A more fundamental concern, however, is to determine why this letter-by-letter reading strategy is necessary in the first place.

Currently, most models assume that normal reading is performed in a hierarchic fashion, with letter units activated in a spatially parallel manner and mapped onto higher level orthographic representations (Adams, 1979; Carr & Pollatsek, 1985; McClelland, 1976; McClelland & Rumelhart, 1981; Morton,

1969; Mozer, 1987; Paap, Newsome, McDonald, & Schvaneveldt, 1982). Within this type of framework, one must ask how the impairment of the selection processes involved in letter identification could be responsible for the word-reading difficulties seen in pure alexia. Faulty selection of letter identities would lead to a decreased signal-to-noise ratio between the target and competing letter units. This implies that the spurious activation of letter representations that are structural neighbors of each letter in the word presented is transmitted to higher levels in the processing hierarchy, thus creating serious problems for the identification of the letter string.

How does this interpretation predict the basic feature of pure alexia, that is, the massive effects of word length on reading performance? Normal readers profit greatly from their knowledge of word and subword forms when identifying visually degraded letters in context (e.g., McClelland, 1976). The fact that such context effects have been demonstrated in cases of pure alexia as well, extending across all letter positions in a four-letter word (e.g., Bub et al., 1989; Reuter-Lorenz & Brunn, 1990), implies that access to higher level orthographic information must still be occurring, yet the pure alexic continues to rely on explicit decoding of individual letters to fully identify the word. The main question then becomes: In what way does the letter-processing deficit in pure alexia allow activation of word-level representations but not complete identification (in the sense that a verbal report of the target is possible) without a further compensatory procedure requiring attention to individual letter elements?

We should note here that the distinction between letter and word units is rather arbitrary when applied to the question of explicit identification. Single characters, after all, have specific pronunciations and can reasonably be thought of as being represented in the same system that maintains the description of whole words. On this account, DM's disturbance in extracting the perceptual identity of letters may be part of a more general deficit within a larger system that deals with the recovery of alphanumeric code. The fact that DM retains the ability to explicitly identify letters but not words (without resorting to a letter-by-letter strategy) can be accounted for in terms of the difference between the density of the neighborhoods of letter and word representations.

Two factors may contribute to this difference. First, whatever the language, the number of characters used for writing is restricted whereas the number of acceptable words is very large. Second, the number of structurally close neighbors of any single character is rather small. If orthographic neighborhood (Coltheart, Davelaar, Jonasson, & Besner, 1977; Scheerer, 1987; Segui & Grainger, 1990) is used as an index of structural closeness for words, then the number of confusable exemplars—the neighborhood density—is much higher for words than for letters. Failure of the selection mechanisms that we consider necessary for perceptual identification may lead to a decreased signal-to-noise ratio in the activation of single-letter representations, and therefore exaggerate the time to produce a response. However, this ratio is even more decreased for word representations due to the density of their neighborhoods, thus completely preventing explicit identification without recourse to a compensatory mechanism that decomposes the word into its constituent letters.

If this interpretation is correct, rapid access to word forms must still be occurring in pure alexia though, as we have argued, at a suboptimal level that precludes complete identification. Interestingly enough, this proposal is congruent with the evidence from some pure alexics regarding the occurrence of a word superiority effect under conditions that preclude word report (Bub et al., 1989; Reuter-Lorenz & Brunn, 1990). We propose that this hypothesis of suboptimal lexical access in pure alexia may also account for the reported capacity of some such patients to classify words without explicit identification (Coslett & Saffran, 1989; Shallice & Saffran, 1986).

ACKNOWLEDGMENTS

This work was supported by a postdoctoral fellowship from the Medical Research Council (MRC) of Canada to Martin Arguin and by a grant from the MRC and by scholarship from the Fonds de la Recherche en Santé du Québec to Daniel N. Bub. We thank DM for his patience, his humor, and his good company.

REFERENCES

Adams, M. J. (1979). Models of word recognition. *Cognitive Psychology, 11,* 133–176.

Arguin, M., & Cavanagh, P. (1988). Parallel processing of two disjunctive targets. *Perception and Psychophysics, 44,* 22–30.

Arguin, M., Joanette, Y., & Cavanagh, P. (1990). Comparing the cerebral hemispheres on the speed of spatial shifts of visual attention: Evidence from serial search. *Neuropsychologia, 28,* 733–736.

Bergen, J. R., & Julesz, B. (1983). Parallel versus serial processing in rapid pattern discrimination. *Nature, 303,* 696.

Briand, K. A., & Klein, R. M. (1987). Is Posner's "beam" the same as Treisman's "glue"?: On the relation between visual orienting and feature integration theory. *Journal of Experimental Psychology: Human Perception and Performance, 13,* 228–241.

Bub, D. N., Black, S., & Howell, J. (1989). Word recognition and orthographic context effects in a letter-by-letter reader. *Brain and Language, 36,* 357–376.

Caplan, L. R., & Hedley-White, T. (1974). Cueing and memory dysfunction in alexia without agraphia. *Brain, 97,* 251–62.

Carr, T. H., & Pollatsek, A. (1985). Recognising printed words: A look at current models. In D. Besner, T. G. Waller, & G. E. MacKinnon (Eds.), *Reading research: Advances in theory and practice* (Vol. 5, pp. 1–82). New York: Academic.

Cave, K. R., & Wolfe, J. M. (1990). Modeling the role of parallel processing in visual search. *Cognitive Psychology, 22,* 225–271.

Coltheart, M. (1981). Disorders of reading and their implications for models of normal reading. *Visible Language, 15,* 245–286.

Coltheart, M., Davelaar, E., Jonasson, J. T., & Besner, D. (1977). Access to the internal lexicon. In S. Dornic (Ed.), *Attention and performance VI* (pp. 535–555). New York: Academic.

Coslett, H. B., & Saffran, E. M. (1989). Evidence for preserved reading in "pure alexia." *Brain, 112*, 317–359.

Dejerine, J. (1892). Contribution à l'étude anatomo-pathologique et clinique des différentes variétés de cécité verbale. [Contribution to the anatomo-pathologic and clinical study of the different varieties of verbal blindness.] *Comptes rendus Hebdomadaires des Séances et Mémoires de la Société de Biologie* (Ninth series), *4*, 61–90

Dejerine, J., & Pélissier, A. (1914). Contribution à l'étude de la cécité verbale pure. [Contribution to the study of pure verbal blindness.] *Encephale, 7*, 1–28.

Eriksen, C. W., & Hoffman, J. E. (1973). The extent of processing of noise elements during selective coding from visual displays. *Perception and Psychophysics, 14*, 155–160.

Farah, M. J. (1990). *Visual agnosia.* Cambridge, MA: MIT Press.

Farah, M. J., & Wallace, M. A. (1991). Pure alexia as a visual impairment: A reconsideration. *Cognitive Neuropsychology, 8*, 313–334.

Friedman, R. B., & Alexander, M. P. (1984). Pictures, images, and pure alexia: A case study. *Cognitive Neuropsychology, 1*, 9–23.

Gilmore, G. C., Hersh, H., Caramazza, A., & Griffin, J. (1979). Multidimensional letter similarity derived from recognition errors. *Perception and Psychophysics, 25*, 425–431.

Grossi, D., Fragassi, N. A., Orsini, A. L., DeFalco, F. A., & Sepe, O. (1984). Residual reading capability in a patient with alexia without agraphia. *Brain and Language, 23*, 337–348.

Henderson, L. (1987). Word recognition: A tutorial review. In M. Coltheart (Ed.), *Attention and performance XII: The psychology of reading* (pp. 171–200). Hillsdale, NJ: Lawrence Erlbaum Associates.

Houck, M. R., & Hoffman, J. E. (1986). Conjunction of color and form without attention: Evidence from an orientation-contingent color aftereffect. *Journal of Experimental Psychology: Human Perception and Performance, 12*, 186–199.

Kay, J., & Hanley, R. (1991). Simultaneous form perception and serial letter recognition in a case of letter-by-letter reading. *Cognitive Neuropsychology, 8*, 249–273.

Kinsbourne, M., & Warrington, E. K. (1962). A disorder of simultaneous form perception. *Brain, 85*, 461–486.

Kinsbourne, M., & Warrington, E. K. (1963). The localizing significance of limited simultaneous visual form perception. *Brain, 86*, 697–702.

Koriat, A., & Norman, J. (1985). Reading rotated words. *Journal of Experimental Psychology: Human Perception and Performance, 11*, 490–508.

LaBerge, D. (1973). Attention and the measurement of perceptual learning. *Memory & Cognition, 1*, 268–276.

LaBerge, D., & Samuels, S. J. (1974). Toward a theory of automatic information processing in reading. *Cognitive Psychology, 6*, 293–323.

Landis, T., Regard, M., & Serrant, A. (1980). Iconic reading in a case of alexia without agraphia caused by a brain tumour: A tachistoscopic study. *Brain and Language, 11*, 45–53.

Levine, D. M., & Calvanio, R. (1978). A study of the visual defect in verbal alexia-simultanagnosia. *Brain, 101*, 65–81.

Loomis, J. M. (1982). Analysis of tactile and visual confusion matrices. *Perception and Psychophysics, 31*, 41–52.

McClelland, J. L. (1976). Preliminary letter identification in perception of words and letters. *Journal of Experimental Psychology: Human Perception and Performance, 2*, 80–91.

McClelland, J. L., & Rumelhart, D. E. (1981). An interactive activation model of context effects in letter perception: Part 1. An account of basic findings. *Psychological Review, 88*, 375–407.

Morton, J. (1969). Interaction of information in word recognition. *Psychological Review, 76*, 165–178.

Mozer, M. C. (1987). Early parallel processing in reading: A connectionist approach. In M. Coltheart (Ed.), *Attention and performance XII: The psychology of reading* (pp. 83–104). Hillsdale, NJ: Lawrence Erlbaum Associates.

Paap, K. R., Newsome, S. L., McDonald, J. E., & Schvaneveldt, R. W. (1982). An activation-verification model for letter and word recognition: The word-superiority effect. *Psychological Review, 89*, 573–594.

Pashler, H., & Badgio, P. C. (1985). Visual attention and stimulus identification. *Journal of Experimental Psychology: Human Perception and Performance, 11*, 105–121.

Patterson, K., & Kay, J. (1982). Letter-by-letter reading: Psychological descriptions of a neurological syndrome. *Quarterly Journal of Experimental Psychology, 34A*, 411–441.

Prinzmetal, W. (1981). Principles of feature integration in visual perception. *Perception and Psychophysics, 30*, 330–340.

Quinlan, P. T., & Humphreys, G. W. (1987). Visual search for targets defined by combinations of color, shape, and size: An examination of the task constraints on feature and conjunction searches. *Perception and Psychophysics, 41*, 455–472.

Rapp, B. C., & Caramazza, A. (1991). Spatially determined deficits in letter and word processing. *Cognitive Neuropsychology, 8*, 275–311.

Reuter-Lorenz, P. A., & Brunn, J. L. (1990). A prelexical basis for letter-by-letter reading: A case study. *Cognitive Neuropsychology, 7*, 1–20.

Scheerer, E. (1987). Visual word recognition in German. In D. A. Allport, D. Mackay, W. Prinz, & E. Scheerer (Eds.), *Language perception and production: Shared mechanisms in listening, speaking, reading and writing* (pp. 227–244). London: Academic.

Schiepers, C. (1980). Response latency and accuracy in visual word recognition. *Perception and Psychophysics, 27*, 71–81.

Segui, J., & Grainger, J. (1990). Priming word recognition with orthographic neighbors: Effects of relative prime-target frequency. *Journal of Experimental Psychology: Human Perception and Performance, 16*, 65–76.

Shallice, T., & Saffran, E. (1986). Lexical processing in the absence of explicit word identification: Evidence from a letter-by-letter reader. *Cognitive Neuropsychology, 3*, 429–458.

Snodgrass, J. G., & Townsend, J. T. (1980). Comparing parallel and serial models: Theory and implementation. *Journal of Experimental Psychology: Human Perception and Performance, 6*, 330–354.

Sperling, G. (1960). The information available in brief visual presentations. *Psychological Monographs, 74*(11).

Stachowiak, F. J., & Poeck, K. (1976). Functional disconnection in pure alexia and colour naming deficit demonstrated by facilitation methods. *Brain and Language, 3*, 135–143.

Staller, J., Buchanon, D., Signer, M., Lappin, J., & Webb, W. (1978). Alexia without agraphia: An experimental case study. *Brain & Language, 5*, 378–387.

Taylor, D. A. (1977). Time course of context effects. *Journal of Experimental Psychology: General, 106*, 404–426.

Townsend, J. T. (1971). Theoretical analysis of an alphabetic confusion matrix. *Perception and Psychophysics, 9*, 40–50.

Treisman, A. (1988). Features and objects. *Computer Vision, Graphics, and Image Processing, 31*, 156–177.

Treisman, A., & Gelade, G. (1980). A feature-integration theory of attention. *Cognitive Psychology, 12*, 97–136.

Treisman, A., & Paterson, R. (1984). Emergent features, attention, and object perception. *Journal of Experimental Psychology: Human Perception and Performance, 10*, 12–31.

Treisman, A., & Sato, S. (1990). Conjunction search revisited. *Journal of Experimental Psychology: Human Perception and Performance, 16*, 459–478.

Treisman, A., & Schmidt, H. (1982). Illusory conjunctions in the perception of objects. *Cognitive Psychology, 14,* 107–141.

Treisman, A., Sykes, M., & Gelade, G. (1977). Selective attention and stimulus integration. In S. Dornic (Ed.), *Attention and performance VI* (pp. 333–361). Hillsdale, NJ: Lawrence Erlbaum Associates.

Van Der Heijden, A. H. C., Malhas, M. S. M., & Van Den Roovaart, B. P. (1984). An empirical interletter confusion matrix for continuous-line capitals. *Perception and Psychophysics, 35,* 85–88.

Warrington, E. K., & Rabin, P. (1971). Visual span of apprehension in patients with unilateral cerebral lesions. *Quarterly Journal of Experimental Psychology, 23,* 423–431.

Warrington, E. K., & Shallice, T. (1980). Word-form dyslexia. *Brain, 103,* 99–112.

Wolfe, J. M., Cave, K. R., & Franzel, S. L. (1989). Guided search: An alternative to the feature integration model for visual search. *Journal of Experimental Psychology: Human Perception and Performance, 15,* 419–433.

7 Neglect Dyslexia: Attention and Word Recognition

Marlene Behrmann*
Rotman Research Institute and University of Toronto

Unilateral neglect, also called unilateral hemispatial neglect or hemispatial inattention (Friedland & Weinstein, 1977; Heilman, Watson, & Valenstein, 1985), is a neurobehavioral disorder in which patients fail to orient or respond to stimuli or events appearing in the hemispace contralateral to the side of the lesion. In its most extreme form, neglect may present as an aberration of behavior with patients showing a complete deviation of the head and eyes toward the ipsilesional side (Bisiach & Vallar, 1988). In milder forms of the disorder, neglect may not be overtly apparent but may still be elicited on tasks such as drawing or line bisection (Black, Vu, Martin, & Szalai, 1990). Figure 7.1 contains examples of the performance of two patients with neglect when given pictures of a daisy and a clock for copying.

Neglect can occur following damage to a number of cortical and subcortical structures, although lesions of the inferior parietal lobule appear to be the most frequent neuroanatomic concomitant (Vallar & Perani, 1986, 1987). This is not surprising given that the parietal lobe is a polymodal sensory association area consisting of multiple reciprocal connections with several areas including unimodal sensory regions, dorsolateral frontal cortex, superior colliculus, limbic cortex, and the reticular nuclei of the brainstem and thalamus (Goldman-Rakic & Selemon, 1986; Kolb & Whishaw, 1990; Mesulam, 1983). Damage to any one of these areas produces partial neglect that may recover whereas damage to multiple regions induces a severe, persistent deficit (Daffner, Ahern, Weintraub, & Mesulam, 1990; Mesulam, 1981, 1990).

---

*The author is now at Carnegie Mellon University.

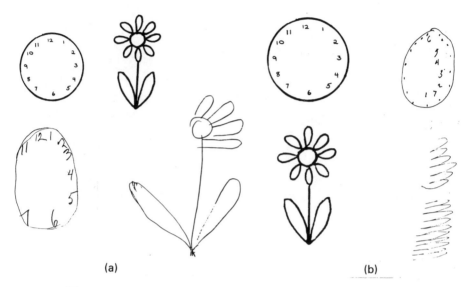

FIG. 7.1. Copying performance of two patients (Subject 1 [a] and Subject 2 [b]) with hemispatial neglect in response to a given picture of a clock and a daisy.

NEGLECT: A DEFICIT IN VISUOSPATIAL ATTENTION

Several explanations have been put forward to account for neglect ranging from a perceptual or sensory deficit (Denny-Brown, Meyer & Horenstein, 1952) to one of impaired access to representations (Bisiach, Capitani, Luzzatti, & Perani, 1981; Bisiach, Luzzatti, & Perani, 1979). One current explanation that has gained much acceptance is that a disruption in attention underlies neglect. Support for an attentional account for neglect comes from the finding that neglect may be absent when a single stimulus is presented (even to the neglected side) but that it may be induced under conditions of simultaneous presentation of bilateral stimuli, that is, when there is competition for attention from the ipsilesional side (Black, Martin, & Dywan, 1991; Karnath, 1988). This phenomenon is often referred to as extinction of the contralesional stimulus (Feinberg, Haber, & Stacey, 1990). Further evidence favoring an attentional account comes from the finding that cueing to the neglected side using digits or letters may reduce left-sided neglect on a variety of tasks such as line bisection, line cancellation, or free report (Butter, Kirsch, & Reeves, 1990; Ishiai et al., 1990; Karnath, 1988; Posner et al., 1984; Riddoch & Humphreys, 1983). Because the subjects' performance may be modified by cueing (Halligan & Marshall, 1989), the deficit cannot be attributed to a fundamental perceptual or sensory loss. Instead, because the left-sided stimulus is able to be processed under certain conditions, a deficit of attention in which attention is not deployed equally to the right and the left sides of space is thought to be responsible for neglect.

Neglect is observed with greater frequency and severity after right-hemisphere damage (Bisiach, Cornacchia, Sterzi, & Vallar, 1984; Colombo, De Renzi, & Faglioni, 1976; but see Ogden, 1985), suggesting a privileged role for the right hemisphere in mediating attention. Another source of evidence favoring this asymmetric control of attention is obtained from studies using patients without focal right-sided damage. For example, epileptic patients undergoing sodium amobarbitol tested preoperatively showed an impairment in contraversive scanning and attentional disruption following unilateral suppression of right-hemisphere function but not following left-sided suppression (Spiers et al., 1990). The finding that the right hemisphere plays a dominant role in attentional processes may explain the asymmetric incidence of neglect following right- versus left-hemisphere brain damage. Because left-sided neglect is more frequent than right-sided neglect, most of the discussion in this chapter is concerned with neglect of the left hemispace.

Despite the general consensus that an attentional disruption gives rise to neglect, there is little agreement as to the exact nature of such a deficit. Heilman and his colleagues (Heilman, Bowers, Coslett, Whelan, & Watson, 1985; Heilman, Bowers, Valenstein, & Watson, 1987; Heilman, Watson, & Valenstein, 1985), for example, have proposed that attentional problems may exist at several functional (and possibly anatomical) levels ranging from impairments in processing incoming sensory input to problems in directing responses to contralesional stimuli. Kinsbourne (1975, 1977, 1987), on the other hand, attributes neglect to the imbalance between the normal equilibrium of the opposing orientational tendencies of the two hemispheres. When one hemisphere is damaged (e.g., the right), the rightward orientation, exercised by the left hemisphere, is increased so that attention is disproportionately deployed to the right side. Support for this idea of an imbalance between the hemispheres is provided by a series of studies that show that, in comparison to normal controls, neglect patients are faster at detecting targets that occupy relative right positions (enhanced ipsilateral processing) whereas attention to the left is markedly decreased (Làdavas, 1987, 1990; Làdavas, Del Pesce, & Provinciali, 1989; Làdavas, Petronio, & Umilta, 1990). An alternative view is that neglect arises from a deficit in selective visuospatial attention (Posner, 1988; Posner, Walker, Friedrich, & Rafal, 1984). According to this view, attention is mediated by two independent but interacting networks, one posterior and the other anterior (Posner & Petersen, 1990; see also chapter 8 of this volume). The anterior system, involving areas of the mid-prefrontal cortex, is critical for tasks requiring subjects to detect target visual stimuli and for monitoring the number of targets presented (Corbetta, Miezen, Dobmeyer, & Shulman; Petersen, 1990; Posner, Petersen, Fox, & Raichle, 1988). The posterior network, including portions of the parietal cortex, is involved in directing attention to relevant locations and in selecting salient information for preferential processing through a series of engage, move, and disengage elementary operations. Empirical studies have demonstrated that patients with parietal lobe lesions (affecting the posterior network), especially those who show hemispatial neglect, are impaired at the disengage operation (Black et al., 1990; Morrow & Ratcliff, 1988; Posner, 1988; Posner et al., 1984; but see Cohen, Romero, & Farah, 1992, for an alternative interpretation). These patients are disproportionately impaired at "disengaging" their attention from the current focus, particularly if their attention is directed to the ipsilesional side. Thus, because they cannot refocus their attention to the left, information appearing in the contralesional hemispace is neglected.

NEGLECT DYSLEXIA

One manifestation of this lack of responsiveness to contralesional stimuli is the failure to read orthographic information that appears in the hemispace opposite to the damaged hemisphere. This phenomenon, termed *neglect dyslexia,* may become manifest in different tasks—the left side of an open book may be ignored and/or the beginning of lines may be omitted by patients when reading text (Caplan, 1987; Friedland & Weinstein, 1977; Kinsbourne & Warrington, 1962). Furthermore, the beginning letters of single words may be neglected, leading to substitution (e.g., *book* → "hook"), omission (e.g., *farm* → "arm"), or addition errors (e.g., *love* → "glove"). Neglect dyslexia, like hemispatial neglect, cannot be attributed to a primary motor or sensory deficit as it may occur in the absence of a hemianopia or hemiplegia (Behrmann, Moscovitch, Black, & Mozer, 1990; Caramazza & Hillis, 1990a; Warrington, 1991). Even in the case of a field defect, a primary visual deficit can be ruled out as an explanation of neglect; when the information is projected entirely to the subjects' intact field, failure to orient to contralesional information may still be evident (Làdavas, 1987; Posner et al., 1984). Neglect dyslexia can also not be attributed to a primary language or developmental reading disturbance as it occurs independently of aphasia and in adults who were premorbidly literate. As with hemispatial neglect, neglect dyslexia is attributed to a deficit in visuospatial attention because the degree of reading impairment can be minimized by cueing or can be exacerbated by bilateral simultaneous stimulus presentation. Riddoch, Humphreys, Cleton, and Fery (1990), for example, showed improved reporting of the left side of a letter string (e.g., *land*) when it was preceded by a cue (*#land*). Also, the simultaneous presentation of two short words produced more left-sided neglect (extinction) than the presentation of a single word to the left or right (Behrmann et al., 1990; Sieroff, 1991; Sieroff & Michel, 1987). Thus, because the degree of the reading impairment is variable, an attentional interpretation rather than a fundamental perceptual problem seems more compatible with the data.

Neglect dyslexia and the breakdown of attention in reading has not been extensively researched and until recently, there has been a marked paucity of detailed case studies. Currently, this phenomenon is enjoying a considerable degree of interest as is reflected by the publication of a special issue of the journal, *Cognitive Neuropsychology,* on neglect and peripheral dyslexias (Parts 1 and 2, edited by M. J. Riddoch). Despite the increasing popularity of research on this topic, many issues concerning the symptoms and underlying mechanism of this phenomenon remain unresolved. This chapter examines how the attentional deficit of neglect affects pattern recognition in general, and more specifically, how the breakdown in attention influences reading. The first section of this chapter considers neglect dyslexia and its relation to generalized hemispatial neglect, examining whether they both arise from the same attentional impairment or not. The next section focuses more specifically on reading with special emphasis on the nature and locus of the attentional deficit in the reading process. Reading (in this case, single-word recognition) requires several stages of processing in the mapping of visually presented letters onto meaning (semantics) and pronunciation (phonology). Stages of processing include low-level encoding of stimulus features (data-driven or bottom-up processes) as well as higher level processing of meaning (conceptual and top-down processes). At present, it is unclear at what stage in processing the attentional deficit has its impact. Experimental data from brain-damaged and normal subjects as well as from a computational model are presented to address this issue and an explanation of the mechanism underlying neglect dyslexia is offered. Insights obtained from examining the co-occurrence of neglect dyslexia and generalized neglect and from investigating the interaction of attention with word recognition may be helpful in understanding how visual-spatial attention normally operates. Furthermore, data from patients with neglect dyslexia may shed light on the contribution of attention to pattern recognition in general.

DISSOCIATIONS AMONG FORMS OF NEGLECT AND NEGLECT DYSLEXIA

The first issue to be addressed in this chapter concerns the extent to which neglect dyslexia is dissociable from hemispatial neglect. The degree to which these phenomena are separable is critical in any account of the role of attention in visuospatial processing. If neglect dyslexia and hemispatial neglect are highly correlated, this would be consistent with a view in which a single attentional mechanism exists and in which damage has far-reaching consequences, affecting all processing that draws from this common mechanism. If, however, neglect and hemispatial neglect are dissociable, a model of attention consisting of multiple attentional subsystems may be more parsimonious. Discrete damage to this latter model in which the subsystems are specialized for different types of perceptual problems may then give rise to the dissociations between hemispatial neglect and neglect dyslexia.

Neglect dyslexia is often considered to be one manifestation of a broader, all-encompassing deficit that affects contralesional information independent of modality of input, task, and domain of processing (Ellis, Flude, & Young, 1987). On some current theoretical accounts, attention is not an independent "module" but rather a central attentional control system subserving all domains and modalities (Moscovitch & Umilta, 1990; Posner, 1988). This view confers a supervisory or central status on attention from which resource allocation may occur and predicts that when attention is disrupted, neglect should be observed concurrently in all processing domains and modalities. Support for a unitary system common to multiple modalities comes from research showing that cueing attention in one modality (e.g., auditory or tactile) can facilitate processing in a second modality (e.g., visual) (Butter, Buchtel, & Santucci, 1989; Farah, Wong, Monheit, & Morrow, 1989). That cross-modality cueing is possible suggests that a common attentional system is responsible and links multiple modalities. In a recent study examining the presence of extinction in three modalities (auditory, tactile, and visual), Black et al. (1990) found that 48% of the sample had a deficit in all three modalities whereas almost all the others had a deficit in two modalities. The high degree of association between the various forms of neglect and extinction favors a single attentional system.

An alternative model of attention that makes allowance for dissociations between domains and modalities is one in which discrete attentional mechanisms operate independently and may be selectively disrupted, giving rise to fractionations of the neglect behavior. This is consistent with many studies that demonstrate dissociations across different modalities. For instance, motor neglect has been described in the absence of hemineglect (Bisiach, Geminiani, Berti, & Rusconi, 1990; Daffner et al., 1990; Leplane & Degos, 1983) and visual neglect has been dissociated from both tactile (Barbieri & De Renzi, 1989; Fujii, Fukatsu, Kimura, Saso, & Kogure, 1991) and auditory neglect (De Renzi, Gentilini, & Pattacini, 1984).

In addition to cross-modality dissociations, dissociations just within the visual modality have been described. For example, Young, De Haan, Newcombe, and Hay (1990) described a case with inattention to the left side of faces with preserved recognition of other objects. In addition, neglect for printed material has been described in isolation from neglect on other visual tasks such as line bisection or symbol detection (Baxter & Warrington, 1983; Warrington, 1991). Also, striking results from two studies show within-subject dissociations with left neglect in reading and right neglect in visuospatial tasks (Costello & Warrington, 1987; Cubelli, Nichelli, Bonito, De Tanti, & Inzhagi, 1991). The double dissociation between neglect dyslexia and generalized visuospatial neglect, however, is not upheld in all studies. In a recent pilot study with 14 subjects with right-hemisphere lesions, Sandra Black and I found that only 8 showed hemispatial neglect on a standardized bedside battery of neglect (Black et al., 1990). Of these eight, only four demonstrated neglect dyslexia. No subject showed neglect dyslexia without visuospatial neglect, suggesting a unidirectional dissociation. A similar unidirectional dissociation has also been noted by Farah (personal communication, June, 1991). One possible reason for the contradictory findings is that there are major methodological differences across studies and across testing procedures. Riddoch (1990) pointed out that testing conditions for hemispatial neglect are far less stringent than those used for assessing reading and that more taxing tests might elicit hemispatial neglect in those few cases with isolated neglect dyslexia.

Models of Attentional Organization

How can an attentional system operate such that it gives rise to the multitude of symptoms and dissociations reported earlier? We have seen that there are dissociations in neglect performance across modalities as well as dissociations just within the visual modality. At this stage, there is little consensus regarding the functional organization of attention vis-a-vis pattern recognition. Any account of selective attention, however, must make provision for the dissociations described previously. To account for the dissociations, one would need to postulate a multicentric model in which individual and independent attentional mechanisms exist, each subserving a particular modality as well as domain of processing. A more parsimonious account, however, would be to show that a single mechanism serves all domains but that the individual modalities and domains might interact differently with attention or might become "disconnected" from the unitary attentional system. A further possibility suggested by Young, Hellawell, and Welch (1992) is that domain specificity is conditional on stage of impairment. Damage at an early stage in the visual processing system where domain-specific representations are not involved, might lead to cross-domain neglect whereas damage at a relatively late stage might give rise to domain-specific forms of neglect. Until such time as further empirical data are available, however, it is difficult to adjudicate between the various hypotheses and the hierarchical organization of attention remains an open issue.

In the next section, the attentional deficit and its contribution to neglect dyslexia is examined in an attempt to clarify more precisely how attention interacts with one specific domain of cognitive processing namely, single-word recognition.

DISSOCIATIONS WITHIN NEGLECT DYSLEXIA

Before providing experimental data and an account of neglect dyslexia, the characteristics and symptoms of the deficit are described in greater detail. Probably the most agreed-upon feature of neglect dyslexia is that there is considerable heterogeneity in its manifestation. The heterogeneity is observed both in type of reading task (single word versus text), frame of reference (viewer-, object-, or environment-centered) and in type of material (symbol type, lexical status, etc.).

Single Word Versus Text Neglect

Some patients produce errors on initial letters in words, while text reading remains intact (Costello & Warrington, 1987; Riddoch et al., 1990), whereas in other patients, both single-word and text deficits are observed (Behrmann et al., 1990; Ellis et al., 1987; Kinsbourne & Warrington, 1962). The dissociation between text and word reading has been suggested as arising from two different sources: Whereas defective location of line beginnings gives rise to text neglect, a lack of compensatory eye movements for a left-sided hemianopia produces single-word errors (Young, Ellis, & Newcombe, 1991). This latter explanation is disputed, however, because single-word neglect may occur in the absence of a field defect and is still observed under conditions in which material is presented entirely in the intact visual field by presenting a red dot or flanker to the left of the stimulus or by tachistoscopic presentation (Ellis et al., 1987; Riddoch et al., 1990).

Another explanation for this dissociation is provided by theories that suggest that different forms of spatial coding underlie word and text reading. Within-object spatial coding combines features that are integral to the identity of a single object (i.e., word) and this occurs within the window of attention (Humphreys & Riddoch, 1990; Humphreys, Riddoch, & Muller, 1991; Riddoch & Humphreys, 1991). Between-object codes are elaborated from the within-object representations and specify the relations between separate objects (i.e., the words in the text). This latter form of coding requires several fixations to construct a map that specifies the relations between separate objects. Although the within-object codes are integral to word recognition, specifying the "what" information, the between-object codes are more concerned with spatial location or "where" the object appears. This separation of information into "what" and "where" fits with the compelling neuroscientific evidence favoring separable systems that compute object identity (ventral, inferotemporal pathway) and those that compute spatial relationships (dorsal, parietal lobe pathway) (Desimone, Schein, Moran, & Ungerleider, 1985; Grady et al., 1992; Ungerleider & Mishkin, 1982). The dissociation between text and single-word reading may be explained, therefore, as arising from selective damage to one of the two visual pathways.

According to Humphreys and his colleagues (Humphreys & Riddoch, 1990; Humphreys et al., 1991), within- and between-object coding rely on different spatial frames of representation. Within-object coding is based on the spatial relations between features as seen from the viewer's perspective (either head-and/or body-centered) and is retinotopically centered. It is assumed to operate in the early stages of processing, prior to recognition, where the physical location of an object in the external world corresponds to its location from the viewer's perspective. Between-object coding provides a map of the entire scene and thus stimuli are represented relative to an environment-based map. This scene-based set of spatial coordinates is thought to be based on nonretinotopic coordinates that allow for stability across successive fixations. A third possible frame of reference that is thought to be important in neglect dyslexia is one that is object-centered and in which the spatial structure of the object is aligned with respect to its canonical representation. Objects appearing in noncanonical orientations must therefore be transformed prior to being represented in this object-centered form. Thus, words that are presented vertically or horizontally ultimately have the same representation in this object coordinate frame but have different representations at a lower, retinotopic level.

Neglect Dyslexia and Frames of Representation

Because neglect dyslexia can arise with respect to different frames of reference, Caramazza and Hillis (1990a) argued that neglect dyslexia may arise at any one of multiple representational levels along a vertical hierarchy from retinocentric to higher level reference frames. A number of patients have been described whose neglect operates with respect to a low-level frame of reference, that is, within a viewer-centered perspective. Thus, vertically presented words are not subject to neglect as is the case with horizontal words. In addition, 180° rotation of words leads to neglect with respect to the left of the viewer's frame rather than with respect to the object frame; for example, these patients make errors such as reading *pearl* → "earl," and when rotated, *lraep* → "pear," showing that information on the left of space rather than the left of the item itself is neglected (Ellis et al., 1987; Young et al., 1991). Other patients, however, show deficits at levels other than this viewer-centered frame. NG (Caramazza & Hillis, 1990a, 1990b), who showed right-sided neglect following a left-hemisphere lesion, continued to make errors on the final letters of the word irrespective of whether strings were presented in their normal horizontal orientation or in vertical or mirror image orientation. For NG, then, the ordinal position of the letters was critical, suggesting that the deficit arose with respect to a word- or object-centered representation rather than with respect to one that was coded from the viewer's vantage point. Interestingly, NG showed a similar pattern of neglect in oral and written spelling suggesting that the impaired word-centered representation underlies both reading and spelling. Of note is the fact that NG had sustained a left-hemisphere lesion— whether similar object-centered effects would be observed in patients with right-hemisphere lesions remains an open question (see Behrmann & Tipper, in press, for related work). Independent of the site of lesion, however, the object-centered effects observed in NG require an explanation. One way to accommodate the data showing that neglect may arise with respect to a viewer-centered and/or an object-centered frame is to assume that attentional deficits arise at different representational levels (Caramazza & Hillis, 1990a, 1990b). Another way, however, is to try and incorporate both results into a single explanation within the viewer-centered frame of reference. Analyzing an item or object might require the mapping of the abstract object- or word-centered representation onto a more concrete viewer-centered frame. This instantiation of the abstract representation may produce an activity pattern that captures the essentials of the stimulus but that does not contain the richness of a true perception. Once the "abstract" representation is mapped, the patient is operating in an "imagined" viewer-centered frame and the stimulus is viewed from a particular vantage point. The attentional system may then operate on the internal representation in the same way as for perception (Bisiach, 1993). The notion of a more concrete mapping is consistent with the report made by Baxter and Warrington's (1983) neglect dysgraphic patient who commented that "attempting to spell [was] like reading off an image in which the letters on the right side were clearer than those on the left" (p. 1075). This mapping process then might lead to deficits that, on the surface, appear to arise with respect to an internal, conceptual representation. This formulation assumes that the same "hardware" is used for imaging stimuli and for processing incoming perceptual stimuli, a notion that has strong support in the literature on the relation between mental imagery and perception (Farah, 1988). It is possible, then, to accommodate data that appear to be the product of a deficit at an object-centered representational level within the viewer-centered framework of attentional selection.

Neglect Dyslexia and Material Specificity

In addition to varying along a vertical hierarchy from low- to higher level spatial frames of reference, neglect dyslexia also shows variability with respect to the type of material that is neglected. Patterson and Wilson (1990), for example, described a case, TB, who omitted the left side of alphanumeric symbols but was able to name the left-hand elements in an array of four geometric figures. Similarly, Cohen and Dehaene (1991) reported a case who, in the absence of clinical signs of hemineglect, made substitution and/or perseveration errors on the left of digits. Because we have no details on this patient's ability to read alphabetic stimuli, we do not know the extent to which this deficit was truly restricted to digits.

A further example of material specificity comes from the finding that neglect dyslexia may be affected by the lexical status of the stimuli. Several cases show superior performance (and less extinction) on reading words than on reporting pronounceable nonwords (Behrmann et al., 1990; Brunn & Farah, 1991; Sieroff, Pollatsek, & Posner, 1988; among others). Additional evidence supporting the idea that lexical constraints affect reading comes from Riddoch et al. (1990) who showed that their two patients found words with more orthographic neighbors more difficult to read than words with few neighbors that are more unique and distinctive orthographically.

NATURE OF THE ATTENTIONAL IMPAIRMENT
IN NEGLECT DYSLEXIA

How does the attentional disruption interact with reading to produce the various symptoms described previously? The most conspicuous role of selective attention in normal reading is to control the order of processing so that words on a page are read from top to bottom and left to right. In addition, attention serves to integrate the results of processing performed by independent subsystems (Treisman, 1977; Treisman & Gelade, 1980). In reading, this function of attention may serve to tie letter or word identities to locations (Ellis et al., 1987; Mozer, 1991). A quite different function of attention is to segment out a stimulus from the background, focusing resources on a small amount of information at any one time. Attention is thus a control mechanism that selects relevant subparts of the input for preferential processing. This is an essential process because visual cognition is fundamentally limited in capacity and there is more sensory input available than can be efficiently processed at any one time. The critical question, then, is on what basis and at what stage this selection takes place. For nearly three decades, cognitive psychologists have debated whether attentional selection occurs early or late in the processing of visual information (see Allport, 1989; chapter 13 of this volume, for recent overview). Early-selection views (Broadbent, 1958; Treisman, 1969) derive their name from the assertion that the "bottleneck" in the flow of information occurs early in the sequence of processing stages and hence, selection takes place prior to stimulus identification and semantic processing.

In contrast, late-selection views (Deutsch & Deutsch, 1963; Norman, 1968; Tipper, 1985; Tipper & Driver, 1988) posit that all stimuli are processed at least to the stage of identification before selection occurs. An important assumption that underlies this early/late dichotomy concerns the presumed monotonic ordering of stages. According to this conventional characterization, early selection is based on low-level features such as the sensory and physical attributes of the stimulus (location, color) whereas late selection is based on high-level features such as stimulus identity and meaning. Explicit predictions arise from this distinction. If selection operates early, then an impairment of attention should result in degradation or attenuation of low-level representations and performance should be affected by manipulations that alter the physical dimensions of the stimulus. Alternatively, if selection occurs late, an attentional disturbance should only come into play after the stimulus has been processed to a high level.

The findings in the neglect dyslexia literature thus far provide a rich but seemingly contradictory source of data regarding the locus of the attentional deficit. On the one hand, neglect dyslexia has been shown to occur with respect to a viewer-centered coordinate frame—as mentioned earlier, orientation (vertical vs. horizontal) affects performance as does 180° rotation of the stimulus. Furthermore, retinal location has been shown to affect performance, even in the right field—the farther to the right the information is presented relative to fixation, the better it is reported (Arguin & Bub, 1991; Behrmann et al., 1990; De Renzi, Gentilini, Faglioni, & Barbieri, 1989; Ladavas, 1987; Rapp, Benzing, & Caramazza, 1991). These findings support the view that attentional selection (and disruption) take place within an early, viewer-centered frame prior to object recognition. On the other hand, there is contradictory evidence indicating that the attentional disruption occurs at later stages of analysis. For example, the nature of the written material affects performance (alphanumeric vs. geometric symbols, words vs. nonwords) suggesting that stimuli must have been encoded to a high level before selection takes place. These paradoxical results rule out simple early- and late-selection views of attention—the early view cannot explain the influence of high-level categorical or semantic properties of stimuli and the late-selection view is contrary to the finding that neglect depends on position and orientation of the stimulus in the visual field.

It is difficult to reconcile these discrepant results if one assumes a monotonic hierarchy of stages of visual processing in which categorical information is encoded at later stages once sensory encoding is complete. Such a stagelike view has predominated in the cognitive and neuropsychological literature (see Seidenberg, 1988 for review). An alternative formulation, based largely on connectionist or parallel distributed processing models, does not assume that the ordering of processing is necessary (McClelland, 1979). A model in which information is processed in parallel and in which later stages of processing can occur while early processing is still ongoing may provide a unifying account of the seemingly discrepant data. Computational models of this dynamic sort assume that information processing takes place in parallel through the competitive and cooperative interaction between a large number of simple processing units. A critical feature of such models is that processing need not be done in an all-or-none fashion and partial activation is possible. Another critical feature of such models is that, because they incorporate distributed rather than localist representations, they are able to complete patterns from partial information. Thus, the activities of the units are guided by the existing knowledge in the network and the stored representations enable them to recover a complete response from degraded input (see McClelland, Rumelhart, & Hinton, 1986; Quinlan, 1991; for overview of psychological research and connectionism). In the last few years, the application of computational models to simulating forms of acquired dyslexia has met with considerable success (Hinton & Shallice, 1991; Patterson, Seidenberg, & McClelland, 1989; Plaut & Shallice, 1993).

In an attempt to synthesize the paradoxical data, a unitary account of neglect, inspired by connectionist models, has been postulated in a series of papers (Behrmann et al., 1990, 1991; Mozer & Behrmann, 1990, 1992). The gist of such an account is as follows: First, we have shown that the attention deficit has its primary locus at an early stage of processing because word recognition is affected by manipulations that alter the physical form and orientation of the stimuli. We have then argued that even if the deficit influences low levels of processing, it may still be possible to demonstrate what appear to be the effects of later stages of processing as a result of influences between lower and higher level processes. Thus, even under damage that occurs early, an effect of the lexical status of the stimulus may still exist through top-down influences, leading to superior reporting of words over nonwords. To illustrate, consider the stimulus "book" in which the left side is affected by the attentional deficit. Contact may nonetheless be made with an existing representation for the item "book" and this may help "clean up" or recover the attenuated input on the left, leading to the correct response "book." This top-down support, however, is not applicable in the case of nonwords, which do not have stored representations. Thus, in response to a stimulus like "wast" in which top-down clean-up of the neglected left side is not possible, the response may be a substitution of another real word like *last* or an omission like "ast." This type of reasoning, in which stored representations may assist in recovering degraded perceptual input degraded by inattention, is similar to that embodied in the well-known *interactive activation model* (IAM; McClelland & Rumelhart, 1981; Rumelhart & McClelland, 1982). In the IAM, under conditions of brief exposure in which input at the letter level is partially degraded, the existing representations at the word level can feed back down to the letter level, thereby enhancing the perception of individual letters and giving rise to the word superiority effect. Because pseudowords overlap with words, they too derive some benefit from word-level representations but this advantage is not afforded to random letter strings. The same reasoning applies in neglect dyslexia: The effects of the low-level deficit may be partially offset by the top-down knowledge that can clean up and recover the stimulus.

Several predictions arise from this interactive view: First, it suggests that the attentional deficit operates early, producing left-sided degradation of the stimulus. Second, it predicts that the effect of stored knowledge will only be observed in those instances in which a prior representation exists; thus, words will be neglected to a lesser extent than nonwords. Finally, this account suggests that the stimulus must be processed to a sufficient degree in order to engage or trigger the stored representation. If, for example, the left side of the stimulus "book" is so severely degraded that it cannot activate the existing representation, then recovery of the stimulus may not be possible. Thus, these conceptual or top-down effects might only be seen in those cases where the attentional deficit is not too severe. In summary, this interactive account of neglect dyslexia would argue that even if the attentional disruption affects processing at an early stage, remote effects might still be observed provided that there is an existing lexical representation and that the deficit is not too severe.

Evidence supporting this interactive account is presented in the following section. Data from two patients with neglect dyslexia (see Behrmann et al., 1990) are presented first and then the findings are considered in the light of a computational model of *M*ultiple *O*bject (word) *R*ecognition and *Se*lective Attention (MORSEL; Mozer, 1987, 1991; Mozer & Behrmann, 1990, 1992). MOR-SEL appears to be a particularly suitable framework within which to consider neglect dyslexia because it embodies a hybrid of early and late attentional selection. Computational simulations of neglect dyslexia, conducted in collaboration with Michael Mozer (now at the University of Colorado at Boulder), demonstrate how such an interactive account can be implemented and also provide a comprehensive, mechanistic account of how both early and late effects can operate simultaneously in neglect dyslexia.

EXPERIMENTAL EVIDENCE

Evidence from Neglect Dyslexic Patients

Case Histories

HR (Subject 1 or S1) and AH (Subject 2 or S2), both right-handed, English-speaking men, demonstrated hemispatial neglect on bedside testing following a single right-hemisphere stroke. The figures illustrated in Fig. 7.1 reflect the performance of these two subjects with panels (a) and (b) containing the copies made by S1 and S2 respectively. Both subjects were mildly dysarthric but neither demonstrated aphasia or diffuse cognitive impairment consistent with dementia. S1 scored 52 on a standardized stroke scale (Adams, Meador, & Sehti, 1987; score above 50 indicates a severe deficit) and, on the Wechsler Adult Intelligence Scale–Revised (WAIS–R), achieved a low average full-scale IQ with an average verbal IQ and a performance IQ in the 20th percentile range. His CT scan revealed a patchy but extensive right middle cerebral artery infarct, involving frontal and parietal areas and the basal ganglia. S2 scored 28 on the Adams et al. (1987) stroke scale (moderate 20–50). On the WAIS-R, he obtained a low average verbal IQ and a performance IQ in the bottom 10th percentile. His CT scan revealed an infarct in the right middle cerebral artery territory involving the basal ganglia, deep white matter, and the temporal and parietal cortex (see Behrmann et al., 1990, for more details and CT scans). Both subjects demonstrated generalized neglect on tests of line cancellation, letter and symbol detection, and spontaneous drawing and copying (Fig. 7.1), more severe in S2 than in S1.

The Attentional Deficit

The nature and extent of the subjects' attentional deficit was measured on two different tasks. In the first task, the subjects' ability to detect the presence of a single oddball letter (C) in a horizontal array of letters (AAAAAA or ACAAAA) was measured in a same/different task, and accuracy as a function of location of the oddball was calculated. In the second task, the subjects were required to report orally the letters in a horizontal array and, again, accuracy of report was measured as a function of serial position. The results of these tasks are shown in Figs. 7.2a and 7.2b below, as a function of string position.

Both subjects showed a gradient of attentional distribution with better performance on the right than on the left. S1's performance on the detection task was superior to that on the report task but the left side was impaired relative to the right on both tasks to an equal extent. It appears that information is being picked up equally on the left and the right in both tasks but when more precise information is required to identify the letters overtly, performance drops. In the rightmost positions, S2 is able to perform the detection and report tasks equally well. His difficulty in the detection task for material on the left side of space, already more pronounced than S1's, is exaggerated in the report task. Although basic information is not being registered well from the left side of the array, when the information is required for precise report, the deficit for S2 becomes even more apparent. The fact that the attentional deficit is more severe in S2 than in S1 is consistent with his poorer performance on the bedside tests of neglect (see Fig. 7.1).

The serial position curves, with a right–left superiority displayed by the subjects, are consistent with the view that, following brain damage, attention is distributed as a gradient across the field with lowest activation on the left and maximal deployment to the right (De Renzi et al., 1989; Friederich, Walker, &

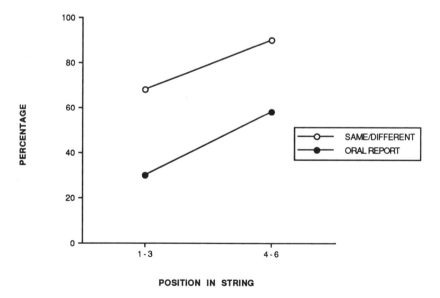

FIG. 7.2a. Percentage correct letter report on same/different and oral report tasks for S1.

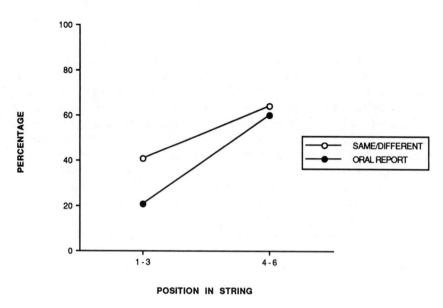

FIG. 7.2b.   Percentage correct letter report on same/different and oral report tasks for S2.

Posner, 1985; Kinsbourne, 1987). The presence of a gradient is also supported by anatomical evidence. Rizzolatti and colleagues (Rizzolatti, Gentilucci, & Matelli, 1985; Rizzolatti, Scandolara, Matelli, & Gentilucci, 1981) have shown that 29% of the neurons in the postarcuate cortex of the monkey have exclusively contralateral fields whereas 3% have exclusively ipsilateral and 68% have bilateral fields. The neurons with bilateral fields predominate and lie across the midline, whereas at the lateral periphery, space representation relies on the contralateral cortex. Damage to the right hemisphere (as in the subjects here) affects the neurons with contralateral receptive fields, thereby impeding processing of left-sided information. Because there are more neurons with bilateral fields and because each hemisphere tends towards equal values as one approaches the midline, the neurons with bilateral fields allow for processing of stimuli in the relative left hemispace (closer to midline) but not in the far hemispace. This results in a gradient with a maximum in the extreme ipsilateral right falling off to a minimum on the extreme contralateral side.

Reading Performance of the Subjects

A series of studies was conducted in which the subjects' reading was assessed under conditions in which the physical features of the stimuli were manipulated to assess the contribution of bottom-up or early processing. Thereafter, a second series of studies was carried out in which the linguistic dimensions of stimuli (lexical status and morphology) were manipulated to reflect later, higher order processing.

Methodology. Testing was carried out on a Macintosh Plus computer and 9-in. diagonal, high resolution, 512 × 342 pixel, bit-mapped display screen using Psychlab software (Bub & Gum, 1988). In all cases a central fixation point appeared 500 ms prior to the stimulus, which was presented in bold black 24-point font on a white background. Responses were manually recorded for error analysis. The patients were seated at a distance of 50 cm and the visual angle subtended was 2.3°, 3.4°, and 4.6° for 3-, 5-, and 7-letter words respectively.

Accuracy of reading is measured. The reading performance of the two patients was examined under the following conditions that might be expected to influence bottom-up or early processing:

1. Stimulus orientation: Words were presented either vertically or horizontally.
2. Retinal location: Words were presented either immediately next to fixation (near condition) or three to four character spaces to the right (far condition).
3. Stimulus length: Words of three to nine letters in length were presented to assess the effect of stimulus length.
4. Horizontal extent: Words were presented either with regular spacing (e.g., ACE) or with a single character space between letters (e.g., A C E) to evaluate the effect of increasing horizontal space on performance.
5. Increased horizontal region: Words of three to five letters were presented in normal form (e.g., DOG) or "stretched," taking up the same horizontal extent as the spaced words in Item 4 (e.g., DOG).

Table 7.1 demonstrates the results of these manipulations, showing whether or not they significantly affect the performance of S1 and S2. The *p* values reflect whether performance on a particular task within a single subject is significantly better (shows less neglect) than on a second task.

These findings demonstrate that both subjects were affected to some extent by manipulations that alter the physical dimensions of the stimuli. This suggests that the attentional impairment has its impact at an early stage of processing in which low-level stimulus features affect performance. Altering the stimulus dimensions appears to have a greater effect on S2 than on S1. This is consistent with the observation that S2 shows more severe neglect on the bedside tasks and a greater deficit on the attentional tasks. According to the prediction of the interactive account, because S1 has a less severe attentional deficit, he should show more conceptual effects on his reading performance. S2, on the other hand, should not be as greatly influenced by the high-level stimulus manipulations.

TABLE 7.1
Effect of Bottom-Up Manipulations on Patients' Performance

	S1	S2
Horizontal > vertical	$p < .001$	$p < .001$
Near > far condition	$p < .05$	$p < .08$
Word length	$p > .05$	$p < .01$
Horizontal extent	$p > .05$	$p < .01$
Regular > stretched	——	$p < .01$

The following experiments manipulate the more abstract, conceptual dimensions of the stimuli, assessing the top-down effects on performance:

1. The effect of *lexicality* was examined in both subjects by giving them words (which have lexical representation) and nonwords (which have no prior lexical entry) for oral reading. Whereas both S1 and S2 showed a word superiority effect, the discrepancy between the stimulus types was more marked in S1 (correct: 63% words, 8% nonwords) than in S2 (correct: 42% words, 3% nonwords), as predicted.

2. A further manipulation that assesses the contribution of stored representations compared the effect of *morphemic composition* on the patients' reading performance. Many reports have suggested that patients with neglect tend to preserve the morphemic status of words even when they produce errors (Friedland & Weinstein, 1977); for example, the word *pretend* is usually read as "tend" or "end" rather than as "retend" or "etend," showing preservation rather than violation of the morphemic boundaries.

To examine the influence of morphemic boundaries on reading performance, the ability of these subjects to report the left-sided member of a pair of words presented simultaneously was examined. Half the pairs consisted of two morphemes that, when joined, formed another morpheme, a compound word, which has a prior lexical entry (e.g., *cow boy*). The remaining half consisted of two words that formed a noncompound word (e.g., *sun fly*). If top-down knowledge really exerts an effect on performance, then we might expect to see less neglect of the left side of those morphemes that form a compound word than of those that make up a noncompound word. According to the interactive account, the top-down effect should be particularly evident in the case of S1 whose processing of left-sided information is better than that of S2. Both subjects neglected the left member of the pair with S1 reporting both members on only 28% of the compound and 9% of the noncompound words. As predicted, S2 performed even more poorly, correctly reading both members of the compound and noncompound words on only 4% and 0% of the trials respectively.

Because the interactive account argues for the simultaneous contribution of both low-level and high-level factors, S1's reading of compound and noncompound words was assessed when the spacing of the items (low-level manipulation) was altered. The same stimuli were re-presented either contiguously (e.g., *cowboy* or *sunfly*) or joined but with an asterisk between the members (e.g., *cow*boy* or *sun*fly*). Because S1's reading is affected by low-level features, the prediction was that he should show least neglect in the contiguous condition, most neglect in the spaced condition, and that the joined condition should fall in between. According to the *additive factor* logic of Sternberg (1969), however, if both low- and high-level factors operate concurrently and affect the same internal processing stage, they will interact, whereas if they affect different processing stages, their effects will be additive. A chi-square analysis of the data incorporating stimulus type (compound, noncompound) and mode (spaced, joined asterisk, contiguous) revealed a significant effect of both variables ($x^2 = 1.9$, $p < .05$), suggesting the joint operation of both high- and low-level variables as predicted by the interactive account.

The data presented previously reflect the bottom-up and top-down processing in S1. According to the interactive account, the emergence of higher order variables on performance is only observed when the attentional deficit is not too severe. To test this notion, a final experiment was conducted with S2. In this task, S2's attention was directed to the left so that the processing of left-sided stimuli could be enhanced through more optimal distribution of attention. Under these conditions, then, when the left-sided stimulus is processed better, the effect of prior lexical entries should be observed (as in the case of S1). The same compound and noncompound stimuli described earlier were presented with a space between the members of a pair. By instructing S2 to report the left item first, the gradient was shifted by directing his attention to the left. With this manipulation, the effect of higher order knowledge was noted with S2 reporting 42% of compound words and 14% of noncompound words (compared to 4% and 0% when no instructions were given). The superiority of items that have a lexical representation over those that do not mirrors the pattern observed in the less severe subject, S1. This is consistent with the view that when left-sided information is sufficiently processed, top-down effects may be triggered and engaged.

Discussion.   The findings from the patients reflect the coexistence of low-level and higher order variables and their relationship to the severity of the deficit. Thus far, the results are consistent with the interactive account of neglect dyslexia outlined in the beginning. These data were then considered in the framework of a connectionist model that contains an attentional mechanism to control the flow and order of information through the capacity limited word recognition system. The next section describes the computational simulations conducted with MORSEL in which the attentional mechanism is "lesioned" to reflect the underlying deficit in neglect dyslexia. As we see, the simulations reveal a remarkably good fit to the behavioral data, supporting the interactive account of neglect dyslexia.

Evidence from Computational Simulations: Data from MORSEL

MORSEL was originally designed to account for a broad spectrum of psychological data, including perceptual errors that arise when several objects appear simultaneously in the field, facilitatory effects of context as well as various attentional phenomena (Mozer, 1987, 1991). In this section, the components of MORSEL are outlined and the simulation methodology is briefly sketched (the interested reader is referred to Mozer & Behrmann, 1990, 1992, for more details). Two simulations are described next to illustrate how the interaction between a low-level attentional deficit and top-down knowledge, observed in the neglect dyslexic subjects, might occur. The first simulation demonstrates the operation of MORSEL's attentional mechanism in its normal and lesioned state and is compatible with a mechanism in which attentional selection occurs early. The second simulation goes on to show the higher order effects that may be observed in the lesioned network under early attentional damage.

Description of Components of MORSEL

MORSEL has three essential components (see Fig. 7.3). The central component is a connectionist network called BLIRNET that *B*uilds *L*ocation *I*nvariant *R*epresentations of visually presented letters and words. BLIRNET has the capacity to analyze multiple strings in parallel, but perceptual inaccuracies arise as the amount of information to be processed increases. Consequently, two additional components are required: a clean-up mechanism that constructs a coherent interpretation of the noisy percepual data provided by BLIRNET, called the pull-out (PO) net; and an attentional mechanism (AM) that guides the operation of BLIRNET and controls the flow of information through the system.

In its typical working condition, when MORSEL is shown a display of two words, *pea* and *boy*, a pattern of featural activity (activated by features such as line segments in four orientations and line-segment terminal detectors) is generated on MORSEL's "retina." The AM then focuses on one retinal region, for example, the word *pea*. Information from this region is processed by BLIRNET, which activates orthographic representations consisting of letter clusters of the target such as **pe*, ***p*, *pea*, **p_a*, **_ea*, as well as perceptually similar clusters such as **pf* and **_er*. Clusters that are mutually compatible, that is, do not conflict in any position (such as *pea* and ***p*, ***p* and **pe*, *pea* and *ea**), are connected by excitatory connections whereas letter clusters that are incompatible and mutually exclusive are connected by inhibitory connection (e.g., ***p* and **r* are incompatible and mutually exclusive). The weights between letter clusters are gradually adjusted until the PO net settles on a plausible and coherent interpreta-

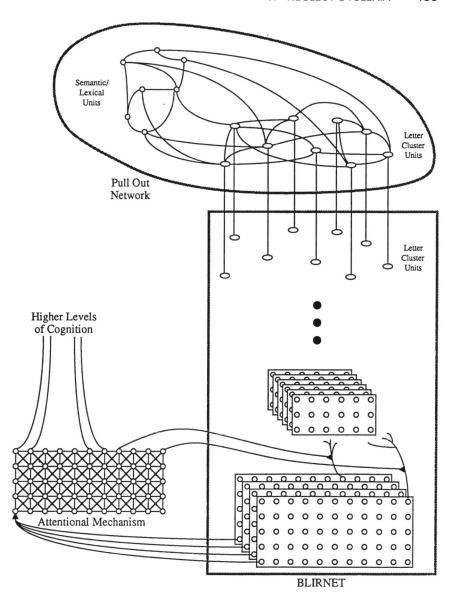

FIG. 7.3.   A sketch of the essential components of MORSEL.

tion of the activated clusters. The settling process is based partly on the bottom-up data but is also assisted by higher order knowledge about valid English words, which is stored in the semlex (semantic-lexical) units. The semlex units provide a higher order linking or statistic of the letter clusters, which then biases the selection of the PO net. When a consistent response has been obtained, the identity of the word is encoded independently of the corresponding location information, which is held by the AM. Next, attention shifts to *boy* and the process is repeated. Thus, the higher order knowledge can feed down onto the perceptual input from BLIRNET and can assist in the interpretation of the incoming information, much as in the case of the Interactive Activation Model.

The critical feature of MORSEL for neglect dyslexia is the AM. The AM receives input from two sources about where to focus. First, attention is guided in a bottom-up manner by stimulus information so selection is biased toward locations in which stimuli appear. Second, higher levels of cognition can supply top-down control on the basis of task demands or expectancies. For instance, if the task instruction is to report the left word first (as in the task with S2 described earlier), selection can be biased in that direction. Once the AM resolves conflicting suggestions about where to focus, a "spotlight," centered on the selected region, is constructed. The spotlight enhances the activation of input features within its bounds relative to those outside. In this way, the AM causes preferential processing of some items, but does not act as an all-or-none filter. As shown in Fig. 7.3, the AM is a set of units in one-to-one correspondence with the retinal feature maps that serve as the input to BLIRNET. Activity in an AM unit indicates that attention is focused on a corresponding retinal region and serves to gate the flow of activity through BLIRNET. Activity of input units in a given location is transmitted with a probability monotonically related to the activity of the AM for that unit. Thus, activations from unattended regions are not inhibited but are transmitted with a lower probability. As activity is propagated through the network, the enhanced region maintains its highlighted status and is consequently chosen by the PO net.

Three properties of the AM turn out to be essential in accounting for the behavior of neglect dyslexia patients:

1. Attention selection by location occurs early in the course of processing.

2. Attention attempts to select a single item. In this regard, a single item is defined as a relatively dense conglomeration of features separated from other features by a relatively sparse region. This crude division on the basis of features does not always suffice but it allows for early segmentation of the image without higher order knowledge.

3. Attention gates the flow of activity through BLIRNET; unattended information receives some analysis because its featural activity is relatively attenuated but not fully suppressed.

A final property of MORSEL is critical in the explanation of neglect dyslexia. After the perceptual data have been processed by BLIRNET in a bottom-up fashion, the clean-up PO net acts on the resulting representation to recover information that is orthographically and semantically meaningful. This clean-up mechanism can compensate for noise and inaccuracy in the recognition system by completing the perceptual pattern using long-term knowledge learned by MORSEL (see Mozer, 1987, 1991, for details on training) and encoded in the weights.

Damaging MORSEL to Produce to Neglect Dyslexia

Damage to the AM involves lesioning the bottom-up connections to the AM from the input feature maps (see Fig. 7.3). The damage to these connections is graded monotonically to reflect the attentional gradient thought to underlie neglect, that is, most severe damage at the extreme left and least severe on the right. The consequences of the damage is to affect the probability that features present on the input maps are detected by the AM. At the left edge of MORSEL's retina, the probability of features being transmitted was 48% and this increased by 2% with each successive pixel location to the right up until a maximum of 90%. To the extent that features are not detected (usually on the left), the AM will fail to focus attention at that location. Damage to the retina itself, rather than to the bottom-up connections, would be more analogous to a field defect or primary sensory problem rather than an attentional one. With this attentional gradient in place, the simulations were conducted.

MORSEL Simulations

Simulations of the AM: Early Attentional Effects.   The first simulation primarily demonstrates the effect of the attentional lesion on the incoming perceptual information, reflecting the neglect pattern. The following data show the extinction or neglect of the left-sided word of a pair of simultaneously presented three-letter words. Neglect of the left-sided item of two simultaneously appearing stimuli is consistent with the view that the visual attentional system attempts to select only one of multiple items in the visual field; in neglect patients, the selection is heavily biased toward the rightmost item. An "item" here is simply defined by the physical adjacency of its components and physical distinctiveness from its neighbors. MORSEL's AM operates exactly in this manner. In the unlesioned model, when any two three-letter words are presented to the AM, attention selects the left word on 41.3% of trials and the right on 40.8%; some combination of the two words is selected on the remaining 17.9% of trials. In the lesioned model, the right word is nearly always selected (88.9%) because the bottom-up input to the AM from the retinotopic feature maps is degraded for the left word, thereby weakening its support. Figure 7.4 illustrates the bottom-up input detected by the lesioned AM upon presentation of two three-letter words (e.g., *sun fly*).

Two regions of activity are apparent in Fig. 7.4, corresponding to the two words but the left-sided region is weaker. The consequence of this left-sided degradation can be seen in Fig. 7.5, which shows the activities of the AM over a

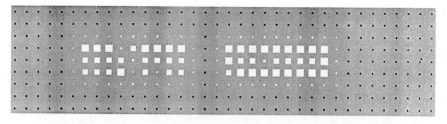

FIG. 7.4. Bottom-up input for two three-letter words detected by the lesioned AM. The area of a white square at a given location in Fig. 7.4 indicates the relative strength of the input at that location in the retinotopic map. The black dots indicate the locations in the map for which there is no input.

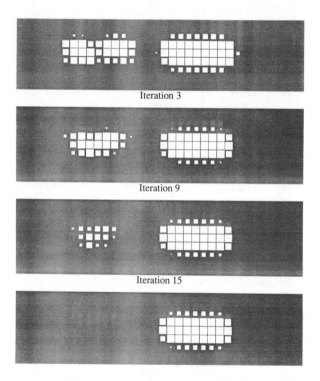

Iteration 3

Iteration 9

Iteration 15

FIG. 7.5. Activities of the AM units over time (under damage) as the right-hand word is selected. At iteration 20, the spotlight forms around the right-hand word and selection is achieved.

TABLE 7.2
Distribution of Attention in the
Lesioned AM for Displays Containing Two
Three-Letter Words (Such as SUN FLY)

Letters Attended	Relative Likelihood of Attentional State
1 2 3 4 5 6	6.6%
2 3 4 5 6	9.7%
3 4 5 6	0.1%
4 5 6	76.2%
5 6	7.2%
6	0.2%

series of iterations (from iteration 3) until the AM settles on the right-sided word (iteration 20) at which time equilibrium is reached and a choice (attentional selection) made.

The distribution of attention in the lesioned model for displays containing two three-letter words was sampled over 1,000 trials (see Table 7.2 for results). Each row of the table indicates the percentage of presentations in which a given combination of letters is selected. "1," "2," and "3" are letters of the left word; "4," "5," and "6" are letters of the right word.

As can be seen from Table 7.2, the right word is selected over 75% of the time, with the remainder of the presentations involving selection of the right word along with the rightmost portions of the left, or selections of only the rightmost portions of the right word. The AM clearly demonstrates extinction of the left item when two words are presented. However, extinction does not occur when the left word is presented alone: The entire word is attended 86% of the time, and its rightmost portion is attended the remaining 14% of the time. Unlike the normal model, which tends to alternate in its selection of the side of the stimulus, the left-sided word in the lesioned model is unlikely to attract attention.

The lesion also affects the distribution of attention even within a single word. Table 7.3 summarizes the distribution of attention for a single six-letter word presented to the AM. The percentages reflect the likelihood of the letters being attended out of a series of 1,000 trials. As is evident from this table, letters appearing in positions 4–6 (row 4 of the table) are most likely to receive attention. Some spillover to the neighboring positions is noted, with letters appearing in position 3 also receiving attention on a high proportion of the trials. Neglect of letters in positions 1 and 2 is clear because they receive attention only on a small proportion of the trials. The difference in distribution between two three-letter words (Table 7.2) and a single six-letter word (Table 7.3), especially for the letter in position 3, comes from the finding that the AM only selects a single item; in the two three-letter word simulation, the letter in position 3 is not selected. In

TABLE 7.3
Distribution of Attention in the Lesioned AM
for Displays of a Single Six-Letter Stimulus

Letters Attended	Relative Likelihood of Attentional State
1 2 3 4 5 6	8.1%
2 3 4 5 6	14.6%
3 4 5 6	30.1%
4 5 6	33.0%
5 6	13.9%
6	0.3%

contrast, it is selected more often when in the context of a single six-letter word. This finding is consistent with the result described in neglect patients who show less intraword extinction or neglect than interword extinction (Behrmann, Moscovitch, & Mozer, 1991; Sieroff, 1991; Sieroff & Michel, 1987).

Although the AM spotlight forms around only one region, the information from the unattended region is not obliterated, but only attenuated, and MORSEL may still detect the unattended information. This depends on the operation of the PO net, which attempts to combine the outputs of BLIRNET into a meaningful whole. Thus, one cannot directly translate the distribution of attention in the AM into a distribution of MORSEL's responses. Nonetheless, the strong right-sided bias will surely affect responses, particularly for simple stimuli that cannot benefit from the PO net's application of higher order knowledge. For instance, in the task of detecting a single flash of light or a pair of simultaneously presented flashes, which are commonly used to test extinction and in which the PO plays no role, responses can only be based on the stimulus strength following attenuation by the AM. In order to see the full effect of the lesion on MORSEL, simulations of the entire system, including the PO net, need to be done. An example of one such simulation appears in the next section. This simulation shows how a lesion to the bottom-up connections that draw attention to a specific region of the retina affects the operation of the AM. What remains to be seen is how such damage affects the final response of MORSEL. The next simulation then illustrates the operation of the word recognition component (including the PO net and the influence of the semlex units), reflecting the interaction between bottom-up and top-down factors in neglect dyslexia.

Simulations of Higher Order Effects in the Lesioned Model.   The simulations described in the previous section illustrate the operation of the AM rather than the overall output of MORSEL. In the following simulations, the response of MORSEL (under AM damage) to various types of stimuli is demonstrated and compared to the pattern of findings observed with the patients. The simulation described next corresponds to the experiment conducted with the patients in which compound and noncompound words are presented for oral reading and extinction is assessed as a function of morphemic status. Both patients showed less extinction in the case of compound words (for S2, this occurred only when attention was manipulated to the left). On the basis of this finding, an interaction between the low-level perceptual input and the influence of higher order knowledge was proposed. In this simulation, the ability of MORSEL to report the leftmost of two words is also influenced by the lexical relationship between the two items. When two items (e.g., *cow boy*) are presented to the lesioned AM, usually the right word is selected (75% of trials). Consequently, BLIRNET strongly activates the clusters of BOY and partially activates the clusters of COW. Because BLIRNET has some difficulty keeping track of the precise ordering of letters, it also weakly activates clusters representing a slight rearrangement of the stimulus letters at the boundaries of the two items (such as *owb* and *wb_y*). These boundary clusters support the full word *cowboy*. The overall pattern of letter cluster activity is thus consistent with *cowboy* as well as with *boy*. Because both of these are real words and thus receive support from the semlex units, the PO net can potentially read out either of them; thus, in the case of *cowboy,* the left morpheme may be read out along with the right. When the morphemes cannot be combined to form a word (as in the case of *sun fly*), however, the semlex units do not support the joined morpheme response, and the PO net is unlikely to read out the two morphemes together. In this way, the bottom-up extinction or selection of the right-sided word is offset by the higher order knowledge, provided that the two morphemes can form a real word with prior lexical representation.

There is another avenue by which the left morpheme may be read out: The patients may be able to shift attention covertly to the left and reprocess the display. This seems a likely possibility because all trials contained two words and the patients' task was to report the entire display. Although the patients were not explicitly told that two words were present, the observation of both words on even a few trials may have provided sufficient incentive to try reporting more than one word per trial. The patients may therefore have had a top-down control strategy to shift attention leftward. MORSEL is likewise able to refocus attention to the left on some trials using top-down control illustrated in Fig. 7.3 (higher levels of cognition). This, however, will cause an increase in reports of the left morpheme both for related and unrelated stimulus pairs.

The 12 word pairs used in the stimulation were taken from the experiment conducted with the patients. Compound words consist of related morphemes whereas unrelated morphemes make up the noncompound condition. Each stimulus was presented 100 times in each attentional state, that is, with attention being directed to letters 1–6, to letters 2–6, to letters 3–6, and so on, to obtain a probability of reporting the joined morpheme (e.g., *cowboy* or *sunfly*) conditional upon the attentional state. In order to obtain a true estimate of MORSEL's

COW BOY

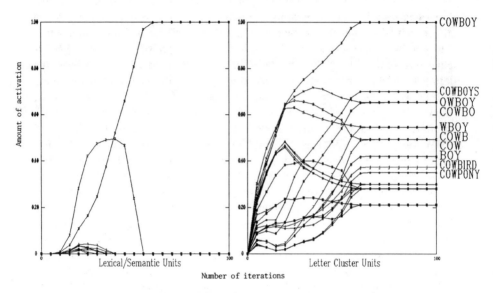

FIG. 7.6.   Activity in the PO net (under damage) as a function of time where the AM has focused on BOY of the stimulus COW BOY. The PO net reads out COWBOY.

response, however, the probability of being in a given attentional state needs to be factored in and thus the conditional probabilities of information reported were then combined with the probability of being in a given attentional state (Table 7.2) to obtain overall response rates. The left morpheme was reported correctly 14.1% on compound words but only on 2.8% of unrelated noncompound words. Even though the exact numbers are small, these findings demonstrate that the strength of lexical/semantic knowledge is sufficient to recover the extinguished information on the left for two morphemes that can be combined to form a word. This, however, does not hold for those pairs that cannot be combined into a single word.

The operation of the PO net on a compound word is illustrated in Fig. 7.6. This shows a graph of activity over time for the semlex units and letter cluster units for the item *cow boy* on a trial where attention of the AM is directed only to *boy* (depicted by the underline on *boy* at the top of the figure). Despite the right-sided selection of attention, the semlex units of *cowboy* and the partial activation from the left morpheme converge eventually to cause the PO net to read out *cowboy* (seen by the highest level of activation in both the letter cluster units and the semlex units).

Assuming that top-down control of the AM allows MORSEL to shift attention to the left and to reprocess the display on some proportion of the trials, say 10%, a good quantitative fit to the data is obtained. This raises the total percentage of trials in which the left morpheme is reported to 24.1% for compound words and 12.8% for noncompound words. These results are in line with S1's data (28% and 9%). Interestingly, on trials in which just the right morpheme is reported, MORSEL occasionally produces left-neglect errors, for example, reporting *roy* for *boy*. S1 produced similar errors. Thus, both left-item interword and left-sided intraword neglect (Sieroff, 1991) can be observed on a single trial. This simulation reveals the interaction between the operation of the attentional mechanism and the PO net most dramatically. Even when a single one of two simultaneous items is selected, both items may be reported and extinction of the left-hand item resisted, provided that higher order lexical/semantic representations exist.

Most of this section has been devoted to simulating S1 who shows the higher order effects rather than S2 who has not demonstrated the effects to the same degree. S2's behavior can also be simulated in the same network in the following way. A more severe attentional gradient would be imposed on the attentional system and information appearing on the left would be transmitted with low probabilities. When this left-sided information is weakly activated, letter clusters for the left side of the stimulus would not be activated and the PO net would not be able to clean up or interpret the left side of the display. Provided that there was some minimal amount of left-sided processing, this might suffice to yield the word/nonword differences produced by S2. The left-sided processing, however, would not be strong enough to produce the other higher order effects.

This computational account of neglect dyslexia has provided considerable explanatory power in accounting for a range of complex neuropsychological phenomena. The simulations have provided a means for mimicking neglect dyslexia and for demonstrating how a range of behaviors could feasibly arise in a single system. Although the behavior of MORSEL is consistent with that of the patients, the claim is not that the underlying mechanism is identical in the two. Rather, MORSEL has provided a comprehensive characterization and theoretical account of a set of neuropsychological phenomena. The model proposed thus far suggests that neglect dyslexia is determined by an interaction between degraded perceptual input caused by an attentional deficit and top-down processes. The primary attentional impairment takes the form of a left–right gradient of attention and information appearing on the right-hand side is processed accurately. Based on this interactive account, there are two main predictions. The first is that the left-sided information, which does not fall in the region of optimal attention distribution, is also processed. The second claim is that this degraded or attenuated contralesional information may be fully recovered through the assistance of top-down processes. This top-down assistance, however, is only helpful in those instances where lexical representations exist. If there are no existing lexical entries, as in the case of nonwords, the benefit from higher order knowledge is not obtained.

Evidence for the Interactive Account from Normal Subjects

The final set of data to be examined in this chapter are those collected from an experiment designed to test the aforementioned predictions in a group of normal subjects (Behrmann et al., 1991). The subjects' attention was directed to one part of the stimulus (as is the case with neglect dyslexia subjects) and then the effect of the "to-be-ignored" or distracting information on performance was measured. Although it was unlikely that normal subjects would restrict their attentional focus as narrowly as neglect subjects, biasing attention to the right might produce the same pattern, but not degree, of reading impairment in normal people as in neglect patients. If this were the case, it would provide a further opportunity for observing the predicted interaction between attention and word recognition. The prediction was that even when attention was drawn to the right side, "unattended" information on the left should still have a significant effect on reading performance and higher order influences should still be observed.

Methods

Stimuli.   The stimuli used were 384 letter strings, ranging in length from 4 to 10 letters. Half the strings were real words whereas the other half were orthographically legal nonwords. In each word, some subset of the letters, ranging in length from three to six letters on the right-hand side was underlined. On half the trials, the underlined target was a real English word, whereas on the other half it was an orthographically legal nonword. A 2 × 2 orthogonal design with lexical status of the whole stimulus or context (word or nonword) crossed with lexical status of the underlined target (word or nonword) was used. Ninety-six stimuli were drawn from each of the following conditions: (a) WORD-IN-WORD: for example, f*arm*; (b) WORD-IN-NONWORD: for example, g*arm*; (c) NONWORD-IN-WORD: for example, e*ast*; and (d) NONWORD-IN-NONWORD: for example, w*ast*. On half the word-in-word trials, the frequency of occurrence of the target word was greater than that of the context word, whereas on the second half, the reverse was true. Mean frequency of the target words was 37 per million (*SD* 34) and mean frequency of the context words was 19 per million (*SD* 78) (Francis & Kučera, 1982).

The stimuli were presented for an unlimited duration on a video screen driven by an IBM microcomputer in amber writing against a black field. Subjects viewed the display binocularly at a distance of approximately 40 cm. Each trial began with the presentation of a centrally placed fixation asterisk that appeared for 500 ms followed by a 500-ms delay. The subjects were instructed to attend to the underlined portion and to indicate whether it constituted a real word or not by pressing the left or right button with the index and middle finger of the dominant hand. The "yes" and "no" buttons were counterbalanced across subjects so that half responded "yes" with the middle finger and half responded "yes" with the index finger. Speed and accuracy of responding were emphasized. Reaction time (RT) was measured using a millisecond clock. The interval between trials, measured from response, was 2 s. A practice block containing 16 novel items, 4 drawn from each condition, was presented first and feedback was given. The 96 stimuli from each of the four conditions were randomized and presented as four blocks of 96 items. All subjects saw all blocks although order of presentation was counterbalanced across subjects.

To demonstrate that the attentional cue was indeed effective in getting subjects to shift their attention to the right, a concurrent dot detection task was included alongside the lexical decision task. The dot detection manipulation draws on the finding that information processing is facilitated when attention is selectively cued to a particular location in visual space prior to the appearance of the target stimulus (Eriksen & Hoffman, 1973; Posner, 1988; Posner, Cohen, & Rafal, 1982). The prediction was that if attention was being selectively cued by the underline bar, information appearing concurrently with the letter string should be processed faster when it fell in the same region as the underline cue than when it fell in the nonunderlined portion of the letter string. An additional 60 letter strings were included in the lexical decision task specifically for the dot detection task. These 60 letter strings appeared simultaneously with a small black dot (located approximately 1 mm above the stimulus) that remained on the screen for 67 ms and then disappeared, leaving the letter string exposed for an unlimited duration. On 30 of the 60 stimuli, the black dot appeared in the region of the underlined section, whereas on the remaining trials it appeared in the nonunderlined region. The exact location of the dot was distributed evenly across all letters of both the underlined and nonunderlined portions of the string. The 60 dot trials were equally divided between the four conditions and randomly presented in the four lexical decision blocks. The subjects were instructed to respond immediately if they detected a small black dot and to forego the lexical decision task. If the trials did not contain a dot, the subjects were to make a lexical decision response. Thus, in addition to the yes/no keys pressed with the right hand (counterbalanced side), the subjects pressed a single key with the left hand for the dot detection. Eight Psychology 100 subjects (five women) participated in this experiment.

Results and Discussion.   On the concurrent dot detection task, subjects failed to detect the dot on less than 6% of the trials. Subjects detected dots appearing in underlined regions significantly faster (mean 490.8 ms) than when the dots appeared elsewhere (mean 539.2 ms) [$t(1,7) = 3.26$, SE = 1.2, $p < .01$]. The results of the subject analysis were confirmed by an item analysis [$t(1,59) = 2.9$, SE = .36, $p < .02$]. The relatively high RTs for the subjects may be attributable to the fact that they were performing two tasks concurrently and were unsure whether or not a dot would appear on each trial. The finding of superior performance of detecting the dot in the attended region suggests that attention is indeed being selectively cued to the right side of the stimulus and that preferential processing is assigned to information appearing on that side.

The analysis of the lexical decision task (see Fig. 7.7) revealed a significant interaction between the lexical status of the underlined item and the status of the whole string [$F(1,7) = 7.8$, MSe = 824.4, $p < .05$] with the effect of the whole string being more marked when the underlined target was a word. Thus, the difference between word-in-word (e.g., f<u>arm</u>; mean 825.2 ms) and word-in-nonword (e.g., g<u>arm</u>; mean 758.5 ms) was greater than the difference between nonword-in-word (e.g., e<u>ast</u>; mean 971.5 ms) and nonword-in-nonword (e.g.,

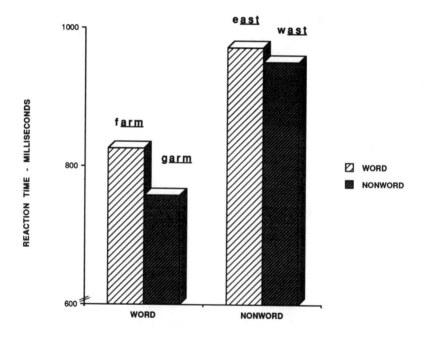

FIG. 7.7. Mean RT (in ms) for normal subjects to make lexical decisions to right-sided underlined word and nonword targets as a function of lexical status of the whole string.

b*ast*; mean 950.4 ms). The main effects of target [$F(1,7) = 50.7, p < .001$] and of whole string [$F(1,7) = 5.9, p < .05$] were also significant. The item analysis confirmed the main effects (underlined target [$F(1,190) = 9.3, p < .001$]; whole string [$F(1,190) = 6.1, p < .05$]), but not the interaction [$F(1,190) = 2.4, p > .05$].

The error analysis across subjects and across items failed to reveal any significant effects for the underlined target or the whole string. Overall, the results from this experiment suggest that even when attention is biased to one side, the information appearing on the opposite side still influences performance. Also, as predicted, the lexical status of the distracting information appears to play a significant role in lexical decision. This result is consistent with the findings from the patient and MORSEL data; the effect of lexical representation or status observed in *cowboy* mirrors that of the word-in-word (and nonword-in-word) condition whereas absence of a prior lexical entry as in *sunfly* is similar to the reduced effect of left-sided information in the word-in-nonword (and nonword-in-nonword) condition.

The results from the experiments with the normal subjects support the interactive account of neglect dyslexia. Information that is not selectively attended is still processed and affects lexical decisions to the attended portions of letter strings. Furthermore, the influence of later, higher order variables is also observed such that performance is affected by the lexical status of the distracting information. To integrate the results from the normal subjects more closely with the interactive explanation, the same experiment conducted with the normal subjects was run with MORSEL. Twelve words from the word-in-word condition of the aforementioned experiment were selected with length of the whole and the underlined component systematically varied (e.g., f*arm*, c*lock*, e*state*, and ce*real*). Rather than generating different stimulus sets for the other three conditions, the same stimuli were used but the whole or context and/or the underlined target were classified as nonwords depending on the condition they fell into. This is possible because a word is distinguished from a nonword in MORSEL only because words are associated with corresponding semlex units. Thus, by simply removing the semlex units for the target to the word in the word-in-word condition, stimuli are transformed into nonword-in-word stimuli, and so forth. The attentional focus was set to correspond to the underlined region of the target and the average number of cycles required for the PO net to settle in each condition was calculated over 100 presentations for each stimulus. This measure is taken as an analogue of reaction time in human subjects. Because the task was lexical decision, some additional assumptions and processes were included such as a verification process and a measure of equilibrium or the point at which minimal changes are observed in the network (settling time). Figure 7.8 shows the average number of cycles required for the PO net to settle as a function of stimulus condition.

The data from the PO net are in qualitative agreement with the normative RT

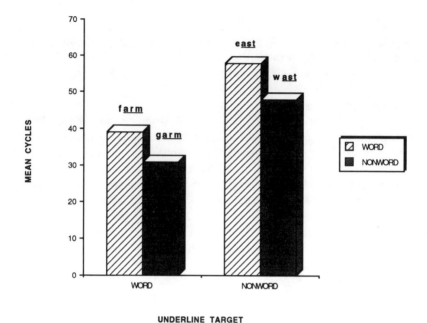

FIG. 7.8.   Mean number of cycles for MORSEL's PO net to settle as a function of lexical status of the whole string.

data in the sense that the rank orderings of the response times are identical; responses to nonword targets are slower than to word targets [$F(1,11) = 42.8, p < .001$], and responses to word distractors are slower than to nonword distractors [$F(1,11) = 13.5, p < .01$], whereas the interaction between target and whole string is not significant [$F(1,11) = 3.3, p < .09$]. These findings, as in the data from the normal subjects, show that even when attention is maximally activated in one region, the minimal activation afforded to the nonattended information is sufficient to allow for processing of the target and the distracting context or whole item. The time taken to settle on an appropriate and stable output leads to an increased number of cycles when the distracting context forms a word, a further illustration of the interactive account of neglect dyslexia.

GENERAL DISCUSSION

The primary goal of this chapter was to examine the neuropsychological phenomenon known as neglect dyslexia in the light of theories of selective visuospatial attention and word recognition. A major issue addressed here concerned the locus of attentional selection, a topic that has generated decades of debate in cognitive psychology. Data from two patients with neglect dyslexia were presented and a theoretical framework was proposed in which attentional selection is thought to take place at an early stage of processing. Evidence for this position comes from demonstrating the influence of the physical features of the stimuli on the patients' reading performance. The attentional disruption takes the form of a left–right gradient in which left-sided information is not abolished but is processed with less accuracy and precision. Support for the gradient hypothesis comes from the same/different and oral report experiments that show optimal attentional processing on the right with gradual decrease from right to left.

How, then, can we explain the effects of higher order variables on neglect dyslexia? If the attentional deficit and gradient is not too severe and left-sided information is registered to a sufficient extent, the processed information may still activate higher order lexical representations. This higher order knowledge may then operate on the encoded perceptual information, cleaning it up and producing the observed higher order effects. The interaction between an attentional deficit and existing knowledge is less obvious when the attentional gradient is severe. Under these conditions, when the left-sided information is so compromised, contact with higher order representations is not possible. In the context of a unitary explanation, then, S1 and S2 are parametric variations of the same underlying attentional disturbance rather than qualitatively different forms of neglect dyslexia. The extent to which the higher order or late effects appear depend on the severity of the primary attentional disturbance.

The explanation just provided is consistent with the theory of attention embodied in MORSEL. First, attention is disrupted at an early stage and affects low-level encoding of information and second, processing is not done in an all-or-none fashion. Provided that sufficient activation is propagated from the left of the retinal display, letter clusters may be generated and fed to the PO net. If the item is a real word, higher order information contained in the semlex units can bias the clean-up process so that even the left side may be accurately recovered. The simulations described earlier show that damage to the connections that draw attention to one side of the display at an early stage of processing has an immediate effect on the AM but also has consequences that permeate up to higher stages.

Based on the observed performance of the patients and of MORSEL, the prediction was that nonattended left-sided stimuli are not entirely ignored but are processed to some extent. Furthermore, the prediction was that the influence of the left-sided information should be more obvious in the case of items that have higher order lexical representations than in the case of items that do not. Studies with normal subjects, using an experimental manipulation in which attention was cued to the right, supported both these predictions. Reaction time to decide whether a right-sided component of a word is an English word or not was slower when the item was embedded in the context of a real word (e.g., f_arm_) than when it was embedded in a nonword (e.g., *garm*). Thus, even when subjects are instructed to ignore the information on the left, it still has an impact on lexical decision times. In a previous experiment, we showed that the presence of any left-sided information slows RT so that decisions to @*arm* are slower than to *arm* (Behrmann et al., 1991). The present experiment, however, reveals a specific effect of the left-sided information; the exact identity of this information is processed so that when the to-be-ignored information is alphabetical (as in f*arm* and g*arm*), there is a differential effect of this left-sided information. Provided the left-sided information constitutes a real word, RT is slowed relative to when it constitutes a nonword, showing that the left-sided information is processed at least to the level of lexical access. The interference observed on the RTs as a function of lexical status of the context reflects the interaction between attention and word recognition suggested by both the patient and MORSEL data.

In summary then, the findings obtained from three empirical sources, patients, MORSEL, and normal subjects, offer strong support for an interactive account of neglect dyslexia. On this account, neglect dyslexia is determined by the degree of attentional impairment operating at an early stage of stimulus representation, as well as by higher order structural and psycholinguistic dimensions of the stimuli that interact with the early representations. This interactional account has now been extended to account for the performance of other patients with hemispatial neglect. BQ (Young et al., 1991) showed visuospatial neglect on object and face recognition under a variety of conditions including brief exposure and varied retinal presentations of the stimulus. Of interest is the fact that BQ, like S1 and S2, showed low-level effects as well; when chimaeric faces were inverted, BQ continued to neglect the side of the chimaeric falling to her left defined from a viewer-centered perspective. Left-sided information, however, could be used if it was critical in determining the identity of an object or face. The authors offer an account of her deficit involving an interaction between moderately defective pickup of left-sided information and preserved access to stored representations of familiar visual stimuli. The interactive account offered here provides a comprehensive explanation of a variety of seemingly contradictory effects observed in hemispatial neglect and neglect dyslexia. Moreover, this account is consistent with, and offers a potential resolution of, the apparently conflicting findings on early versus late selection in normal attentional processing (e.g., see Allport, 1989) and neglect patients (chapter 13 of this volume).

ACKNOWLEDGMENTS

This research was supported by a scholarship and operating grant from the Medical Research Council of Canada. My thanks to Martha Farah, Mike Mozer, Morris Moscovitch, and David Plaut for their comments and suggestions.

REFERENCES

Adams, R. J., Meador, K. J., & Sethi, K. D. (1987). Graded neurological scale for use in acute hemisphere stroke treatment protocols. *Stroke, 18,* 665–669.

Allport, A. (1989). Visual attention. In M. I. Posner (Ed.), *Foundations of cognitive science* (pp. 631–682). Cambridge, MA: MIT Press.

Arguin, M., & Bub, D. (1993). Evidence for an independent stimulus-centered spatial reference frame from a case of visual hemineglect. *Cortex, 29,* 349–357.

Barbieri, C., & De Renzi, E. (1989). Patterns of neglect dissociation. *Behavioral Neuroscience, 2,* 13–24.

Baxter, D., & Warrington, E. K. (1983). Neglect dysgraphia. *Journal of Neurology, Neurosurgery and Psychiatry, 46*(13–24), 1073–1078.

Behrmann, M., Moscovitch, M., Black, S. E., & Mozer, M. (1990). Perceptual and conceptual factors in neglect dyslexia: Two contrasting case studies. *Brain, 113*(4), 1163–1883.

Behrmann, M., Moscovitch, M., & Mozer, M. (1991). Directing attention to words and nonwords in normal subjects and in a computational model: Implications for neglect dyslexia. *Cognitive Neuropsychology, 8*(3/4), 213–248.

Behrmann, M., & Tipper, S. P. (in press). Object-based attentional mechanisms: Evidence from patients with unilateral neglect. In C. Umilta & M. Moscovitch (Eds.), *Attention and performance XV.* Cambridge, USA: MIT Press.

Bisiach, E. (1993). The Twentieth Bartlett Memorial Lecture: Mental representation in unilateral neglect and related disorders. *Quarterly Journal of Experimental Psychology, 46A, 3,* 435–461.

Bisiach, E., Capitani, E., Luzzatti, C., & Perani, D. (1981). Brain and conscious representation of outside reality. *Neuropsychologia, 19,* 543–551.

Bisiach, E., Cornacchia, L., Sterzi, R., & Vallar, G. (1984). Disorders of perceived auditory lateralization after lesions of the right hemisphere. *Brain, 107,* 37–52.

Bisiach, E., Geminiani, G., Berti, A., & Rusconi, M. L. (1990). Perceptual and premotor factors of unilateral neglect. *Neurology, 40,* 1278–1291.

Bisiach, E., Luzzatti, C., & Perani, D. (1979). Unilateral neglect, representational schema and consciousness. *Brain, 102,* 609–618.

Bisiach, E., & Vallar, G. (1988). Hemineglect in humans. In F. Boller & J. Grafman (Eds.), *Handbook of neuropsychology* (Vol. 1, pp. 195–222). Amsterdam, Netherlands: Elsevier Science Publishers.

Black, S. E., Martin, D., & Dywan, C. (1991). Brain behaviour relationships in tactile, auditory, and visual extinction. *Neurology, 41,* 265.

Black, S. E., Vu, B., Martin, D., & Szalai, J. P. (1990). Evaluation of a bedside battery for hemispatial neglect in acute stroke. *Journal of Clinical and Experimental Psychology, 12,* 102.

Broadbent, D. E. (1958). *Perception and communication.* London: Pergamon.

Brunn, J. L., & Farah, M. (1991). The relation between spatial attention and reading: Evidence from the neglect syndrome. *Cognitive Neuropsychology, 8*(1), 59–75.

Bub, D., & Gum, T. (1988). *Psychlab software.* Montreal: McGill University, Neurolinguistics Department.

Butter, C. M., Buchtel, H. A., & Santucci, R. (1989). Spatial attention shifts: Further evidence for the role of polysensory mechanisms using visual and tactile stimuli. *Neuropsychologia, 27*(10), 1231–1240.

Butter, C. M., Kirsch, N. L., & Reeves, G. (1990). The effect of lateralized dynamic stimuli on unilateral spatial neglect following right hemisphere lesions. *Restorative Neurology and Neuroscience, 2,* 39–46.

Caplan, B. (1987). Assessment of unilateral neglect: A new reading test. *Journal of Experimental and Clinical Neuropsychology, 9*(4), 359–364.

Caramazza, A., & Hillis, A. E. (1990a). Spatial representation of words in the brain implied by studies of a unilateral neglect patient. *Nature, 346,* 267–269.

Caramazza, A., & Hillis, A. E. (1990b). Levels of representation, co-ordinate frames and unilateral neglect. *Cognitive Neuropsychology, 7*(5/6), 391–446.

Cohen, J., Romero, R. D., & Farah, M. J. (1992). Disengaging from the disengage function: The relation of macrostructure to microstructure in parietal attentional deficits. *Journal of Clinical and Experimental Neuropsychology, 14,* 1, 49 (abstract).

Cohen, L., & Dehaene, S. (1991). Neglect dyslexia for numbers? A case report. *Cognitive Neuropsychology, 8*(1), 39–58.

Colombo, A., De Renzi, E., & Faglioni, P. (1976). The occurrence of visual neglect in patients with unilateral cerebral disease. *Cortex, 12,* 221–231.

Corbetta, M., Miezin, F. M., Dobmeyer, S., Shulman, G. L., & Petersen, S. E. (1990). Selective attention modulates neural processing of shape, color and velocity in humans. *Science, 248,* 1556–1559.

Costello, A. D., & Warrington, E. K. (1987). The dissociation of visual neglect and neglect dyslexia. *Journal of Neurology, Neurosurgery and Psychiatry, 50,* 1110–1116.

Cubelli, R., Nichelli, P., Bonito, V., De Tanti, A., & Inzhagi, M. (1991). Different patterns of dissociation in unilateral spatial neglect. *Brain and Cognition, 15,* 139–159.

Daffner, K. R., Ahern, G. L., Weintraub, S., & Mesulam, M. M. (1990). Dissociated neglect behaviour following sequential strokes in the right hemisphere. *Archives of Neurology, 28*(1), 97–101.

Denny-Brown, D., Meyer, J. S., & Horenstein, S. (1952). The significance of perceptual rivalry resulting from parietal lesions. *Brain, 75,* 433–471.

De Renzi, E., Gentilini, M., Faglioni, P., & Barbieri, C. (1989). Attentional shifts towards the rightmost stimuli in patients with left visual neglect. *Cortex, 25,* 231–237.

De Renzi, E., Gentilini, M., & Pattacini, F. (1984). Auditory extinction following hemisphere damage. *Neuropsychologia, 22*(6), 733–744.

Desimone, R., Schein, S. J., Moran, J., & Ungerleider, L. G. (1985). Contour, color and shape analysis beyond the striate cortex. *Vision Research, 25*(3), 441–452.

Deutsch, J. A., & Deutsch, D. (1963). Attention: Some theoretical considerations. *Psychological Review, 70,* 80–90.

Ellis, A. W., Flude, B., & Young, A. W. (1987). Neglect dyslexia and the early visual processing of letters in words and nonwords. *Cognitive Neuropsychology, 4,* 439–464.

Eriksen, C. W., & Hoffman, J. E. (1973). The extent of processing noise elements during selective coding from visual displays. *Perception and Psychophysics, 14,* 155–160.

Farah, M. J. (1988). Is visual imagery really visual? Overlooked evidence from neuropsychology. *Psychological Review, 95,* 307–317.

Farah, M. J., Wong, A. B., Monheit, M., & Morrow, L. A. (1989). Parietal lobe mechanisms of spatial attention: Modality specific or supramodal? *Neuropsychologia, 27*(4), 461–470.

Feinberg, T. E., Haber, L. D., & Stacey, C. B. (1990). Ipsilateral extinction in the hemineglect syndrome. *Annual Review of Neuroscience, 47,* 802–804.

Francis, W. N., & Kučera, H. (1982). *Frequency analysis of English usage.* Boston: Houghton Mifflin.

Friedland, R. P., & Weinstein, E. A. (1977). Hemi-inattention and hemisphere specialisation: Introduction and historical review. In E. A. Weinstein & R. P. Friedland (Eds.), *Advances in neurology 18: Hemi-inattention and hemisphere specialisation* (pp. 1–31). New York: Raven.

Friedrich, T. J., Walker, J., & Posner, M. I. (1985). Effects of parietal lesions on visual matching: Implications for reading errors. *Cognitive Neuropsychology, 2,* 253–264.

Fujii, T., Fukatsu, R., Kimura, I., Saso, S., & Kogure, K. (1991). Unilateral spatial neglect in visual and tactile modalities. *Cortex, 27,* 339–343.

Goldman-Rakic, P., & Selemon, L. D. (1986). Topography of corticostriatal projections in nonhuman primates and implications for functional parcellation of the neostriatum. In E. G. Jones & A. Peters (Eds.), *Cerebral cortex* (Vol. 5). New York: Plenum.

Grady, C. L., Haxby, J. V., Horowitz, B., Schapiro, M. B., Rapoport, S. I., Ungerleider, L. G., Mishkin, M., Carson, R. E., Herscovitch, P. (1992). Dissociation of object and spatial vision in human extrastriate cortex: Age-related changes in activation of regional cerebral blood flow measured with [150]-water and positron emission tomography. *Journal of Cognitive Neuroscience, 4,* 1, 23–34.

Halligan, P. W., & Marshall, J. (1989). Perceptual cueing and perceptuo-motor compatibility in visuo-spatial neglect: A single case study. *Cognitive Neuropsychology, 6,* 423–435.

Heilman, K. M., Bowers, D., Coslett, H. B., Whelan, H., & Watson, R. T. (1985). Directional hypokinesia. *Neurology, 35,* 855–859.

Heilman, K. M., Bowers, D., Valenstein, E., & Watson, R. T. (1987). Hemispace and hemispatial neglect. In M. Jeannerod (Ed.), *Neurophysiological and neuropsychological aspects of spatial neglect* (pp. 115–150). Amsterdam, Netherlands: North-Holland.

Heilman, K., Watson, R. T., & Valenstein, E. (1985). Neglect and related disorders. In K. M. Heilman & E. Valenstein (Eds.), *Clinical neuropsychology* (pp. 243–293). New York: Oxford University Press.

Hinton, G. E., & Shallice, T. (1991). Lesioning an attractor network: Investigations of acquired dyslexia. *Psychological Review, 98*(1), 74–95.

Humphreys, G. W., & Riddoch, M. J. (1993). Interactions between object and space systems revealed through neuropsychology. In D. E. Meyer & S. Kornblum (Eds.), *Attention and performance XIV.* Cambridge, MA: MIT Press.

Humphreys, G. W., Riddoch, M. J., & Muller, H. (1991). *Where, what and why: On the interaction between ventral object vision and dorsal space vision in humans.* Manuscript submitted for publication.

Ishiai, S., Sugushita, M., Odajima, N., Yaginuma, M., Gono, S., & Kamaya, T. (1990). Improvement of unilateral spatial neglect with numbering. *Journal of Neurology, Neurosurgery and Psychiatry, 40,* 1395–1398.

Karnath, O. H. (1988). Deficits of attention in acute and recovered hemi-neglect. *Neuropsychologia, 26*(1), 27–43.

Kinsbourne, M. (1975). The mechanism of hemispheric control of the lateral gradient of attention. In P. M. A. Rabbitt & S. Dornic (Eds.), *Attention and performance V* (pp. 81–99). Hillsdale, NJ: Lawrence Erlbaum Associates.

Kinsbourne, M. (1977). Hemi-neglect and hemisphere rivalry. In E. Weinstein & R. Friedland (Eds.). *Hemi-inattention and hemispheric specialization: Advances in neurology 18* (pp. 41–49). New York: Raven.

Kinsbourne, M. (1987). Mechanisms of unilateral neglect. In M. Jeannerod (Ed.), *Neurophysiological and neuropsychological aspects of spatial neglect* (pp. 69–86). Amsterdam, Netherlands: North-Holland.

Kinsbourne, M., & Warrington, E. K. (1962). A variety of reading disability associated with right hemisphere lesions. *Journal of Neurology, Neurosurgery and Psychiatry, 25,* 339–344.

Kolb, B., & Whishaw, I. Q. (1990). *Fundamentals of human neuropsychology.* New York: Freeman.

Làdavas, E. (1987). Is hemispatial deficit produced by right parietal damage associated with retinal or gravitational coordinates. *Brain, 110,* 167–180.

Làdavas, E. (1990). Selective spatial attention in patients with visual extinction. *Brain, 113,* 1527–1538.

Làdavas, E., Del Pesce, M., & Provinciali, L. (1989). Unilateral attention deficits and hemispheric asymmetries in the control of visual attention. *Neuropsychologia, 27*(3), 353–366.

Làdavas, E., Petronio, A., & Umilta, C. (1990). The deployment of attention in the intact field of hemineglect patients. *Cortex, 26,* 307–317.

LePlane, D., & Degos, J. D. (1983). Motor neglect. *Journal of Neurology, Neurosurgery and Psychiatry, 46*, 152–158.

McClelland, J. L. (1979). On the time relations of mental processes: An examination of systems of processes in cascade. *Psychological Review, 86*, 287–330.

McClelland, J. L., & Rumelhart, D. E. (1981). An interactive activation model of context effects in letter perception: Part 1. An account of basic findings. *Psychological Review, 88*(5), 375–407.

McClelland, J. L., Rumelhart, D. E., & Hinton, G. E. (1986). The appeal of parallel distributed processing. In D. E. Rumelhart, J. L. McClelland, & the PDP research group (Eds.), *Parallel distributed processing: Explorations in the microstructure of cognition: Vol. 1. Foundations* (pp. 272–235). Cambridge, MA: MIT Press.

Mesulam, M. M. (1981). A cortical network for directed attention and unilateral neglect. *Annals of Neurology, 10*, 309–325.

Mesulam, M. M. (1983). The functional anatomy and hemispheric specialization for directed attention: The role of the parietal lobe and its connectivity. *Trends in Neurosciences,* September, 382–387.

Mesulam, M. M. (1990). Large scale neurocognitive networks and distributed processing for attention, language and memory. *Annals of Neurology, 28*, 597–613.

Morrow, L. A., & Ratcliff, G. G. (1988). The disengagement of attention and the neglect syndrome. *Psychobiology, 16*, 261–269.

Moscovitch, M., & Umilta, C. (1990). Modularity and neuropsychology. In M. Schwartz (Ed.), *Modular deficits in Alzheimer's disease* (pp. 1–59). Cambridge, MA: MIT Press/Bradford.

Mozer, M. C. (1987). Early parallel processing in reading: A connectionist approach. In M. Coltheart (Ed.), *Attention and Performance XII; The psychology of reading* (pp. 83–104). Hillsdale, NJ: Lawrence Erlbaum Associates.

Mozer, M. C. (1991). *The perception of multiple objects: A connectionist approach.* Cambridge, MA: MIT Press/Bradford.

Mozer, M. C., & Behrmann, M. (1990). On the interaction of selective attention and lexical knowledge: A connectionist account of neglect dyslexia. *Journal of Cognitive Neuroscience, 2*(2), 96–123.

Mozer, M. C., & Behrmann, M. (1992). Reading with attentional impairments: A brain-damaged model of neglect and attentional dyslexia. In R. Reilly & N. Sharkey (Eds.), *Connectionist approaches to natural language processing* (pp. 409–460). Hillsdale, NJ: Lawrence Erlbaum Associates.

Norman, D. (1968). Towards a theory of memory and attention. *Psychological Review, 75*, 522–536.

Ogden, J. A. (1985). Contralesional neglect of constructed visual images in right and left brain-damaged patients. *Neuropsychologia, 23*, 273–277.

Patterson, K. E., Seidenberg, M., & McClelland, J. L. (1989). Connections and disconnections: Acquired dyslexia in a computational model of reading. In R. G. Morris (Ed.), *Parallel distributed processing: Implications for psychology and neuroscience* (pp. 131–181). Oxford, England: Oxford University Press.

Patterson, K. E., & Wilson, B. (1990). A ROSE is a ROSE or a NOSE: A deficit in initial letter identification. *Cognitive Neuropsychology, 7*(5/6), 447–477.

Plaut, D., & Shallice, T. (1993). Deep dyslexia: A case study of connectionist neuropsychology. *Cognitive Neuropsychology, 10*(5), 377–500.

Posner, M. I. (1988). Structures and functions of selective attention. In T. Boll & B. Bryant (Eds.), *Clinical neuropsychology and brain function: Research, measurement and practice* (pp. 173–202). Washington, DC: American Psychological Association.

Posner, M. I., Cohen, A., & Rafal, R. (1982). Neural systems control of spatial orienting. *Philosophical Transactions of the Royal Society of London, 298*, 187–198.

Posner, M., & Petersen, S. E. (1990). The attention system of the human brain. *Annual Review of Neuroscience, 13*, 25–42.

Posner, M. I., Petersen, S., Fox, P. T., & Raichle, M. (1988). Localization of cognitive functions in the human brain. *Science, 240*, 1627–1631.

Posner, M. I., Walker, J. A., Friedrich, F. J., & Rafal, R. D. (1984). Effects of parietal injury on covert orienting of visual attention. *Journal of Neuroscience, 4*, 1863–1874.

Quinlan, P. (1991). *Connectionism and psychology.* Chicago: University of Chicago Press.

Rapp, B., Benzing, L., & Caramazza, A. (1991, May). *Stimulus characteristics and visual neglect.* Poster presented at TENNET, Montreal.

Riddoch, M. J. (1990). Neglect and the peripheral dyslexias. *Cognitive Neuropsychology, 7*(5/6), 369–390.

Riddoch, M. J., & Humphreys, G. W. (1983). The effect of cueing on unilateral neglect. *Neuropsychologia, 21*, 589–599.

Riddoch, M. J., & Humphreys, G. W. (1991). Visual aspects of neglect dyslexia. In D. M. Willows, R. S. Kruk, & E. Corcos (Eds.), *Visual processes in reading and reading disabilities* (pp. 111–136). Hillsdale, NJ: Lawrence Erlbaum Associates.

Riddoch, M. J., Humphreys, G. W., Cleton, P., & Fery, P. (1990). Levels of coding in neglect dyslexia. *Cognitive Neuropsychology, 7*(5/6), 479–518.

Rizzolatti, G., Gentilucci, M., & Matelli, M. (1985). Selective spatial attention: One centre, one circuit or many circuits. In M. I. Posner & O. S. M. Marin (Eds.), *Attention and performance XI* (pp. 251–265). Hillsdale, NJ: Lawrence Erlbaum Associates.

Rizzolatti, G., Scandolara, C., Gentilucci, M., & Matelli, M. (1981). Afferent properties of perarcuate neurons in macaque monkeys. *Behavioural Brain Research, 2*, 147–163.

Rumelhart, D. E., & McClelland, J. L. (1982). An interactive activation model of context effects in letter perception: Part 2. The contextual enhancement effects and some tests and extensions of the model. *Psychological Review, 89*, 60–94.

Seidenberg, M. (1988). Cognitive neuropsychology: The state of the art. *Cognitive Neuropsychology, 5*, 403–426.

Sieroff, E. (1991). Focusing in/on verbal visual stimuli in patients with parietal lesions. *Cognitive Neuropsychology, 7*(5/6), 519–554.

Sieroff, E., & Michel, F. (1987). Visual verbal extinction in right/left hemisphere lesion patients and the problem of lexical access. *Neuropsychologia, 25*, 907–918.

Sieroff, E., Pollatsek, A., & Posner, M. I. (1988). Recognition of visual letter strings following injury to the posterior visual spatial attention system. *Cognitive Neuropsychology, 5*(4), 427–449.

Spiers, P. A., Schomer, D. L., Blume, H. W., Kleefield, J., O'Reilly, G., Weintraub, S., Osborne-Shaefer, P., & Mesulam, M. M. (1990). Visual neglect during intracarotid sodium amobarbitol testing. *Neurology, 40*, 1600–1606.

Sternberg, S. (1969). The discovery of processing stages: Extensions of Donders' method. *Acta Psychologica, 30*, 276–315.

Tipper, S. P. (1985). The negative priming effect: Inhibitory effects of ignored primes. *Quarterly Journal of Experimental Psychology, 37A*, 571–590.

Tipper, S. P., & Driver, J. (1988). Negative priming between pictures and words: Evidence for semantic analysis of ignored stimuli. *Memory & Cognition, 16*, 64–70.

Treisman, A. (1969). Strategies and models of selective attention. *Psychological Review, 76*, 282–299.

Treisman, A. (1977). Focused attention in the perception and retrieval of multidimensional stimuli. *Perception and Psychophysics, 22*, 1–11.

Treisman, A., & Gelade, G. (1980). A feature-integration theory of attention. *Cognitive Psychology, 12*, 97–136.

Ungerleider, L. G., & Mishkin, M. (1982). Two cortical visual systems. In D. J. Ingle, M. A.

Goodale, & R. J. W. Mansfield (Eds.), *Analysis of visual behavior* (pp. 549–586). Cambridge, MA: MIT Press.

Vallar, G., & Perani, D. (1986). The anatomy of unilateral neglect after right-hemisphere stroke lesions: A clinical/CT scan correlation study in man. *Neuropsychologia, 24,* 609–622.

Vallar, G., & Perani, D. (1987). The anatomy of spatial neglect in humans. In M. Jeannerod (Ed.), *Neurophysiological and neuropsychological aspects of spatial neglect* (pp. 235–258). Amsterdam, Netherlands: Elsevier Science Publishers.

Warrington, E. K. (1991). Right neglect dyslexia: A single case study. *Cognitive Neuropsychology, 8*(3/4), 193–212.

Young, A. W., De Haan, E. H. F., Newcombe, F., & Hay, D. C. (1990). Facial neglect. *Neuropsychologia, 28,* 391–415.

Young, A. W., Hellawell, D. J., & Welch, J. (1992). Neglect and visual recognition. *Brain, 115,* 51–71.

Young, A. W., Newcombe, F., & Ellis, A. W. (1991). Different impairments contribute to neglect dyslexia. *Cognitive Neuropsychology, 8*(3/4), 177–191.

III TOP-DOWN PROCESSES IN VISION: ATTENTION AND IMAGERY

8 Visual Attention

Michael I. Posner
Peter G. Grossenbacher
Paul E. Compton
University of Oregon

Attention, like many concepts in psychology, has had a complex of meanings during its history. At the turn of the century the concept was closely related to subjective awareness of the world around us (James, 1890). With the advent of behaviorism, the study of subjective experience was discouraged and studies of attention declined. When attention was reintroduced with the development of information-processing psychology (Broadbent, 1958), studies emphasized the interference between overlapping signal processing and the limited ability to time share between tasks. Although interference between signals remains an important method for indicating attention demands, the idea of a necessary limited-capacity bottleneck became less appealing as psychological theories developed more enthusiasm for massively parallel processing (Allport, 1989). Instead, emphasis has been placed on the necessity to coordinate information in order to limit incompatible responses (Allport, 1989) and reduce cross talk in relaying messages between separate modules (Schneider, 1985).

In empirical studies, evidence for selection of some portions of input for higher processing has remained a stubborn fact (Bourke, 1991; Posner, 1982). In recent years the concept of attention has derived its meaning in contrast to the idea of a purely automatic processing that occurs without attention. Although the reasons for automaticity and appropriate indicants for it remain quite controversial, this dichotomy has continued to play an important role in defining attention (Logan, 1988; Posner, 1982). The varying definitions of attention, its relation to subjective concepts, and the tendency to use attention as an explanatory principle rather than as something that itself must be explained have all led to the thought that the concept of attention is necessarily vague and may not even have explicit mechanisms (Neisser, 1976).

This situation has changed dramatically in the last few years as some of the neural systems underlying attention have become understood (LaBerge, 1990; Näätänen, 1990; Posner & Petersen, 1990; Posner, Petersen, Fox, & Raichle, 1988). By means of a cognitive neuroscience approach it is now possible to view attention as a neural system for the selection of information similar in many ways to the visual, auditory, or motor systems. Like vision, attention involves a complex of networks that perform particular operations or computations. These networks can be specified anatomically in terms of the neural areas involved. The computations can be specified, like all cognitive operations, in terms of the transformation between input and output to a given processor. As is true for the visual and auditory systems we do not yet know all of the neural areas involved, nor can we always specify how the operations are performed in synaptic terms, but the way seems to be open for acquisition of more refined knowledge at all levels. It is not clear how many attentional networks there are, but in previous work we have discussed three such networks: for visual orienting, for detecting targets, and for maintenance of the alert state (Posner & Petersen, 1990).

In this chapter we are concerned mainly with reviewing evidence that supports the network approach. For illustrative purposes, the network chosen for review is the one that selects information from visual locations. This visual orienting network is used to illustrate how attention can be studied in terms of the functional anatomy, circuitry, development, and pathologies. This selection of topics is designed to foster the analogy to vision or audition, which can also be examined in each of these ways. One of the most important aspects of the evidence that we consider is the convergence of many different methods. Convergence of this sort is particularly important for cognitive neuroscience because it is important to be able to coordinate animal studies that give promise of anatomical specificity and human studies that can observe how the network operates within the time constraints of cognitive tasks. Recent studies using positron emission tomography (PET) and studies of patients with known areas of damage have allowed us to examine the general anatomical areas involved when humans carry out tasks involving spatial selection and the links between this anatomy and cellular studies of alert monkeys.

FUNCTIONAL ANATOMY

A remarkable aspect of the studies using PET during cognitive tasks has been the clear evidence for localization of component mental operations (Posner et al., 1988). There have now been replicated studies showing very restricted localization in such visual tasks as detection of color, form, and motion (Corbetta, Miezin, Dobmeyer, Shulman, & Petersen, 1990; Zeki et al., 1991), integrating visual letters into words, obtaining word names, and producing their semantic associates (Frith, Friston, Liddle, & Frackowiak, 1991; Petersen, Fox, Miezin, & Raichle, 1988; Petersen, Fox, Snyder, & Raichle, 1990).

Studies of orienting attention to visual locations have found parietal activation (Corbetta, Meizin, Shulman, & Petersen, 1993) when subjects attend to spatial locations, and pulvinar activation (LaBerge & Buchsbaum, 1990) when they select a location from competing information at other locations. These brain areas provide component operations that comprise part of the posterior attention system underlying visual spatial selection (Posner & Petersen, 1990). The act of detecting targets irrespective of input modality seems to be invariably accompanied by activation in the anterior cingulate gyrus, a cortical region that is also active during Stroop conflict (Pardo, Pardo, Janer, & Raichle, 1990), and passive perception of auditory words (Petersen, Fox, Posner, Mintun, & Raichle, 1989) and of painful stimuli (Talbot et al., 1991). Alternating bands of connectivity between this area and both parietal and dorsolateral prefrontal cortex (Goldman-Rakic, 1988) make this area a likely candidate for providing circuitry controlling the operation of the posterior attention system based on planning operations that could be provided by frontal areas. This anterior attention system is also involved in tasks not involving spatial selection, and there is some evidence that the posterior attention system may not always work in close coordination with this anterior circuitry.

Most of the PET studies involve the measurement of cerebral blood flow within relatively restricted areas of the brain. There is good evidence from studies of retinal mapping (Fox, Miezin, Alklman, Van Essen, & Raichle, 1987) that these areas of blood flow do follow quite well changes in neural activity where we have sufficient information to relate to the two. Thus there is good reason to believe that changes in blood flow reflect neural activity whether inhibitory or excitatory. Of course, measurements of these forms of activation have thresholds, which may be rather high. Thus failure to detect activation in an area certainly does not mean that no computations are occurring there. There are also cases in which significant reductions in blood flow, suggesting that tasks may induce a reduction of neural activity within restricted areas (Frith et al., 1991). The relationship of these anatomically restricted computations to underlying synaptic activity remains to be worked out. Fortunately, in the area of visual attention, the close relation between results with alert monkeys and humans should allow such understanding to occur, but that largely remains for the future.

The localization found in most recent PET studies rests upon subtracting two tasks, one called experimental and the other control. With this subtractive method the central tendency of differences found between conditions can be localized within a few millimeters. On the other hand there are also criticisms of subtractive approaches of this type (Sternberg, 1969). One certainly has to be cautious in trying to attribute functions to a particular activated area. In the language studies reported by Petersen et al. (1988, 1989), there were several tasks (e.g., passive viewing, read aloud, semantic association) allowing different levels of subtraction. It was possible to see if large subtractions (semantic − passive) generated the areas expected by smaller subtractions (read aloud − passive) and no others. It was also possible to ask whether there were significant negative subtractions (passive — read aloud). The absence of these effects in these data helped to make interpretation relatively straightforward. However, there is no question that these interpretations require converging evidence from other techniques.

It is remarkable that at the millimeter range of precision most studies have shown it possible to sum activations over subjects who perform in the same tasks in order to obtain significance. This suggests that even high-level semantic tasks have considerable anatomical specificity in different subjects and is perhaps the most important results of the PET work. Because it is well known that tasks like visual word reading are performed differently by individuals (Baron & Strawson, 1976), it seems most likely that these individual differences may be reflected anatomically at more microlevels than has been currently explored by the PET studies cited.

How can we understand the functional significance of these anatomical areas when we do see them activated? With good luck, the PET studies themselves may suggest likely functions for these areas. For example, when the locus of blood flow moves from one area to another as a stimulus moves from one retinal location to another, it seems reasonable that one is mapping the neural activity related to a retinal location (Fox et al., 1987). Moreover, much is known from cellular studies of the organization of the primate visual cortex and the results can be directly compared with these primate studies.

A similar, although perhaps less compelling strategy has been adopted for the study of visual words (Petersen et al., 1989; Petersen et al., 1990; Posner & Carr, 1991). Of course, there are no cellular studies of visual words, but there is a history of cognitive studies with normal adults and neuropsychological studies with brain-lesioned patients. These studies have been used to infer a functional analysis of these anatomical areas. In our PET studies of visual word reading there were areas of the left ventral occipital lobe (prestriate) active. It seemed possible that these areas were related to the visual word form (Shallice, 1988). The visual word form is a chunk of visual information that corresponds to the orthography of the word. This would be a strong confirmation of the idea from cognitive studies that visual information is used to compute an orthographic representation. Later studies compared real words, orthographically regular non-words, and consonant strings. The results showed an area of the left ventral occipital lobe that is active for real words and orthographically regular nonwords but not consonant strings, just as would be anticipated by cognitive theory. A later study of visual words by another PET group also showed activity in this ventral occipital lobe area. They used slower presentation and also found active, a more anterior inferior temporal area on the left side (Chertkow, Bub, Evans, Meyer, & Marrett, 1990). One possibility is that the ventral occipital and anterior temporal area share aspects of the visual word form and it is also possible that the more anterior area involves memory processes not active during faster presentation conditions of the earlier study. Further studies are probably necessary to sort through these possibilities, but it is remarkable that they provide strong convergence for strict localization, lateralization, and even probably a similar network of areas.

As in most areas of cognition and neuroscience, new methods become established as their results influence ways of thinking that allow convergence with other sources of information. For visual spatial attention it is possible to compare the newer PET results in systematic ways with decades of work consisting of primate cellular studies and lesion studies of both humans and primates. So far a remarkable degree of convergence has developed that supports a view of attention as an anatomically separate system that interacts with sensory pathways.

Site and Source

A feature of the PET studies has been the separation of anatomical areas during passive processing and those active during tasks that might be said to involve attention. In the neurobiology of vision based on primate studies, there is a well-known distinction between a "what" system (pattern recognition) and a "where" system (localization information) (Ungerleider & Mishkin, 1982). When human subjects are asked to maintain attention at a given location or to select one location from among other competing locations, there is very considerable evidence from both PET and cellular recording methods of activity in a network of areas that include the parietal lobe, pulvinar, and perhaps the superior colliculus (see Posner & Petersen, 1990, for reviews; see also Posner et al., 1988).

There is also clear evidence that lesions of these areas produce specific deficits in processing visual information. Clinically these disorders may be lumped together as involving aspects of "neglect." To study the details of the neglect induced by different types of lesions we have used cueing tasks in which the subject's attention is brought to one location, then the target usually occurs at that location, but sometimes the target occurs at another location. There is a great deal of evidence from normal subjects that this task involves a covert shift of attention from one location in the visual field to another (Posner, 1980). This covert shift is confirmed by advantages of efficiency of target detection when the target is at the location of the cue.

Studies of patient deficits have led to the idea that there are three main operations involved in shifts of attention (Posner et al., 1988). The parietal lobe seems to be involved in higher levels of functioning (LaBerge & Buchsbaum, 1990; Posner et al., 1988). For the attention-shifting task, this has been described as a deficit in disengaging the subjects' attention from a prior source of visual information. The midbrain seems more closely related to the shift of attention from the coordinates of a particular stimulus to those of the target and in inhibiting the former target location once attention is moved elsewhere. The thalamus seems to be involved with the readout of information from the chosen target location. Studies of the details of these computations can probably be better carried on with alert monkeys where the lesion method can be used in conjunction with cellular recording. Although there is already some agreement on the general functions outlined earlier, it is also probable that they are not correct in detail. However, what is most important is that the attentional computations are carried out by a complex but specifiable anatomical network and that each area of the network has its own computations. These principles are applicable to other attention networks and to other cognitive systems as well.

Are the computations of the posterior attention system really attentional? Perhaps they relate only to the location of information and not to the priority selection that is the hallmark of attention. To check on this idea it is important to study a task in which there is complex pattern recognition and observe how attention affects this process. One promising candidate is visual search (Treisman & Gormican, 1988). This task has been studied with normal persons who are cued to attend to a particular location (Prinzmetal, Presti, & Posner, 1986). The major results are very straightforward. When people attend to a location there is more efficient processing of individual features in target detection, but as Treisman has shown the influence of attention is increased when the task requires selection of an item that shares some features with the background. Although attention does influence even simple feature search, it has more major effects upon the search for conjunctions. When subjects with parietal lesions were studied in these same tasks, it was clear that the lesion produced devastating effects upon search rate for conjunctions when they were contralateral to the lesion (Cohen & Rafal, 1991; Friedrich, Walker, & Posner, 1985). Moreover, when cues were placed to draw attention to the contralesional field this deficit was reduced. If cueing is used as a way of studying the posterior attention system, these studies argue that attention has the expected influence upon visual search and that lesions of this system act very much as though the subject was now less able to attend. These results link the functional anatomy of the posterior attention system with visually demanding information-processing tasks and support the view that attention to a visual task involves an interaction with a data-processing module.

These studies also move us well beyond the sterile argument of 25 years about whether attention can affect perceptual processing. There is clear evidence from cellular recording (Moran & Desimone, 1985) and lesion data from V4 in the monkey (Schiller & Lee, 1991), that V4 is one site of action of attention within the visual system. In the PET studies showing amplification in prestriate areas for color, form, and motion, targets occurred at all locations in the display. There was no evidence of activation in the posterior attention system, but basal ganglia and anterior cingulate were activated. Thus the posterior attention system appears specialized for covert orienting of attention to select locations and not other features even of visual stimuli. Amplification of prestriate areas comes from the activity of the parietal lobe when subjects are required to attend to a location or search successive locations, but from more anterior areas (anterior cingulate) when they are required to select on the basis of multiple nonlocation cues. This distinction may relate to results in cognitive studies that location is a very much more powerful cue for visual selection than color or form (Sperling, 1960; Wurst & Sperling, 1992) and the finding that selection by location produces a straightforward amplification of the electrical event related potential (ERP) recorded above prestriate areas (Mangun & Hillyard, 1990), whereas other forms of selection produce different and later (Harter & Aine, 1984) changes in the waveform.

CIRCUIT TRACING

The anatomical separation of the attention system from the pattern recognition system provides an unusual opportunity to study the details of their interaction. If the brain is modular, we now have two anatomically separate modules that are clearly designed to interact. Attention seems to amplify even simple feature detection, whether one measures by reaction time, percentage correct, electrical activity, or blood flow. There is a very important lesson to be learned from this degree of convergence. It has sometimes been argued that although attention can affect visual efficiency it does so only in a relatively indirect way, through a change in the bias or criterion that subjects assume to be typical of the conditions of the experiment. This argument is based upon the distinction between sensitivity (d') and criterion (Beta) statistics of signal detection theory. Indeed, this argument has been going on for nearly 15 years and although recent studies suggest a d' change (Downing, 1988; Hawkins, Luck, Mustapha, Downing, & Woodward, 1990), it is unlikely to be finally settled. If one considers only the cognitive literature the d' versus Beta issue seems a very crucial one. After all, if the change is in the sensory evidence, all subsequent decisions will be changed. If attention merely changes criterion, no change in the perceptual experience is likely. However, now that we know that attentional effects occur as early as V4 and other prestriate areas within the occipital lobe and that patients with damage to the spatial attention system miss signals they are capable of perceiving, it is clear that aspects of the perceptual signal that have important consequences are being changed. Even if changes were not found in d', the perceptual consequences of attentional amplification would still be manifest.

Amplification of the visual signal by attention allows us to attempt to trace the interaction of attention and pattern recognition by observing the aspects of signal processing that are altered when subjects' attention is focused on some aspects of the visual input. Although PET allows us to see the brain areas involved (functional anatomy), only time dynamic measures can provide information on the details of the interaction. Much of the available information comes from studies of cognitive tasks with normal or brain injured subjects. We examine this evidence first. In an effort to obtain closer convergence between the functional anatomy obtained from PET and the patterns of interaction from cognitive studies, we have turned to the use of scalp electrode arrays to determine if the scalp distribution is consistent with the generators obtained from the blood-flow studies. The last part of this section examines the evidence obtained from these studies.

Cognitive Studies

Two major dimensions of control have been attributed directly to the visual spatial attention system. First, attention can be allocated to different coordinates of visual space. This location selection is sometimes called the "spotlight" of attention, and underlies the finding that targets at cued locations are responded to with higher efficiency than targets at uncued locations. Second, the selected spatial scale may involve either local detail or broader global aspects of the visual stimulus. This scale selection is sometimes called the "zoom lens" of attention. When centered at a given location, attention may affect a greater or lesser amount of the visual field depending on this focus. Just how the location selection is related to the selection of global or local aspects of a figure is not completely clear. However, these two aspects of selection must be coordinated. It seems misguided to see these various parameters as in conflict with one another or as competing models of attention. It would also be a mistake to suppose that these parameters are set without regard to what is being recognized. In fact, they seem to interact with the visual scene. In an empty field the fovea appears to play no special role and attention can be moved freely about the field. Empirically, costs are as large for foveal targets when one is cued to the periphery as the reverse (Posner, 1978). In visual search of a cluttered field, the fovea does play a special role, probably because of the acuity demands that arise, and attention is constrained so that the most efficient processing is always close to the fovea. Locus of attentional selection in visual space can be determined by both learning and the currently performed task, such as reading, where attention seems to show a strong bias to the right of fixation when reading English, and the reverse with Hebrew (Pollatsek, Bolozky, Well, & Rayner, 1981). These cognitive findings support a highly interactive model relating attention to pattern recognition.

A major vehicle for the empirical study of the interaction between attention and pattern recognition has been the processing of visual letter strings (see Behrmann, chap. 7, this volume). There are many reasons for this choice. Letters are easy stimuli to produce, they can be searched for or chunked into higher units, and a great deal of interest lies in the distinction between strings of letters that make words and those that do not. Sieroff and Posner (1989) cued subjects to the left or right of a foveal-centered letter string. They found that for strings of consonants, whole reports were greatly biased by the direction of attention, but for orthographically regular wordlike stimuli there was little or no difference. This should not be taken as evidence that the location cue was ineffective at drawing attention to one side when the stimulus was a word. After all, location cues affect the efficiency of processing light flashes, colors, digits, and letters when there is position uncertainty (Posner, 1978). How could they not affect words? Indeed, a considerable effect of cues on the perception of words was found when the words were lateralized and thus their location was unpredictable (Posner, 1987), and this has been confirmed in later more extensive experimentation (Behrman, Moscovitch, & Mozer, 1991). Rather than claiming that the stimulus determined whether a shift in the distribution of attention in visual space following a lateralized precue occurred or not, the Sieroff and Posner argument was that chunking the letters into a word form did not seem to require attention. The basic idea here is that a visual word for a skilled reader is a single item, whereas a four-letter orthographically irregular string is four items. If the word is one item it is not necessary for attention to scan the items in order to integrate their features, although attention might still amplify the chunk for higher priority to later processes. At the time, little was known about how and where such chunking might take place. However, the likelihood that this occurs in the ventral occipital lobe fits well with the idea that it might, like feature registration, be a process in which attention plays only a small role. We know attention is important in the development of visual word forms when adults learn a new language (Givón, Yang, & Gernsbacher, 1990), thus it would seem wrong to suppose that attention cannot affect this level. The argument is that one ought to expect a sparing of this chunking process in skilled readers even when attention is unavailable.

In support of this argument, many patients with lesions of the parietal lobe, who show clear evidence of spatial attention deficits in luminance detection, also have great trouble in conjunction search and letter search contralateral to the lesion, although they show little or no deficit in reporting letters when they make words (Behrman et al., 1991; Brunn & Farah, 1991; Sieroff, Pollatsek, & Posner, 1988). Moreover, there is some evidence that the spatial distribution of attention in these patients may differ for words and nonwords (Brunn & Farah, 1991). Although this conclusion seems to have a great deal of documentation in the literature, there have been some reports of studies in which patients do not show this form of the word superiority effect (Ellis, Flude, & Young, 1987). If we attend to the cognitive neuropsychology literature alone, then things remain ambiguous. However, the convergence with cueing studies of normals and the suggestive neuroanatomy of the process certainly make it reasonable to suppose that patients with attention deficits are getting a benefit from the spared process of chunking into a visual word form. This suggests that, in the skilled reader, attention is more involved with the output of the visual word form computation than the input to it.

The relative independence of visual word forms from attention finds support in two other recent findings. Friedrich, Henik, and Tzelgov (1991) studied normal persons making lexical decisions and found that when the prime had to be searched for a target letter, semantic facilitation was largely blocked, but repetition priming was not changed. Similarly, when subjects are required to shadow a complex message during an interference task, it has been found that semantic priming is greatly reduced but repetition priming is not (Posner, Sandson, Dhawan, & Shulman, 1989). If, as we think reasonable, repetition priming is based on activation of the visual word-form system, then these results suggest that dual tasks that make use of either the posterior (letter search) or anterior (shadowing) attention networks do not affect the ability of visual word stimuli to activate their customary visual pathways and prime visually similar items.

Models of the relation between attention and pattern recognition (LaBerge, 1990; Mozer & Behrman, 1990; Phaf, Van der Heijden, & Hudson, 1990) generally reflect a high degree of interaction between the two systems. They appear to be on the right general track although there is clearly much to be learned about these interactions from new empirical studies. In order for models to be most useful in advancing our understanding in this area, they should attempt to specify influences of both location and scale dimensions of visual spatial selectivity.

Electrical Recording

There is a long history of efforts to record brain potentials during visual word processing (Fischler, 1990). This work has been effective in working on the time course of processing information. However, there are great difficulties in going from the far field potentials measured at the scalp to the underlying generators. During the last few years there has been substantial progress in this effort, with the use of current source density analysis and of algorithms designed to make optimal matches between scalp distributions and underlying generators. These new methods have been applied effectively to the study of visual spatial attention (Harter, Miller, Price, LaLonde, & Keyes, 1989; Mangun & Hillyard, 1990) and are starting to be applied to study the interaction between spatial attention and visual word forms (Compton, Grossenbacher, Posner, & Tucker, 1991; Posner & Carr, 1991).

Recently Mangun and Hillyard (1990) cued subjects to a spatial position and studied the event-related potentials to visual targets at that location in comparison with nonattended locations. They found a clear amplification of the attended signal that started about 80 ms after input. By use of current source density analysis they were able to build up a map of the scalp distribution and potential generators of the amplification. The data clearly suggested a prestriate generator in the hemisphere opposite the target. When the targets differed in color, the location of this generator approximated one of the areas found active in PET studies of selection by color. These data confirm the cellular recording and PET data as suggesting prestriate areas as the site of selection of input information by attention. Moreover, they confirm the time course proposed from cellular studies of attentional effects at about 80–90 ms after input.

What causes the delayed effect in the prestriate area? According to the pro-posal by Posner (1988) and LaBerge (1990), the cue sets up a process involving parietal, midbrain, and pulvinar areas that influences prestriate activation. Due to the lack of precise localization afforded by ERP methodology, there is less than compelling ERP data on the source of these selective effects. Harter et al. (1989) reported slow wave activity recorded maximally over the contralateral parietal lobe during the time the cue was present. Whether this slow wave activity is related to the underlying processes of the posterior attention system is not at all clear, but it is of obvious importance for future research.

Can we relate these attentional effects to the recognition of visual letter strings? There is evidence that selection of different aspects of word information leads to different forms of amplification of the event-related potential (Rugg, 1987). Rugg compared repetition priming with semantic priming. He found that primed letter strings differed from nonprimed ones over the posterior areas of the brain when the priming was by repetition and over the anterior parts when it was by semantics. Moreover, the anterior priming was rather late, peaking at about 500 ms, whereas the posterior priming was early, starting at about 200 ms. There is reason to suppose that the repetition priming involves the visual word-form system. We have shown (Posner et al., 1989) that this form of priming is not affected by shadowing whereas semantic priming is drastically altered. Because repetition priming involves the same pathways for the prime and target and occurs passively, it would be reasonable that the changes would occur in sys-tems sensitive to the visual word form. On the other hand, semantic priming requires information about associations and would seem to require more anterior areas including the semantic network and anterior attentional areas. Thus, the Rugg data fit quite well with the story obtained from the PET functional anatomy.

To test these ideas further, we (Compton et al., 1991) employed arrays of 32 electrodes that allow better ideas of the scalp distribution than had been obtained previously. Our tasks included passive perception, thick letter detection, letter case detection, and lexical decision. The thick letter task was designed to amplify feature-level information. The case detection task was designed to require use of letter-level (conjunction) information and the lexical decision task was thought to involve semantic analysis. Each block of trials included equal numbers of words and consonants strings.

There was good evidence from reaction time (RT) data that the various tasks did tap different forms of search process. All blocks had both four- and six-letter strings displayed centrally. For feature search, RTs for target detection were fastest at fixation and slower as one moved away from fixation. For letter search, however, there was a clear increase of RT from left to right. The lexical decision latencies did not vary as a function of string length.

Our findings so far indicate two close correspondences with the functional anatomy found in the PET studies. First, we found that for the passive condition, the distinction between words and strings is marked first at leads over the occipital and posterior temporal lobes. This occurs about 200 ms after onset. Although both left and right posterior leads showed this effect, there was a small asymmetry consistent with the medial left-hemisphere areas of activation found in PET. These results fit well with Rugg's (1987) finding during repetition priming and support the idea that repetition priming involves the visual word-form system. Second, in addition to the difference between words and strings, another feature of the ERP patterns is a large difference between left and right scalp recordings, centered in the mid-temporal lobe, which starts by 80 ms after stimulus onset regardless of string lexicality (Compton et al., 1991). PET studies (Petersen et al., 1990) showed that both words and consonant strings produced a strong focus of blood flow in the right posterior temporal lobe. It was also found that this area appeared to be related to the analysis of visual features irrespective of the type of input string.

The degree of convergence between PET and ERP results found so far is encouraging. A great deal of additional work must go on. The close agreement between different methods necessitates the ability to precisely translate between the spatial and neuroanatomical frameworks employed by different researchers. The results reviewed in this section show we can use subjects' attention to different aspects of the task to amplify computations. This allows us to trace the time course of these computations and thus develop an idea of the circuitry involved in the task studied.

DEVELOPMENT

Following work on the anatomy and physiology of the visual cortex, important physiological experiments were designed to understand the plasticity of the organization of the visual cortex during early development (Hubel, 1988). A similar strategy for attention would be to examine the development of the attentional network we have been describing. Of course, there is a great deal of interest in infant development and its biology. In part this is because infant studies allow us to observe how temperament and socialization interact. In the first year of life there is a remarkable transition in the infant that is obvious to all observers. An organism largely under the control of others and of its own biological rhythms begins to show "a mind of its own." This form of self-regulation should be closely related to the mechanisms of attention.

With these goals in mind it is important to have a way of linking observations on human infants with the underlying circuitry of attention. Johnson (Johnson, Rothbart & Posner, 1991; see also Johnson, chap. 9, this volume) outlined important concepts for doing so. He stressed the laminar development of the visual system over the first few months of life. As the laminae develop they make possible the transmission of information over particular pathways. The development of these pathways can be observed in the behavior of infants in particular marker tasks. We have exploited this idea to study the development of the posterior attention network (Clohessy, Posner, & Rothbart, 1991; Johnson, Posner, & Rothbart, 1991; Rothbart, Posner, & Boylan, 1990).

Development of Posterior Attention

Our results suggest that the posterior attention system undergoes its most significant development from 3 to 6 months. As one example, consider the phenomenon we call inhibition of return. This is the tendency to avoid returning the eyes or attention to an already inspected location. Our studies in normal subjects and patients suffering from a degenerative midbrain disorder have suggested that this operation involves the superior colliculus (Posner, Inhoff, Friedrich, & Cohen, 1987) and that the necessary and sufficient conditions for obtaining it is for the person to program, but not necessarily to execute an eye movement to a given location (Rafal, Calabresi, Brennan, & Scioloto, 1989).

At 3 months, infants can move their eyes to visual targets in an empty field located 30° from fixation, but they do so in several jerky steps. Unlike adults three month old infants do not seem to have a program for locating the target prior to the start of the eye movement. Rather they appear to search for the target location just as adults do when the field is cluttered with distractors. At 3 months, they are more likely to return their eyes to the same location just fixated than to choose a novel location. By 6 months, eye movements to the target are direct like those of adults. Six-month-old infants also show the preference for the new location (inhibition of return) to about the same degree as adults. These data confirm our previous finding that the superior colliculus is a structure involved, not only in eye movement control, but also in elements of covert attention. Although the visual system of infants relies more on collicular control than is true of adults, the colliculus is itself developing at this age and we can observe this development by studying the computations that it supports.

The widespread influence of attentional systems on overt behavior of adults makes it reasonable to suppose that the maturation of these systems in infants will influence much of their other behavior. The maturation of the posterior attention system appears to support the ability of infants to disengage attention to deal with new targets. During the period from 1 to 4 months, infants show a strong tendency to maintain fixation on visual objects and difficulty in breaking away from them (obligatory looking). When the object is a parent, this is often interpreted as a form of "love" on the part of the infant. When the object is a checkerboard, the inability to disengage may lead to distress. By 6 months, when the disengage operation has matured, the parents tend to employ visual distraction (e.g., blowing bubbles) as a means of soothing. As the infant matures further it becomes important that the means to soothe (e.g., by distraction) comes under their own control.[1]

Adult self-report studies show that the more attentional control they report, the less their experience with negative emotion (Derryberry & Rothbart, 1988), presumably because attention can serve to produce self-distraction. These observations support the importance of understanding the maturation of attentional networks as one way of illuminating the development of self-regulation.

Development of Lexical Access

One of the most remarkable things about the PET data on the visual word-form system that we have been discussing is that one learns to read only at about 5 years of age. At this time there appears to be a reorganization of what is a relatively early part of the visual system. Parts of the occipital lobe become sensitive to the particular organization of English words (native language symbols). Thus the acquisition of initial literacy may be an important model for understanding how a very high-level human skill affects brain organization of both the ventral occipital lobe and the related posterior attention system.

A puzzle that has arisen from the PET studies of visual and auditory words is how the left lateral frontal area claimed to underlie the associations to individual words can be reconciled with the usual claim that the semantics of language involves posterior areas at the parieto-temporal junction (Wernecke's area). It should not be particularly surprising that more than one area of the brain is involved in semantic associations. After all, some 20 retinotopic maps in the posterior cortex of the monkey are thought to perform computation related to visual perception and pattern recognition. Surely there could be more than one brain area underlying human processing of meaning. One possibility is that the left frontal association area is related to single-word association and that it arises in the frontal cortex in early infancy (8–10 months) when the first words are learned, frequently in close connection with gestures (Dore, Franklin, Miller, & Ramer, 1976). Only some 10 months later do infants start using multiword strings. Perhaps the need for memory involved in the use of such strings makes the posterior temporal area a useful one for the assembly of word meanings into phrases. A prediction that would be compatible with this idea is that pathways from frontal to parieto-temporal areas should develop in close connection with the start of multiword phrases. We know of no evidence currently on this possibility. It might also be possible to dissociate the activation of word association to individual items from the ability to assemble meaningful language in adult studies. There is some evidence that lesions of Wernecke's area leave intact the

---

[1]Dr. Mary K. Rothbart developed these ideas on the role of the ability to disengage in infant social-emotional behavior.

priming of individual words while causing a virtual inability to assemble or comprehend meaningful language (Milberg & Blumstein, 1981).

PATHOLOGY

Many neurological and psychiatric disorders have been said to involve pathologies of attention. These include neglect, Balint's syndrome, depression, schizophrenia, attention deficit disorder, anxiety, obsessive-compulsive disorder, and others. However, without a real understanding of the neural substrates of attention, this list has constituted a collection of various unexplained syndromes, without benefiting from a classification scheme that would help determine etiology or treatment. This situation should be changed with the systematic application of our (admittedly primitive) understanding of attentional networks to pathological issues. On this topic we have so far worked mainly on neglect (Posner & Rafal, 1986), schizophrenia (Early, Posner, Reiman, & Raichle, 1989), and attention deficit disorder (Swanson et al., 1991).

In each case we have found it possible to document a deficit in attention that was surprisingly specific and implied a particular anatomical basis for the disorder. In each case the disorder involves portions of the cortex that compute attentional operations, but also abnormal regulation by transmitter systems that influence these computations. This association between neurochemistry and functional brain networks could explain why certain pharmacological interventions can be successful in ameliorating some of these syndromes. Understanding the relation between neurophysiology and network function could reveal the mechanisms by which the brain accomplishes mental operations. To illustrate the general principle involved, this section deals with the way in which the norepinephrine (NE) system interacts with computations of the posterior visual spatial attention system and discusses how these influence neglect.

Previous sections of this article have reviewed the computations of the parietal lobe, pulvinar, and colliculus that constitute the posterior visual spatial attention system. From work in monkeys (Morrison & Foote, 1986) it is known that each of these areas receives a very heavy input of NE from the locus coeruleus. NE input to these areas is much greater than to the classical geniculo-striate pathway or to the areas along the ventral pathway from primary visual cortex to the inferior temporal lobe visual areas. This anatomy corresponds well to a view of visual pattern recognition put forward many years ago based solely on cognitive experiments (Posner, 1978). This view suggests that arousal, such as induced by task-relevant warning signals, influences the operation of attention but has relatively little direct influence on the pattern recognition system. The basis for this idea was that the time course of retrieval of information from internal codes appeared little changed by providing a warning signal; what was changed was the probability and speed that the subject would become aware of these retrieved products and could thus note them, store them, and respond to them. In anatomical terms, the warning signal induces changes in the posterior attention network that allow faster interaction with pattern recognition and thus produce a more efficient routing of visual information to the anterior attention network.

By far the most common lesion site to produce contralateral neglect of visual stimuli is the posterior parietal lobe. It is well documented that damage to this area produces a specific abnormality in dealing with visual stimuli contralateral to the lesion. Shortly after the lesion there is widespread disregulation of metabolic activity that might extend over the whole hemisphere, but after about 6 months this usually has cleared (Duell & Collins, 1984). Although neglect as a clinical syndrome has many features, the lasting deficit appears to be primarily attentional. Subjects may appear to be generally normal, but if tested in a way that allows us to study their ability to deal with a contralateral target when they are already attending to visual information, the impairment is revealed in terms of a greatly magnified cost in reaction time. These basic results have now been replicated with many parietal patients and the time course of recovery has also been thoroughly traced (Morrow & Ratcliff, 1988). Nor does the parietal damage have to result from trauma. Recently a subset of Alzheimer's patients with reduced metabolism of the parietal lobe consequent to their degenerative process were studied (Parasuraman, Greenwood, Haxby, & Grady, 1992). These patients showed the same attentional deficit as the stroke patients and the degree of deficit was correlated with the amount of reduction in metabolism in this area.

It has been known for many years that neglect as a clinical syndrome is more prevalent with right- than with left-hemisphere damage (Heilman & Van Den Abell, 1980; Mesulam, 1981) This has led these authors to suppose that the right hemisphere controls attention to both sides of space but the left only to the contralateral space. Indeed, recent PET studies (Corbetta et al., 1993) have confirmed the presence of bilateral maps of space in the right superior parietal lobe but only contralateral ones in the left superior parietal lobe.

A second difference between patients with right- and left-sided lesions also showed up in our studies. In the attention-shifting task we have been describing, the cue to draw attention also serves as a warning signal for the upcoming target. If the cue is omitted on some trials RTs slow down even for normals. Patients with right parietal lesions are extremely slow to targets in the left visual field after omission of the cue. Although it is difficult to make direct comparisons between groups of subjects, in most of our data and in Ladavas, Pesce, and Provinciali's (1989) work, the right parietal patients are generally quite slow in comparison to those with left parietal lesions. In sum, the warning signal appears to interact with the efficiency of the visual spatial attention system in parietal patients.

A rather surprising aspect of this story is that the NE system appears to be asymmetric in its organization. The right cerebral hemisphere appears to be specialized for maintaining the alert state (Posner & Petersen, 1990). There is abundant evidence that patients with right-sided lesions have reduced ability to stay alert during vigilance tasks. This corresponds to findings that lesions of the right but not the left hemisphere of rats can deplete NE input to the cortex. Heilman (Heilman & Van Den Abell, 1980) has argued for many years that the right hemisphere has a special role in arousal. In this he appears to be quite correct. However, he seemed to think of arousal as being the same as the operation of attention, whereas our view has been that arousal modifies specific orienting computations by the posterior attention system.

Recently, it was possible to illustrate the asymmetric nature of these arousal affects in normal persons (Whitehead, 1991). In these studies, subjects received a warning signal followed by intervals of from 3 to 30 s arranged so that the length of delay did not affect the likelihood of a signal. The striking effect of four such studies was that for delay intervals of 12 s and up, response times to stimuli presented to the left visual field were significantly shorter than those for the right visual field. For intervals of 3 s or less, there was a tendency for responses to right visual field stimuli to be faster. The asymmetry produced by longer delay intervals appears to be due to the facility with which subjects can orient attention to the target event. This was shown by two converging operations. In one study a noninformative auditory stimulus sometimes accompanied the target. It was shown previously that such an stimulus produces a change in phasic alertness (Posner, Nissen, & Ogden, 1977). The presence of the accessory completely eliminated the asymmetry. In addition, the asymmetry was shown to interact with central cues presented at the start of a trial suggesting that the asymmetry in-volved some of the same mechanisms as are involved in the cueing effect (poste-rior visual spatial attention system). The way in which we interpret these results is as follows. The right hemisphere maintains its alert state by innervations of the posterior attention system of the right hemisphere from the locus coeruleus. Initial activation also affects the left hemisphere. However, over time the left hemisphere becomes relatively depleted of NE and thus shows less sustained activation. This view supposes that there are really two separate mechanisms: the first involving the actual operations used to shift attention and the second mod-ulating the relative efficiency of this first mechanism.

It might seem more parsimonious to suppose that the NE (arousal) system is itself involved in the computations of the posterior attention system, rather than serving as a modulator of its efficiency. Indeed, this is just the link between arousal and attention proposed by Heilman (Heilman et al., 1980). However, a number of recent results suggest that the NE system operates in quite a different way. Recall that patients with parietal damage show greatly exaggerated costs when attention is cued to their good side, but the target goes to the bad side. This increase in cost due to parietal lesions contrasts markedly with the reduction in costs that occurs from blocking NE. In one study the norepinephrine system was reduced in efficiency by administration of the drug clonodine (Clark, Geffen, & Geffen, 1989). The results showed a very specific effect on attention shifting, but it was opposite to that found with parietal lesions. Subjects showed a reduction in cost. Although a reduction in cost might, at first, be thought of as improved performance, it also has a strong adaptive disadvantage. What we call cost in this attention-shifting paradigm is a decrement in measures of how well one can restrict attention to the locus of the target. Difficulty in doing so may well be what in normal life we would call abnormal distractibility. Another situation in which there is a reduction of NE (as well as serotonin) is the REM sleep state (Hobson, 1990). When Hobson awakened subjects from REM and tested them in an attention-shifting paradigm, he also found a reduction of cost much as that reported with clonodine. These two results are not necessarily very specific to NE but they do show that whatever transmitter(s) are involved, they operate in a specific way quite different than the parietal system they modulate.

How does the evidence for asymmetries in arousal relate to neglect? A striking feature of the clinical data is the differences obtained between right- and left-hemisphere patients. The relatively slow RTs for right-hemisphere patients and their relatively poor performance in natural situations where neglect may be manifest could well relate to their failure to maintain the alert state. Moreover, changes in arousal over time may relate to the well-known variability of the symptoms of individual patients. It would be incorrect to suppose that we can predict the natural behavior of patients from our current understanding of the attentional and arousal deficits involved. For example, it is not at all clear why either of these factors should lead patients to deny that they are ill, yet right parietal damage often produces anosognosia. However, we are starting to have some idea of the complex underlying factors that relate to the neglect disorder. These include not only the computations of the complex vertically arrayed network that comprises the posterior attention system, but also the modulation of this system by transmitters. The interaction of transmitters and attentional computations carried out in the cerebral cortex seems central, not only to our understanding of the neglect syndrome, but also to the analysis of schizophrenia and attention deficit disorder.

CONCLUSION

The major theme of this chapter is that attention can best be viewed from a joint cognitive and neuroscience perspective as involving networks of neural areas that carry out quite specific computations. From this perspective, questions of anatomy, circuitry, neurochemistry, development, and pathology become natural ones. We have found that within each of these topics there is already substantial development and the techniques are available for sustained progress.

In this chapter we have confined our examination to the network that selects information from locations in the visual field. That should not be taken as meaning that this network operates in isolation from the rest of the attention system. In addition to the potential knowledge that might come from learning more about individual attentional networks, there is also hope that we will learn more concerning the relationship between attention as a system and subjective issues of awareness and feelings of self-control. The study of blindsight, amnesia, and unconscious priming have all shown that important higher level processing can be dissociated from the form of awareness that leads to the ability to report or recall events. Similarly, studies of mental illness and of normal dreaming have shown that awareness can be dissociated from the feelings of control that usually accompany self-generated ideas. Elsewhere we (Posner & Rothbart, 1991) have examined in some detail the hypothesis that these subjective aspects might be the output of attention and specifically of the anterior attention network. Although there is a strong temptation to see the problem of attention only in terms of the selection of some or all forms of sensory input, it is also important to keep in mind that attention as a whole is a system designed to support critical aspects of mental life. Whereas discussion of these issues raises many difficult philosophical and scientific issues, progress with them may now be more possible with the combined perspectives of cognition and neuroscience.

ACKNOWLEDGMENTS

This research was supported by the Office of Naval Research Contract N 0014-89-J3013 and the Center for the Cognitive Neuroscience of Attention supported by the Pew Memorial Trust and the James S. McDonnell Foundations. This article was presented to the Carnegie Conference of Cognition in May 1991.

REFERENCES

Allport, D. A. (1989). Visual attention. In M. I. Posner (Eds.), *Foundations of cognitive science* (pp. 631–682). Cambridge, MA: MIT Press.

Baron, J., & Strawson, C. (1976). Use of orthographic and word specific knowledge in reading words aloud. *Journal of Experimental Psychology: Human Perception and Performance, 2,* 386–393.

Behrman, M., Moscovitch, M., & Mozer, M. (1991). Directing attention to words and nonwords in normal subjects and in a computational model: Implications for neglect dyslexia. *Cognitive Neuropsychology, 8,* 213–248.

Bourke, P. A. (1991). *A general factor involved in dual task performance decrement.* Unpublished doctoral dissertation, University of Cambridge, Cambridge, England.

Broadbent, D. E. (1958). *Perception and communication.* London: Pergamon.

Brunn, J. L., & Farah, M. J. (1991). The relation between spatial attention and reading: evidence from the neglect syndrome. *Cognitive Neuropsychology, 8,* 59–75.

Chertkow, H., Bub, D., Evans, A., Meyer, E. I., & Marrett, S. (1990). Cerebral activation during silent naming studied with positron emission tomography: A cortical correlate for subvocalization. In *Annual meeting of the Neuroscience Society,* Abstract.

Clark, C. R., Geffen, G. M., & Geffen, L. B. (1989). Catecholamines and the covert orientation of attention in humans. *Neuropsychologia, 27*(2), 131–139.

Clohessy, A. B., Posner, M. I., & Rothbart, M. K. (1991). The development of inhibition of return in early infancy. *Journal of Cognitive Neuroscience, 3,* 345–356.

Cohen, A., & Rafal, R. D. (1991). Attention and feature integration: Illusory conjunctions in a patient with aparietal lobe lesion. *Psychological Science, 2,* 106–110.

Compton, P., Grossenbacher, P., Posner, M. I., & Tucker, D. (1991). A cognitive-anatomical approach to attention in lexical access. *Journal of Cognitive Neuroscience, 3,* 304–312.

Corbetta, M., Miezin, F. M., Dobmeyer, S., Shulman, G. L., & Petersen, S. E. (1990). Attentional modulation of neural processing of shape, color, and velocity in humans. *Science, 248,* 1556–1559.

Corbetta, M., Meizin, F. M., Shulman, G. L., & Petersen, S. E. (1993). Shifting attention in space: Direction versus visual hemifield: Psychophysics and PET. *Journal of Neuroscience 13(3),* 1202–1226.

Derryberry, D., & Rothbart, M. K. (1988). Arousal, affect, and attention as components of temperament. *Journal of Personality and Social Psychology, 55,* 953–966.

Dore, J., Franklin, M. B., Miller, R. T., & Ramer, A. L. H. (1976). Transitional phenomenon in early language acquisition. *Journal of Child Language, 3,* 13–27.

Downing, C. J. (1988). Expectancy and visual-spatial attention: Effects of spatial quality. *Journal of Experimental Psychology: Human Perception and Performance, 14,* 188–202.

Duell, R. M., & Collins, R. C. (1984). The functional anatomy of frontal lobe neglect in the monkey: Behavioral and quantitative 2 DG studies. *Annals of Neurology, 15,* 521–529.

Early, T. S., Posner, M. I., Reiman, E., & Raichle, M. E. (1989). Hyperactivity of the left striato-pallidal projection. Part I: Lower level theory. *Psychiatric Developments, 2,* 85–108.

Ellis, A. W., Flude, B. M., & Young, A. W. (1987). "Neglect dyslexia" and the early processing of letters in words and nonwords. *Cognitive Neuropsychology, 4,* 439–464.

Fischler, I. S. (1990). Comprehending language with event related potentials. In J. W. Rohrbaugh, R. Parasuraman, & R. Johnson (Eds.), *Even related brain potentials* (pp. 165–177). New York: Oxford University Press.

Fox, P. T., Miezin, F. M., Alklman, J. M., Van Essen, D. C., & Raichle, M. E. (1987). Retinotopic organization of human visual cortex mapped with positron emission tomography. *Journal of Neuroscience, 7,* 913–922.

Friedrich, F. J., Henik, A., & Tzelgov, J. (1991). Automatic processes in lexical access and spreading activation. *Journal of Experimental Psychology: Human Perception and Performance, 17,* 792–806.

Friedrich, F. J., Walker, J. A., & Posner, M. I. (1985). Effects of parietal lesions on visual matching: Implications for reading errors. *Cognitive Neuropsychology, 2,* 250–264.

Frith, D. C., Friston, K. J., Liddle, P. F., & Frackowiak, R. S. J. (1991). Willed action and the prefrontal cortex in man: A study with PET. *Proceedings of The Royal Society of London,* B, *244:*241–246.

Givón, T., Yang, L., & Gernsbacher, M. A. (1990). *The processing of second language vocabulary from attended to automated word recognition* (Tech. Rep. No. 90-4). Eugene: University of Oregon, Institute of Cognitive and Decision Sciences.

Goldman-Rakic, P. S. (1988). Topography of cognition: Parallel distributed networks in primate association cortex. *Annual Review of Neuroscience, 11,* 137–156.

Harter, M. R., & Aine, C. J. (1984). Brain mechanisms of visual selective attention. In R. Parasuraman & D. R. Davies (Eds.), *Varieties of attention* (pp. 293–318). New York: Academic.

Harter, M. R., Miller, S. L., Price, N. J., LaLonde, M. E., & Keyes, A. L. (1989). Neural processes involved in directing attention. *Cognitive Neuroscience, 1,* 223–237.

Hawkins, H. L., Luck, S. A., Mustapha, M., Downing, C. J., & Woodward, D. P. (1990). Visual attention modulates signal detectability. *Journal of Experimental Psychology: Human Perception and Performance, 16,* 802–811.

Heilman, K. M., & Van Den Abell, T. (1980). Right hemisphere dominance of attention: The mechanisms underlying hemispheric asymmetries in inattention (neglect). *Neurology, 30,* 327–330.

Hobson, J. A. (1990). Sleep and dreaming. *Journal of Neuroscience, 10*(2), 371–382.

Hubel, D. H. (1988). Eye, brain and vision. New York: Scientific American Library.

James, W. (1890). *Principles of psychology.* New York: Holt.

Johnson, M. H. (1990). Cortical maturation and the development of visual attention in early infancy. *Journal of Cognitive Neuroscience, 2,* 81–95.

Johnson, M. H., Posner, M. I., & Rothbart, M. K. (1991). Components of visual orienting in early infancy: Contingency learning, anticipatory looking and disengaging. *Journal of Cognitive Neuroscience, 3,* 335–344.

LaBerge, D. (1990). Thalamic and cortical mechanisms of attention suggested by recent positron emission tomographic experiments. *Journal of Cognitive Neuroscience, 2,* 358–372.

LaBerge, D., & Buchsbaum, M. S. (1990). Positron emission tomographic measurements of pulvinar activity during an attention task. *Journal of Neuroscience, 10*(2), 613–619.

Ladavas, E., Pesce, M. D., & Provinciali, L. (1989). Unilateral attention deficits and hemispheric asymmetries in the control of visual attention. *Neuropsychologia, 27,* 353–366.

Logan, G. D. (1988). Toward an instance theory of automatization. *Psychological Review, 95,* 492–527.

Mangun, G. R., & Hillyard, S. A. (1990). Electrophysiological studies of visual selective attention in humans. In A. B. Scheibel & A. F. Wechsler (Eds.), *Neurobiology of higher cognitive function* (pp. 271–294). New York: Guilford.

Mesulam, M. M. (1981). A cortical network for directed attention and unilateral neglect. *Annals of Neurology, 10,* 309–325.

Milberg, W., & Blumstein, S. E. (1981). Lexical decision and aphasia: Evidence for semantic processing. *Brain and Language, 14,* 371–385.

Moran, J., & Desimone, R. (1985). Selective attention gates visual processing in extrastriate cortex. *Science, 229,* 782–784.

Morrison, J. H., & Foote, S. L. (1986). Noradrenergic and seretoninergic innervation of cortical, thalamic and tectal visual structures in Old and New World monkeys. *Journal of Comparative Neurology, 243,* 117–128.

Morrow, L. A., & Ratcliff, G. (1988). The disengagement of covert attention and the neglect syndrome. *Psychobiology, 16,* 261–269.

Mozer, M. C., & Behrman, M. (1990). On the interaction of selective attention and lexical knowledge: A connectionist account of neglect dyslexia. *Cognitive Neuroscience, 2,* 96–123.

Näätänen, R. (1990). The role of attention in auditory information processing as revealed by event-related potentials and other measures of cognitive function. *Behavioral and Brain Sciences, 13,* 201–288.

Neisser, U. (1976). *Cognition and reality.* San Francisco: Freeman.

Parasuraman, R., Greenwood, P. M., Haxby, J. V., & Grady, C. L. (1992). Visuspatial attention in dementia of the alzheimer type. *Brain, 115,* 711–733.

Pardo, J. V., Pardo, P. J., Janer, K. W., & Raichle, M. E. (1990). The anterior cingulate cortex mediates processing selection in the stroop attentional conflict paradigm. *PNAS, 87,* 256–259.

Petersen, S. E., Fox, P. T., Miezin, F. M., & Raichle, M. E. (1988). Modulation of cortical visual responses by direction of spatial attention measured by PET. *Association for Research in Vision and Opthamology* (Abstract), 22.

Petersen, S. E., Fox, P. T., Posner, M. I., Mintun, M., & Raichle, M. E. (1989). Positron emission tomographic studies of the processing of single words. *Journal of Cognitive Neuroscience, 1,* 153–170.

Petersen, S. E., Fox, P. T., Snyder, A. Z., & Raichle, M. E. (1990). Activation of extrastriate and frontal cortical areas by visual words and word like stimuli. *Science, 249*, 1041–1044.

Phaf, R. H., Van der Heijden, A. H. C., & Hudson, P. T. W. (1990). SLAM: A connectionist model for attention in visual selection tasks. *Journal of Cognitive Psychology, 22*, 273–341.

Pollatsek, A., Bolozky, S., Well, A. D., & Rayner, K. (1981). Asymmetries in the perceptual span of Israeli readers. *Brain and Language, 14*, 123–130.

Posner, M. I. (1978). *Chronometric explorations of mind.* Hillsdale, NJ: Lawrence Erlbaum Associates.

Posner, M. I. (1980). Orienting of attention. *Quarterly Journal of Experimental Psychology, 32*, 3–25.

Posner, M. I. (1982). Cumulative development of attentional theory. *American Psychologist, 37*, 268–179.

Posner, M. I. (1988). Structures and functions of selective attention. In T. Boll & B. Bryant (Eds.), *Master lectures in clinical neuropsychology and brain function: Research measurement and practice* (pp.171–202). American Psychological Association.

Posner, M. I., & Carr, T. H. (1992). Lexical access and the brain: Anatomical constraints on cognitive models of word recognition. *American Journal of Psychology, 105*, 1–26.

Posner, M. I., Inhoff, A. W., Friedrich, F. J., & Cohen, A. (1987). Isolating attentional systems: A cognitive-anatomical analysis. *Psychobiology, 15*, 107–121.

Posner, M. I., Nissen, M. J., & Ogden, W. C. (1977). Attended and unattended processing modes: The role of set from spatial location. In H. J. Pick (Ed.), *Modes of perception* (pp. 137–157). Hillsdale, NJ: Lawrence Erlbaum Associates.

Posner, M. I., & Petersen, S. E. (1990). The attention system of the human brain. *Annual Review of Neuroscience, 13*, 25–42.

Posner, M. I., Petersen, S. E., Fox, P. T., & Raichle, M. E. (1988). Localization of cognitive operations in the human brain. *Science, 240*, 1627–1631.

Posner, M. I., & Rafal, R. D. (1986). Cognitive theories of attention and the rehabilitation of attentional deficit. In R. J. Meir, L. Diller, & A. C. Benton (Eds.), *Neuropsychological rehabilitation* (pp. 187–201). London: Churchill-Livingston.

Posner, M. I., & Rothbart, M. K. (1991). Attentional mechanisms and conscious experience. In D. Milner & M. Rugg (Eds.), *The neuropsychology of consciousness* (pp. 91–112). New York: Academic.

Posner, M. I., Sandson, J., Dhawan, M., & Shulman, G. L. (1989). Is word recognition automatic? A cognitive-anatomical approach. *Journal of Cognitive Neuroscience, 1*, 50–60.

Prinzmetal, W., Presti, D., & Posner, M. I. (1986). Does attention affect feature integration? *Journal of Experimental Psychology, 12*, 361–369.

Rafal, R. D., Calabresi, P., Brennan, C., & Scioloto, T. (1989). Saccade preparation inhibits reorienting to recently attended locations. *Journal of Experimental Psychology: Human Perception and Performance, 15*, 673–685.

Rothbart, M. K., Posner, M. I., & Boylan, A. (1990). Regulatory mechanisms in infant development. In J. T. Enns (Ed.), *The development of attention: research and theory* (pp. 47–65). North-Holland: Elsevier Science Publishers.

Rugg, M. D. (1987). Dissociation of semantic priming, word and non-word repetition by event related potentials. *Quarterly Journal of Experimental Psychology, 39A*, 123–148.

Schiller, P. H., & Lee, K. (1991). The role of the primate extrastriate area V4 in vision. *Science, 251*, 1251–1253.

Schneider, W. (1985). Toward a model of attention and the development of automatic processing. In M. I. Posner & O. S. M. Marin (Eds.), *Attention and performance XI* (pp. 475–492). Hillsdale NJ: Lawrence Erlbaum Associates.

Shallice, T. (1988). *From neuropsychology to mental structure.* Cambridge, England: Cambridge University Press.

Sieroff, E., Pollatsek, A., & Posner, M. I. (1988). Recognition of visual letter strings following injury to the posterior visual spatial attention system. *Cognitive Neuropsychology, 5*(4), 427–449.

Sieroff, E., & Posner, M. I. (1989). Cueing spatial attention during processing of words and letter strings in normals. *Cognitive Neuropsychology, 5*(4), 451–472.

Sperling, G. (1960). The information available in brief visual presentations. *Psychological Monographs, 74,* 498.

Sternberg, S. (1969). The discovery of processing stages: Extensions of Donder's method. *Acta Psychologica, 30,* 276–316.

Swanson, J. M., Posner, M., Potkin, S., Bonforte, S., Youpa, D., Fiore, C., Cantwell, D., & Crinella, F. (1991). Activating tasks for the study of visual-spatial attention in ADHD children: A cognitive anatomic approach. *Journal of Child Neurology, 6,* S119–S127.

Talbot, J. D., Marrett, A., Evans, A. C., Meyer, E., Bushnell, M. C., & Duncan, G. H. (1991). Multiple representation of pain in human cerebral cortex. *Science, 251,* 1355–1357.

Treisman, A. M., & Gormican, S. (1988). Feature analysis in early vision: evidence from search asymmetries. *Psychological Review, 95,* 15–18.

Ungerleider, L. G., & Mishkin, M. (1982). Two cortical visual systems. In D. J. Ingle, M. A. Goodale, & R. J. W. Mansfield (Eds.), *Analysis of visual behavior* (pp. 540–580). Cambridge, MA: MIT Press.

Whitehead, R. (1991). Right hemisphere processing superiority during sustained visual attention. *Journal of Cognitive Neuroscience, 3,* 329–334

Wurst, S. A., & Sperling, G. (1992). Selective attention does not produce early perceptual filtering. In D. Meyer & S. Kornblum (Eds.), *Attention and performance XIV* (pp. 265–298). Cambridge, MA: MIT Press.

Zeki, S., Watson, J. D. G., Lueck, C. J., Friston, K. J., Kennard, C., & Frackowiak, R. S. J. (1991). A direct demonstration of functional specialization in human visual cortex. *Journal of Neuroscience, 11*(3), 641–649.

9

Dissociating Components of Visual Attention: A Neurodevelopmental Approach

Mark H. Johnson
Carnegie Mellon University

It has become clear in recent years that attention is not a unitary phenomenon, but rather that it can be dissociated into a variety of components or systems. To date, most of the evidence in support of this multiple system view has come from studies in which the neural basis of attention was studied in adult patients with brain damage, positron-emission tomography (PET) scanning studies, and lesion studies in the nonhuman primate (see chapter 8, this volume, for review). In this chapter evidence from a different approach to studying the neural basis of attention is reviewed: the investigation of how the postnatal development of cortical structures and pathways give rise to advances in visual attention in human infants. As well as providing converging evidence for some of the conclusions drawn from the other approaches to investigating the neural basis of attention, the neurodevelopmental approach outlined in this chapter provides some new insights and perspectives on the adult literature.

The approach taken in this chapter to studying the development of infant attention is based on the idea that certain tasks can be designed that engage one cortical pathway or system more than any other, the *marker task* approach. Such tasks can be used to test predictions about the sequence of development of attentional pathways resulting from postnatal cortical maturation. As we will see, predictions about the sequence of development of attention pathways can be made from consideration of the details of maturation of cortical architectonics. This approach contrasts with two others commonly taken to the study of infant visual orienting and attention: theories based on the psychophysical limitations of the eye and early visual channels, and information-processing level cognitive theories. An example of the former type of theory is the linear systems model (Banks & Salapatek, 1981). This model aims to predict infants preferences among a range of stimuli in terms of the filtered amplitude spectrum of the stimuli in question. Although such theories are very successful in predicting visual preferences in certain testing situations, there is some question over their generality (e.g., Morton, Johnson, & Maurer, 1990). More important, like all theories based on the assumption that the development of visually guided behavior in the infant can be accounted in terms of the development of the psychophysical limitations at the retinal level, it has difficulty in accounting for observations such as that the extent of the measurable visual field of the infant declines between birth and 1 month, before gradually expanding to reach adult size (Schwartz, Dobson, Sandstrom, & van Hof-van Duin, 1987).[1] In other words, it is becoming increasingly evident that to account for the development of visually guided behavior in the human infant changes in central attention mechanisms are at least as important as changes in peripheral sensitivity. On the other hand, cognitive information-processing accounts of aspects of visual attention in infants (e.g., Cohen, 1988) have, as yet, rarely been related to any neural structures or pathways.

In the first section of the chapter, the existing state of knowledge about the components of overt orienting (attentional shifts involving head and eye movements) and their development in the human infant is reviewed. It is argued that these developments can be understood in terms of the underlying cortical maturation. In the second section, evidence for covert attentional processes (shifts of attention that occur independently of eye or head movements) in the human infant are discussed, with the emphasis again being on how changes in abilities can be understood in terms of the maturation of the underlying neural circuitry. In the final section, the role that attention plays in the postnatal organization of cortical functions is outlined, before a discussion of what these developmental analyses tell us about the structure of adult attentional processes and their breakdown.

OVERT VISUAL ORIENTING

In an article now commonly regarded as a classic, Gordon Bronson (1974) proposed that the primary visual pathway does not gain control over sensory motor behavior in the human infant until around 2 months after birth. Prior to this age, he claimed, the infant is primarily responding to visual stimuli by means of subcortical visual processing. The detailed evidence in support of this contention comes from a variety of sources including the similarities between the visually guided behavior of young infants and that of animals with particular kinds of cortical damage. Because this evidence in support of Bronson's claim has been

---

[1] A multistage retinal account of this phenemenon put to me by Alan Cowey is discussed in a later section.

extensively reviewed elsewhere (Atkinson, 1984; Bronson, 1974, 1982; Johnson, 1990a), I only briefly review one source here, that from evoked potentials.

Many studies of visually evoked potentials (VEPs) in young infants have been performed (see Atkinson, 1984; Vaughan & Kurtzberg, 1989, for reviews). In general, these studies show that components of the VEP thought to be related to subcortical structures are present from birth, and some components related to the striate cortex are present from around the time of birth. More specific components of cortical origin (fast, high-frequency wavelets), however, do not appear in infants under 4 weeks. Further, the responses to changes in the orientation of moving bars do not appear until 6 weeks (Atkinson, Wattam-Bell, Anker, & Tricklebank, 1988).[2] Thus, the electrophysiological evidence gives general credence to the idea that cortical functioning develops over the first few months, and that some major changes occur in the 2nd month of life. However, the evidence is also indicative of some cortical activity at birth.

In recent years the notion of a shift from subcortical to cortical visual processing in early infancy has come under criticism for several reasons. First, the increasing evidence for apparently sophisticated perceptual abilities in early infancy (e.g., Bushnell, Sai, & Mullen, 1989; Slater, Morison, & Somers, 1988; Slater, 1988). Second, neurophysiological studies have brought into question the notion of one cortical visual pathway: Recent evidence suggests that there are multiple pathways for visual information processing (e.g., deYoe & Van Essen, 1988; Van Essen, 1985). These considerations have led several authors to propose some form of partial cortical functioning at birth (e.g., Atkinson et al., 1988; Maurer & Lewis 1979; Posner & Rothbart 1980). As yet, however, this partial cortical functioning remains poorly specified.

I recently proposed a hypothesis regarding the development of visual attention and its relation to cortical maturation. This hypothesis specifies the extent of cortical functioning in the newborn, and accounts for changes in the development of overt visual orienting over the first few months in terms of the maturation of three cortical pathways (Johnson, 1990a, 1990b). These three pathways and a fourth, subcortical pathway, are derived from proposals initially put forward to account for adult primate electrophysiological and lesion data by Schiller (1985; see Fig. 9.1). The four pathways are:

1. A pathway from the retina to the superior colliculus, the *SC pathway,* is thought to be involved in the generation of eye movements toward simple, easily discriminable stimuli, and fed mainly by the peripheral visual field.

2. This is a cortical pathway that goes both directly to the superior colliculus from the primary visual cortex and also via the middle temporal area (MT), the

---

[2]But see recent papers by Slater, Morison, and Somers (1988) and reply by Atkinson, Hood, Wattam-Bell, Anker, and Tricklebank (1988).

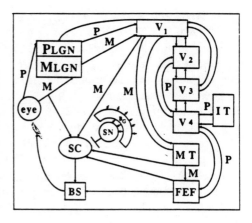

FIG. 9.1. A schematic representation of the model proposed by Schiller (1985) for the neuroanatomical pathways thought to underlie oculomotor control in primates. LGN = Lateral geniculate nucleus; SC = Superior colliculus; SN = Substantia nigra; BG = Basal ganglia; BS = Brain stem; FEF = Frontal eye fields; BB = Broadband (magnocellular) stream; CO = Color opponent (parvocellular) stream. From Johnson (1990). Copyright 1990 by MIT Press.

MT pathway. This pathway is exclusively driven by the broadband or magnocellular system, and is thought to be involved in the detection and smooth tracking of moving stimuli.

3. Third is a cortical pathway that converges both broadband and color-opponent streams of processing in the frontal eye fields, the *FEF pathway,* and that is thought to be involved in the temporal sequencing of eye movements within complex arrays, and the performance of predictive or "anticipatory" saccades.

4. The final pathway for the control of eye movements is an inhibitory input to the colliculus from several cortical areas via the substantia nigra and basal ganglia, the *nigral pathway.* Schiller proposed that this final pathway ensures that the activity of the colliculus can be regulated.

The specific proposals put forward by Johnson (1990a) are that, first, the characteristics of visually guided behavior of the infant at particular ages is determined by which of these pathways is functional, and second, which of these pathways is functional is determined by the maturational state of the visual cortex. The logic of this theoretical approach at the neuroanatomical level lies in three sets of observations:

1. The primary visual cortex is the major "gateway" through which information to be processed by the three cortical pathways mentioned earlier (MT, FEF, & nigral) has to pass (Schiller, 1985).[3]

2. The primary visual cortex, like other cortical regions, shows an "inside-out" pattern of growth with the deeper layers (5 & 6) developing in

---

[3]See later for some exceptions to this statement.

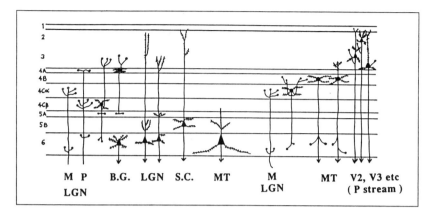

FIG. 9.2. A schematic representation of primary visual cortex with some of the main efferents and afferents shown. For abbreviations see legend to Fig. 9.1 and main text from Johnson (1990). Copyright 1990 by MIT Press.

advance of the more superficial ones (2 & 3) (Conel, 1939/1967; Purpura, 1975; Rabinowicz, 1979).

3. There is a restricted pattern of inputs and outputs from primary visual cortex (e.g., the efferents to V2 depart from Layers 2 and 3 only) (Maunsell & Van Essen, 1983; Rockland & Pandya, 1979; see Fig. 9.2).

It is evident that because the projections from V1 to the three cortical pathways mentioned earlier depart from different layers of the primary visual cortex, and because cortical development shows an inside-out pattern of growth it should be possible to predict the developmental sequence with which they will influence the infant's behavior. Employing this logic, Johnson (1990a) attempted to account for characteristics of the visually guided behavior of the infant in terms of the sequential development of pathways underlying visual orienting (see Table 9.1). Briefly, the stages proposed by Johnson were as follows.

The Newborn. On the basis of neuroanatomical evidence (e.g., Conel, 1939/1967; Rabinowicz, 1979) it is likely that only the deeper layers of the primary visual cortex are capable of supporting organized activity in the human newborn. Because the majority of feedforward cortico-cortico projections depart from outside Layers 5 and 6, some of the cortical pathways mediating orienting (the MT and FEF pathways) may not be functional at this age. However, evidence from various sources supports the notion that information from the eye is entering the primary visual cortex and that feedback from this structure to the lateral geniculate is operating in the newborn. Thus, although agreeing with

TABLE 9.1
Stages in the Development of Visual Orienting

Age	Functional Anatomy	Behavior
Newborn	SC pathway + Layer 5 & 6 output to LGN and colliculus	-Saccadic pursuit tracking -Preferential orienting to temporal visual field
1 Month	As above + nigral pathway to colliculus via BG	-As above + obligatory attention
2 Months	As above + MT pathway to the colliculus	-Onset of smooth tracking -Increased sensitivity to nasal visual field
3 Months and over	As above + FEF pathway to colliculus and brainstem	-Onset of anticipatory tracking -Fixed scanning patterns

Bronson's (1974) proposal that most of the newborn's visual behavior can be accounted for in terms of processing in the subcortical pathway, in the Johnson (1990a) account it is not denied that there is some information processing occurring in the deeper cortical layers at birth. One of the many behavioral manifestations of this immature state of cortical development concerns the visual tracking of a moving stimulus. Aslin (1981) reported that tracking in very early infancy has two characteristics. The first is that the eye movements follow the stimulus in a *saccadic* or steplike manner, as opposed to the smooth pursuit found in adults and older infants. The second characteristic is that the eye movements always lag behind the movement of the stimulus, rather than predicting its trajectory (see Fig. 9.3a). When a newborn infant visually tracks a stimulus therefore, it could be described as performing a series of reorientations. Such behavior is consistent with collicular control of orienting (see Johnson, 1990a, for further details).

One Month of Age. During the first few weeks of life, the nigral pathway (4) becomes increasingly functional by this account. This is due to maturation in lower Layer 4 of the primary visual cortex allowing the projection to basal ganglia and substantia nigra. These developments were proposed to result in regulation of the colliculus by non-specific inhibition of its activity. This may have the result that stimuli impinging on the peripheral visual field no longer elicit an orientation as readily as they do in younger infants (see Johnson, 1990a, for details). This, in turn, is hypothesized to result in the commonly reported phenomenon of *obligatory attention* whereby infants from around 1 month of age have great difficulty in disengaging their gaze from a stimulus. This generalized inhibition of the colliculus may also give rise to the decrease in head turning to a sound source observed at around this age (Muir, Clifton, & Clarkson, 1989).

(a) 20°

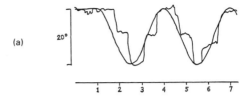

1   2   3   4   5   6   7

(b) 20°

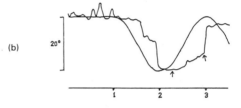

1   2   3

FIG. 9.3. The visual following of a moving target by (a) a typical 5-week-old, (b) a typical 8-week-old, and (c) a typical 3-month-old infant (the arrow indicates areas of smooth pursuit with gain greater than 1.0. At these two points the movement of the eye anticipates the future location of the object). The smooth line indicates the movement of the target whereas the other line indicates the movement of the eyes while attempting to track the stimulus. From Johnson 1990. Copyright 1990 by MIT Press.

(c) 20°

Two Months of Age. Although their eye movements still lag behind the movement of the stimulus, by around 2 months of age infants begin to show periods of smooth visual tracking of moving targets (see Fig. 9.3b). Furthermore, they become more sensitive to stimuli placed in the nasal visual field (Aslin, 1981). The onset of these behaviors is postulated to coincide with maturation of the rest of Layer 4 of the primary visual cortex and the consequent "enabling" of the MT pathway. The enabling of this pathway is hypothesized to provide the cortical magnocellular stream with control over the superior colliculus.

3 Months of Age and Over. After around 3 months of age, the FEF pathway is proposed to be enabled by maturation of Layers 2 and 3 of primary visual cortex, resulting in the ability of the infant to make anticipatory eye movements and to make organized sequential scanning patterns toward familiar objects. For example, with regard to the visual tracking of a moving object infants now not only show periods of smooth tracking, but their eye movements often predict the movement of the stimulus in an anticipatory manner (Fig. 9.3c).

Recent Evidence Relating to the Johnson (1990a) Account of the Development of Overt Visual Orienting

Further Anatomical Considerations

The account put forward in the previous section depended on three sets of neuroanatomical observations. Evidence pertaining to each of these observations has been rapidly accruing over the past few years. Some of these new reports may eventually require some modifications to the account proposed, whereas others actually reinforce the conclusions reached earlier.

The Primary Visual Cortex Is the Major Gateway Through Which Information from the Retina Reaches the Three Cortical Pathways.   One common misconception is that there are projections from the LGN to areas V2, V3, and so on, in the human. This misconception is based on the evidence for such projections in other mammals such as cats, but in primates it is clear that the LGN projects more or less exclusively to the primary visual cortex (Lund, 1988). There is, however, some evidence that visual areas downstream of V1 may receive some visual input from the retinocollicular pathway. For example, in a recent article Rodman, Gross, and Albright (1989) reported that they were able to record stimulus selective activity from about 50% of cells in macaque area MT after lesions to, or cooling of, the primary visual cortex (such effects are not found in V2 or the inferotemporal cortex). This strongly suggests that there are independent routes from the retina to this region, probably via the colliculus and pulvinar. That this might also be true in humans is suggested by studies of blindsight patients (see Cowey & Stoerig, 1991, for review).

Although the visual input to MT from subcortical structures is probably not the major projection, it may still be argued that this region will influence visuomotor behavior in the infant before the ages predicted by the maturational account discussed earlier.[4] In my view, however, it is unlikely that this projection, which circumvents V1, will significantly alter the predictions with regard to the sequence of development of cortical pathways underlying orienting put forward earlier, because Area MT would have to be developmentally in advance of V1 for it to do so. The evidence available (Conel, 1939/1967) suggests that, if anything, MT is some way behind the primary visual cortex in terms of the

---

[4]It is also the case that area MT receives projections from the deeper layers of V1. See Johnson (1990a) for reasons why this projection is unlikely to alter the predictions of the theory substantially.

maturational factors mentioned earlier. Thus, although there may be multiple sources of input to MT, the region will not start to influence behavior at least until the maturation of Layer 4, the adult termination site of these projections. Having said this, the definite conclusion of this matter must await further developmental neuroanatomical evidence.

The Primary Visual Cortex Shows an Inside-Out Pattern of Growth with the Deeper Layers Developing in Advance of the More Superficial. The original report of Conel (1939/1967) that, in most regions of the human cortex, postnatal growth proceeds from deeper layers to more superficial ones has been broadly confirmed by subsequent investigators who have made quantitative measurements concerning the length and order of branching of dendrites in the human primary visual cortex. For example, Becker, Armstrong, Chan, and Wood (1984) reported that the mean total length of dendrites for pyramidal cells in Layer 3 is only about 30% of the maximum at birth, whereas in Layer 5 the equivalent figure is about 60% of maximum. Furthermore, a higher degree of dendritic branching is found in Layer 5 than in Layer 3. This layerwise pattern of development has also been quantitatively described in human motor cortex (e.g., Marin-Padilla, 1970). It is worth noting that although the inside-out layerwise pattern of cortical growth has been observed for many aspects of neural development, it does not seem to be the case for the characteristic postnatal decrease in synaptic density (e.g., Huttenlocher, 1990). This class of postnatal neural event occurs later than those on which the account given earlier is based (e.g., in primary visual cortex the peak of synaptic density is reached around 8–10 months). At present the computational significance of this class of event is unknown (but see Johnson & Karmiloff-Smith, 1992).

There Is a Restricted Pattern of Inputs and Outputs from Primary Visual Cortex. The fact that the macaque and some other primate primary visual cortices have layer-specific projection patterns has been clearly established for a number of years (e.g., Rockland & Pandya, 1979). Only recently have similarly detailed neuroanatomical studies been performed with the human visual cortex. Burkhalter and Bernardo (1989) reported that the pattern of interconnectivity between V1 and V2 in the human are very similar to those found in nonhuman primates, giving confidence that the broad patterns of cortico-cortico projections described in nonhuman primates are also applicable to humans.

The Disengage Function

In the adult literature it is still unclear whether there is a specific neurocognitive system that underlies the ability to disengage attention from a spatial location (as argued by Posner et al., chapter 8 of this volume) or whether the ability to disengage attention from a location is a product of the interaction between two or more systems. This distinction is also apparent with regard to the phenomenon of obligatory attention found in infants from 1 to 3 months of age (Stechler & Latz 1966; Tennes et al. 1972). One view is that the end of this period is due to the onset of a covert attention mechanism subserved by parietal structures (Rothbart, Posner, & Boylan 1990; see also chapter 8 of this volume). Covert attention mechanisms, and the evidence for their involvement in the ability to disengage in infants, are discussed later in this chapter.

The alternative view, and that put forward in this chapter, favors the idea that the end of obligatory attention is due to the interactive action of at least two systems. Specifically, I argued earlier that the development of the nigral pathway before the MT and FEF pathways resulted in the phenomenon of obligatory attention due to non-specific inhibition of the colliculus. If this is the case then we would predict that infants difficulty in disengaging from one stimulus to attend toward another should decrease following the development of one or more of the other pathways. Johnson, Posner, and Rothbart (1991) designed an experiment (the details of which are given later; also see Fig. 9.5) in which infants ability to disengage from a centrally presented stimulus to orient toward a peripheral one was studied at the same time as some functions attributed to the FEF pathway. Consistent with the predictions of the Johnson (1990a) maturational account, a sharp increase in the ability to disengage from the central stimulus coincided with the onset of functions attributed to the FEF pathway.

It should be stressed, however, that the investigation of the puzzling phenomenon of obligatory attention has only just begun, and that explanations other than that given in this chapter are certainly worth further exploration. For example, Hood (personal communication 1990) is developing an account in terms of the differential development of the control of head and eye movements. By this account, although infants are able to orient their head toward a peripheral stimulus, they are unable to move their eyes. This leads to the observation (which I have noticed myself) that whereas the infant's head may attempt to orient toward the novel stimulus, the eyes stay fixed on the original location. Perhaps it is this dissociation that often leads to the distress associated with the termination of these episodes.

Another possibility is an account partially in terms of retinal development (Cowey, personal communication, May 1991). In the newborn, the temporal visual field part of the retina is more developed than the nasal part (see earlier). This biases the infant to attend more to stimuli outside the central visual field. By 1 month, the argument goes, the nasal visual field has caught up to some extent with the temporal. The infant then fixates stimuli within the nasal field due to their "novelty" compared to when they appear in the temporal field. The end of obligatory attention is presumably attributable to the appearance of stimuli in the nasal visual field no longer being novel. One of several problems with this account is defining novelty and accounting for its long duration.

One intriguing possibility as to the function of obligatory attention is that it is essential for the development of binocularity. Held (1985) demonstrated that

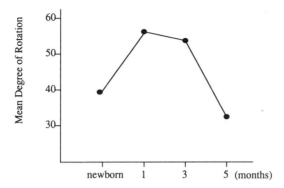

FIG. 9.4.   The mean extent of visual tracking (eye movements) to the same stimulus in infants of four different ages. The newborn infants (Johnson et al., 1991; Experiment 2) were tested in a slightly different manner from the older infants that may slightly overestimate their tracking relative to the older groups (Johnson et al., 1991; Experiment 3). The stimulus used was a "scrambled" face. See Johnson et al., 1991, for further details.

binocular vision comes in at about 4 months of age in the human infant. Assuming that the mechanisms underlying the development of binocularity are similar to those studied in the cat, it is reasonable to suppose that preceding the onset of binocularity is a sensitive period in which it is essential that equivalent visual stimulation is received by both eyes (see, e.g., Hirsch, Tieman, Tieman, & Timosa, 1987). It may be that prolonged exposure to the same stimulus within both nasal visual fields is necessary for this binocularity to develop properly in the human. If this is the case we might expect obligatory attention to be object centered (in the sense that some aspects of adult covert visual attention have been argued to be).[5] Some support for this suggestion comes from the observation that infants in the midst of the obligatory attention period will, nevertheless, readily track a stimulus moving relative to its background (Johnson, Dziurawiec, Ellis, & Morton, 1991). Figure 9.4 shows the extent of tracking of the same stimulus at four different ages. The maximum extent of tracking occurs during the period of obligatory attention, 1–3 months of age, suggesting that the phenomenon may indeed be object centered.

The Perception of Motion

From neurophysiological studies on nonhuman primates, the MT pathway (including area MST) have been associated with the ability to smoothly track a moving target. However, neurones within MT have also been closely associated

---

[5]I thank Glyn Humphries for originally suggesting to me the idea that obligatory attention might be object centered.

with the perception of motion. Newsome and colleagues have conducted a series of experiments in which they have obtained evidence for MT being involved in motion processing in the nonhuman primate (for review, see Newsome & Wurtz, 1988). These experiments normally use stimuli composed of a number of dots that either move in the same direction, or in which they have uncorrelated movement. Using such stimuli to assess psychophysical thresholds, Newsome and Pare (1988) found a massive increase in the threshold for detecting common motion following discrete acid lesions to MT in the macaque. Furthermore, the sensory thresholds of single neurons in MT match, or even exceed, the behavioral performance of the whole animal in the motion discrimination task (Newsome, Britten, & Movshon, 1989), and weak, spatially localized electrical stimulation to MT influences the perceptual decision in a selective manner (Salzman, Britten, & Newsome, 1990). This evidence strongly suggests that the moving dots with correlated motion stimulus may be an effective behavioral marker for MT functioning. It is therefore a prediction of the Johnson (1990a) maturational account that the perception of motion should (a) coincide in age of onset with the development of smooth tracking (2 months of age) and (b) should proceed the development of abilities attributed to the frontal eye field pathway.

Spitz and Kleffner (1992) studied the perception of coherent motion in infants by exposing them to stimuli composed of random moving dots. These dots either moved with coherent motion, in the same direction, or in random directions. Adults perceive directional motion flow in the first case but not in the second. These authors found that infants at the youngest age they tested, 4 months, were able to discriminate these stimuli suggesting that they could detect the motion. More recently, Spitz (personal communication, January 1992) has found evidence for the perception of coherent motion in infants as young as 8 weeks, the same age as Aslin (1981) reports the onset of smooth tracking.[6] However, strong evidence for the model presented earlier will only be obtained when marker tasks for both MT and FEF pathway functioning are studied within the same infant.

The Development of Visual Expectancies

As mentioned earlier, the ability of infants to initiate a saccade toward a location before a target appears, an anticipatory saccade, has been associated with the FEF pathway. A prediction of the maturational account presented earlier is therefore that the ability of infants to consistently show anticipatory saccades should first appear after about 3 months of age. Evidence in support of this claim comes from recent studies by Haith and his collaborators. In an initial study, 3.5-month-old infants viewed one of two series of slides that appeared either on the right- or on the left-hand side of the infant either alternating with regular inter-

---

[6]Although Condry, Gentile, and Yonas (1991) failed to find a preference for an illusory moving stimulus in 4-month-olds, they attribute this to the particular method employed.

stimulus intervals (ISI) or with an irregular alternation pattern and ISI (Haith, Hazan, & Goodman, 1988). The regular ISI generated more stimulus anticipations, and reaction times (RTs) to make an eye movement were reliably faster than in the irregular series. The authors argued that infants of this age are able to develop expectancies for noncontrollable spatiotemporal events. Canfield and Haith (1991) tested 2- and 3-month-olds in a similar experiment that included more complex sequences (such as left-left-right, left-left-right). Although they failed to obtain significant effects with 2-month-olds, 3-month-olds appeared to be able acquire at least some of the more complex sequences.[7] Furthermore, if the acquired sequence is changed to another sequence, infants of 3 months make errors consistent with having acquired the first sequence (Arehart & Haith, 1991). Thus, consistent with the predictions of the Johnson (1990a) maturational account, between 2 and 3 months of age the ability to make anticipatory eye movements may develop. Preliminary evidence from Canfield (1991) suggests that once these abilities do develop, individual differences remain fairly stable from 4 to 6 months.

In the experiment of Johnson, Posner, and Rothbart (1991; described next; see Fig. 9.5) the ability of infants to make an anticipatory saccade toward the location where they expected a target stimulus to appear was investigated. The results of this experiment were largely concordant with those obtained in the studies from Haith's laboratory. During the later phases of the experiment, 4-month-old infants showed more than twice the percentage of anticipatory looks than did younger infants, although a low baseline of anticipatory looking was also found in these groups.

Johnson, Posner, and Rothbart (1991) also inquired into the ability of infants to do something more complex, namely to use a centrally presented cue stimulus to predict the location in which a target stimulus should appear. The procedure used in Johnson et al. is illustrated in Fig. 9.5. In brief, infants faced three monitor screens on which colored dynamic stimuli were presented. During the first half of the experiment, the training phase, the infant viewed a number of training trials that began with a stimulus appearing on the central screen. This central stimulus served both to attract the infant's gaze to the center screen at the start of a trial, and as a cue to predict the location (left- or right-hand side screen) in which a target stimulus would subsequently appear. In other words, for each infant there was a contingent relationship between which of two patterns were presented on the central screen, and whether the target stimulus would subsequently appear on the left- or on the right-hand side screen. During the training trials there was a 1 s gap between the offset of the central stimulus and the onset of the target stimulus.

---

[7]A recent report that the performance of 2-month-olds in such tasks can be improved by extending the stimulus durations (Wentworth & Hood, 1991) does not alter this conclusion because age differences remained regardless of stimulus duration.

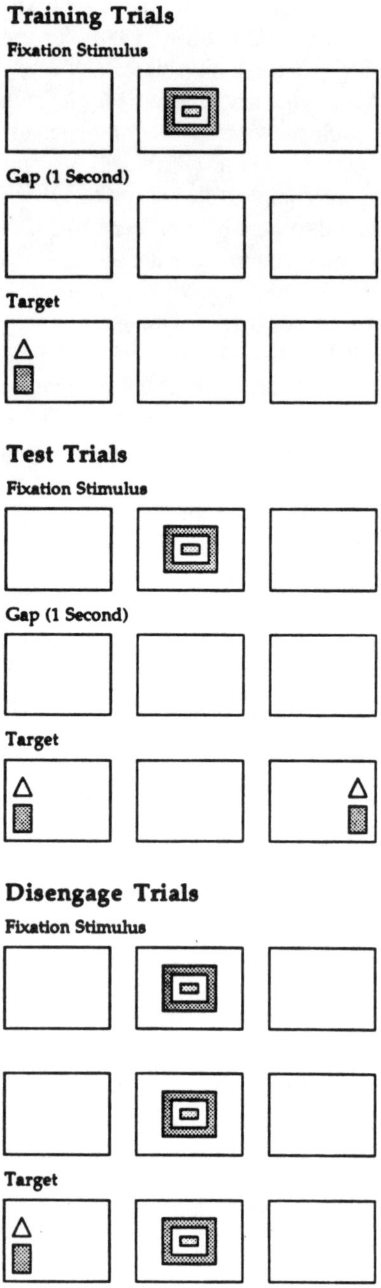

Training Trials

Fixation Stimulus

Gap (1 Second)

Target

Test Trials

Fixation Stimulus

Gap (1 Second)

Target

Disengage Trials

Fixation Stimulus

Target

FIG. 9.5. The three types of trials in the experiment of Johnson, Posner, and Rothbart (1991). The infant faced three monitor screens on which colored moving stimuli appeared in certain sequences.

The second phase of the experiment involved three types of trials: first, training trials as just described; second, disengage trials in which the central stimulus stayed on even when the target appeared (the infant had to disengage its gaze from the first stimulus to orient toward the target—these trials were discussed earlier); and third, test trials that were identical to the training trials except that the target stimulus appeared in both possible locations. In these latter types of trials, infants who have learned to use the central stimulus as a cue to predict the location of the target should orient more frequently to the contingent location, despite the target being presented in both locations. It was only in the 4-month-old group that significant evidence for learning the contingent relationship between the central stimulus and the location of the target was obtained (although trends in the same direction were found in the other groups). Although this effect was not a strong one, it is reinforced by the observation that during the training phase of the experiment it was only the 4-month-old group that showed a significant decrease in mean RT to make a saccade toward the target. There were no significant changes in mean RT as a result of training in the other age groups.

A recent series of studies by Colombo, Mitchell, Coldren, and Atwater (1990) investigated the ability of infants of 3, 6, and 9 months old to fixate toward a particular stimulus or lateral position as a result of reinforcement with an auditory stimulus. They established that whereas all age groups could acquire the contingency, 3-month-olds could not retain the stimulus discrimination after a 5-min delay. The younger infants also seemed to be more dominated by the positional, rather than the stimulus, cues. Although exact age information was not provided in this study, the finding that infants of around 3 months can learn about such a contingency may at first seem to conflict with those of Johnson, Posner, and Rothbart (1991). This need not be the case however, for two reasons. First, the authors themselves acknowledged that their findings with 3-month-olds should be interpreted with caution due to the high proportion of infants who failed to learn the response. Second, the procedure differed from that of Johnson et al. in ways that may make the task easier. Unlike the Johnson et al. task, in the Colombo et al. task the infant is presented with stimuli in the two possible locations from the outset. It only has to attend toward the correct one of the two locations (or stimuli) to obtain the auditory reward. In contrast to this, in the Johnson et al. task the infant begins a trial by attending to a cue. It then has to infer from the cue at what location the reward will appear.

COVERT VISUAL ATTENTION

The analysis of overt visual orienting discussed in the previous section accounts for at least some of the phenomena associated with the development of the control of eye movements and overt shifts of attention. The analysis did not, however, address the development of covert (internal) shifts of attention. In the adult literature it has been demonstrated internal covert attention mechanisms can be dissociated from eye movements (for review, see Posner & Peterson, 1990). A metaphor commonly applied to such a covert mechanism is that of "spotlight" or "beam" of attention that moves around the visual field. The discovery of such a mechanism in early infancy would be exceptionally important because it may represent the first indications of "top-down" control over behavior: that is, behavior seemingly initiated by the infant as opposed to being "input-driven." How might the operation of such a covert attention mechanism become apparent in the behavior of the infant?

In the previous section, the experiment by Johnson, Posner, and Rothbart (1991) was discussed. In this experiment, the 4-month-old group of infants were able to learn the contingency between a central stimulus and the location (right or left) in which a target would appear. This ability to use the first stimulus as a cue to predict the location of the second could be accounted for in two ways:

1. The onset of this ability is another manifestation of the functioning of the frontal eye field pathway, a pathway often thought to be involved in the acquisition of sequential looking patterns.
2. The onset of this ability indicates the ability to shift attention covertly.

The first possibility would be consistent with the finding that other functions attributed to the FEF pathway appear at about the same age. By this view it is no accident that the ability to make regular anticipatory saccades appears to coincide with the onset of the ability to perform the learning task: They are both manifestations of development in the same underlying mechanism.

The second account of the developments seen in the 4-month-old is that it is only at this age that covert attention mechanisms mature. This account would not rule out that there may be coincidental development of the frontal eye field pathway. This coincidental development may give rise to the onset of regular anticipatory saccades, but would be independent (developmentally) of the ability to use the central stimulus as a cue.

The latter argument would be supported if (a) structures known to subserve covert attention showed approximately the right developmental neuroanatomical time course, and (b) for any given infant of 4 months of age there was no significant correlation between their frequency of anticipatory looking and their ability to use the cue to predict the location of the target.

The correlations between the three aspects of the Johnson, Posner, and Rothbart (1991) task are shown in Table 9.2. There were no significant correlations between any of the measures within any age group. Indeed, in the 4-month-old group, most of the correlations are weak negative ones, reinforcing the conclusion that these abilities reflect the functioning of at least partially independent neural systems that happen to coincide in their developmental onset.

TABLE 9.2
Correlations Between the Three Measures of Orienting
for the Three Age Groups

	Anticipation/ Disengage	Disengage/ Preference	Preference/ Anticipation
2 Months	+0.42	+0.24	+0.17
3 Months	+0.12	−0.17	−0.30
4 Months	−0.27	+0.20	−0.27

Thus, it is possible that two independent developments underlie the changes between 3 and 4 months observed in the Johnson, Posner, and Rothbart (1991) study: first, the maturation of the frontal eye field pathway that allows anticipatory looking to occur more frequently; and, second, the independent development of covert attention subserved by the parietal cortex. It is this latter development that underlies the successful use of a central cue to predict the location where the target will appear. These facets of orienting are uncorrelated within any individual infant because they are mediated by at least partially different neural circuits.

In a recent experiment a further attempt was made to unravel these two mechanisms by training 4-month-olds to use a peripherally presented cue to predict the presentation of a target on the opposite side (Johnson, Posner, & Rothbart, 1990). Also included were trials in which the location of the cue is altered, and trials in which the target appears in the same location as the cue. The latter type of trials allowed a dissociation between a sequential looking strategy and a covert attention one. Specifically, infants had to learn that a cue stimulus on one of three screens can be used to predict that a target stimulus would subsequently appear on the opposite screen (right or left of the center screen; Fig. 9.6). Two mechanisms could be used by infants in this task. One is that they acquire a sequential looking pattern of the form "if left then right and if right then left." Another mechanism that be could employed is a covert attention spotlight that shifts from central fixation to the location of the cue. The information from the cue can then be used to generate a saccade in the opposite direction.

It is known from adult studies that, at short latencies, the presence of covert attention at a particular spatial location facilitates subsequent eye movements to that location (Maylor, 1985). Therefore we might expect the target stimulus to be oriented toward more rapidly if it appeared in this location very shortly after the offset of the cue. In other words, if infants used a covert attention mechanism in this task we would expect that they (a) not make a saccade toward the (briefly) presented cue stimulus, and (b) show a faster mean RT to make a saccade toward the target if it appeared in the cue location shortly after the cue offset. In contrast to this, if infants used a sequential looking strategy we would expect that they (a)

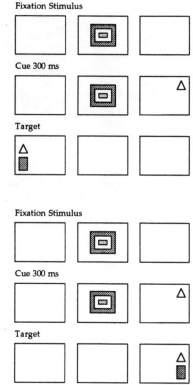

FIG. 9.6. Two of the types of trials employed in the experiment of Johnson, Posner and Rothbart (1990).

would regularly make a saccade toward the cue stimulus, and (b) would show a slower mean RT to orient toward the target if it appeared in an unexpected location such as under the cue. Of course, if infants adopted neither strategy we would expect them to show the same mean RT to make a saccade toward the target regardless of the spatial location in which it appears. After 16 training trials (Fig. 9.6 top) a test phase of the experiment began in which training trials were mixed in with test trials (in which the target appeared under the cue with very short latency—100ms; see Fig. 9.6 bottom).

Videotapes of the infants' eye movements during the experiment were subsequently coded by persons not directly involved in the testing, and mean RTs for each of the trials were established for each infant. Following the logic outlined earlier, the total sample of subjects was divided into three groups depending on the extent to which they shifted their gaze toward the cue stimulus during the training trials. One group of infants never looked toward the cue stimulus during the training phase (nonorienters), a second group were composed of those who shifted their gaze toward the cue intermittently (partial orienters), and a third group shifted their gaze toward the cue most of the time (real orienters).

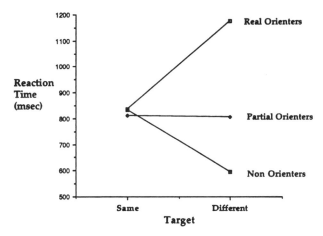

FIG. 9.7.   The mean RTs to orient toward the target stimulus for the training and test trials during the test phase of the experiment of Johnson, Posner, and Rothbart (1990). Groups of infants are defined according to their performance in the training phase of the experiment (see text for further details).

Figure 9.7 shows the difference in mean RT to orient toward the target when it appears under the cue as opposed to its expected location on the opposite screen. An analysis of variance performed on the means of means revealed no significant main effects of trial type or group, but a highly significant interaction between trial type and group ($F(2,19) = 4.92, p < .02$). That is, performance during the training phase of the experiment determined RT to orient toward the target when it appeared in the same spatial location as the cue.

To reiterate the argument outlined earlier, infants who employ a sequential looking mechanism during the experimental procedure should (a) make saccades toward the cue during training, and (b) show a slower mean RT to orient toward the target when it appears in the unexpected location (under the cue). In contrast, infants who employ a covert attention mechanism (a) will not make a saccade to the cue during training, and (b) will show a faster mean RT to make a saccade toward the target when it appears in the covertly attended location (where the cue appeared). Infants who adopt neither strategy should (a) intermittently look toward the cue during training, and (b) show no difference in mean RT to make a saccade toward the target, regardless of the location where it appears.

Looking at Fig. 9.7, it can be seen that all of these groups were represented within the sample of normal 4-month-olds. Why should the infants in our sample have adopted different strategies in the task? It is unlikely that age is a critical factor in determining strategy because the range of ages of the infants in our sample was very small. It is worth noting that most of the infants who adopted the covert strategy were boys whereas most of the infants who adopted the sequential looking strategy were girls. However, when we reanalyzed our data by gender, instead of by performance during the training phase, the significance of the effect was reduced suggesting that the degree of (overt) orienting toward the cue during training was a more accurate predictor of test performance in the test phase. Nevertheless, it is possible that this sex bias reflects the first manifestation of subsequent adult sex differences in visuo-spatial ability.

Inhibition of Return

The phenomenon of *inhibition of return* is also thought to be a reflection of covert attention mechanisms, and in some ways can be regarded as the opposite to the facilitation of saccades toward a covertly attended location discussed in the previous section. While *facilitation* of detection and saccades toward a covertly attended location occurs if the target stimulus appears very shortly after the cue offset, with longer latencies *inhibition* of saccades toward that location occurs (see Posner, this volume). In adults facilitation is observed when targets appeared at the cued location within about 100ms of the cue, whereas targets that appear between 300 and 1300msec after a peripheral cue result in longer latency saccades (e.g., Posner & Cohen 1980, 1984; Maylor 1985).

Concordant with the suggestion that maturation of a covert attention mechanism may be responsible for the changes observed in the study just described is the observation that inhibition of return may also develop between 3 and 6 months of age (Chlossey, Posner, Rothbart, & Vecera, 1991). In these experiments, infants have a stimulus briefly presented on one of two side screens. Following this they returned their gaze to the center screen, before an identical stimulus was presented bilaterally on both side screens. Between 4 and 6 months of age infants start to orient more toward the opposite side from that on which the initial stimulus appeared. The authors argue that this preferential orienting toward the opposite side is indicative of inhibition of return. This result has recently been replicated by Hood and Atkinson (1990).

Sustained Attention

Just because an infant is gazing at a stimulus this does not mean that it is actively processing it. Indeed, Richards (1989a, 1989b, 1991) has established by means of both behavioral and heart-rate measures that there are distinct temporal phases of visual attention toward a stimulus. The first phase is referred to as *automatic interrupt* and involves detecting the presence of a new stimulus. This phase is associate with a brief biphasic deceleration-acceleration of heart rate. The next stage is in one in which the infant orients toward the stimulus, *stimulus orienting*, and is accompanied by a larger deceleration of heart rate lasting about 5 s. The

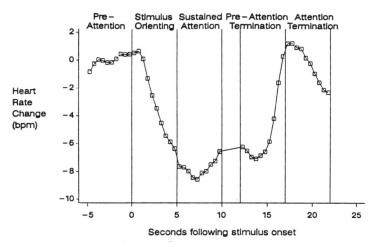

FIG. 9.8.   The heart rate defined information-processing phases. From Richards & Casey, 1991. Copyright 1991 by *Society for Psychophysiological Research*. Reprinted by permission.

extent of this stage is to some extent dependent on the novelty of the stimulus. The third stage is referred to as *sustained attention* and involves the maintaining of the heart-rate deceleration. The length of this phase depends on a variety of factors such as the novelty of the stimulus and the age of the infant, and varies from 2 to 3 s to 15 or 20 s. The final phase discussed by Richards is attention termination where the infant continues to gaze at the stimulus but does not continue to process information about it. During this phase heart rate returns to its prestimulus levels (over about 6 s). The heart-rate variations in these temporal phases of infant attention are shown in Fig. 9.8.

In one experiment, Richards (1989a, 1989b) used an *interrupted stimulus method* in which a peripheral stimulus (a flashing light) is presented while the infant is gazing at a central stimulus (a TV screen with a complex visual pattern). By varying the length of time between the onset of the TV image and the onset of the peripheral stimulus, he was able to ascertain the latency to orient toward the peripheral stimulus during different phases of attention to the TV screen. In accordance with his prediction, Richards found that during the periods when heart rate was decreased (sustained attention) it took twice as long for the infant to shift their gaze toward the peripheral stimulus as when heart rate had returned to prestimulus levels (attention termination). Thus, during periods of sustained attention the infant is less easily distracted by peripheral stimuli.

How do these observations relate to the neural pathways underlying attention discussed earlier? In general, the lack of distractibility by a peripheral stimulus is likely to be due to cortically mediated pathways inhibiting input-driven saccades generated by collicular mechanisms.[8] The time course of heart-rate changes are thought to reflect activation in cortical circuits processing visual information because both are consequences of excitation in the mesencephalic reticular formation (see Richards, 1991). If we assume that the cortically mediated pathways responsible for the inhibition of input-driven saccades are the MT and FEF pathways mentioned earlier, then we should expect there to be no clearly definable period of sustained attention in infants under 2 months. Concordant with this suggestion, Richards (1989b) reported that the clearly defined differences in distractibility in relation to heart rate are not found, or are at least very slight, in infants of 8 weeks of age.

ATTENTION AND DEVELOPMENT: IMPLICATIONS FOR ADULT NEUROPSYCHOLOGY

Aside from dissociating components of visual attention, there are several ways in which information from neurodevelopmental studies such as those described in this chapter can inform and complement studies of adult neuropsychology. Some of these are:

1. Following certain kinds of cortical damage or disorder, adult patients may show symptoms that are a regression to an earlier developmental state. One example of this is the observation that schizophrenic patients (often claimed to have frontal deficits) show an intrusion of saccades when attempting smooth pursuit of a moving target (Frith & Done, 1988). This, and some other abnormalities of visual attention in schizophrenics, may be attributed to the loss of frontal inhibition over collicular circuits (see also Cohen & Servan-Schreiber, 1992).

2. Brain injury occurring in the adult is normally "vertical" in the sense that it rarely effects particular cortical layers while leaving others intact. In early infant development we have the opportunity to study the layerwise development of cortical areas and their implications for other neural pathways. Due to the selective nature of cortico-cortico efferents and afferents with regard to the layers in which they originate and terminate, this offers a potentially powerful technique for dissociating neural pathways more "cleanly" than often occurs following gross injury.

---

[8]A recent experiment with 3- and 6-month-olds has provided further support for the idea that collicular orienting mechanisms are inhibited during sustained attention (Richards, 1991). In this experiment it was found that saccades toward a peripheral stimulus during sustained attention to a central stimulus were less accurate than normal, and involved multiple jumps, patterns of behavior often found in much younger infants.

3. The neurodevelopmental approach leads to a particular view of the relationship between classes of representations and the control mechanisms underlying attention. The rest of this section is devoted to outlining the viewpoint.

Throughout this chapter I have implicitly argued that the development of visual attention can be characterized in terms of increasing levels of hierarchical control.[9] Each new attention or orienting mechanism that develops has some degree of influence, either by differential excitation or inhibition, over those that preceded it. For example, the collicular control of orienting was superseded by the MT system, which was to some extent superseded by the FEF and covert mechanisms. At each transition, the earlier stage of control is not lost, but merely becomes incorporated as part of the machinery of a higher level of control. Clearly, under the right conditions, the earlier developing systems can still operate independently even in the adult (e.g., Rafal, Henik, & Smith, 1991).

One characteristic of the progression of levels of attentional control in the infant is worth noting. This is that the later developing systems seem to be more concerned with the prediction of future events. Thus, although the collicular level of control responds to stimuli appearing within the peripheral visual field, the FEF system was argued to be involved in the generation of saccades before the actual appearance of a target. That this progression toward more anticipatory mechanisms should take place is not surprising, given that the ability to anticipate future events would be likely to be a key ability for understanding and interpreting aspects of the external world.

During ontogeny a parallel development to that in levels of attentional control may occur in the classes of representations that are encoded, and that influence behavior. Let us take the development of face recognition as an example of this. In the newborn, a stimulus such as three high-contrast blobs in the correct location for eyes and a mouth may be sufficient to obtain a discriminatory response (Johnson, Dziurawiec, Ellis & Morton, 1991). Although simple monochromatic facelike stimuli are also sufficient to elicit a preference in infants of 2 months of age, the elements require to resemble the features of a face (Johnson, Dziurawiec, Bartrip & Morton, 1992). By 5 months of age, the features must be moving in a facelike manner in order to elicit a preference (Johnson et al., 1992), suggesting that, by this age, the infant's "mental image" of a face has incorporated dynamic aspects of the stimulus. I have argued elsewhere that classes of representations relating to conspecifics become increasingly "predictive" during ontogeny (Johnson & Leslie, in preparation). That is, infants' perception of conspecifics goes from being viewer-centered to object-centered to goal-centered to a level of representation based on the supposition that the object being viewed

---

[9]The idea that the brain can be characterized by the hierarchical arrangement of systems is, of course, not a new one (see Jackson, 1884/1958).

has a mind similar to one's own ("theory of mind" is the phrase coined for this class of representations by Premack & Woodruff, 1978).

The thesis that I have attempted to defend elsewhere is that particular levels of attentional control are associated with particular classes of representation. This is due to the ontogenetic fact that the sensory input to the developing cortical circuitry that will come to subserve a particular class of representation, is partly determined by the level of attentional control operating at that age. Thus, when attentional mechanisms are sophisticated enough to predict future events (such as the spatial location where an interesting target stimulus will appear), the infant will be able to develop more dynamic representations concerned with these events or stimuli.

What are the implications of these developmental considerations for adult neuropsychology? First, that we should expect that multiple levels of attentional control will be involved in most tasks. Although this fact may not be surprising to many, it is sometimes overlooked in the adult literature. For example, the fact that patients with collicular damage are impaired in tasks purported to measure some component of attention, does not mean that this is the brain structure that was primarily controlling the behavior. The structure may simply be implementing saccades generated elsewhere.

A second implication for adult neuropsychology is that we should expect the brain to contain multiple representations of some classes of stimuli important for survival. Thus, by this view, it is unlikely that there is only one cortical region involved in the processing of faces. Rather, there will be several classes of representations associated with the recognition of faces and their expressions. These classes of representations may even have different developmental histories. Taking this argument to its extreme leads to the prediction that there will be several varieties of disorder related to prosopagnosia.[10] Whether these classes of representations related to conspecifics are identified or not largely depends on the stimulus materials used in testing patients, or while recording from neurones in the monkey. Seen in this light, the apparent fractionation of face recognition abilities with different types of testing methods and materials (see chapter 11 of this volume) is hardly surprising.

Perhaps the most speculative implication of the view put forward in this section is that there may be an association between patterns of breakdown in attentional control and classes of representation. Thus, for example, collicular control of orienting may be associated with representations at the level of Marr's 2.5-dimensional sketch, and we might expect deficits in some aspects of covert attention to be intimately associated with deficits in representations that have a dynamic component. This suggests that we should be more circumspect in classi-

---

[10]Of course, some of these may never fractionate cleanly following brain damage. For example, there is evidence for face-sensitive cells in the primate amygdala. Even localized damage to this region, however, is likely to cause widespread effects on behavior.

fying adult patients as having either attentional problems or recognition deficits. The two may often coexist in ways that will tell us much more about the architecture of the human mind.

ACKNOWLEDGMENTS

Financial support from the McDonnell foundation, the Human Frontiers science program, the MRC (UK), NSF (grant DBS-9120433) and Carnegie Mellon contributed to some of the experiments described in this chapter. Leslie Tucker and Chris Hirt assisted in its preparation.

REFERENCES

Arehart, D. M., & Haith, M. M. (1991, April). *Evidence for visual expectation violations in 13-week old infants.* Paper presented at meeting of Society for Research in Child Development, Seattle.

Aslin, R. M. (1981). Development of smooth pursuit in human infants. In D. F. Fisher, R. A. Monty, & S. W. Senders (Eds.), *Eye movements: Cognition and visual perception* (pp. 31–51). Hillsdale, NJ: Lawrence Erlbaum Associates.

Atkinson, J. (1984). Human visual development over the first six months of life: A review and a hypothesis. *Human Neurobiology, 3,* 61–74.

Atkinson, J., Hood, B., Wattam-Bell, J., Anker, S., & Tricklebank, J. (1988). Development of orientation discrimination in infants. *Perception, 17,* 587–595.

Banks, M. S., & Salapatek, P. (1981). Infant pattern vision: A new approach based on the contrast sensitivity function. *Journal of Experimental Child Psychology, 31,* 1–45.

Becker, L. E., Armstrong, D. L., Chan, F., & Wood, M. M. (1984). Dendritic development in human occipital cortical neurons. *Developmental Brain Research, 13,* 117–124.

Bronson, G. W. (1974). The postnatal growth of visual capacity. *Child Development, 45,* 873–890.

Bronson, G. W. (1982). Structure, status and characteristics of the nervous system at birth. In P. Stratton (Ed.), *Psychobiology of the human newborn* (pp. 99–114). Chichester, England: Wiley.

Burkhalter, A., & Bernardo, K. L. (1989). Organization of corticocortical connections in human visual cortex. *Proceedings of the National Academy of Sciences, 86,* 1071–1075.

Bushnell, I. W. R., Sai, F., & Mullin, J. T. (1989). Neonatal recognition of the mother's face. *British Journal of Developmental Psychology, 7,* 3–15.

Canfield, R. L. (1991, April). Stability of RT and visual expectancies from 4 to 6 months of age. Paper presented at the meeting of the Society for Research in Child Development, Seattle.

Canfield, R. L., & Haith, M. M. (1991). Young infants' visual expectations for symmetric and asymmetric stimulus sequences. *Developmental Psychology, 27,* 198–208.

Clohessy, A. B., Posner, M. I., Rothbart, M. K., & Vecera, S. (1991). The development of inhibition of return in early infancy. *Journal of Cognitive Neuroscience, 3,* 345–350.

Cohen, J., & Servan-Schreiber, D. (1992). Contex, cortex and dopamine: A connectionist approach to behavior and biology in schizophrenia. *Psychological Review.*

Cohen, L. B. (1988). An information processing approach to infant cognitive development. In L. Weiskrantz (Ed.), *Thought without language* (pp. 211–228). Oxford, England: Clarendon.

Colombo, J., Mitchell, D. W., Coldren, J. T., & Atwater, J. D. (1990). Discrimination learning during the first year: Stimulus and positional cues. *Journal of Experimental Psychology: Learning, Memory and Cognition, 16,* 98–109.

Condry, H., Gentile, D. A., & Yonas, A. (April, 1991). *Four and seven month old infants' perception of global structure with kinetic illusory contour displays.* Paper presented at the meeting of the Society for Research in Child Development, Seattle.

Conel, J. L. (1967). *The postnatal development of the human cerebral cortex* (Vols. 1–8). Cambridge, MA: Harvard University Press. (Original work published 1939)

Cowey, A., & Stoerig, P. (1991). The neurobiology of blindsight. *Trends in the Neurosciences, 14,* 140–145.

de Yoe, E. A., & Van Essen, D. C. (1988). Concurrent processing streams in monkey visual cortex. *TINS, 11,* 219–226.

Frith, C. D., & Done, J. (1988). Towards a neuropsychology of schizophrenia. *British Journal of Psychiatry, 153,* 437–443.

Haith, M. M., Hazan, C., & Goodman, G. S. (1988). Expectation and anticipation of dynamic visual events by 3.5-month old babies. *Child Development, 59,* 467–479.

Held, R. (1985). Binocular vision: Behavioral and neural development. In J. Mehler & R. Fox (Eds.), *Neonate cognition: Beyond the blooming, buzzing confusion* (pp. 37–44). Hillsdale, NJ: Lawrence Erlbaum Associates.

Hirsch, H. V. B., Tieman, D. G., Tieman, S. B., & Tumosa, N. (1987). Unequal alternating exposure: Effects during and after the classical critical period. In J. P. Rauschecker & P. Marler (Eds.), *Imprinting and cortical plasticity: Comparative aspects of sensitive periods.* New York: Wiley.

Hood, B., & Atkinson, J. (1990). Inhibition of return in infants. *Perception, A47.*

Huttenlocher, P. R. (1990). Morphometric study of human cerebral cortex development. *Neuropsychologia, 28,* 517–527.

Jackson, J. H. (1958). The evolution and dissolution of the nervous system, Lecture II. In J. Taylor (Ed.), *Selected writings of John Hughlings Jackson* (Vol. 2). New York: Basic. (Original work published 1884)

Johnson, M. H. (1990a). Cortical maturation and the development of visual attention in early infancy. *Journal of Cognitive Neuroscience, 2,* 81–95.

Johnson, M. H. (1990b). Cortical maturation and perceptual development. In H. Bloch & B. K. Bertenthal (Eds.), *Sensory motor organisation and development in infancy and early childhood* (pp. 145–162). Dordrecht, Netherlands: Academic.

Johnson, M. H., Dziurawiec, S., Bartrip, J., & Morton, J. (1992). The effects of movement of internal features on infants' preferences for face-like stimuli. *Infant Behavior and Development, 15,* 129–136.

Johnson, M. H., Dziurawiec, S., Ellis, H. D., & Morton, J. (1991). Newborns' preferential tracking of face-like stimuli and its subsequent decline. *Cognition, 40,* 1–23.

Johnson, M. H., & Karmiloff-Smith, A. (1992). Can neural selectionism be applied to cognitive development and its disorders? *New Ideas in Psychology, 10,* 35–46.

Johnson, M. H., & Leslie, A. M. (In preparation). A neural circuit analysis of the capacity to acquire a "theory of mind".

Johnson, M. H., Posner, M. I., & Rothbart, M. K. (1990). *Covert attention and sequential looking patterns in four month olds.* Unpublished manuscript.

Johnson, M. H., Posner, M. I., & Rothbart, M. K. (1991). Components of visual orienting in early infancy: Contingency learning, anticipatory looking, and disengaging. *Journal of Cognitive Neuroscience, 3,* 335–344.

Lund, J. (1988). Anatomical organization of macaque monkey striate visual cortex. *Annual Review of Neuroscience, 11,* 253–288.

Maunsell, J. H. R., & Van Essen, D. C. (1983). The connections of the middle temporal visual area (MT) and their relation to a cortical hierarchy in the macaque monkey. *Journal of Neuroscience, 3,* 2563–2586.

Maurer, D., & Lewis, T. L. (1979). A physiological explanation of infants' early visual development. *Canadian Journal of Psychology, 33*, 232–252.

Maylor, E. A. (1985). Facilitatory and inhibitory components of orienting in visual space. In M. I. Posner & O. M. Marin (Eds.), *Attention & performance XI*. Hillsdale, NJ: Laurence Erlbaum Associates.

Morton, J., Johnson, M. H., & Maurer, D. (1990). On the reasons for newborns' responses to faces. *Infant Behavior and Development, 13*, 99–103.

Muir, D. W., Clifton, R. K., & Clarkson, M. G. (1989). The development of a human auditory localization response: A U-shaped function. *Canadian Journal of Psychology, 43*, 199–216.

Newsome, W. T., Britten, K. H., & Movshon, J. A. (1989). Neuronal correlates of a perceptual decision. *Nature, 341*, 52–54.

Newsome, W. T., & Pare, E. B. (1988). A selective impairment of motion processing following lesions of the middle temporal visual area (MT). *Journal of Neuroscience, 8*, 2201–2211.

Newsome, W. Y., & Wurtz, R. H. (1988). Probing visual cortical function with discrete chemical lesions. *Trends in the Neurosciences, 11*, 394–400.

Premack, D. G., & Woodruff, G. (1978). Does the chimpanzee have a theory of mind? *Behavioral and Brain Sciences, 1*, 515–526.

Posner, M. I., & Cohen, Y. (1980). Attention and the control of movements. In G. E. Stelmach & J. Roguiro (Eds.), *Tutorials in motor behavior*. Amsterdam, Netherlands: North Holland.

Posner, M. I., & Cohen, Y. (1984). Components of visual orienting. In H. Bouma & D. G. Bouwhis (Eds.), *Attention and performance* X. Hillsdale, NJ: Lawrence Erlbaum Associates.

Posner, M. I., & Peterson, S. E. (1990). The attention system of the human brain. *Annual Review of Neuroscience, 13*, 25–42.

Posner, M. I., & Rothbart, M. K. (1980). The development of attentional mechanisms. In J. H. Flower (Ed.), *Nebraska symposium on motivation* (pp. 1–52). Lincoln: University of Nebraska Press.

Purpura, D. P. (1975). Normal and aberrant neuronal development in the cerebral cortex of human fetus and young infant. In N. A. Buchwald & M. A. B. Brazier (Eds.), *Brain mechanisms of mental retardation* (pp. 141–169). New York: Academic.

Rabinowicz, T. (1979). The differential maturation of the human cerebral cortex. In F. Faulkner & J. M. Tanner (Eds.), *Human growth: Vol. 3, Neurobiology and nutrition*. New York: Plenum.

Rafal, R., Henik, A., & Smith, J. (1991). Extrageniculate contribution to reflex visual orienting in normal humans: A temporal hemifield advantage. *Journal of Cognitive Neuroscience, 3*, 322–328.

Richards, J. E. (1989a). Development and stability of HR-defined, visual sustained attention in 14, 20, and 26 week old infants. *Psychophysiology, 26*, 422–430.

Richards, J. E. (1989b). Sustained visual attention in 8-week old infants. *Infant Behavior and Development, 12*, 425–436.

Richards, J. E. (1991). Infant eye movements during peripheral visual stimulus localization as a function of central stimulus attention status. *Psychophysiology, 28*.

Richards, J. E., & Casey, B. J. (1991). Heart rate variability during attention phases in young infants. *Psychophysiology, 28*, 43–53.

Rockland, K. S., & Pandya, D. N. (1979). Laminar origins and terminations of cortical connections of the occipital lobe in the rhesus monkey. *Brain Research, 179*, 3–20.

Rodman, H. R., Gross, C. G., & Albright, T. D. (1989). Afferent basis of visual response properties in area MT of the macaque. I. Effects of striate cortex removal. *Journal of Neuroscience, 9*, 2033–2050.

Rothbart, M. K., Posner, M. I., & Boylan, A. (1990). Regulatory mechanisms in infant temperament. In J. Enns (Ed.), *The development of attention: Research and theory*. Amsterdam, Netherlands: North Holland.

Salzman, C. D., Britten, K. H., & Newsome, W. T. (1990). Cortical microstimulation influences perceptual judgements of motion direction. *Nature, 346,* 174–177.

Schiller, P. H. (1985). A model for the generation of visually guided saccadic eye movements. In D. Rose & V. G. Dobson (Eds.), *Models of the visual cortex.* Chicester, England: Wiley.

Schwartz, T. L., Dobson, V., Sandstrom, D. J., & van Hof-van Duin, J. (1987). Kinetic perimetry assessment of binocular visual field shape and size in young infants. *Vision Research, 27,* 2163–2175.

Slater, A. (1988). Habituation and visual fixation in infants: Information processing, reinforcement and what else? *European Bulletin of Cognitive Psychology, 8,* 517–523.

Slater, A., Morison, V., & Somers, M. (1988). Orientation discrimination and cortical function in the human newborn. *Perception, 17,* 597–602.

Spitz, R. V., & Kleffner, D. (1992). The perception of coherent motion in infancy: Estimates from the displacement limit at 4- and 7 months. Unpublished manuscript.

Stechler, G., & Latz, E. (1966). Some observations on attention and arousal in the human infant. *Journal of the American Academy of Child Psychiatry, 5,* 517–525.

Tennes, K., Emde, R., Kisley, A., & Metcalf, D. (1972). The stimulus barrier in early infancy: An exploration of some formulations of John Benjamin. In R. R. Holt & E. Peterfreund (Eds.), *Psychoanalysis and contemporary science.* New York: Macmillan.

Van Essen, D. C. (1985). Functional organisation of primate visual cortex. In A. Peters & E. G. Jones (Eds.), *Cerebral cortex* (Vol. 3). New York: Plenum.

Vaughan, H. G., & Kurtzberg, D. (1989). Electrophysiologic indices of normal and aberrant cortical maturation. In P. Kellaway & J. L. Noebels (Eds.), *Problems and concepts in developmental neurophysiology.* Baltimore: Johns Hopkins University Press.

Wentworth, N., & Hood, R. (1991, April). The effect of stimulus duration on young infants' visual expectations. Paper presented at the meeting of the Society for Research in Child Development, Seattle.

10 Visual Mental Images in the Brain: Current Issues

Stephen M. Kosslyn
Harvard University

Lisa M. Shin
Harvard University

Visual mental imagery occurs when visual information is retained or when stored visual information is activated, creating a short-term memory representation that is accompanied by the experience of "seeing with the mind's eye." In this chapter we review key issues surrounding, and much of the recent empirical findings about, visual mental imagery. However, we have chosen not to review the findings exhaustively; the literature on visual mental imagery has been surveyed many times in the recent past, notably by Farah (1988), Finke (1989), and Finke and Shepard (1986); prior to this, Paivio (1971), Kosslyn (1980), and Shepard and Cooper (1982) provided detailed reviews of the earlier literature. We have no desire to duplicate previous efforts; hence, we focus on major current issues about the brain mechanisms that underlie imagery, and review only findings that have a direct relation to these issues.

The issues we consider bear on the mechanisms that produce a set of imagery abilities. We concentrate on the aspects of imagery that allow us to use it to recall information and to reason about spatial properties. For example, consider the following imagery task: One is packing a truck with furniture, and first studies the furniture that is sitting at curbside. One then visualizes a sofa in the truck, imagining how it would look in particular positions: against the far wall or against the side wall. After settling on a position and holding the image of the sofa, one then visualizes a chair and tries to "see" how the chair would fit relative to the sofa. It happens that by turning the chair upside down, it fits snugly against one side of the sofa. One then turns to an end table, and so on. Eventually, one has visualized a configuration of the furniture that appears to use the space efficiently.

This task illustrates four of our imagery abilities. First, one can "inspect" patterns in images, "seeing" whether the pieces of furniture fit tightly together. Second, one can generate images of specific objects, adding additional objects to the imaged scene. Third, one can retain the image while adding new objects. Fourth, one can mentally transform the scene, imagining furniture shifting and turning in various ways.

We consider key issues about each of these abilities, and for each we summarize recent findings that bear on the nature of the neural mechanisms that underlie the ability. Many of the inferences we discuss are based on material that is treated in more detail elsewhere (Kosslyn, 1987; Kosslyn, Flynn, Amsterdam, & Wang, 1990; Kosslyn & Koenig, 1992). To avoid excessive redundancy with these earlier publications, we only briefly summarize this material here.

We begin with a fundamental issue, the relationship between the mechanisms that subserve imagery and those that subserve like-modality perception. This issue is critically important because we now know a large amount about the neural mechanisms underlying visual perception. Thus, if imagery can be assumed to share these mechanisms, we gain enormous leverage in developing theories of imagery. We then turn to the question of what is an image representation, taking advantage of the assumption that imagery shares mechanisms with like-modality perception. Following this, we consider issues about the nature of image inspection, and then turn to image generation. We then discuss image maintenance, which appears to be closely tied to some forms of image generation. Finally, we consider the mechanisms underlying image transformation.

IMAGERY AND PERCEPTION

Imagery is often characterized as "seeing with the mind's eye," "hearing with the mind's ear," and the like. These characterizations suggest that mental imagery shares mechanisms with like-modality perception, and in fact, there is much evidence that this is true (Farah, 1988). Let us consider a few representative findings.

Are Neural Structures Used in Visual Perception Used in Visual Imagery?

Studies of regional cerebral blood flow show that visual areas of the brain are active during visual mental imagery. For example, Roland and Friberg (1985) instructed subjects to imagine walking out of their front door and turning alternately right and left. Regional cerebral blood flow was measured using the intracarotid ^{133}Xe injection technique. Compared to a mental subtraction task and a verbal task, the visual mental imagery task resulted in increased blood flow to the posterior superior parietal, the superior temporal, and the posterior inferior temporal areas, all of which are also involved in visual perception. (Unfortunately, most of the occipital lobe was not monitored in this study.)

Similarly, Goldenberg, Podreka, Steiner, and Willmes (1987) used single photon emission computed tomography (SPECT) with IMP (123-I-N-isopropylamphetamine) to measure regional cerebral blood flow. Their subjects were instructed to memorize a list of auditorily presented concrete nouns. One group of subjects used visual imagery to memorize the list, and another group used either simple rehearsal or no particular strategy at all. The results showed high blood flow in the left inferior occipital lobe for some subjects who used visual mental imagery, and Goldenberg et al. concluded that regions of the medial occipital and inferior temporal lobe are involved in visual mental imagery.

In another experiment, Goldenberg et al. (1989) asked subjects to listen to high-imagery statements (such as, "The forelegs of a cat are longer than its hind legs"), low-imagery statements (such as, "The Vatican is in Rome, but it is a state of its own and not part of Italy"), or the words *yes* and *no*. The subjects were asked to flash a light whenever they heard a false statement (or a "no," for subjects in the third condition). While they were performing the task, the amount of blood flow in different regions of their brains was assessed using the SPECT technique. The results showed activity in the occipital, temporal, and parietal lobes when the high-imagery statements were evaluated, and all of these areas are also involved in visual perception. In addition, there was significantly more activity in the left inferior occipital regions in the high-imagery condition than in the other two conditions.

Event-related potentials (ERPs) have also been used to examine the relationship between imagery and perception. Farah, Peronnet, Gonon, and Giard (1988) asked subjects to image either an *H* or a *T*, and then presented them with faint *H* and *T* stimuli while ERPs to the faint *H* and *T* stimuli were recorded. Previous studies suggested that mental imagery selectively facilitates perception so that if subjects image the letter *H*, they are more likely to detect a faint letter *H* than they are to detect a faint letter *T* and vice versa (Farah, 1985). In order to discover whether imagery selectively affects the visual ERP to the stimuli, Farah et al. separately averaged the ERPs from the trials on which the image matched the stimulus and the trials on which the image did not match the stimulus. Results showed that the effect of imagery was greatest in the occipital and the posterior-temporal scalp areas, consistent with the hypothesis that imagery shares these visual cortical regions with perception.

In addition, Kosslyn, Alpert et al. (1993) used positron emission tomography (PET) to study visual mental imagery and found very similar patterns of activation when an imagery and an analogous perception task were compared. Specifically, they found activation in the medial occipital, inferior temporal, posterior parietal, and dorsolateral prefrontal lobes, as well as several subcortical structures. We discuss these findings in more detail shortly. The important point for present concerns is that in all of the activation studies, most of the areas that are activated by imagery are also active in perception.

Does Brain Damage Disrupt Imagery and Perception Together?

We would not expect imagery and perception always to be disrupted by the same lesions; they are, after all, different functions. Thus, we expect that some lesions should disrupt processes that are unique to imagery or perception. However, if some mechanisms are shared, then we also expect to find patients who have correlated deficits. As we argue later, the mechanisms underlying the "mind's eye" (i.e., the processes that "inspect" imaged objects) seem particularly likely to be shared by the two functions. And in fact, there is good evidence that brain damage that disrupts "seeing" objects or spatial relations in imagery often disrupts perception in the same way, and vice versa. For example, Bisiach and Luzzatti (1978) found that brain-damaged patients who neglect (ignore) one half of space during perception also neglect one half of space during imagery. They asked such patients to imagine standing at one end of a plaza and to describe what they could "see" in their images. These patients neglected the buildings and landmarks that would have been on the left side of the plaza, but they described what would have been on the right (nonneglected) side. Following this, the subjects were asked to imagine standing at the opposite end of the plaza, looking back toward their previous location. When asked to describe what they could "see" from this vantage point, they mentioned buildings and landmarks that they had previously ignored, but they ignored those that they had previously described.

Hemianopia, as well as hemispatial neglect, can also be manifest in imagery. Kosslyn, Cave, and Gabrieli (1989) studied patients who had "field cuts" (blind regions) so that they could see objects only when they subtended a relatively small visual angle. These patients were simply asked to visualize objects against a screen, and to point to where the left and right side of the object would be if they were actually seeing it. The visual angle subtended was measured, and Kosslyn et al. found that these patients could form images of objects only when they subtended a relatively small visual angle. Indeed, it appeared that the larger the field cut in perception, the smaller the angle at which images could be formed. Farah, Soso, and Dasheiff (1992) used Kosslyn's (1978) method for measuring the visual angle of the mind's eye to examine the scope of imagery in a female patient (MGS) before and after unilateral occipital lobectomy. After this surgery, which left her with a dense left homonymous hemianopia, her images were confined to a smaller maximum size. These results are consistent with the claim that imagery does in fact share common mechanisms with perception. For a good review of similar findings, see Farah (1988).

THE IMAGE REPRESENTATION

If we assume that visual imagery occurs in parts of cortex that also are used in visual perception, then we gain insight into the nature of the representations that underlie imagery. Visual mental imagery must make accessible the local geometry of remembered shapes; one purpose of imagery is to help one recall such information. For example, one may use imagery to determine the shape of an enclosed space (e.g., the space within the upper case version of the letter *a*) or whether a banana or cucumber is more bow-shaped. Kosslyn (1980) reviewed much evidence that image representations preserve the spatial structure of objects.

Many areas of cortex process visual information; see chapter 1 of this volume for an up-to-date review. Many areas preserve the spatial structure of at least part of the retina, and hence are called *retinotopically mapped*. These areas are physically organized so that a pattern of activation within them mirrors the pattern of activation on the retina, displaying a planar projection of an object. In most of these retinotopically mapped areas, the image is distorted because more cortical area is allocated to the fovea than to the periphery. Nevertheless, these areas depict the spatial structure of an object, as seen from a single point of view. These retinotopically mapped areas are at the "lower" and "intermediate" levels in the visual system; areas that are further along in the processing sequence are less likely to be topographically organized (see chapter 1 of this volume; see also Felleman & Van Essen, 1991; Van Essen, 1985).

During visual perception, the retinotopically mapped areas of cortex receive input from lower visual areas that intervene between the eyes and cortex. In addition, they also receive input from higher areas. Indeed, virtually all visual areas that send input to another area also receive input from that area (see chapter 1 of this volume; see also Felleman & Van Essen, 1991; Van Essen, 1985). Therefore, it is plausible that "high-level" areas that store visual information can evoke patterns of activation in the retinotopically mapped areas even when no input is arriving from the eyes. This top-down processing would evoke a pattern of activation in at least some of these areas, which would be a visual mental image proper.

This idea is consistent with the finding that the occipital lobe, which contains many retinotopically organized areas, is activated during imagery, as noted earlier. Fox et al. (1986) used PET scanning to document that an area in the medial occipital cortex is retinotopically mapped in humans. Thus, it is of interest that the same area may have been activated by imagery. In fact, as illustrated in Fig. 10.1, Kosslyn, Alpert et al. (1993) showed that more anterior portions of this area were activated by images that subtended large angles, whereas more posterior portions were activated by images that subtended small angles. The locations of activation were close to what was expected based on perceptual results—even though subjects closed their eyes in the imagery task.

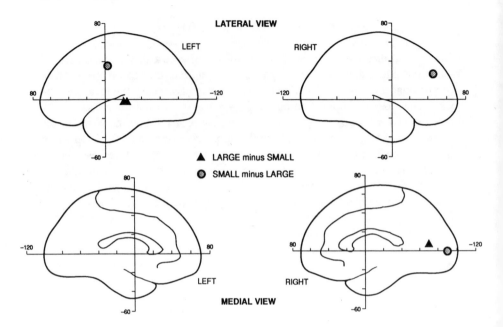

FIG. 10.1.   PET results: Lateral and medial views. The triangles indicate loci where large images activated the brain more than small images, and circles indicate loci where small images activated the brain more than large images. Copyright 1993 by MIT Press. Reprinted by permission.

In addition, Kosslyn (1980) summarized evidence that subjects require more time to "see" small properties of imaged objects. This finding makes sense if the structure that supports images (the "visual buffer") has a "grain" because of spatial summation, the neural averaging over variations within a given region. If this property affects all representations in the structure, then it follows that that spatial variations of objects will be obscured if they are too small, both when we view them and image them.

A Dedicated System?

It seems unlikely that the rich pattern of efferent (backwards) connections in the visual system evolved expressly to form visual mental images. Rather, we suspect that these connections had a different purpose, but once they were present they could be recruited into this new context. In this respect, imagery is a little like the nose; the nose presumably evolved to warm and filter air, but once it was present it could be used to hold up glasses (Gould & Lewontin, 1979).

We speculate that the original purpose of the efferent fibers was to help the system deal with fragmentary and "noisy" input during perception; because of occlusion, less than ideal viewing conditions, and the like, such fragmented and noisy input is the norm. Because of this problem, many researchers in computer vision have found that it is useful to supplement the input with stored information (Lowe, 1985). The anatomy of the visual system suggests that "cooperative computation" may occur, with each level sending feedback to earlier areas to help resolve the noise (see Kosslyn & Koenig, 1992). Kosslyn, Alpert et al. (1993) used PET scanning to provide evidence that imagery may be used when one encodes degraded input.

A Mental Screen?

We identify the set of retinotopically mapped areas that can be activated from memory as the "visual buffer" posited by Kosslyn (1980). This line of thinking leads us to suspect that Kosslyn's earlier characterization of the visual buffer as a mental "screen" was misguided. Kosslyn conceived of the visual buffer as a static structure, analogous to an array in a computer. But according to the present view, the visual buffer is much more than a static array; it performs a great deal of computation. During perception, the visual buffer defines regions of homogeneous color and texture, and actively computes edges by filling in missing portions. When an image is created from stored information, there may be gaps in patterns; it is unlikely that we record faithfully all of the details, even if we do perceive them in the first place (which is unlikely). The visual buffer may fill in these gaps using bottom-up processes that complete colinear fragments, regions of color, and so forth.

Consistent with these inferences, Kosslyn, Alpert et al. (1993) found greater activation in the medial occipital lobe during imagery than during a corresponding perceptual task. Apparently the visual buffer had to work harder to fill in information during imagery than during perception; this assumption makes sense because stored visual memories may be more fragmentary than on-line percepts, and hence imagery requires additional computation to fill in edges and the like. Indeed, when the perceptual stimulus was degraded, the difference between imagery and perception was eliminated.

Kosslyn, Alpert et al. used a variant of a task developed by Podgorny and Shepard (1978). In Kosslyn, Alpert et al.'s experiment, the subjects first were asked to memorize a set of block letters drawn within a 4 × 5 grid. Later they were shown grids that contained only a single X mark with a script version of a letter underneath, and were asked whether the X would be covered by a specific block letter if it were present in the grid. Podgorny and Shepard had earlier shown that this task requires imagery.

This imagery task, however, involves processes that encode the probe, make the comparison, reach a decision, and generate a response. To remove the contribution of such processes, the subjects participated in a task that was identical to the experimental one except that light gray letters were actually presented in the grids; thus, no imagery was required. These pairs of tasks were very similar to those used by Podgorny and Shepard (1978), which is important because they found that a host of factors—such as the number of probes and size of the display—had identical effects in the imagery and perceptual version of the task. Using the logic of additive factors analysis (Sternberg, 1969), this result suggests that the two tasks share numerous processes. Thus, it seemed reasonable to subtract the blood flow evoked by the perceptual task from that evoked by the imagery task; the remainder should reflect the effects of imagery per se.

The imagery version of the task was developed by Kosslyn, Cave, Provost, and Von Gierke (1988), who modified the original task to allow them to study image generation. They presented the lower case cue very quickly, not allowing subjects enough time to finish forming the image before the X appeared. Thus, at least part of the response time reflected the time to form the image. Perhaps the most interesting result was that subjects evaluated the probe more or less quickly depending on its location, and the ordering of response times suggested that the subjects imaged the letters a segment at a time. Indeed, the relative time to evaluate a probe was predicted by the order in which other subjects drew the segments of uppercase letters in grids; for example, the left vertical bar of an *F* was drawn first, the top horizontal one next, and so on. This result occurred only when the image had to be generated on the spot; if a light gray letter was present in the grid, or if subjects were allowed to form the image before the X was presented, there was no effect of probe position. Thus, this effect indicates that response times do indeed reflect the image generation process. We defer discussing the PET results that bear on image generation until we consider this process later in the chapter.

Kosslyn, Alpert et al. (1993) were concerned that any differences between the conditions might reflect the effects of seeing more lines in an empty grid, or moving one's eyes over the grid. Thus, they tested a second group of subjects in a sensory-motor control task. These subjects saw empty grids with an X mark and simply waited for the X mark to be removed before responding. The X mark was presented for variable amounts of time, but the mean exposure time was the same as in the imagery condition. Thus, it is of interest that the selective activity in the occipital lobe did not occur in this control task when it was compared to the perceptual control task (the same as that received by subjects in the imagery group).

IMAGE INSPECTION

Pylyshyn (1973) attacked the idea that imagery is a distinct form of internal representation. This attack rested on apparent paradoxes in the concept. One such paradox was noted in the title of his article, "What the Mind's Eye Tells the

Mind's Brain: A Critique of Mental Imagery." Pylyshyn was worried about "who sees" objects in images. Do we need to posit an homunculus to look at the object? If so, do we need another one in his head? And how can these little people see, when there is no light in the brain? (For a review of the arguments, see chapter 2 of Kosslyn, 1980.)

What Is the Mind's Eye?

The fundamental issue concerns how we can "see" objects we are imaging. If we assume that imagery and perception share common mechanisms, we can put to rest the worry that this idea is paradoxical; we can understand how objects are inspected during visual mental imagery by examining the mechanisms used to inspect an object during perception.

During perception, the visual buffer contains more information than can be processed at any one time; hence, there is a mechanism that gives one region in the buffer higher processing priority than other regions. We call this mechanism the *attention window*. The attention window selects a contiguous region of the visual buffer for further processing, inhibiting other areas from sending information further into the system.

At least since the time of Sperling (1960), it has been known that humans can shift attention covertly across space, even when eye movements are not possible. We conceive of such shifts as movements of the attention window. The attention window not only can be shifted to different locations in the visual buffer, but also can be adjusted to take in different sized regions of the buffer (Larsen & Bundesen, 1978; Treisman & Gelade, 1980). In fact, the time needed to adjust the size of the window increases linearly with the amount of adjustment needed (Cave & Kosslyn, 1989; Larsen & Bundesen, 1978). These adjustments of the attention window may be involved in at least one imagery ability. Specifically, the location of the attention window can be shifted over an imaged object, even when one's eyes are closed. Indeed, the farther one scans across an imaged object, the more time is required (Kosslyn, 1973, 1980).

Because the attention window is the "gate keeper," its properties affect the sorts of information that are stored—and hence are later available to be used in mental imagery. Thus, it is of interest that the attention window appears to exhibit a "scope/resolution tradeoff": If one attends to a larger area of space, one encodes the information with less resolution than if one attends to a smaller region of space (Shulman & Wilson, 1987). For example, one could attend to an entire room full of people, but would not be aware of the details of any one person's face; alternatively, one could attend to a single face and note such details, but not notice much about the surrounding people. Navon (1977) found that we typically encode the general shape envelope of an object before attending to its details.

How Does One Inspect Shape, Color, and Texture in Mental Images?

The attention window passes information in images deeper into the visual system. The issue is how these later phases of processing allow us to identify shapes, colors, and textures. Imagery is often used when one has encoded information incidentally, and needs to reconstruct the physical structure of an object or scene to recall the information. For example, subjects use imagery to determine whether Snoopy has pointed ears, whether a Christmas tree is darker green than a frozen pea, and whether a golf ball is bumpier than a grapefruit. We know more about these properties of objects than we have encoded explicitly, and use imagery as a "second chance" to examine the objects. Thus, image inspection plays a critical role in information processing.

Our group has developed a theory of how objects are visually identified that also serves as a theory of how imaged objects are inspected. This theory posits a set of processing subsystems that work together to identify shapes and specify their locations (Kosslyn, 1987, 1991; Kosslyn et al., 1990; Kosslyn & Koenig, 1992). A processing subsystem corresponds to a neural network or a set of related neural networks, and is characterized by the kind of input it receives, the operation it performs on the input, and the kind of output it produces. We briefly describe these subsystems and explain how they operate in visual imagery. The components of visual object identification and imagery we have inferred are shown in Fig. 10.2.

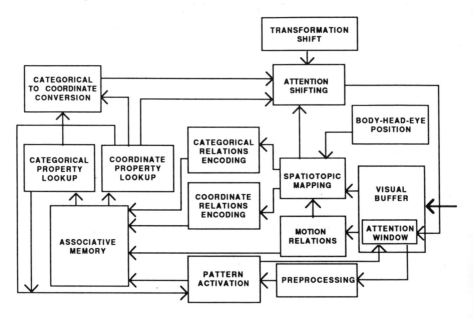

FIG. 10.2.   The subsystems hypothesized by Kosslyn (1991).

The output from the attention window is sent along at least two major anatomical pathways. These pathways contain numerous areas, which serve to extract information from the input and interpret it. The *ventral system* refers to the pathway that runs from the occipital lobes down to the inferior temporal lobes. It has been shown that this system is concerned with object properties, such as shape and color (Maunsell & Newsome, 1987; Mishkin, Ungerleider, & Macko, 1983). Ungerleider and Mishkin (1982) referred to the ventral system as the "what" system. According to Kosslyn et al. (1990), this system may be broken down into three subsystems.

Encoding Properties and Units.   Kosslyn et al. (1990) hypothesized a *pre-processing subsystem,* which encodes two kinds of stimulus characteristics during the process of object recognition. First, it extracts "nonaccidental properties," which are likely to remain invariant over various transformations of the stimulus (Biederman, 1987; Lowe, 1987a 1987b). For example, parallel edges project roughly parallel lines over all viewing angles, a symmetrical shape is likely to project a symmetrical image and so forth (Biederman provided a good summary of Lowe's theory of nonaccidental properties).

Second, the preprocessing subsystem encodes perceptual units. In many cases, these units are defined by regions of a single color or texture; indeed, it is possible that separate "streams" are used to encode the different properties (see chapter 1 of this volume; see also Cavanagh, 1987; DeYoe & Van Essen, 1988; Zeki, 1975). In addition, the preprocessing subsystem can be "trained" by higher areas to encode more easily any visual characteristics that have proven to be useful in the past (see Kosslyn & Koenig, 1992). For example, if one becomes an expert at selecting male baby chicks, the relevant ratios of parts of the cloaca may come to be seen at a glance because the preprocessing subsystem has been "tuned" to encode them (Biederman & Shiffrar, 1987).

The preprocessing subsystem also is used to inspect imaged objects, especially when they are combined in novel ways. For example, if one images an upper case letter *d* rotated 90° counterclockwise, and then imagines an upper case letter *j* beneath it, one can see the emergent pattern of an umbrella (Finke, Pinker, & Farah, 1989). The preprocessing subsystem extracts the new points of intersection, symmetries, and collinear segments, which are used subsequently to identify the new shape.

Encoding Motion Relations.   Movement can be a valuable source of information in object identification. For example, because fragments that move in the same way are grouped together, the visual system can infer the overall structure of the stimulus (Ullman, 1979). In addition, we are able to recognize human forms and identify specific individuals solely on the basis of patterns of movement (Cutting & Kozlowski, 1977; Cutting & Proffitt, 1981).

The computations used to encode motion information are very different from those used to encode static stimulus properties. Thus, it is not surprising that areas MT and MST of the macaque brain appear to play a special role in encoding motion (Maunsell & Newsome, 1987). Kosslyn (1991) inferred a *motion relations subsystem,* which works the same way in imagery and perception: It allows one to detect characteristic patterns of movement in either novel or remembered images.

Freyd and her colleagues (e.g., Freyd & Finke, 1984) showed that subjects "automatically" anticipate motion from a series of still pictures, and this may involve imagery; however, we cannot assert this with confidence, because she never looked for the hallmarks of imagery processing. If imagery is in fact used in her task, the results are interesting because they suggest that subjects often continue a trajectory after it has in fact stopped (displaying "representational momentum"). It is possible that this tendency represents a kind of priming during image generation, where anticipation of movement primes the motion relations subsystem to see movement. We consider issues about priming and dynamic properties of imagery in more detail shortly.

Matching Patterns. An object is recognized if the input matches a stored visual memory. Perrett, Oram, Hietanen, and Benson (chapter 2 of this volume) discuss the psychology and physiology of this process in detail. Within our model, visual memories correspond to perceptual units, which may be whole objects or parts of objects. Such visual memories apparently are stored (at least in part) in the inferior temporal lobe (see chapter 2 of this volume; see also Ungerleider & Mishkin, 1982). Kosslyn et al. (1990) hypothesize a *pattern activation subsystem,* which receives information from the preprocessing and motion relations subsystems. If the input from these two subsystems matches the corresponding aspects of a particular pattern stored in the pattern activation subsystem, then the object is recognized. When it only partially matches, we suspect (following Lowe, 1987a, 1987b), that information flows backward to the preprocessing subsystem and the visual buffer, supplementing the input. If this additional information is appropriate, it "reinforces the input;" if it is not, it conflicts with the input and does not aid perception. As noted earlier, this "backflow" allows one to visualize objects.

Lowe (1987a, 1987b) argued that patterns of nonaccidental properties are matched to stored information using the *viewpoint consistency constraint:* It does not matter how an object is oriented, only that the various parts are positioned such that they are consistent with seeing an object from a single point of view. This idea is important in part because it may allow us to explain Farah and Hammond's (1988) finding that a patient who could not mentally rotate imaged objects nevertheless could identify misoriented objects. If the objects were simple enough, and seen often enough that key parts and characteristics were encoded, mental rotation should not have been necessary. In this case, a part or two may have been enough to identify the object, given that the viewpoint consistency constraint allowed the input to match a stored visual representation.

In contrast, if the object is complex, it may be perceptually organized differently when in different orientations (Rock, 1973). Our visual systems often appear to organize patterns relative to the gravitational upright, especially if the object has no strong "intrinsic" axis. In this case, the viewpoint consistency constraint will not operate effectively for the entire object because different parts will be present in the input and in memory, and only a few parts and characteristics may match stored representations. In such situations, one may be forced to seek out specific parts or characteristics (e.g., a distinctively shaped spot) to confirm an hypothesis formed on the basis of a partial match (using search processes described later). Presumably, the farther one must rotate or scan to locate a sought part or characteristic, the more time will be required—and the farther objects are misoriented from the standard upright, the more such rotation or scanning typically will be required. When the picture is upside down, however, it may be relatively easy to locate sought material. Jolicoeur (1990) provided compelling evidence that subjects do require more time to identify pictures that are rotated farther from the standard upright, but are relatively fast for upside-down pictures.

In general, we assume that once there is a pattern of activation in the visual buffer, a region can be selected by the attention window for further processing; the same processes then operate, regardless of whether the pattern is a percept (evoked by input from the eyes) or an image (evoked by input from higher areas). Thus, one can "inspect" an imaged object, recognizing shapes, colors, and textures that were previously not named but were implicit in the image.

How Many Types of Visual Memory?

It has long been known that damaging the right temporal lobe disrupts memory for pictures more than damaging the left temporal lobe (e.g., Milner, 1968). However, these tasks all involved recognizing specific pictures, and it is possible that the right temporal lobe plays a special role in encoding individual exemplars—not in all visual memories. Marsolek, Kosslyn, and Squire (1992) used a stem-completion task (Graf & Schacter, 1985) to test the idea that the right hemisphere stores specific exemplars. The subjects first were given words (either spoken or presented visually), and asked to rate how much they liked each word. They were later shown the first three letters of various words in the left or right visual field, and were asked to say the first word that came to mind when they saw each cue. (They were not asked to recall words from the initial list.) The number of completions to words that were shown during the exposure phase was taken as an index of priming. Marsolek et al. found that subjects only exhibit modality-specific and font-specific priming when stimuli are presented to the right hemisphere.

Thus, it is possible that there are two kinds of visual memories; one sort is very specific, whereas another represents the product of averaging inputs to form a prototype. The appropriate experiments to demonstrate this distinction have not yet been performed, however.

How Does One Inspect Location, Size, and Orientation in Mental Images?

People also use imagery to recall spatial properties, such as location, size, and orientation. For example, one can use imagery to recall the locations of food on the shelves of a refrigerator, to determine whether a German shepherd dog has a longer nose than a collie, or whether the angle formed by the hands of a clock at 3:00 is larger than that formed at 9:55. These imagery abilities also appear to parallel corresponding perceptual abilities. Thus, it is of interest that a second major anatomical pathway is concerned with spatial properties, such as location, size, and orientation (Maunsell & Newsome, 1987; Ungerleider & Mishkin, 1982). This pathway runs from the occipital lobe up to the parietal lobes, and hence has been called the *dorsal system*. Levine, Warach, and Farah (1985) and Farah, Hammond, Levine, and Calvanio (1988) described dissociations between the imagery functions of the ventral system and the dorsal system.

Getting Off the Retina.   The location, size, or orientation of an object on the retina is not very useful; this representation changes when one shifts one's eyes or tilts one's head. To navigate or reach, one needs to know where objects are located in space, not where their images lie on one's retinas. It seems likely that there is a *spatiotopic mapping subsystem* that uses the location of a stimulus within the retinotopically mapped areas and body, head, and eye position to compute the location of objects (or portions of objects) relative to other objects (or portions of objects).

The processes that perform this coordinate transformation would be most useful if they could set the origin of the space to one's own body or to another object, including someone else's body. If so, then when one observes someone else moving in a specific way, one could encode the locations of his or her limbs relative to his or her body. One then could attempt to mimic the action, now representing the locations of one's own limbs relative to one's own body. The two representations could be compared (in associative memory, as noted later); in this way, one could learn a motor skill by imitating someone else (see chapter 7 of Kosslyn & Koenig, 1992). As noted later, the same processes may occur in imagery.

Encoding Metric Information.   Navigation and reaching require one to encode precise metric information, but explicit representations of precise metric information are rarely useful for recognition. We are not claiming that metric relations among parts of shapes (e.g., features of a face) are not encoded during recognition, only that they typically are implicit in a visual input—and are not encoded explicitly as separate spatial relations representations. When separate representations of metric distance are encoded, they typically are used to guide action. Such information can be stored and later used to traverse a familiar room, even in the dark.

Kosslyn (1987) inferred a *coordinate spatial relations encoding subsystem* that encodes spatial coordinates that can be used to guide actions; these coordinates specify the locations of targets in a way that can be used to compute trajectories (see chapter 7 of Kosslyn & Koenig, 1992). According to Andersen (1987) and Hyvarinen (1982), many neurons in the posterior parietal lobes fire prior to the initiation of a movement or are sensitive to the consequences of a movement. It is of interest that information about spatial properties is conveniently located in nearby cortex, given that such information is critical for guiding and monitoring movements.

Presumably, this subsystem plays a critical role when imagery is used to "mentally practice" an action. Richardson (1967) reviewed much evidence that people can improve a motor skill (up to a point) by visualizing themselves performing it. In this case, one visualizes a movement and encodes the coordinates of the limbs, and these coordinates can be used to guide later action. In addition, as is discussed later, the coordinate spatial relations encoding subsystem plays a role in both image generation and image inspection.

Categorizing Spatial Relations. Spatial relations not only can be encoded to guide movements, but also can be categorized in a way that is useful for identifying a scene. For example, one can categorize a location as "above," "left of," "connected to," or "on" another. These representations convey spatial information without reference to precise metric measures of distance. According to recent research, a *categorical spatial relations encoding subsystem* is probably more effective in the left cerebral hemisphere (Kosslyn, Chabris, Marsolek, & Koenig, 1992). Consistent with this idea is the finding that Gerstmann's syndrome, a component of which is left–right confusion, occurs following lesions to the left angular gyrus (De Renzi, 1982).

The categorical spatial relations subsystem sometimes is called into play when one is using imagery to recall information, such as deciding whether a race horse's tail falls above or below its rear knees. Thus, it is of interest that the left parietal lobe appears to be involved in using imagery to evaluate some kinds of stored information (see Kosslyn, Alpert et al., 1993).

How Does One See Combinations of Object and Spatial Properties in Mental Images?

In many cases, we must integrate object properties and spatial properties to identify an object during perception or to inspect an imaged object. For example, a landmark—seen or imaged—is defined as an object in a specific location; to encode information about a landmark, one must register the relation between object properties and spatial properties. Kosslyn et al. (1990) inferred an *associative memory,* which receives and stores information about object properties from the ventral system and information about spatial properties from the dorsal system. Goldman-Rakic (1987) summarized evidence that the ventral and dorsal systems ultimately project into the frontal lobes, where their outputs are stored in special short-term memory structures. Presumably, the frontal lobes also play a role in cross-indexing this information.

During perception, if an object is too large to be seen in one fixation, associative memory will accumulate input over the course of multiple fixations, allowing one to identify the object. In order to do so, associative memory must include something like a "structural description" of objects (Marr, 1982; Palmer, 1977). Such a description specifies the arrangement of parts. Hence, as one moves one's eyes, different parts will be encoded via the ventral system, and their spatial relations will be encoded via the dorsal system. These two kinds of information will be matched to stored information about the arrangements of parts of specific objects, allowing one to identify the stimulus.

Unlike the pattern activation subsystem, associative memory stores many different types of information; associative memory registers the outputs from the modality-specific recognition subsystems, and also stores information about categories, contexts in which events or objects occur, and so forth. Associative memory also must play a critical role in language comprehension (Kosslyn & Koenig, 1992).

Associative memory plays several important roles in visual mental imagery. For one, it allows language to index an associated visual code, which in turn can activate a visual memory in the pattern activation subsystem in response to a request. But more than that, the associative properties of this structure are often used to build up a visual mental image a part at a time, as is discussed later.

Why Is Image Inspection Limited?

Chambers and Reisberg (1985) found that if one encodes an ambiguous figure in one way, it is difficult to "see" the other reading when later imaging it; for example, if one sees an ambiguous shape as a duck, one later has difficulty reorganizing it in an image to see a rabbit. It is important to note that images are built up on the basis of the visual units that were previously encoded. If an object is presented at one orientation, it will be perceptually organized from that point of view and stored differently than if it is presented at another orientation (see Rock, 1973).

In perception, it is difficult to see a pattern that cuts across perceptual units. For example, Reed and Johnsen (1975) found that subjects required more time to see the parallelogram embedded in a Star of David than to see a triangle; the figure presumably was organized as two overlapping triangles, and seeing the parallelogram required reorganizing it. This reorganization process is particularly difficult in imagery because images do not linger for very long. If the visual buffer is also used in perception, then it should not hold patterns of activation for long, in order to avoid "smearing" as we move our eyes. The same property, the equivalent of "fast fade phosphor" on a screen, also affects imagery, making images decay very quickly.

IMAGE GENERATION

How are visual mental images produced? In some cases, we may see an object briefly and retain the perceptual input. But more typically, we are reminded of something, and its image springs to mind. The process whereby stored information is used to create an image is called *image generation*. As we noted earlier, the basic process of forming an image may have evolved in the service of fundamental perceptual processes. However, the simple idea that stored information evokes a pattern of activation in the visual buffer is not sufficient to explain the range of our image generation abilities.

For example, most Americans can determine whether Bill Clinton would be able to see over the top of an elephant's head if he were riding on its shoulders. But they have never witnessed such a scene. The image was generated on the spot, as needed, by visualizing previously seen objects combined in a new way. This flexibility is one of the reasons imagery is useful; we can visualize novel circumstances, and try to anticipate what they will look like.

Why Are Images Often Built Up a Part at a Time?

Kosslyn (1980, chapter 6) reviews much evidence that objects are often visualized a part at a time. Why? One account rests on the scope/resolution tradeoff of the attention window (noted previously). Because of this tradeoff, visual encodings of the overall shape of an object often will not have a high resolution. Thus, to form an image of an object with high resolution, or to "see" a specific part or characteristic clearly, one will need to activate additional visual memories. Furthermore, these parts or characteristics will have to be placed at the proper locations in the image. We hypothesize that the same subsystems that are used to direct attention to the likely location of an important part or characteristic during perception also guide one to add parts or characteristics to an imaged object when necessary.

For example, if asked whether a cat has pointed ears, one initially may image the overall shape of a cat. But this image may be too fuzzy to allow one to "see" the shape of the ears. Hence, the system uses stored information to guide the attention window to the top of the head, and allows this information to activate the appropriate visual memory—which in turn sends feedback that fills out the image, allowing one to "see" the pointed shape of the ears. (This mechanism relies on vector completion, a property of many neural networks models; see McClelland & Rumelhart, 1986).

How Does One Position Parts in the Visual Buffer?

How can one place a new part in the proper position in an image? This ability can be understood if we consider another aspect of perception, the use of knowledge to guide attention to a specific location. In most situations, one may be able to identify an object in a single glance; its image subtends a small enough visual angle that it can be seen in its entirety with relatively high resolution. The size of an image is critical, however, because one sees only about two degrees of visual angle with high resolution. Thus, in some cases one must move one's eyes over the object or scene in order to see all of it clearly.

Logically, there are only three ways to guide eye movements. First, one could move one's eyes randomly; second, one could move them using bottom-up information, directing them to locations of sudden movement, changes in luminance, or the like; and third, one could move them using stored information (top-down). Yarbus (1967) and many others have shown convincingly that knowledge is often used to guide eye movements. Such processing would greatly streamline the task of identifying an object when only a single part is initially seen.

For example, if one initially sees only the tail of a cat, the shape, texture, color, and motion pattern may match a specific tail pattern in the pattern activation subsystem, and the fact of this match is sent to associative memory. At the same time, the size, location, and orientation of the part are encoded via the dorsal system, and sent to associative memory. However, this information may not be enough to infer conclusively that one is viewing a cat. Hence, other properties of cats are accessed in its structural description, and attention is moved to a likely location of a salient part (e.g., its face). Such top-down search is very effective. In the following section we consider a set of subsystems involved in accessing and using stored information to shift attention to guide encoding during perception (Kosslyn et al., 1990).

The same processes that shift the attention window during perception can also be used to shift the attention window during imagery. And once the attention window has been shifted to a target location, an image of a new part or object can be generated at that location. This process would allow one to build up an image of distinct parts or objects in specific spatial relations.

Using Stored Coordinate Spatial Relations.   We have inferred that information about spatial properties can be encoded in two ways, in terms of metric coordinates or spatial categories. Presumably each form of information then can be stored. We infer that coordinate information can be stored, and that it has a special role in guiding actions.

Consider the following task: Visualize the locations of the furniture in your living room. When most people do this, their eyes shift; indeed, none of the 25 people we observed began to describe the room prior to making an eye movement, and all moved their eyes more than once in the course of describing the room. This observation is consistent with the idea that the locations of the furniture were stored to help one to navigate, and one needed to run a motor program to access these coordinates before they could be used to insert objects in the appropriate locations in an image. Thus, it is possible that multipart images may be constructed by using coordinate spatial relations to position the parts.

If so, then in some situations images may be generated more effectively by the right cerebral hemisphere, if indeed coordinate information is processed more effectively there (as argued by Kosslyn et al., 1992). Sergent (1989) reported an experiment in which subjects did in fact form images more quickly when cues were presented to the left visual field, and hence were processed initially in the right hemisphere.

Categorical Property Lookup.   Similarly, in principle, categorical spatial relations may be used to form images of scenes or multipart objects. In this case, one would position parts less accurately, using rather coarse specifications of location such as "above," "right of," and so forth. Pylyshyn (1973) noticed that people often make errors when arranging parts in an image, which led him to assert that imagery relies on stored descriptions. We are suggesting that in some cases he is correct; a categorical spatial relation representation is a type of description, and when it is used to arrange parts in images, people may make errors.

Farah (1986) provided evidence that the left hemisphere sometimes is better than the right at generating images of letters. Similarly, Farah, Gazzaniga, Holtzman, and Kosslyn (1985) and Kosslyn, Holtzman, Gazzaniga, and Farah (1985) showed that images of letters were formed more effectively by the left hemispheres than by the right hemispheres of split-brain patients. In contrast, Kosslyn et al. (1985) found that images of individual perceptual units—which could be formed without using explicit representations of spatial relations—were generated equally easily in both hemispheres.

Kosslyn, Hamilton, Maljkovic, Horwitz, and Thompson (in press) explored the circumstances in which an image would be generated using categorical or coordinate spatial relations. They used variants of the task developed by Kosslyn et al. (1988). In these experiments, however, the subjects received the stimuli lateralized in the left or right visual field (and hence were processed initially by the right or left hemisphere, respectively). In one condition, the subjects first memorized a description of a pattern of segments in a rectangle. They later were shown rectangles that contained only a single X mark, which were presented in the left or right visual field. The subjects were asked whether the X would be covered by one of the memorized patterns if it were in the grid. Kosslyn, Hamilton et al. found that subjects were faster in this condition if the grid was presented in the right visual field. This finding was expected because the description forced the subjects to use categorical relations to later construct the image. In contrast, another group of subjects learned patterns by seeing the segments appear one at a time, and "mentally gluing" them together. Again, the subjects later saw a rectangle with an X mark, and were asked to determine whether the X would have been covered by one of the stimuli. Now the subjects were faster when the probe was presented to the left visual field, so that the right hemisphere received the information first. This was expected because the image was presumably generated using coordinate spatial relations.

Kosslyn et al. (in press) conducted a series of convergent experiments and control conditions. For example, they found that subjects were faster to image letters in grids when the grids were presented to the left hemisphere. Presumably the grid lines were a kind of crutch, allowing subjects to use categorical descriptions of spatial relations to image the segments of letters. For example, an *F* could be stored as "a vertical bar on the left, a horizontal bar at the top, and a horizontal bar in the middle row." In contrast, other subjects memorized letters within four brackets, which were placed at the corners of a rectangle. These stimuli were created by taking the grid stimuli used before, and then eliminating all of the grid lines and all of the perimeter of the grid except the lines at the corners. A set of four brackets, which contained only a single X mark placed within the enclosed space, was lateralized. Subjects again were cued to image a specific letter, and now were faster when the stimuli were presented initially to the right hemisphere. This right-hemisphere advantage was expected because the grid lines were no longer present, and subjects were forced to use coordinate spatial relations to construct the image. Additional experiments have supported this interpretation.

This grid imagery task was also used in two PET experiments reported by Kosslyn, Alpert et al. (1993). They not only found that the occipital lobe was activated, but also found that dorsolateral prefrontal cortex (Areas 44 and 46) was activated bilaterally. These results did not depend on how long the grid was visible. In contrast, when the grid remained in free view, the left pulvinar was activated; this structure is apparently involved in selective attention (LaBerge & Buschsbaum, 1990), and Podgorny and Shepard (1978) conceived of this imagery task as requiring selective attention to specific regions of the grid. In contrast, when the grids were presented for only 200 ms, and so attention could not be shifted easily over them, the pulvinar was not activated. Rather, inferior temporal regions were activated. This result suggested that subjects activated a visual memory when they could not easily form an image by engaging attention at the appropriate locations in the grid.

What Is the Relation Between Imagery and Attention?

Attention is the selective aspect of perception. The attention window carries out one form of selection, defined over space. But there are other types of attentional processes that occur in some forms of imagery. Two mechanisms may be involved, one that primes a particular object or part in the ventral system and one that shifts the attention window to a specific location and size in the visual buffer.

Priming.   When the system is engaging in top-down search for a specific part, it not only shifts attention to the supposed location of the part or characteristic, but also may prime the pattern activation subsystem to encode that part or characteristic. The frontal lobe is clearly involved in accessing stored information (Luria, 1980; Petersen, Fox, Snyder, & Raichle, 1990), and it must access information about the identity of a part before it can access the associated information about its location. Thus, it would not be a large step to use the information about the identity of the part to activate the corresponding visual representation. This process would sensitize the pattern activation subsystem, so that it could encode a shape with less stimulus information. Indeed, if the pattern activation subsystem were sensitized enough, it would act as if it were receiving low-grade input and would provide feedback to the visual buffer, and thereby induce an image (cf. Finke, 1989). Thus, the priming process could be responsible for initiating the process of forming an image of a single part or overall shape.

Attention Shifting.   In perception, the aim of top-down processing is to encode new information effectively. As noted, a critical part of this process is directing the attention window to a specific location. According to Posner, Inhoff, Friedrich, and Cohen (1987; see also Posner & Petersen, 1990), at least three subsystems are involved in actually shifting attention: one that disengages attention from the initial location (which appears to rely on the parietal lobe), one that shifts attention to a new location (which appears to rely on the superior colliculus), and one that engages attention at the new location (which appears to rely on the thalamus, probably the pulvinar nucleus).

In imagery, the attention shifting subsystems adjust the location and size of the attention window in the visual buffer, thus allowing some forms of image scanning and zooming. In addition, the engage process may allow one to form "attentional images" (Podgorny & Shepard, 1978). If one is attending to a regular grid work, such as a tile floor, one can see patterns by organizing rows and columns of tiles. This process is distinctly different from activating a stored visual memory. In one of their PET studies, Kosslyn, Alpert et al. (1993) found that when subjects formed images in grids, the temporal lobe did not become activated. But the pulvinar, which presumably was engaging attention at specific regions of the grid, was activated. In addition, the appropriate parts of the frontal lobes (involved in looking up information to shift attention) and the parietal lobes (monitoring the locations) were activated. As noted earlier these results contrast with those obtained when it was difficult to attend to distinct rows and columns; they also contrast with results of SPECT studies in which subjects had to image shapes with specific colors and textures—and hence it makes sense that the object-properties system was engaged.

IMAGE MAINTENANCE

We noted earlier that image inspection is limited in large part because images fade very quickly. Thus, to use imagery effectively, images must be retained. However, very little is known about the nature of image maintenance.

A Special Mechanism?

Perhaps the most important issue about the mechanisms responsible for maintaining images concerns their role in other processes. Are there distinct mechanisms that retain a pattern of activation in the visual buffer, or do the mechanisms responsible for forming an image simply keep operating, refreshing the pattern frequently? This issue has yet to be explicitly studied.

What Is the Role of Organizational Strategies?

It is clear that organizational strategies can help one to use imagery effectively as a memory aid (Bower, 1972; Paivio, 1971). We have found that if subjects can effectively organize material in images into relatively few perceptual units, they can maintain more information in images. For example, in one study (unpublished), we asked 81 people to visualize a sequence of line segments forming a pathway. The subjects heard directions, such as "northwest, southwest, west . . ." and were asked to visualize a 1-in. line segment for each direction, and to connect them end-to-end. The sequence included several repeated patterns, such as inverted U shapes and zig-zags. Over 90% of the people who were able to recall the entire sequence had noticed the repeating patterns. Kosslyn and Koenig (1992) discussed such strategies in more detail, outlining the mechanisms that may allow one to reorganize visual patterns.

IMAGE TRANSFORMATION

A pervasive finding in the behavioral literature on imagery is that objects are transformed incrementally, in relatively small steps (Shepard & Cooper, 1982). But why? Shepard and Cooper suggested that the brain has become structured to perform such transformations over the course of evolution; these kinds of transformations mimic the corresponding physical transformations, and hence allow one to anticipate possible consequences of specific actions. Although this idea may be correct, it—like most evolutionary theories—is devilishly difficult to test.

Kosslyn (1987) offered a mechanistic alternative. He suggested that because images are constructed a part at a time, the representation itself preserves the part organization. Furthermore, each part is transformed individually, for example by being shifted around a central pivot during rotation. This shifting process may itself be based in the parietal lobe, as suggested by the finding that patients with damage to the parietal lobe have difficulty rotating images (Butters, Barton, & Brody, 1970; Ratcliff, 1979). However, the shifting process is noisy, so each part is not moved an equivalent amount. Thus, frontal lobe processes are involved in accessing a stored description of the proper arrangement of the parts. This "clean-up" operation involves shifting the image in much the same way that the attention window can be shifted. Deutsch, Bourbon, Papanicolaou, and Eisenberg (1988) found actuation in the right frontal and right parietal lobes in a mental rotation task, which is consistent with this view.

Are There Multiple Ways of Imagining Movement?

Logically, there are at least two ways to image movement. The first is by simply reactivating a visual memory of a moving object; recall that the motion relations subsystem provides information to visual memory, and this information presumably can be stored. For example, imaging a running dog would require only reactivating a visual memory of a dog running. But if the object were encoded without motion information, one could image movement by adding motion information to a static image. This second way to image movement may alter spatial representations in the dorsal system. Preliminary evidence suggests that one may perform motor operations on these spatial representations in order to alter them.

What Is the Role of Image Transformations in Scanning?

When one scans images, one does not "bump into the edge" of the visual buffer. Instead, one seems to be able to scan continuously around the walls of a room or the like. New parts of the image must be added to one side while parts are deleted from the opposite side (similar to scrolling down a computer screen; Kosslyn, 1980). At issue is whether this process draws on the same processes that allow one to translate objects in images, which is a kind of image transformation. To our knowledge, patients who have problems transforming imaged objects have not been systematically studied with an eye toward discovering whether the mechanisms used in transforming images are also used when scanning long distances across images.

CONCLUSIONS

In this chapter we outlined a number of issues about visual mental imagery, and discussed relevant empirical findings. We also provided many hypotheses about how various issues may be resolved. A major virtue of attempting to understand how the brain generates and uses visual mental images is that new distinctions are often hypothesized. These new distinctions in turn should lead to additional empirical research.

In this chapter, we drew many distinctions; if we combine them, we are led to distinguish 24 possibly distinct types of visual mental images. These images differ in part by being generated in different ways. These different types of imagery are as follows; we note whether the left or right hemisphere should be relatively more effective at different phases of processing (however, the hemispheric specializations will be ones of degree, not absolute differences):

1. A single visual unit is activated, which corresponds to a stored exemplar; this unit is activated more effectively in the right cerebral hemisphere.

2. A single visual unit is activated, which corresponds to a stored prototype; this unit is activated more effectively in the left cerebral hemisphere.

3. A composite image is formed, built from visual memories of exemplars (right cerebral hemisphere), which are composed using categorical spatial relations (left cerebral hemisphere).

4. A composite image is formed, built from visual memories of prototypes (left cerebral hemisphere), which are composed using categorical spatial relations (left cerebral hemisphere).

5. A composite image is formed, built from visual memories of exemplars (right cerebral hemisphere), which are composed using coordinate spatial relations (right cerebral hemisphere).

6. A composite image is formed, built from visual memories of prototypes (left cerebral hemisphere), which are composed using coordinate spatial relations (right cerebral hemisphere).

7. A composite image is formed, built from allocating attention using coordinate spatial relations (right cerebral hemisphere).

8. A composite image is formed, built from allocating attention using categorical spatial relations (left cerebral hemisphere).

9. If motion is included, it could be of either type (replay or added), bringing the total to 16 types of imagery with motion, plus another eight types of static images, as noted.

Until recently, this sort of exercise would have seemed futile in the extreme. But now that PET scanning and related techniques are available, and sensitive behavioral techniques have been devised to study patients with focal lesions, such hypotheses can be rigorously tested. The idea that imagery may come in so many flavors is consistent with the conjecture that imagery grew out of other functions, which evolved in large part in the service of perception.

REFERENCES

Andersen, R. A. (1987). The role of the inferior parietal lobule in spatial perception and visual-motor integration. In F. Plum & V. B. Mountcastle (Eds.), *Handbook of physiology: The nervous system* (Vol. 5, pp. 483–518). Bethesda, MD: American Physiological Society.

Biederman, I. (1987). Recognition-by-components: A theory of human image understanding. *Psychological Review, 94*, 115–147.

Biederman, I., & Shiffrar, M. M. (1987). Sexing day-old chicks: A case study and expert systems analysis of a difficult perceptual-learning task. *Journal of Experimental Psychology: Learning, Memory and Cognition, 13,* 640–645.

Bisiach, E., & Luzatti, C. (1978). Unilateral neglect of representational space. *Cortex, 14,* 129–133.

Bower, G. H. (1972). Mental imagery and associative learning. In L. Gregg (Ed.), *Cognition in learning and memory* (pp. 51–88). New York: Wiley.

Butters, N., Barton, M., & Brody, B. A. (1970). Role of the right parietal lobe in the mediation of cross-modal associations and reversible operations in space. *Cortex, 6,* 174–190.

Cavanagh, P. (1987). Reconstructing the third demension: Interactions between color, texture, motion, binocular disparity, and shape. *Computer Vision, Graphics, and Image Processing, 37,* 171–195.

Cave, K. R., & Kosslyn, S. M. (1989). Varieties of size-specific visual selection. *Journal of Experimental Psychology: General, 118,* 148–164.

Chambers, D., & Reisberg, D. (1985). Can mental images be ambiguous? *Journal of Experimental Psychology: Human Perception and Performance, 11*(3), 317–328.

Cutting, J. E., & Kozlowski, L. T. (1977). Recognizing friends by their walk: Gait perception without familiarity. *Bulletin of the Psychonomic Society, 9,* 353–356.

Cutting, J. E., & Proffitt, D. R. (1981). Gait perception as an example of how we may perceive events. In R. D. Walk & H. L. Pick (Eds.), *Intersensory perception and sensory integration* (pp. 249–273). New York: Plenum.

De Renzi, E. (1982). *Disorders of space exploration and cognition.* New York: Wiley.

Deutsch, G., Bourbon, W. T., Papanicolaou, A. C., & Eisenberg, H. M. (1988). Visuospatial experiments compared via activation of regional cerebral blood flow. *Neuropsychologia, 26,* 445–452.

DeYoe, E. A., & Van Essen, D. C. (1988). Concurrent processing streams in monkey visual cortex. *Trends in Neurosciences, 11,* 219–226.

Farah, M. J. (1985). Psychophysical evidence for a shared representational medium for visual images and percepts. *Journal of Experimental Psychology: General, 114,* 93–105.

Farah, M. J. (1986). The laterality of mental image generation: A test with normal subjects. *Neuropsychologia, 24,* 541–551.

Farah, M. J. (1988). Is visual imagery really visual? Overlooked evidence from neuropsychology. *Psychological Review, 95,* 307–317.

Farah, M. J., Gazzaniga, M. S., Holtzman, J. D., & Kosslyn, S. M. (1985). A left hemisphere basis for visual mental imagery? *Neuropsychologia, 23*(1), 115–118.

Farah, M. J., & Hammond, K. M. (1988). Mental rotation and orientation-invariant object recognition: Dissociable processes. *Cognition, 29,* 29–46.

Farah, M. J., Hammond, K. M., Levine, D. N., & Calvanio, R. (1988). Visual and spatial mental imagery: Dissociable systems of representation. *Cognitive Psychology, 20,* 439–462.

Farah, M. J., Peronnet, F., Gonon, M. A., & Girard, M. H. (1988). Electrophysiological evidence for a shared representational medium for visual images and visual percepts. *Journal of Experimental Psychology: General, 117,* 248–257.

Farah, M. J., Soso, M. J., & Dasheiff, R. M. (1992). Visual angle of the mind's eye before and after unilateral occipital lobectomy. *Journal of Experimental Psychology; Human Perception and Performance, 18,* 1–6.

Felleman, D. J., & Van Essen, D. C. (1991). Distributed hierarchical processing in primate cerebral cortex. *Cerebral Cortex, 1,* 1–47.

Finke, R. A. (1989). *Principles of mental imagery.* Cambridge, MA: MIT Press.

Finke, R. A., Pinker, S., & Farah, M. (1989). Reinterpreting visual patterns in mental imagery. *Cognitive Science, 13,* 51–78.

Finke, R. A., & Shepard, R. N. (1986). Visual functions of mental imagery. In K. R. Boff, L.

Kaufman, & J. P. Thomas (Eds.), *Handbook of perception and human performance* (pp. 37-1–37-55). New York: Wiley-Interscience.

Fox, P. T., Mintun, M. A., Raichle, M. E., Miezen, F. M., Allman, J. M., & Van Essen, D. C. (1986). Mapping human visual cortex with positron emission tomography. *Nature, 323,* 806–809.

Freyd, J. J., & Finke, R. A. (1984). Representational momentum. *Journal of Experimental Psychology: Learning, Memory and Cognition, 10,* 126–132.

Goldenberg, G., Podreka, I., Steiner, M., & Willmes, K. (1987). Patterns of regional cerebral blood flow related to memorizing of high and low imagery words—An emission computer tomography study. *Neuropsychologia, 25,* 473–485.

Goldenberg, G., Podreka, I., Steiner, M., Willmes, K., Suess, E., & Deecke, L. (1989). Regional cerebral blood flow patterns in visual imagery. *Neuropsychologia, 27,* 641–664.

Goldman-Rakic, P. S. (1987). Circuitry of primate prefrontal cortex and regulation of behavior by representational knowledge. In F. Plum & V. Mountcastle (Eds.), *Handbook of physiology* (pp. 373–417). Washington, DC: American Physiology Society.

Gould, S. J., & Lewontin, R. C. (1979). The spandrels of San Marco and the Panglossian paradigm: A critique of the adaptationist programme. *Proceedings of the Royal Society, Series B, 205,* 581–598.

Graf, P., & Schacter, D. L. (1985). Implicit and explicit memory for new associations in normal and amnesic subjects. *Journal of Experimental Psychology: Learning, Memory and Cognition, 11,* 501–518.

Hyvarinen, J. (1982). Posterior parietal lobe of the primate brain. *Physiological Reviews, 62,* 1060–1129.

Jolicoeur, P. (1990). Identification of disoriented objects: A dual-system theory. *Mind and Language, 5,* 387–410.

Kosslyn, S. M. (1973). Scanning visual images: Some structural implications. *Perception and Psychophysics, 14,* 90–94.

Kosslyn, S. M. (1980). *Image and mind.* Cambridge, MA: Harvard University Press.

Kosslyn, S. M. (1978). Measuring the visual angle of the mind's eye. *Cognitive Psychology, 10,* 356–389.

Kosslyn, S. M. (1987). Seeing and imagining in the cerebral hemispheres: A computational approach. *Psychological Review, 94,* 148–175.

Kosslyn, S. M. (1991). A cognitive neuroscience of visual mental imagery: Further developments. In R. H. Logie & M. Denis (Eds.), *Mental images in human cognition* (pp. 351–381). Amsterdam, Netherlands: North-Holland.

Kosslyn, S. M., Alpert, N. M., Thompson, W. L., Maljkovic, V., Weise, S. B., Chabris, C. F., Hamilton, S. E., Rauch, S. L., & Buonanno, F. S. (1993). Visual mental imagery activates topographically organized visual cortex: PET investigations. *Journal of Cognitive Neuroscience, 5,* 263–287.

Kosslyn, S. M., Cave, C. B., & Gabrieli, J. D. E. (1989). Imagery in the blind side: Three case studies. Unpublished manuscript, Harvard University, Cambridge, MA.

Kosslyn, S. M., Cave, C. B., Provost, D., & Von Gierke, S. (1988). Sequential processes in image generation. *Cognitive Psychology, 20,* 319–343.

Kosslyn, S. M., Chabris, C. F., Marsolek, C. J., & Koenig, O. (1992). Categorical versus coordinate spatial representations: Computational analyses and computer simulations. *Journal of Experimental Psychology: Human Perception and Performance, 18,* 562–577.

Kosslyn, S. M., Flynn, R. A., Amsterdam, J. B., & Wang, G. (1990). Components of high-level vision: A cognitive neuroscience analysis and accounts of neurological syndromes. *Cognition, 34,* 203–277.

Kosslyn, S. M., Hamilton, S. E., Maljkovic, V., Horwitz, G., & Thompson, W. L. (in press).

Image generation in the cerebral hemispheres: Different strategies produce different patterns of lateralization. *Neuropsychologia.*

Kosslyn, S. M., Holtzman, J. D., Gazzaniga, M. S., & Farah, M. J. (1985). A computational analysis of mental image generation: Evidence from functional dissociations in split-brain patients. *Journal of Experimental Psychology: General, 114,* 311–341.

Kosslyn, S. M., & Koenig, O. (1992). *Wet mind: The new cognitive neuroscience.* New York: Free Press.

LaBerge, D., & Buchsbaum, M. S. (1990). Positron emission tomography measurements of pulvinar activity during an attention task. *Journal of Neuroscience, 10,* 613–619.

Larsen, A., & Bundesen, C. (1978). Size scaling in visual pattern recognition. *Journal of Experimental Psychology: Human Perception and Performance, 4,* 1–20.

Levine, D. N., Warach, J., & Farah, M. J. (1985). Two visual systems in mental imagery: Dissociation of "what" and "where" in imagery disorders due to bilateral posterior cerebral lesions. *Neurology, 35,* 1010–1018.

Lowe, D. G. (1985). *Perceptual organization and visual recognition.* Boston: Kluwer Academic.

Lowe, D. G. (1987a). Three-dimensional object recognition from single two-dimensional images. *Artificial Intelligence, 31,* 355–395.

Lowe, D. G. (1987b). The viewpoint consistency constraint. *International Journal of Computer Vision, 1,* 57–72.

Luria, A. R. (1980). *Higher cortical functions in man.* New York: Basic Books.

Marr, D. (1982). *Vision: A computational investigation into the human representation and processing of visual information.* New York: Freeman.

Marsolek, C. J., Kosslyn, S. M., & Squire, L. R. (1992). Form-specific visual priming in the right cerebral hemisphere. *Journal of Experimental Psychology: Learning, Memory and Cognition, 18,* 492–508.

Maunsell, J. H. R., & Newsome, W. T. (1987). Visual processing in monkey extrastriate cortex. *Annual Review of Neuroscience, 10,* 363–401.

McClelland, J. L., & Rumelhart, D. E. (1986). *Parallel distributed processing: Explorations in the microstructure of cognition.* Cambridge, MA: MIT Press.

Milner, B. (1968). Visual recognition and recall after right temporal-lobe excision in man. *Neuropsychologia, 6,* 191–210.

Mishkin, M., Ungerleider, L. G., & Macko, K. A. (1983). Object vision and spatial vision: Two cortical pathways. *Trends in Neurosciences, 6,* 414–417.

Navon, D. (1977). Forest before trees: The precedence of global features in visual perception. *Cognitive Psychology, 9,* 353–383.

Paivio, A. (1971). *Imagery and verbal processes.* New York: Holt, Rinehart & Winston.

Palmer, S. E. (1977). Hierarchical structure in perceptual representations. *Cognitive Psychology, 9,* 441–474.

Petersen, S. E., Fox, P. T., Snyder, A. Z., & Raichle, M. E. (1990). Activation of extrastriate and frontal cortical areas by visual words and word-like stimuli. *Science, 249,* 1041–1044.

Podgorny, P., & Shepard, R. N. (1978). Functional representations common to visual perception and imagination. *Journal of Experimental Psychology: Human Perception and Performance, 4,* 21–35.

Posner, M. I., Inhoff, A. W., Friedrich, F. J., & Cohen, A. (1987). Isolating attentional systems: A cognitive-anatomical analysis. *Psychobiology, 15,* 107–121.

Posner, M. I., & Petersen, S. E. (1990). The attention system of the human brain. In W. M. Cowan, E. M. Shooter, C. F. Stevens, & R. F. Thompson (Eds.), *Annual review of neuroscience* (pp. 25–42). Palo Alto, CA: Annual Reviews.

Pylyshyn, Z. W. (1973). What the mind's eye tells the mind's brain: A critique of mental imagery. *Psychological Bulletin, 80,* 1–24.

Ratcliff, G. (1979). Spatial thought, mental rotation and the right cerebral hemisphere. *Neuropsychologia, 17,* 49–54.

Reed, S. K., & Johnsen, J. A. (1975). Detection of parts in patterns and images. *Memory & Cognition, 3,* 569–575.

Richardson, A. (1967). Mental practice: A review and discussion I & II. *Research Quarterly, 38,* 95–107, 262–273.

Rock, I. (1973). *Orientation and form.* New York: Academic.

Roland, P. E., & Friberg, L. (1985). Localization of cortical areas activated by thinking. *Journal of Neurophysiology, 53,* 1219–1243.

Sergent, J. (1989). Image generation and processing of generated images in the cerebral hemispheres. *Journal of Experimental Psychology: Human Perception and Performance, 15,* 170–178.

Shepard, R. N., & Cooper, L. A. (1982). *Mental images and their transformations.* Cambridge, MA: MIT Press.

Shulman, G. L., & Wilson, J. (1987). Spatial frequency and selective attention to local and global information. *Perception, 16,* 89–101.

Sperling, G. (1960). The information available in brief visual presentations. *Psychological Monographs, 74* (11, Whole No. 498).

Sternberg, S. (1969). The discovery of processing stages: Extensions of Donders' method. In W. G. Koster (Ed.), *Attention and performance II* (pp. 276–315). Amsterdam: North-Holland.

Treisman, A. M., & Gelade, G. (1980). A feature integration theory of attention. *Cognitive Psychology, 12,* 97–136.

Ullman, S. (1979). *The interpretation of visual motion.* Cambridge, MA: MIT Press.

Ungerleider, L. G., & Mishkin, M. (1982). Two cortical visual systems. In D. J. Ingle, M. A. Goodale, & R. J. W. Mansfield (Eds.), *Analysis of visual behavior* (pp. 549–586). Cambridge, MA: MIT Press.

Van Essen, D. (1985). Functional organization of primate visual cortex. In A. Peters & E. G. Jones (Eds.), *Cerebral cortex* (pp. 259–329). New York: Plenum.

Yarbus, A. L. (1967). *Eye movements and vision.* New York: Plenum.

Zeki, S. M. (1975). The functional organization of projections from striate to prestriate visual cortex in the rhesus monkey. *Cold Spring Harbor Symposium on Quantitative Biology, 40,* 591–600.

IV HIGH-LEVEL VISION WITH AND WITHOUT AWARENESS

11 Mechanisms of Implicit Reading in Alexia

H. Branch Coslett
Eleanor M. Saffran
Temple University School of Medicine

The phenomenon of severely impaired reading in the context of well-preserved language and, in particular, spelling abilities ("alexia without agraphia"), first described by Dejerine almost 100 years ago (1892), is a well-recognized manifestation of posterior left-hemisphere injury. The traditional account (Dejerine, 1892; Geschwind & Fusillo, 1966) of this disorder attributes the syndrome to a "disconnection" of visual information, which is restricted to the right hemisphere, from the left-hemisphere word recognition system. Alternative accounts of the disorder are discussed in chapter 6 of this volume and later in this chapter.

Though these patients do not appear to be able to read in the sense of fast, automatic word recognition, many are able to use a compensatory strategy that involves naming the letters of the word in serial fashion; they read, in effect, letter by letter. Use of the letter-by-letter procedure, which is slow and inefficient, was long thought to be the sole mechanism for word recognition in these patients. Recently, however, several investigators have demonstrated that alexic patients are able to perform tasks such as lexical decision and semantic categorization on letter strings presented too rapidly to permit effective use of the letter-by-letter procedure (Coslett & Saffran, 1989a; Landis, Regard, & Serrat, 1980; Shallice & Saffran, 1986). Though lexical decision and categorization are performed at above-chance levels, the patients are able to explicitly identify only a small percentage of these words at rapid presentations. Similar residual reading capacities have been demonstrated in an alexic patient who was unable to name letters and was consequently unable to offer any explicit responses to written words (Coslett & Saffran, 1989a).

In this chapter we review the evidence supporting the claim that at least some patients with pure alexia access lexical-semantic information for words that they do not explicitly identify as well as reports in which implicit processing was not demonstrated. Data from five patients with pure alexia and two patients with *optic aphasia* studied in our laboratory are presented in some detail. We conclude with a discussion of possible accounts and implications of the implicit reading demonstrated by these patients.

BACKGROUND TO THE PRESENT STUDIES

Although most reports of pure alexia have emphasized the profound nature of the reading deficit, often stating that patients were utterly incapable of reading without recourse to a letter-by-letter procedure (Geschwind & Fusillo, 1966), a number of investigators have reported data demonstrating that alexic patients are able to perform some kinds of tasks with printed words. Kreindler and Ionasescu (1961) described a patient with a right homonymous hemianopia who, despite the absence of aphasia, was unable to read aloud a single word. However, he matched a picture to a set of words correctly on 16 of 20 trials and was 100% correct on auditory-to-written word matching.

Caplan and Hedley-White (1974) described a patient who was impaired at naming letters and was unable to read aloud any words. However, when shown a letter string containing a real word as well as extraneous letters, she was able to indicate which letters were not part of the word. She was also able to match auditory to written words fairly accurately (9 of 13 correct) and to point to words that corresponded to a designated semantic category (color, temperature) though she was unable to name them correctly. Thus, she pointed to *red, cold,* and *warm* while saying "warm," "cold," and "hot," respectively.

Albert, Yamadori, Gardner, and Howes (1973) described a patient who, although able to read aloud only a small portion of short, high-frequency words, was nonetheless able to match written words to objects with 90% accuracy and match written and spoken words perfectly on 10 trials. The patient also performed perfectly on a number of different lexical decision tests. Interestingly, like the patient reported by Caplan and Hedley-White (1974), this patient also made semantic errors on oral reading and reading comprehension tasks.

Another example of at least partial access to semantic information appropriate to words that could not be explicitly identified was provided by Landis et al. (1980). These investigators described a 39-year-old man with a left occipital tumor who exhibited pure alexia with letter-by-letter reading. Of greatest interest was the patient's performance with tachistoscopic presentation and the change in this performance over time. Initially, though unable to identify words or even letters at 30 ms, he successfully matched the stimulus word to an item from a large array of objects on five of seven trials. When tested again seven weeks later, he was able to read letters at 10 ms and correctly read 4 of 10 words at 20 ms. On the other six trials, he selected the matching object only once; intriguingly, this was the only trial on which he did not identify any letters.

Thus, some patients with pure alexia are able to match spoken to written words and to derive some semantic information appropriate to visually presented words that they are unable to report. These data are subject to a number of caveats. First, for most of the reports the number of observations was quite small, raising the possibility that the reported effects were simply chance occurrences. Second, the stimuli were often presented free-field for an indefinite interval; under such conditions, subjects may have covertly employed a letter-naming strategy or responded on the basis of partial letter information.

Perhaps the first compelling demonstration of preserved reading capacities in a patient with pure alexia was reported by Shallice and Saffran (1986). Their patient, ML, explicitly identified words quite readily by means of a letter-by-letter strategy; of particular interest, however, was the demonstration that the patient performed better than chance on lexical decision tests and some (but not all) semantic categorization tasks in which words were presented too briefly to be explicitly identified. One additional striking aspect of the patient's performance was the apparent use of alternative reading "strategies" for the different tasks; whereas ML used a serial letter identification approach when asked to name words, he stated that he used a very different approach in his attempts to derive semantic information from written words. ML's introspection appeared to be supported by his behavior on these tasks; when asked to name words he scrutinized the stimulus for the entire 2-s period during which it was present, whereas when making a semantic category judgment he often averted his eyes after only a quick glance at the stimulus.

Additional evidence that some patients with pure alexia are able to comprehend words that they are unable to explicitly identify was reported by Howard (1990). Two pure alexics were tested on a cued-word definition task in which they were asked to define a polysemous word that was preceded by a briefly presented word that, if processed semantically, would bias the patient's definition. On one trial, for example, the word *tree* was presented for a brief interval (either 150 or 250 ms) and was overwritten by the word *palm,* which remained in view until the patient responded; on another trial, the target *palm* was preceded by *hand.* Neither patient reported seeing any of the cue words. One patient (KW) exhibited a significant biasing effect of the cue though the other (PM) showed no such effect. Also of note is that KW performed well on a task in which he was asked to categorize rapidly presented words that he was unable to explicitly identify; PM performed at chance on this task.

A different type of evidence supporting the claim that at least some patients with pure alexia are able to access stored lexical information for words they are unable to identify has been provided by the elegant work of Bub, Black, and Howell (1989). These investigators tested the ability of their patient to identify letters in familiar words, orthographically legal pseudowords, and random letter strings. They found that the patient with pure alexia, like normals, performed better at identifying letters in the real words and pseudowords as compared to random letter strings. This word (or orthographic) superiority effect suggests that the patient is, indeed, able to access stored lexical information. It should be noted, however, that other alexics tested on this paradigm have not shown this effect (see Behrman, Black, & Bub, 1990).

Not all investigators, however, have found evidence of implicit reading in pure alexics. Warrington and Shallice (1980) reported a patient (RAV) with letter-by-letter reading who read aloud 42 of 50 words presented for 500 ms; he performed at chance on this and another task, however, when asked to match words he had been unable to read to a picture. Patterson and Kay (1982) evaluated four patients with pure alexia and letter-by-letter reading on a variety of lexical decision and word comprehension tasks; they found no compelling evidence that their patients were able to comprehend words that they could not explicitly identify. In a similar vein, Behrman et al. (1990) reported a patient with pure alexia and letter-by-letter reading who performed at chance on a series of three investigations in which she was asked to categorize a word presented for 3 s.

As we have argued elsewhere (Coslett & Saffran, 1989a; Shallice & Saffran, 1986), however, the failure to demonstrate access to stored information for words that are not explicitly identified may be attributable to differences in patient strategy; those investigators who did not demonstrate implicit processing emphasized explicit word identification or did not discourage the use of a letter-by-letter strategy by presenting words for a sufficiently brief period at which this strategy would be clearly ineffective. The possible role of strategic factors is discussed later.

The data reviewed to this point suggest that at least some patients with pure alexia are able to access lexical and, in some instances, semantic information appropriate to words that they are unable to explicitly identify. In the following section we report data from seven patients, five with pure alexia and two with optic aphasia, which confirm and extend these observations. In addition, we discuss the procedures by which this reading is mediated and propose an explanation for at least some of the heterogeneity of performance exhibited by these patients.

PATIENTS

Pure Alexics.   We report data from five patients with pure alexia; four of the patients (JG, TL, JC, AF) were described in a previous publication (Coslett & Saffran, 1989a).

The fifth patient, JWC, is a 62-year-old right-handed man who noted the sudden onset of mild right-sided weakness and loss of vision on the right. He had finished 11th grade and had worked as a laborer until retiring several years ago. JWC stated that he scanned the newspaper most days but read little else. He rarely wrote. Neurological examination performed approximately 5 weeks after the onset of symptoms revealed only a dense right homonymous hemianopia and a profound alexia. JWC named words only after explicitly naming the constituent letters, frequently misnaming letters with resultant failure in word identification. The clinical diagnosis of stroke was confirmed by a computerized axial tomography (CAT) scan performed 8 days after the onset of symptoms, which demonstrated a left occipital lobe infarction.

Optic Aphasics. Data from two patients with optic aphasia are presented. Optic aphasia is a visual modality-specific naming disorder in which patients are unable to name visually presented stimuli that they are able to name from description or palpation. The disorder is differentiated from a visual object agnosia by the fact that the patients are able to access stored information pertinent to visually presented objects, as evidenced by their ability to provide the appropriate gesture for an object or sort objects or pictures by semantic category although they are unable to name the object. Though alternative hypotheses have been proposed (Coslett & Saffran, 1989b; Riddoch & Humphreys, 1987), optic aphasia, like pure alexia, has classically been attributed to a disconnection between visual information restricted to the right hemisphere and the left-hemisphere systems that subserve naming (Freund, 1889).

We report data from two patients with this disorder. The first, CB, was the subject of a previous report (Coslett & Saffran, 1989b). The second, EM, was a 67-year-old right-handed retired insurance adjuster with a college education who developed right-sided weakness, loss of vision on the right, word-finding problems, and alexia. CAT scan performed 1 week after the onset of symptoms demonstrated an infarction involving the left occipital lobe and posterior, inferior temporal lobe.

The patient was grossly impaired in naming both pictures and objects presented visually but was able to name many objects by palpation. On a task that examined naming as a function of mode of presentation, EM named 19 of 28 (68%) of objects from their description, 17 of 25 (68%) by palpation (3 items were not tested in this condition), and 6 of 28 (21%) by visual inspection. EM performed well, however, on tasks that assessed knowledge of visually presented objects. Given a set of 20 objects, he named only 3 but provided appropriate gestures for the other 17; he also performed normally (97% correct) on a task modeled on the functional similarity test of Warrington and Taylor (1978), which required him to match objects on the basis of their functions.

Though EM performed well on tests of oral spelling and naming spelled words, he was unable to read words aloud and failed to name any letters correctly. There was no consistent visual similarity between letter targets and the named letter.

Thus, like the patient (CB) we previously reported (Coslett & Saffran, 1989b), EM exhibited the characteristics of both optic aphasia and pure alexia.

In summary, it should be noted that all of the seven subjects whose data are summarized here were right-handed and exhibited right homonymous hemi-anopias. All but one patient suffered left occipital infarcts; the exception, JG, sustained infarctions in the left lateral geniculate and the splenium of the corpus callosum; the functional consequence of these lesions would be to prevent visual information from directly reaching the left hemisphere and to prohibit transfer of visual information from the right occipital lobe to the left hemisphere by means of transfer through the splenium of the corpus callosum. Finally, it should be noted that when asked to read, the five patients with pure alexia who were able to identify letters employed an explicit letter-by-letter approach.

SINGLE WORD ORAL READING

Unlike normal readers or patients with other types of alexia (e.g., deep dyslexia), patients with pure alexia typically exhibit an effect of word length on reading latency. This is frequently, but not invariably, associated with the explicit use of a letter-by-letter strategy in which subjects name letters and subsequently attempt to produce the word on the basis of the serial letter information. To verify that the alexic patients were indeed employing a letter-by-letter reading strategy, they were asked to name words of three, four, five, six, and seven letters presented free-field. The time required to correctly identify each word was measured with a stopwatch.

As shown in Table 11.1, a clear effect of word length (in letters) was observed in the five patients who were able to name letters (This task could not be performed by the optic aphasics, who failed to name a single letter or word.) As is also apparent in Table 11.1, there were substantial differences in reading latency across subjects, reflecting, at least in part, differences in letter-naming ability.

TABLE 11.1
Speed of Oral Reading as a Function of
Word Length (in Seconds)

Patient	Number of Letters				
	3	4	5	6	7
JG	9	13	17	27	28
TL	2	3	3	5	4
JC	2	6	17	16	30
AF	31	83	...	...	...
JWC	16	21	26	26	60
CB	no letter naming or oral reading				
EM	no letter naming or oral reading				

Some investigators have noted that patients with pure alexia explicitly identify some words (at least relatively) normally but are quite slow with other stimuli for which they employ a letter-by-letter strategy (Howard, 1990; Warrington & Shallice, 1980). Rapid, correct responses were rare in our patients, occurring in only 1%–5% of trials.

These data suggest that, with rare exceptions, these five pure alexics were unable to explicitly identify visually presented words except by means of a letter-by-letter strategy.

LEXICAL DECISION TESTS

All seven subjects denied that they were able to see visually presented letter strings "as a whole"; the five who could name letters stated that they were only able to identify or even achieve a sense of word identity by employing a letter-by-letter strategy. One of the optic aphasics, CB, occasionally denied even having "seen" a word written on a card and presented free-field for an indefinite time. A series of lexical decision tests was performed to assess the possibility that words were being processed as such without awareness.

Lexical Decision with High- and Low-Frequency Words

The first test included 60 high-frequency words (mean frequency of 445.8 counts per million; Kucera & Francis, 1967), 60 low-frequency words (all 1 count per million), 60 "wordlike" nonwords such as *shart* (mean N of 10.9; Coltheart, Davelaar, Jonasson, & Besner, 1977), and 60 nonwords with unusual or illegal orthographic sequences such as *twilk* (mean N of 1.3) for a total of 240 stimuli. Stimuli in the four experimental conditions were matched for length, which ranged from three to five letters. Items were presented singly on a computer screen.

The patient was told that it was not necessary to explicitly identify the stimulus but to attempt to determine if the letter string was a real, familiar word. Prior to and on many occasions during the course of the experiment, the subject was reminded that he or she was simply to determine if the word looked familiar or to "get a feel for the whole word" rather than to name the word. Despite these continued admonitions, patients frequently attempted to identify the constituent letters and often reported seeing a single letter; patients were discouraged from reporting the individual letters but were asked to notify the investigator if they thought they could identify the word.

The results, expressed as percentage of "yes" responses, are presented in Table 11.2. All subjects responded more accurately with high- as compared to low-frequency words and with Hi-N as compared to Lo-N nonwords. Although

TABLE 11.2
Lexical Decision at Brief Exposures

		Words			Nonwords			
				% "Yes" Responses				
Patient	Exp.	HiFreq	LoFreq	Hi + Lo	Hi − N	Lo − N	Hi + Lo	d'
L-By-L	*ms*	*N = 60*	*N = 60*	*N = 120*	*N = 60*	*N = 60*	*N = 120*	
JG	250	75	37	56	35	25	30	0.68*
TL	150	82	78	80	63	38	50	0.84*
JC	250	78	52	65	28	11	19	1.3*
AF	250	80	53	67	42	18	30	0.96*
JWC	249	93	48	71	57	43	45	.55*
No Ltr Ident								
EM	250	92	58	75	20	12	16	1.63*
CB	unlim	88			34			1.59*

*p < .05

TABLE 11.3
Effect of Length on Lexical Decision Performance

String Length	Percent Correct		
	Words	Nonwords	Total
3	67.9	70.1	69
4	68.6	62.6	65.6
5	65.4	73	69.2

Note. Means $F(4)$ patients (JG, JC, TL, JWC).

performance was far from perfect, analysis with a d' statistic demonstrated that all subjects reliably discriminated words from nonwords ($P < .05$ for all patients). Thus, despite their frequent protestations and claims not to have seen the letter string, all seven patients were accessing lexical information from briefly presented words.

As noted earlier, word-length effects are a defining characteristic of letter-by-letter reading, and were clearly in evidence when these patients were identifying words explicitly at unlimited exposures (see Table 11.1). When the effects of word length were examined in a post hoc analysis of the lexical decision data (see Table 11.3), no significant effect was noted. (These data were not available for AF.) Though the range of word lengths employed in this task (three, four, and five letters) was limited, other investigators (Ellis, Young, & Anderson, 1988) obtained length effects with stimuli in this range. The absence of a word-length effect suggests that the patients were not encoding the stimuli in a serial, letter-by-letter fashion in this task.

A further indication that the patients were using a different mode of processing in this task comes from an examination of the lexical decision performance as a function of exposure time, which we carried out in two patients (JG, AF). For JG, the lexical decision test described previously was repeated on five occasions at least 1 week apart. As can be seen in Table 11.4, JG performed above chance with very brief (50 ms) and very long (mean of over 1 min) exposure; only at 2,000 ms did he fail to perform better than chance. Informal observations of the patient's behavior revealed that with longer exposure times (i.e., 2,000 ms and unlimited) he explicitly identified letters, whereas he did not do so with brief exposure. At 2,000 ms he generally failed to identify all of the letters.

The effect of stimulus duration was tested in AF using a 40-item lexical decision test (see Coslett & Saffran, 1989a, for details). With 2,000-ms exposure, AF responded yes to 58% of words and 50% of nonwords for an overall chance performance (54% correct); with 250-ms exposure, however, she responded yes to 85% of nonwords and 35% of nonwords; this performance is significantly above chance (d' $= 1.42$, Z $= 4.50$, $p < .05$).

TABLE 11.4
Lexical Decision Test as Function of
Exposure Duration—JG (% "Yes" Responses)

	50 ms	250 ms	500 ms	2,000 ms	Unlimited
Words	49%	59%	55%	51%	86%
Hi F	57	68	70	64	
Lo F	40	57	40	37	
Nonwords	22%	36%	21%	54%	8%
Hi N	27	33	25	68	
Lo N	18	28	18	40	
d' =	.75	.72	.93	.13	2.49
z =	4.36	4.40	5.38	.775	7.32

Thus, these patients performed better on lexical decision at brief exposures, when a letter-by-letter strategy could not be employed, than at a longer exposure that allowed only partial recovery of the letter string by means of letter-by-letter encoding. The effect of exposure time, together with the lack of a word length effect in the lexical decision data, argue quite compellingly for two distinct modes of processing in these alexic patients, one that is fast and parallel but rarely yields explicit identification of the letter string, and another that is slow and serial but generally effective (given enough time) in achieving explicit identification.

Lexical Decision Test with Suffixed Stimuli

The previous experiment demonstrated that all seven subjects were able to discriminate between words and nonwords at above chance levels at exposures too rapid to allow effective use of letter-by-letter reading. As noted, however, the performance of our patients was far from perfect; like the case reported by Shallice and Saffran (1986), the patients tended to reject low-frequency words and to make false positive responses to nonwords that were visually similar to familiar words. A further deficiency noted by Shallice and Saffran is that the patient (ML) was insensitive to the appropriateness of suffixes; thus, he accepted words that were inappropriately suffixed (e.g., *elephanting*) as often as properly suffixed words (e.g., *elephants*). To further characterize the lexical decision capabilities of our patients, we replicated their study with three of our alexic subjects and performed a modified version with three others.

Three patients (JG, JC, EM) were given the test developed by Shallice and Saffran (1986). Stimuli for this task included 63 root morphemes (nouns, adjectives, and verbs) between five and nine letters in length. Each root morpheme was presented in three forms: unaffixed (e.g., *elephant*), appropriately suffixed (e.g., *elephants*), and inappropriately suffixed (e.g., *elephanting*). Stimuli also included 63 nonwords generated by changing two letters in each of the 63 root morphemes; each nonword appeared twice, once unsuffixed and once in conjunction with the suffix appropriate to the word from which it was derived.

As three (less well-educated) patients performed at chance with the stimuli just described, a second version of this test was constructed employing higher frequency root morphemes. Stimuli for this test included 40 unsuffixed words (20 nouns, 20 verbs), 40 appropriately suffixed words, 40 root morphemes with inappropriate suffixes (e.g., *wifed*), 20 unsuffixed nonwords, and 20 suffixed nonwords. For all subjects except CB, the stimuli were presented with a microcomputer; exposure durations for the individual patients are indicated in Table 11.5.

The results are presented in Table 11.5. Several points warrant mention. First, as in the previous experiment, all subjects reliably discriminated unsuffixed words from unsuffixed nonwords (all $p < .05$). Of greatest interest in this context, however, is the comparison between appropriately and inappropriately suffixed words. Five of the six patients failed to reliably distinguish appropriately from inappropriately suffixed words; only EM performed significantly better by virtue of rejecting more inappropriately suffixed nonwords ($X^2 = 7.0, p < .05$). Even EM, however, incorrectly accepted two thirds of inappropriately suffixed words. No patient explicitly identified more than two words.

TABLE 11.5
Sensitivity to Appropriateness of Suffixes in Lexical Decision

			% "Yes" Responses				
			Lexical Root Morphemes			*Nonlexical Roots*	
	Exp.	*N*	*No Suffix*	*Correct Suffix*	*Incorrect Suffix*	*No Suffix*	*Suffixed*
Patient	*ms*		*(broad)*	*(broadest)*	*(broading)*	*(narrid)*	*(narridest)*
L-By-L							
JG	250	63	63	63	65	19	37
TL	100	40	88	78	75	13	13
JC	250	63	84	79	73	40	32
AF	250	40	85	75	65	18	18
No Ltr Ident							
EM	250	63	83	87	67	10	10
CB	unlim.	40	93	63	68	30	20

Although this study confirmed the finding that alexics are able to discriminate words from nonwords, it also demonstrated a marked insensitivity to the appropriateness of stem-affix combinations. As Shallice and Saffran (1986) demonstrated that their patient was sensitive to the difference between true affixes and other terminal letter groups that occur frequently in English words, such as -ain and -ent, this performance pattern is unlikely to reflect insensitivity to word endings per se. Rather, as Shallice and Saffran suggested, this insensitivity could reflect "shallow" processing of lexical input. An alternative interpretation is that it reflects an "asyntactic" mode of processing that is characteristic of the right hemisphere (Coslett & Saffran, 1989b).

WORD COMPREHENSION

In light of the demonstration that these patients were able to determine the lexical status of letter strings that they could not explicitly identify (as well as previous demonstrations that patients with pure alexia were able to access semantic information in the absence of explicit word identification), a series of word categorization tests was performed.

Semantic Categorization. In the first study, patients were asked to indicate whether a rapidly presented word was an animal name. Stimuli consisted of 25 animal names (e.g., *mouse*), 25 words judged to be visually similar to the animal names (e.g., *mount*), and 25 words judged not to be visually or phonologically similar to the animal names (e.g., *rally*). Visually similar foils shared at least the first two letters with the matched animal name. The three types of stimuli were matched for frequency. Animal names and foils differed in length by no more than one letter. In the second study, in which the targets were names of food items, the foils were matched to the targets in a similar manner. In both studies, the patients were instructed to say "yes" if the word was the name of a member of the designated category (e.g., food). Except for CB, stimuli were presented with a microcomputer for the time indicated in Table 11.6. Stimuli were presented to CB free-field until he responded.

As in the lexical decision tests, patients were encouraged to attend to the whole word and derive a "feeling for" or "impression" about the word. Serial letter identification was strongly discouraged. Though emphasis was placed on the importance of the category judgment rather than explicit word identification, patients were asked to inform the investigator if they believed they had identified a word.

Results for the seven patients are presented in Table 11.6. All correctly categorized most animal names and responded more accurately with foils that were not visually similar to the animal names. Summed across all three types of stimuli, all patients responded significantly better than chance.

TABLE 11.6
Category Decision at Brief Exposures

		% Correct				
			Animal?			Edible?
Patient	Exp.	Animal	Visual Foil	Unrel. Foil	Total	Total
L-By-L	ms	(e.g., Mouse)	(e.g., Mount)	(e.g., Rally)		
		N = 25	N = 25	N = 25	N = 75	N = 75
JG	250	80	72	72	75	80
TL	100	96	52	60	69	67
JC	250	68	92	96	85	79
AF	250	80	60	72	71	76
JWC	249	80	68	72	73	76
No Ltr Ident						
EM	250	100	92	100	97	96
CB	unlim.	84	76	84	81	79

An analysis of the explicit responses offered by the patients is presented in Table 11.7 Four patients failed to correctly identify any words; JC correctly identified 6.7% of the stimuli but incorrectly named an equal number of stimuli. Excluding the correctly named stimuli from the analysis did not alter the outcome of the analysis: All subjects performed better than chance in categorizing briefly presented words that they were unable to identify.

Incorrect explicit responses that might be considered "semantic errors" (categorized as within-category substitutions, e.g., *tiger* → "lion") were produced in small numbers by all patients on this or other semantic categorization tasks. Additionally, all subjects produced responses on this and other tasks that were categorized as partial semantic information. Such responses, which in the vast majority of instances were provided in response to words that were members of the semantic category in question, were particularly frequent in the output of JWC and EM. The following are examples of responses scored as partial semantic information: *tiger* → "stripes on it"; *lobster* → "lives in water"; *oyster* → "funny name, body flat, like a duckbill, lives in water"; *zebra* → "stripes, like horse"; *trout* → "fish-like, big, sharp teeth"; *alligator* → "awful long"; and *rabbit* → "has big ears, something about Easter." Semantically related responses in the food names task included: *sandwich* → "you can eat it, not a meal though . . . a snack, or maybe lunch"; *salad* → "helps to add to a meal"; *chocolate* → "coke or candy"; and *potato* → "served frequently to add to a meal."

TABLE 11.7
Explicit Responses to Animal Name Categorization Test (% of Trials)

Response	JG	TL	JC	AF	JWC
Correctly named	1.3	2.6	6.7	0	0
Incorrectly named	2.7	1.3	6.7	7.9	0
Unrelated	2.7	1.3	2.7	5.2	0
Within cat. subst.	0	0	4.0	2.7	0
Partial semantic info.	0	0	0	1.3	16

Word-to-Picture Matching.   Evidence for word comprehension in the absence of explicit word identification was also sought with two forced-choice tasks requiring the matching of a rapidly presented word to one of two pictures.

In the first test, the names of items pictured in the Boston Naming Test or Peabody Picture Vocabulary Test were used to generate 31 pairs of words that shared the first two letters and differed in length by no more than two letters (e.g., *house/horse, whistle/whale, propeller/pretzel*).

The 62 words were presented in random sequence on a computer screen. Following each word, subjects were shown the sheet of paper on which the drawing appropriate to the stimulus and its matched word had been copied and was asked to point to the appropriate picture. With two exceptions, (*snake/snail* and *broom/brush*), the members of each pair were drawn from different semantic categories.

The data are presented in Table 11.8. All patients performed significantly above chance. As no patient correctly named more than three words, eliminating the trials on which the stimuli were explicitly identified did not alter the results.

A second, within-category forced-choice word-to-picture matching task was performed in which patients were asked to match animal names to pictures. For this task, 14 pairs of animal names were generated. Because of the smaller number of possible stimuli, matching of the initial portion of the letter strings was less rigorous than in the cross-category task. Thus, for 10 of the pairs the names shared only the first letter; the other 4 pairs shared the first two letters.

Data for the four patients tested on this task are included in Table 11.8. All patients performed well above chance on this task. Although there are a number of factors that make a direct comparison between performance on the two tasks difficult, it is interesting to note that all patients performed at least as well on the within- as compared to the across-category task.

Data from these experiments demonstrate that all seven patients were able to derive semantic information from words that they were unable to explicitly identify. These data do not, of course, demonstrate that the patients were able to access full semantic representations; judgment tasks of the type described previously may well be performed on the basis of incomplete semantic information.

TABLE 11.8
Word-to-Picture Matching

Patient	Exp.	Percent Correct	
		Different Category	Within Category
	ms	n = 62	n = 32
L-By-L		(house/horse)	(snake/snail)
JG	500	87	90
TL	100	69	....
JC	250	74	87
AF	250	66	73
JWC	249	84	....
No Ltr Ident			
EM	250	87	88

One possible account of the preservation of categorization in the absence of explicit responses is that subjects adopted a conservative response bias, that is that patients refrained from offering an explicit response to the target words because they were unsure and did not want to be wrong. On this hypothesis, one would expect responses to be correct when the patients felt sufficiently confident to offer them. As demonstrated by the analysis of responses in Table 11.7, this was not the case; the patients' explicit responses were wrong as often as right. A conservative response bias would, therefore, appear to be an unlikely explanation for the patients' performance.

ACCESS TO PHONOLOGY

Data presented to this point suggest that the subjects were able to contact a catalog of stored word forms as well as at least some semantic information appropriate to briefly presented words that they could not explicitly identify. The following tasks were performed to determine whether phonologic information could also be accessed from these words. Data on this task are only available for subject EM.

On this task, the patient was required to determine if two serially presented words rhymed. Stimuli included 64 pairs of words. Half of the pairs of words rhymed; half of the rhyming word pairs were visually similar (e.g., *break/steak*) whereas the other half were visually dissimilar (e.g., *bean/scene*). Of the overall corpus of 64 word pairs, half were visually similar, half of these rhymed (e.g., *break/steak*), and half did not rhyme (e.g., *height/freight*).

Each word was presented on a computer screen for 250 ms with a 1,000-ms unfilled interval between the two stimuli in each pair. EM was instructed to say "yes" if the two words rhymed; he was told that it was not important to identify the words but he was told to report any word that he thought he had recognized.

He performed at chance on the rhyming task, responding correctly to 17 of 32 trials on which the words rhymed and 14 of 32 trials on which they did not rhyme (48% correct overall). His performance was influenced by the visual similarity of the stimuli; EM responded "yes" to 13 of 16 visually similar but nonrhyming pairs as compared to 6 of 16 pairs that rhymed but that were visually dissimilar, a difference that is significant ($X^2 = 6.35, p < .05$).

EM performed no better on a second rhyming task in which one of the words was presented auditorily. In fact he declined to complete the task, claiming that it "simply can't be done."

EM was therefore unable to perform rhyme matches for rapidly presented words at exposure durations that support judgments of lexical status as well as access to semantic information. It appears that phonological information does not become available under these conditions, though it should be noted that the rhyming task is, at least with respect to demands on short-term storage, more difficult than the tasks in which lexical and semantic access were demonstrated.

EVIDENCE FOR DIFFERENT READING PROCEDURES

One account of the performance pattern demonstrated by the five subjects who were able to identify letters is that these patients were able to derive lexical-semantic information by means of at least two different procedures. The first involves serial letter naming and subsequent explicit word identification. The second may involve access to a lexical-semantic system in the absence of explicit word identification. As noted earlier, we have suggested that this performance is mediated by the right hemisphere (Coslett & Saffran, 1989a, 1989b).

Although some subjects such as ML, the patient studied by Shallice and Saffran (1986), may voluntarily switch between these procedures, the patients studied in our laboratory appeared reluctant to forgo the certain identification that can be achieved by letter-by-letter reading and only with repeated practice and coaching have proven willing to act upon knowledge not confirmed by the ability to explicitly identify the word.

To experimentally test the hypothesis that two distinct and possibly incompatible procedures are available to these patients we carried out an additional study in our most recent patient, JWC.

We reasoned that if JWC utilized one procedure for purposes of explicit identification but a different procedure to access semantic information for briefly displayed words, his performance with the same stimuli should differ as a function of task demands. More specifically, we predicted that when asked to explicitly identify words he would be able to name a proportion of stimuli but perform poorly on semantic judgment tasks for the stimuli he was not able to name. In contrast, when asked to make a semantic judgment about a stimulus, JWC would be expected to perform well at that task but perform poorly in terms of explicit word identification.

The tasks administered and results are presented in Table 11.9. The first task in this session was to indicate if a rapidly presented letter string was a male or female name. JWC was also instructed to provide the name if he thought he recognized it. JWC correctly categorized all 30 of the names; his only attempt at naming a word was his response of "Andrew" to the target "Andy."

The second task was the animal categorization test described earlier, which had last been administered 7 weeks previously. As is evident from Table 11.9, JWC performed very well on this task, though only three of the animal names were named correctly.

Next, JWC was shown sets of five three-, four-, five-, and six-letter words printed on 5-in. × 7-in. cards and asked to name the words. Although JWC was somewhat faster than he had been 2 months previously, he was still pathologically slow and continued to display an obvious effect of word length, requiring an average of 9 s to name four-letter and 44 s to name six-letter words. This task

TABLE 11.9
Performance as a Function of Task Type (JWC)

Task Order	Task	Exposure	N	No. Named	% Correct
1	Categorization male or female name?	249 ms	30	1−	100
2	Categorization animal?	249 ms	75	3+	85
3	Name word	Unlimited			(only trials not named)
4	Name, then edible?	2,000 ms	25 foods	16+, 3−	
			25 vis. foils	0+, 12−	
			25 unrel. foils	0+, 4−	
			Total		51
5	Categorization	249 ms	25 foods	3+	
			25 vis. foils		
			25 unrel. foils	1+	
			Total		86

was performed not only to demonstrate that the patient continued to employ a letter-by-letter strategy for explicit word identification but also to induce him to revert from the "whole-word" procedure with which he had become quite comfortable and reengage the letter-by-letter procedure.

A second task requiring explicit letter identification was then performed. Stimuli for this task included the 75 words from the "edible" categorization task described earlier. The instructions to JWC on this administration were quite different, however. He was told that each letter string would be visible for 2,000 ms and was instructed to attempt to name the target word. He was also told that if unable to identify the target, he would be asked if the word designated something edible.

Performance on the word identification task at 2,000 ms was poor (Table 11.9). JWC correctly named only 16 words, all names of foods. When unable to name a word, he always named one or more of the initial letters from the word string. Word substitution errors were in all cases food names (e.g., *apple* to the related foil *apply; seafood* to the unrelated foil *safer*).

On the judgment task, JWC's performance at 2,000 ms was poor. Overall, JWC correctly categorized the target on 39 of 75 (52%) trials. Excluding all trials on which JWC offered an explicit response (either correct or incorrect), JWC responded correctly on 4 of 9 trials with food names, 4 of 13 trials with visually similar foils, and 14 of 21 trials with unrelated foils for a total of 22 of 43 (51%).

To ensure that JWC's failure to categorize the words on the last task was not attributable to specific visual or semantic features of the stimuli, a randomized version of the same stimuli were presented once again after a 15-min interval filled with conversation. On this administration, he was told that words would be presented for a very brief interval (that is, 249 ms) and he was asked to judge whether the word referred to something that was edible. He was told that the primary task was to judge whether the referent of the word was edible; he was also instructed to name the word if he recognized it.

JWC correctly categorized 23 of 25 food names, 17 of 25 visually similar foils, and 25 of 25 unrelated foils for a total of 65 of 75 (87%); he correctly named three food names (*sandwich, apple,* and *fruit*) and one unrelated word (*ocean*). Excluding the four trials on which he correctly identified the word, JWC responded correctly on 61 of 71 trials (86%), a performance far better than chance ($X^2 = 21.0, p < .01$). In contrast to his performance on the previous task when asked to name the words, JWC did not report information about initial letters on any trials.

Data from this series of tests, therefore, conform to the predictions outlined previously. When asked to explicitly identify words, JWC accurately reported words on 21% of trials and reported partial letter information on all trials on which he did not report a word; he performed at chance when asked to determine if the referent of the word was edible. When asked to produce a semantic category judgment, JWC performed well on three tasks, including one employing stimuli with which he had performed at chance when attempting to name words. When making judgments about the stimuli, he correctly named only 5% of words and never reported partial letter information. These data suggest that JWC was, indeed, able to employ two distinct reading procedures.

EXPLICIT WORD IDENTIFICATION DURING RECOVERY FROM PURE ALEXIA

When first tested, all of the five letter-by-letter readers reported seeing only a series of single letters. With repeated admonitions to see the whole word and to attempt to get a feel for the word, the overt behavior of the patients changed; in conjunction with a relinquishment of an explicit letter-by-letter strategy, the patients began to display processing capabilities of which they seemed unaware and that they initially denied possessing. As these patients became more confident of their ability to access information about words without utilizing serial letter identification, three of them (JG, JC, TL) regained the ability to explicitly identify a sizeable proportion of briefly presented words. AF, who was presumed to have suffered bihemispheric damage, failed to demonstrate substantial improvement in explicit word recognition. The other patient, JWC, declined further testing.

The following series of investigations was undertaken to characterize the nature of this recovered reading performance. Specifically, as we hypothesized that the reading of these patients was mediated by the right hemisphere, the effects of part of speech and imagery, variables hypothesized to influence the reading performance of the right hemisphere (Coltheart, 1980; Saffran, Bogyo, Schwartz, & Marin, 1980), were investigated.

Part of Speech

The possible effects of part of speech were assessed by asking subjects to read aloud a randomized list of 30 functors and 30 nouns matched for frequency and length. The exposure times are indicated in Table 11.10.

The percentages of nouns and functors correctly read aloud by JG, TL, and JC are expressed in Table 11.10. JG and JC identified significantly more nouns than functors ($X^2 = 5.71$, $X^2 = 10.33$, df = 1, respectively, both $p < .05$); although TL also identified a greater proportion of functors, the difference did not reach significance ($X^2 = 3.45$, df = 1, $.10 > p > .05$). Although the small numbers make a formal analysis difficult, it would appear that the major difference in the errors to functors and nouns was the greater frequency of functor omissions. No semantic errors were noted. Two normal controls tested at exposures that yielded error rates approximating those of the patients produced equivalent numbers of errors on nouns and functors.

TABLE 11.10
Characteristics of Recovered Oral Reading

Patient	Exposure (ms)	Effect of (% Correct):					
		Imageability		Word Class		Morphology	
		Hi-Imag N = 40	Lo-Imag N = 40	Noun N = 30	Functor N = 30	Suffix (flowed) N = 40	Pseudo (flower) N = 40
JG	250	88	63	77	47	30	73
TL	100	...	...	77	50	50	88
JC	250	98	65	83	40	33	83

Word Imagery

Methods: The effect of word imagery on oral reading was assessed by asking subjects to read aloud a randomized list of 40 nouns of high (> 5.0) and 40 nouns of low (< 3) imagery (Paivio, Yuille, & Madigan, 1968), half of each high (> 60) and half low (< 20) in frequency (Kucera & Francis, 1967).

Data for this task are summarized in Table 11.10. Both patients read aloud high-imagery words significantly more accurately than low-imagery words. ($X^2 = 12.86$, df = 1, $p < .001$, and $X^2 = 13.87$, df = 1, $p < .001$, respectively). Collapsing across word imagery, JC was significantly more accurate with high-than low-frequency words ($X^2 = 6.65$, $p < .01$); JG also performed better with high- than low-frequency words but this effect was not significant. Most incorrect responses were visual errors or omissions; 13 of the 14 omissions were noted with low-imagery words.

Thus, all subjects with pure alexia who regained the ability to explicitly identify rapidly presented words performed better with nouns than functors and better with high- than low-imagery words. As previously pointed out by Allport and Funnell (1981), the part of speech effect may reduce to an imageability effect because functors are low in imageability (but see Coslett, 1991, for an example of a dissociation in performance between the effects of imagery and part of speech). In any case, both effects are consistent with reports of right-hemisphere performance patterns (e.g., Zaidel, 1978).

Oral Reading of Suffixed Words

The previous experiment in which JG, JC, and TL were asked to read aloud nouns and functors demonstrated that the patients were significantly more accurate in reading aloud open-class as compared to freestanding closed-class items. The following experiment was performed to determine if these subjects were also impaired in the oral reading of bound closed-class morphemes.

Forty pairs of words containing the same potential freestanding root mor pheme (e.g., *flow*) were generated; one of the pair of words was suffixed (e.g., *flowed*), whereas the other word was not suffixed but ended in a letter sequence that, in a different context, could be a suffix (e.g., "-er" as in *flower*). The two sets of words were equivalent in length and frequency. Stimuli were presented with a microcomputer using the exposure intervals indicated in Table 11.10. Patients were asked to read each word aloud.

The results are presented in Table 11.10. All subjects read aloud significantly more pseudosuffixed than suffixed words ($p < .001$ for all). The nature of the errors on this task is also informative. For all three subjects, the most common errors were suffix omissions; in many cases, the root was correctly read but the suffix omitted (e.g., *flowed → flow*); the number of errors of this type for each subject is indicated in parentheses next to the total number of suffix omissions in Table 11.11.

In contrast, the analogous error with pseudosuffixed words, the omission of pseudosuffixes to yield a legal freestanding root morpheme (e.g., *flower →* *flow*), was rare; the precise number of such omissions is recorded in parentheses under the category of suffix omissions for pseudosuffixed words. JG also made two errors to pseudosuffixed words that might be interpreted as "suffix" substitu- tions (*wallet → walls, sparkle → sparked*).

Thus, when asked to read aloud suffixed and pseudosuffixed words matched for frequency and sharing the same potential root morpheme, patients manifested a significantly greater impairment in reading aloud suffixed as compared to pseudosuffixed words. These data suggest that the impairment in reading these words reflects impaired processing of suffixes rather than simply a neglect of word endings. Again, these results are consistent with reported characteristics of right-hemisphere reading performance (Zaidel, 1978; Zaidel & Peters, 1981).

TABLE 11.11
Oral Reading of Suffixed Versus Pseudosuffixed Words:
Error Analysis (# of Errors)

	Subject					
	JG		TL		JC	
	Suf.	P-S	Suf.	P-S	Suf.	P-S
Root						
Omission	1	2	0	0	4	3
Vis. errors	16	9	7	4	21	14
Suffix (P-S)						
Omission	20(7)	(1)	16(11)	(0)	35(12)	(1)
Sub.	3	(2)	1	(0)	2	(0)
Add.	0	(0)	0	(1)	1	(0)

DISCUSSION

To summarize, there is evidence that at least some proportion of patients who read letter by letter also demonstrate the ability to process words as entities, albeit only implicitly. The implicit reading performance of these patients, which is manifested at presentation rates too rapid to sustain letter-by-letter reading, has a number of consistent features:

1. Though above chance, performance is (with some exceptions) not highly accurate. Lexical decision d's are often in the range of .5–.8 and semantic categorization performance is in the range of 70%–90%. In lexical decision, patients tend to miss low-frequency words and to accept nonwords that are orthographically similar to words.

2. Performance is sensitive to imageability, and insensitive to the appropriateness of affixes.

3. Phonological information is not accessed.

4. Evidence for implicit reading emerges only when letter-by-letter reading is suppressed. It is also noteworthy that when patients who demonstrate implicit reading regain the ability to identify words explicitly, their reading performance is subject to similar constraints: Word naming is sensitive to imageability, and affixes are often read incorrectly.

How Do We Account for Implicit Reading in Letter-by-Letter Readers?

Implicit processing has also been demonstrated in the context of other neurologically based impairments, including amnesia, hemianopia, and prosopagnosia. Thus, for example, amnesic patients who demonstrate little retention of word lists as tested by recall or recognition tests show normal priming by the same word lists in word completion tasks (e.g., Schacter & Graf, 1986). Hemianopic patients display accurate reaching to stimuli in the blind field (Weiskrantz, 1986), and patients with prosopagnosia produce galvanic skin responses (GSRs; Bauer, 1984; Tranel & Damasio, 1985) and other implicit responses (e.g., Young & De Haan, 1988) to photographs of individuals that they fail to recognize explicitly. There is, however, an important distinction between the performance of these patients and the pattern we have described in pure alexia. Most of the alexics we have studied are able to achieve explicit recognition when words are presented long enough to read them letter by letter. Patients with these other forms of neuropsychological deficit do not appear to have an alternative, explicit processing mode.

Implicit reading phenomena have also been demonstrated in normal subjects, under conditions of brief presentation and backward masking. Though the stimuli are not perceptible under these conditions, subjects are able to perform lexical decision at above-chance levels, and demonstrate some recovery of semantic information as well (Cheesman & Merikle, 1985; Marcel, 1983). Replacement of the letter string by the pattern mask presumably prevents the stable binding of visual pattern and stored word-level representation that supports conscious perception of the graphemic stimulus (cf. Coslett & Saffran, 1991). When the pattern mask is removed, normal subjects have no difficulty identifying the letter string. Letter-by-letter reading parallels the situation in normals in that the patient demonstrates implicit processing under reduced presentation conditions and explicit processing with unlimited exposure. In contrast to the normal case, however, the reading performance of the alexic does not simply become "better" with increased exposure. Letter-by-letter reading is sensitive to different parameters than implicit recognition and has different characteristics.

This point is critical for consideration of the nature of the underlying deficit in letter-by-letter reading. Although it is certainly plausible to attribute the two types of reading performance in normal subjects to differential activation of the same reading system, it is difficult to account for the behavior of letter-by-letter readers in terms of a single system. Consider the alternative accounts of pure alexia. A number of investigators, including Farah and Wallace (1991), Kinsbourne and Warrington (1962), and Levine and Calvanio (1978), have proposed that the disorder is a manifestation of a more general visual impairment that compromises the rapid identification of multiple visual forms. Although there is little doubt that at least some patients with pure alexia have such an impairment, it is not clear how this could account for the implicit reading demonstrated in alexic patients by ourselves and others. It seems paradoxical that these patients would find it necessary to engage in serial processing with unlimited presentation yet succeed in processing letter strings in parallel under tachistoscopic conditions. Similarly, on Patterson and Kay's (1982) account, which takes impeded parallel access of letter information to visual word forms to be the primary limitation in letter-by-letter readers, it is difficult to understand why the word-form system should yield weak output (a possible characterization of implicit processing) when addressed in a parallel mode and more adequate (explicit) output when addressed serially.[1]

Howard (1990) offered an alternative account of the multiple forms of reading behavior in letter-by-letter readers in terms of a single system. He argued that the fundamental deficit in letter-by-letter readers is an impairment in letter identification. When letter identification processes do yield correct output, word identification is accomplished in the normal, parallel, fashion; processing of the letter string is fast and identification is explicit. Most of the patients described as letter-

---

[1]One possible consideration, however, is that the processing of multiple letter forms induces inhibition, at the letter or possibly at the word level, which effectively weakens activation of the target at the lexical level.

by-letter readers produce at least some responses of this type; that is, they respond rapidly and correctly at unlimited exposures. When a letter identification error occurs, there are several possibilities, according to Howard:

1. Letter misidentification yields an incorrect word, in which case the response is fast and explicit, but incorrect.

2. Letter misidentification yields a nonword, which generally causes the patient to shift to the slow, serial, letter-by-letter strategy.

3. Should the patient be induced to respond before the strategy can be applied, as in categorization tasks under tachistoscopic conditions, "the pattern of activation across representations in a lexicon" induced by the stimulus is "likely to be consistent with a correct response" (p. 74), though the level of activation is presumably insufficient to yield an explicit response.

On this account, then, implicit processing and letter-by-letter reading are both due to difficulties in letter identification. If so, performance on implicit processing tasks should depend on the discriminability of the graphemic stimuli: Performance on implicit tasks should be better with uppercase than lowercase letters, which are more confusable, and particularly poor on strings that contain confusable letters (like *b, d, p* or *W, M, N*). These predictions have not been tested.

Though Howard's (1990) proposal acknowledges the use of two different strategies for reading, both are presumed to rely on the same letter recognition system, which is characterized as error-prone and inefficient. There are aspects of the patient's performance, however, that strongly suggest the use of two different systems. For example, ML, the patient studied by Shallice and Saffran (1986), often failed to take advantage of the full 2-s exposure allowed him in lexical decision and categorization tasks; he would typically glance at the card and quickly look away. This behavior is difficult to reconcile with a letter recognition problem, as is the demonstration, in JWC, that performance on categorization tasks was significantly worse at longer (2 s) than shorter (250 ms) exposures. These phenomena are more naturally accounted for in terms of two distinct (and possibly incompatible) mechanisms for processing printed words, one capable of processing letters in parallel that supports implicit reading performance and another that affords explicit information by means of serial letter identification.

One such account, suggested by Shallice and Saffran (1986), is that implicit processing is carried out by an impaired but still partially functional word-form system, whereas letter-by-letter reading is mediated by the spelling system (see Warrington & Shallice, 1980). As Shallice and Saffran pointed out, the characteristics of implicit reading performance are consistent with use of an impaired system:

   . . . lexical decision performance at above chance, but well below normal levels; recognition of morphemes, but insensitivity to the appropriateness of their combination; limited access to semantic information. These limitations, including the failure to identify the stimulus explicitly, could . . . be explained in terms of decreased levels of activation within the system that normally subserves explicit identification . . . , a view which is compatible with cascade-type models of the reading process. . . . Weak input from an impaired word-form system could allow sufficient activation of the corresponding semantic representation to activate other representations by spreading activation, but not enough to inhibit the competing possibilities which explicit identification requires. (p. 452)

The viability of this account depends, however, on the plausibility of an independent mechanism for letter-by-letter reading. The inverse spelling hypothesis proposed by Warrington and Shallice has not, to our knowledge, been put to empirical test.[2] A further objection to this line of explanation is that "weak activation" accounts of patients' performance are very difficult to falsify.

We have proposed a different type of dual mechanism account that invokes lateralized processing as an explanatory principle (Coslett & Saffran, 1989a; Shallice & Saffran, 1986). According to this account, letter-by-letter reading is accomplished by accessing the left-hemisphere word-form system, or orthographic input lexicon, in serial rather than parallel fashion. We assume, with Dejerine (1892), that visual input in the alexic patient is initially analyzed in the right hemisphere and that, for purposes of explicit word identification, letter information must be transmitted in serial fashion to the word-form system on the left; like Patterson and Kay (1982), we assume that this system is intact, but isolated from its normal (parallel) sources of orthographic input. The task of reading the word aloud engages left-hemisphere reading mechanisms that have direct output to language production mechanisms. Input to this system in the alexic patient is serial, slow, and inefficient, but output—provided that letters are successfully identified and memory is not overloaded—is generally correct. This system is not available to patients like the optic aphasics CB and EM, presumably because their ability to transfer letter information from right to left is even more impeded than it is in letter-by-letter readers.

As noted earlier, there is no obvious way to account for implicit reading phenomena in terms of the postulated limited-capacity letter transfer and encoding mechanism. Moreover, the fact that at least some of the patients who demonstrate implicit reading (the optic aphasics CB and EM) are unable to access this mechanism is a further argument against an explanation of this type. We suggest that the implicit reading performance demonstrated in alexics, both those who

---

[2]Evidence interpreted as contrary to this hypothesis has been reported by Rapcsak, Rubens, and Laguna (1990). They studied a letter-by-letter reader who demonstrated different error patterns in spelling and reading. On the assumption that reverse spelling hypothesis predicts parallel performance in spelling and letter-by-letter reading, they argued that their patient provides counterevidence to the hypothesis. However, the requirement for parallelism may be too strong, given the different processing demands of the two tasks.

read letter by letter as well as those who do not, is subserved by a separate right-hemisphere word recognition system. We take the characteristics of implicit reading to be a reflection of (a) limitations inherent to the right-hemisphere reading system and (b) limitations on information transfer from that system to the left-hemisphere language system. We suggest, in addition, that the left-hemisphere system controls performance in reading tasks, in the patients as well as in normals. The instruction to read a letter string is construed by the alexic as it normally is, that is, as a request to name the word, a task that engages left-hemisphere language mechanisms. In order to report information generated by the right-hemisphere system, it is necessary to suppress activation of the left-hemisphere reading and phonologic output systems. Instead, the letter string must be treated as an object with certain characteristics (Does it look like a word? Does it stand for an animal?) rather than as a stimulus that is to be encoded phonologically (the usual construal of a command to "read the word"). We assume that to perceive a letter string as such-and-such-a-word, a record of the visual information must be in registration with, or bound to, a phonological representation in the left-hemisphere language system (Coslett & Saffran, 1991). The lesion, which interrupts the normal interhemispheric transfer of information, prevents the critical binding between a visual representation of the letter string and the corresponding word- (or phoneme-) level representations in the left hemisphere.

As we have observed elsewhere (Coslett & Saffran, 1989a; also, Shallice & Saffran, 1986), the characteristics of implicit reading performance in letter-by-letter readers are similar, in a number of respects, to that of the isolated right hemisphere, as demonstrated in hemispherectomy and commissurotomy cases (see Baynes, 1990, for a recent review). Though the data on right-hemisphere reading (and language performance more generally) are subject to caveats of various sorts, and the patterns are not entirely consistent across patients, it seems safe to draw the following generalizations: (a) The isolated right hemisphere has some capacity for printed word recognition, though this capacity is in varying degree limited; (b) semantic and syntactic processing of printed words is also limited; and (c) right-hemisphere capacity for print-to-sound conversion is rarely demonstrable. Whether these limitations represent general characteristics of a restricted or degraded (in terms of number of nodes) reading system (cf. Hinton & Shallice, 1991) or reflect limitations intrinsic to right-hemisphere representational capacities is presently unclear.

There are additional parallels between implicit reading performance in letter-by-letter readers and phenomena associated with commissurotomy. When stimuli are flashed to the right hemispheres of split-brain patients, verbal report is generally absent or confabulatory, though other kinds of responses can be made to these stimuli. It has been shown, furthermore, that some cross-hemispheric integration of information can occur even in the absence of callosal connections. Sergent (1990) showed that although commissurotomy patients are generally unable to perform identity matches for stimuli presented separately to the two visual fields, they can make judgments on the basis of more general characteristics (e.g., which of two digits is the larger). Asked to report on visual stimuli presented to the left visual field, Sergent's patients sometimes provided descriptive information similar to the responses generated by our alexic subjects. Like the commissurotomy cases, the alexics often denied seeing anything at all when presented with letter strings under tachistoscopic conditions, yet they were able to respond to forced-choice queries about these stimuli (word/not word; animal/not animal; food/not food) at above-chance levels and to match words to pictured alternatives as well. It is worth noting that ML, the patient studied by Shallice and Saffran (1986), performed well on most binary classification tasks but poor on a five-alternative categorization task. It may be that the semantic information activated by the letter string can only be apprehended if attention is focused on a particular semantic field. Although the lesions that result in alexia spare callosal transmission anteriorly, they do interrupt interhemispheric pathways posteriorly, either by direct damage to callosal fibers or by injury to the left hemisphere and its underlying white matter (Damasio & Damasio, 1983).

In some patients with alexia, the inability to name visually presented stimuli applies to objects as well as words; that is, the patients are optic aphasic as well as alexic. Data from two such patients, CB (Coslett & Saffran, 1989b) and EM, have been presented in this chapter. Though unable to read aloud or even to name letters, both patients showed implicit reading phenomena similar to those demonstrated by letter-by-letter readers. Elsewhere, we have argued that optic aphasia, like alexia, reflects a block in the transmission of visual information processed in the right hemisphere to the left-hemisphere language system. In most of the letter-by-letter readers we have tested, however, picture naming was relatively intact and vastly superior to the ability to name words.

How do we account for the superiority of picture naming over word naming in these patients? Due to the lesion in left-hemisphere visual pathways and the interruption of callosal transfer of (at least) low-level visual information, early visual processing is presumably restricted to the right hemisphere. But at what level of encoding does information cross to the left hemisphere, and to what processing components does this information go? To answer these questions, we need not only to have a visual information processing (box and arrow) model for each hemisphere but also to specify how the two models are interconnected.

Ideally, such a model should be constrained by knowledge of regional interhemispheric connectivity patterns and, in order to make use of that information, by knowledge of intrahemispheric localization of function. Information gaps in the latter domain are well known to neuropsychologists. More surprising is that there is little detailed knowledge of regional interhemispheric connectivity patterns in the human brain. Some guidelines can, however, be obtained from studies of primates, which indicate that though some projections have a diffuse distribution, the majority of callosal connections are homotopic (Pandya & Seltzer, 1986). In postulating links between information-processing modules in the two hemispheres, it seems reasonable, therefore, to constrain such connections to modules that might be expected to be homotopically represented, that is, to modules of the same general type. (This would rule out, e.g., a direct connection between a right-hemisphere conceptual system and the lexical system in the left hemisphere.)

The model outlined in Fig. 11.1 respects this constraint, as well as one other.[3] We took a conservative stance with respect to the types of functional systems that are likely to be homotopically represented; specifically, we assumed homotopic representation only for functional systems that have a venerable phylogenetic history. Thus, on the assumption that phylogenetically old functions with bilateral representation are subserved by homotopic areas of the two cerebral hemispheres, we allowed direct transmission links between early visual processing modules, between object recognition modules, and between the two conceptual systems. By the same token, we were reluctant to assume homologous representation for the mechanisms that subserve written language, which is phylogenetically recent, culturally determined, and generally acquired with some effort—and hence likely to be variable in its anatomical substrate.[4]

In alexia, the output of early visual processes cannot be transmitted from the right hemisphere to the left hemisphere. According to the model in Fig. 11.1, the only way that visual letter information can reach the left hemisphere is via the object recognition system. This system is presumably able to process individual letters as familiar visual forms. It is not, however, endowed with the capabilities of a word-form system: It is unable to process letter strings in parallel and it does not recognize a string of letters as a unitary perceptual object. We take letter recognition via the object recognition system to be the mechanism that supports letter-by-letter reading; the letters are named and then processed by the word-form system by means of the mechanisms that support the recognition of orally spelled words, which are generally well preserved in letter-by-letter readers. In alexics whose lesions extend to the pathway that connects the two object recognition systems, the naming impairment should include visually presented objects and letters, as well as words. Recall that CB and EM, the two patients with optic aphasia, were unable to name letters and did not demonstrate letter-by-letter reading.

We have still to account for the characteristics of implicit reading performance in alexia, which we attribute to the right-hemisphere system. As noted earlier, the right hemisphere is assumed to have limited lexical and syntactic abilities, and to lack the capacity for phonological encoding.[5] But these are limitations on

---

[3]The development of this model owes much to discussions with Max Coltheart.

[4]See Farah and Wallace (1991) for a similar argument about reading.

[5]As there appears to be some variability in language lateralization patterns in the population, there may well be individual differences in right-hemisphere reading capacities.

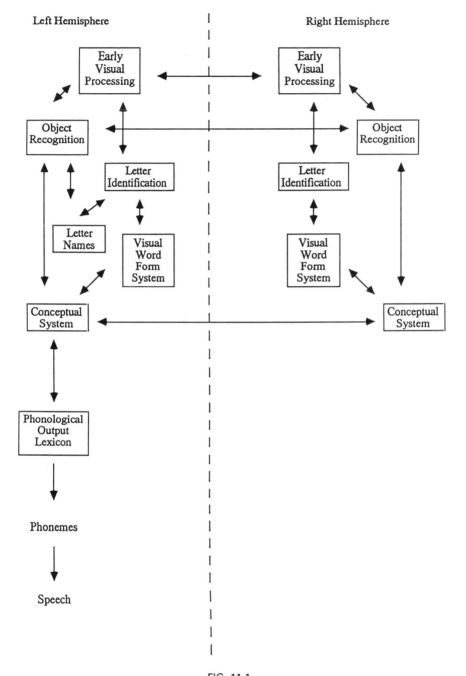

Left Hemisphere

Right Hemisphere

FIG. 11.1.
An information processing account of the process involved in single word reading.

the types of words that the right hemisphere system can process. We still need to explain why the information computed by this system is so difficult to access. Interference from letter-by-letter reading is likely to be part of the problem. The efficiency of information transmission from the right-hemisphere conceptual system to the left-hemisphere system may be another factor. In order to name the word, the information that reaches the left-hemisphere lexical system has to be specific enough to activate the correct lexical entry. The vague descriptions that the patients are sometimes able to offer are probably a good index of the quality of the information that is filtered through two conceptual systems and their connecting pathways; because neither system is hard-wired, it is an open question whether they are linked in a manner that supports highly specific information transmission. Our working assumption is, however, that increased efficiency in this pathway accounts for the improvement in word recognition that we have seen in some of the patients after repeated testing on implicit tasks; recall that this "recovered" performance retains characteristics associated with right-hemisphere reading (Table 11.10).

This line of argument is, of course, highly speculative. It does, however, suggest a somewhat different way of looking at the problem of letter-by-letter reading, and puts this disorder into the context of a wider spectrum of disturbances involving the conscious perception and the verbal identification of visual patterns. Examined from this perspective, alexia and letter-by-letter reading could prove to have broader implications for the neuropsychology of cognition than has hitherto been suspected.

REFERENCES

Albert, M. L., Yamadori, A., Gardner, H., & Howes, D. (1973). Comprehension in alexia. *Brain, 96,* 317–328.

Allport, D. A., & Funnell, E. (1981). Components of the mental lexicon. *Philosophical Transactions of the Royal Society of London B, 295,* 297–310.

Bauer, R. M. (1984). Autonomic recognition of names and faces in prosopagnosia: A neuropsychological application of the guilty knowledge test. *Neuropsychologia, 22,* 457–470.

Baynes, K. (1990). Language and reading in the right hemisphere: Highways or byways of the brain? *Journal of Cognitive Neuroscience, 2,* 159–179.

Behrman, M., Black, S. E., & Bub, D. (1990). The evolution of pure alexia: A longitudinal study of recovery. *Brain and Language, 39,* 405–427.

Bub, D., Black, S. E., & Howell, J. (1989). Word recognition and orthographic context effects in a letter-by-letter reader. *Brain and Language, 36,* 357–376.

Caplan, L. R., & Hedley-Whyte, T. (1974). Cueing and memory dysfunction in alexia without agraphia: A case report. *Brain, 97,* 251–262.

Cheesman, J., & Merikle, P. M. (1985). Word recognition and consciousness. In D. Besner, T. G. Waller, & G. E. Mackinnon (Eds.), *Reading research: Advances in theory and practice* (Vol. 5). New York: Academic.

Coltheart, M. (1980). Deep dyslexia: A right hemisphere hypothesis. In M. Coltheart, K. Patterson, & J. C. Marshall (Eds.), *Deep dyslexia* (pp. 326–380). London: Routledge & Kegan Paul.

Coltheart, M., Davelaar, E., Jonasson, J. T., & Besner, D. (1977). Access to the internal lexicon. In S. Dornic (Ed.), *Attention and performance VI* (pp. 535–555). Hillsdale, NJ: Lawrence Erlbaum Associates.

Coslett, H. B. (1991). Read but not write "idea": Evidence for a third reading mechanism. *Brain and Language, 40,* 425–443.

Coslett, H. B., & Saffran, E. M. (1989a). Evidence for preserved reading in pure alexia. *Brain, 112,* 327–329.

Coslett, H. B., & Saffran, E. M. (1989b). Preserved object recognition and reading comprehension in optic aphasia. *Brain, 112,* 1091–1110.

Coslett, H. B., & Saffran, E. M. (1991). Simultanagnosia: To see but not two see. *Brain, 114,* 1523–1545.

Damasio, A. R., & Damasio, H. (1983). The anatomic basis of pure alexia. *Neurology, 33,* 1573–1583.

Dejerine, J. (1892). Contribution a l'etude anatomo-pathologique et clinique des differentes varietes de cecite verbale [Contributions to the anatomic, pathologic, and clinical investigation of different varieties of word blindness]. *C. r. Seanc. Soc. Biol., 4,* 61–90.

Ellis, A. W., Young, A. W., & Anderson, C. (1988). Modes of word recognition in the left and right cerebral hemispheres. *Brain and Language, 35,* 254–273.

Farah, M. J., & Wallace, M. A. (1991). Pure alexia as a visual impairment. *Cognitive Neuropsychology, 8,* 313–334.

Freund, D. C. (1889). Uber Optische Aphasie und Seelenblindheit [Regarding optic aphasia and mind-blindness]. *Archiv. Psychiatrie und Nervenkrankheiten, 20,* 276–297.

Geschwind, N., & Fusillo, M. (1966). Color-naming defects in association with alexia. *Archives of Neurology, 15,* 137–146.

Hinton, G. E., & Shallice, T. (1991). Lesioning an attractor network: Investigations of acquired dyslexia. *Psychological Review, 98,* 74–95.

Howard, D. (1990). Letter-by-letter readers: Evidence for parallel processing. In D. Besner & G. Humphreys (Eds.), *Basic processes in reading* (pp. 34–76). Hillsdale, NJ: Lawrence Erlbaum Associates.

Kinsbourne, M., & Warrington, E. K. (1962). A disorder of simultaneous form perception. *Brain, 85,* 461–485.

Kreindler, A., & Ionasescu, Y. (1961). A case of "pure" word blindness. *Journal of Neurology, Neurosurgery and Psychiatry, 24,* 275–280.

Kucera, H., & Francis, W. N. (1967). *Computational analysis of present-day American English.* Providence, RI: Brown University Press.

Landis, T., Regard, M., & Serrat, A. (1980). Iconic reading in a case of alexia without agraphia caused by a brain tumor: A tachistoscopic study. *Brain and Language, 11,* 45–53.

Levine, D. N., & Calvanio, R. (1978). A study of the visual defect in verbal alexia-simultanagnosia. *Brain, 101,* 65–81.

Marcel, A. J. (1983). Conscious and unconscious perception. Experiments on visual masking and word recognition. *Cognitive Psychology, 15,* 197–237.

Paivio, A., Yuille, J. C., & Madigan, S. A. (1968). Concreteness, imagery, and meaningfulness values for 925 nouns [Monograph]. *Journal of Experimental Psychology, 76*(Suppl. 1), 1–25.

Pandya, D. N., & Seltzer, B. (1986). The topography of commissural fibers. In F. Lepore, M. Ptito, & H. H. Jasper (Eds.), *Two hemispheres—One brain.* New York: Liss.

Patterson, K., & Kay, J. (1982). Letter-by-letter reading: Psychological descriptions of a neurological syndrome. *Quarterly Journal of Experimental Psychology, 34A,* 411–441.

Patterson, K., Vargha-Khadem, F., & Polkey, C. F. (1989). Reading with one hemisphere. *Brain, 112,* 39–63.

Rapcsak, S. Z., Rubens, A. B., & Laguna, J. F. (1990). From letters to words: Procedures for word recognition in letter-by-letter reading. *Brain and Language, 38,* 504–514.

Riddoch, M. J., & Humphreys, G. W. (1987). Visual object processing in optic aphasia: A case of semantic access agnosia. *Cognitive Neuropsychology, 4,* 131–186.

Saffran, E. M., Bogyo, L. C., Schwartz, M. F., & Marin, O. S. M. (1980). Does deep dyslexia reflect right-hemisphere reading? In M. Coltheart, K. Patterson, & J. C. Marshall (Eds.), *Deep dyslexia* (pp. 381–406). London: Routledge & Kegan Paul.

Schacter, D. L., & Graf, P. (1986). Preserved learning in amnesic patients: Perspectives from research on direct priming. *Journal of Clinical and Experimental Neuropsychology, 8,* 727–743.

Sergent, J. (1990). Furtive incursions into bicameral minds. *Brain, 113,* 537–568.

Shallice, T., & Saffran, E. M. (1986). Lexical processing in the absence of explicit word identification: Evidence from a letter-by-letter reader. *Cognitive Neuropsychology, 3,* 429–458.

Tranel, D., & Damasio, A. R. (1985). Knowledge without awareness: An autonomic index of facial recognition by prosopagnosics. *Science, 228,* 1453–1454.

Warrington, E. K., & Shallice, T. (1980). Word-form dyslexia. *Brain, 103,* 99–112.

Warrington, E. K., & Taylor, A. M. (1978). Two categorical stages of object recognition. *Perception, 7,* 695–705.

Weiskrantz, L. (1986). *Blindsight: A case study and implications.* Oxford, England: Oxford University Press.

Young, A. W., & De Haan, E. H. F. (1988). Boundaries of covert recognition in prosopagnosia. *Cognitive Neuropsychology, 5,* 317–336.

Zaidel, E. (1978). Lexical organization in the right hemisphere. In P. Buser & A. Rougeul-Buser (Eds.), *Cerebral correlates of conscious experience* (pp. 263–284). Amsterdam: Elsevier.

Zaidel, E., & Peters, A. M. (1981). Phonological encoding and ideographic reading by the disconnected right hemisphere: Two case studies. *Brain and Language, 14,* 205–234.

12 Covert Recognition

Andrew W. Young
MRC Applied Psychology Unit, Cambridge

One of the most remarkable findings to arise from investigations of visual recognition impairments due to brain injury has been that patients who do not seem to show normal, overt recognition of things they see may nonetheless demonstrate a form of nonconscious, covert recognition if appropriate tests are used. These patients do not seem to suffer any general alteration of consciousness, but one specific aspect, awareness of recognition, is lost.

If correct, this finding fundamentally changes the way in which we think about recognition impairments, and has implications for our understanding of awareness itself. It is therefore appropriate to give it careful scrutiny. In this chapter, I provide a tutorial review of findings of covert recognition, concentrating on those arising in cases of prosopagnosia, but sketching their relation to other neuropsychological phenomena. I then consider some of the issues which arise and accounts of the phenomena that have been attempted, in the context of recent findings.

BACKGROUND

In order to understand work on covert recognition, it is necessary to have some background information concerning prosopagnosia, to examine the findings obtained with electrophysiological and behavioral measures, and to consider the extent to which these hold across faces familiar before and after the patients' illnesses. I also draw attention to the fact that not all prosopagnosic patients show covert recognition, and explore briefly the relation of covert recognition in prosopagnosia to other forms of neuropsychological impairment.

Prosopagnosia

Most of the work on covert recognition after brain injury has arisen from studies of prosopagnosia. Prosopagnosic patients are unable to identify familiar faces overtly, and rely on voice, context, name, or sometimes clothing or gait to achieve recognition of people they know. A review of the clinical findings is given by Hécaen and Angelergues (1962). The patients know when they are looking at a face, and can describe its features, but the loss of any sense of overt recognition is often complete, with no feeling of familiarity to even the most well-known faces.

Prosopagnosia was first identified as a distinct neuropsychological problem by Bodamer (1947). The underlying pathology involves lesions affecting occipito-temporal regions of cerebral cortex. Usually these are bilateral lesions (Damasio, Damasio, & Van Hoesen, 1982; Meadows, 1974), but several cases apparently involving unilateral lesions of the right cerebral hemisphere have been reported (e.g., De Renzi, 1986b; Landis, Cummings, Christen, Bogen, & Imhof, 1986; Sergent & Villemure, 1989; see Benton, 1990, for a recent review). The neuroanatomical correlates are discussed in detail by Damasio et al. (1982) and Damasio, Tranel, and Damasio (1990).

Covert Recognition from Electrophysiological Responses

Bauer (1984) measured skin conductance (galvanic skin responses or GSRs) while a prosopagnosic patient, LF, viewed a familiar face for 90 s and listened to a list of five names being read out. When the name belonging to the face being viewed was read out, there was a greater skin conductance change than when someone else's name was read out. Yet if LF was asked to choose which name in the list went with the face, his performance was at chance level. These findings are summarized in Table 12.1, which makes it clear that the same effect was found to personally known faces (LF's family) and famous faces he would only have encountered in the mass media.

TABLE 12.1
Percentages of Famous Faces and Family Faces
for Which LF Showed Spontaneous Naming, Selection of the
Correct Name from Five Alternatives, and Maximum GSR
to the Correct Name in the List of Five Alternatives

	Spontaneous Naming	Name Selection	Maximum GSR to Correct Name
Famous faces	0%	20%	60%
Family faces	0%	25%	63%

Bauer's (1984) study showed compellingly a difference between overt recognition, which was at chance level for LF, and some form of preserved covert recognition, as evidenced by his skin conductance responses. In a subsequent study, Bauer and Verfaellie (1988) demonstrated that it is the correspondence between the specific identity of the face and name that is crucial, rather than the mere presence of some kind of match, because differential GSR was not found for a matching task with unfamiliar faces.

Bauer's (1984; Bauer & Verfaellie, 1988) findings profoundly affect our conception of the nature of prosopagnosia, because they show that it is inadequate to think of it as simply involving loss of recognition mechanisms. Instead, at least some degree of recognition does take place; what has been lost is *awareness of recognition*.

Comparable findings were reported by Tranel and Damasio (1985, 1988), using a different technique in which the patients simply looked at a series of familiar and unfamiliar faces. GSR changes were greater to familiar than unfamiliar faces. This shows that it is possible to demonstrate a preserved electrophysiological response to the familiarity of the face alone (i.e., without any accompanying name), which is a useful adjunct to Bauer's (1984) procedure.

A further electrophysiological demonstration of covert recognition in prosopagnosia comes from Renault, Signoret, Debruille, Breton, and Bolgert's (1989) work on evoked potentials.

Behavioral Indices of Covert Recognition

Findings of covert recognition are not restricted to electrophysiological measures. Bruyer et al. (1983) asked their prosopagnosic patient, Mr. W., to learn names to sets of five faces. Some of the data from this study are shown in Table 12.2, which summarizes the conditions in which famous faces were used. On each trial, Mr. W was given a written name for each of five famous faces, and allowed 30 s to examine them. The faces were then removed, and he was asked to pair them up with the names, which were reordered at random. As can be seen, Mr. W seemed better able to learn "true" names to the faces (i.e., the person's actual name) than "untrue" names, which were the names of other

TABLE 12.2
Mr. W's Learning of Different Types of Name to Sets of Five Famous Faces

		Trials					Overall Percentage Correct
Visual Stimuli	Verbal Stimuli	1	2	3	4	5	
Famous male faces	True names	3	5	5	5	5	92%
Famous male faces	Untrue names	1	3	3	5	3	60%
Famous male faces	Male first names	1	1	3	3	3	44%

FIG. 12.1. Examples of stimuli from a condition of de Haan, Young, and Newcombe's (1987a, Task 4) study in which there was significant interference of the distractor face on classification of the name as being that of a politician or nonpolitician. The nonpolitician Frank Bough's name is combined with the face of the politician Neil Kinnock, and vice versa. As can be seen, the two faces are of similar appearance. Copyright 1987 by Lawrence Erlbaum Associates. Reprinted by permission.

people in the set of faces. As Bruyer et al. noted, this superior learning of true than untrue pairings demonstrates some form of preserved recognition of the faces, even though Mr. W was not able to access this overtly.

Bruyer et al. (1983) must be given credit for introducing this conveniently simple learning technique, which has been adapted for use in several subsequent demonstrations of covert recognition of familiar faces (e.g., de Haan, Young, & Newcombe, 1987a; Sergent & Poncet, 1990; Young & de Haan, 1988), and has been extended to examine covert recognition of stimuli from other visual categories (de Haan, Young, & Newcombe, 1991).

Covert recognition has also been demonstrated with a number of other behavioral indices including eye movement scanpaths (Rizzo, Hurtig, & Damasio, 1987), reaction times for face matching across transformations of orientation or age (faster to familiar than unfamiliar faces: de Haan et al., 1987a, Task 1; Sergent & Poncet, 1990), matching of internal and external facial features (faster for familiar than unfamiliar faces with internal features only; de Haan et al., 1987a, Task 2), and interference from distractor faces belonging to the "wrong" semantic category in a name classification task (politician's name versus nonpolitician's name: de Haan, Young, & Newcombe, 1987a, 1987b). Figure 12.1 shows an example taken from de Haan et al. (1987a, Task 4), which illustrates

TABLE 12.3
Reaction Times (in Milliseconds) for Correct Responses to
Target Names of Familiar People Preceded by Related, Neutral,
or Unrelated Face or Name Primes for PH (Young, Hellawell, &
de Haan, 1988) and MS (Newcombe, Young, & de Haan, 1989)

	Related	Neutral	Unrelated
PH:			
Face primes	1016	1080	1117
Name primes	945	1032	1048
MS:			
Face primes	1260	1276	1264
Name primes	1178	1370	1439

that interference was found even when each of the photographs of the faces in a particular category was matched quite closely in appearance to one of the photographs of the faces in the opposite category.

A very useful procedure has been to examine associative priming from face or name primes onto name targets. Associative priming tasks examine the influence of one stimulus on the recognition of a related stimulus; for instance, the effect of seeing John Lennon's face on recognition of Paul McCartney's name. Recognition of a target stimulus is facilitated by an immediately preceding prime stimulus that is a close associate of the target (Bruce & Valentine, 1986).

Using this technique, we were able to demonstrate that the prosopagnosic patient PH shows associative priming from faces he does not recognize. Table 12.3 shows PH's mean correct reaction times for classification of target names as familiar when they are preceded by face or name primes (reaction times to unfamiliar names are not shown). The data are taken from Young, Hellawell, and de Haan (1988), who presented primes to PH for 450 ms each, with a 50 ms interstimulus interval before onset of the target name. Three types of prime were used: related (e.g., John Lennon as a prime for the target name "Paul McCartney"), neutral (an unfamiliar prime with a familiar target name), or unrelated (e.g., Ronald Reagan as a prime for the target name "Paul McCartney").

As the data in Table 12.3 show, PH recognized familiar target names more quickly when they were preceded by related face primes than when they were preceded by neutral or by unrelated face primes. Hence he showed associative priming from faces he did not recognize overtly. Lack of overt recognition was confirmed by a separate posttest given immediately after the experiment, in which PH could only recognize 2 of the 20 familiar faces used (shown to him with unlimited exposure duration), despite the fact that these faces had all been presented many times in the course of the experiment. The associative priming effect was measured (and statistically tested) across all the primes used, so there is no question of the result simply being due to these two faces that could be recognized overtly after the experiment.

It is possible to compare the size of the priming effect across face primes (which PH mostly did not recognize overtly) and printed name primes (which he could recognize). These are exactly equivalent; the possibility of overt recognition of name primes made no additional contribution to the associative priming effect.

In absolute terms, PH's response latencies (Table 12.3) were quite long for this type of task. However, slow responding is a common consequence of certain types of brain injury (van Zomeren & Deelman, 1978). The important point is that the pattern of PH's reaction times across conditions is the same as that found for normal people, with faster reaction times in the related condition regardless of whether face or name primes are employed.

Learning New Faces

The findings I have presented thus far mostly involve tasks in which prosopagnosic patients are shown faces of people who would have been familiar to them before their illnesses. But what about people who have only been encountered since the patient's illness? Would there be covert recognition effects for these as well?

One of the patients studied by Tranel and Damasio (1985, Case 2) could recognize overtly the faces of people familiar to her before her illness, but did not recognize overtly faces of people she had only met since her illness. This clinical pattern is somewhat different to prosopagnosia, which involves both a retrograde recognition deficit (faces known before the patient's illness) and an anterograde deficit (faces met since the illness). Tranel and Damasio (1985, 1988) referred to their patient as having an "anterograde prosopagnosia," and other authors have described similar cases in which old but not new faces can be recognized (Hanley, Pearson, & Young, 1990; Ross, 1980, Case 2).

Tranel and Damasio (1985, Case 2) found that their patient showed larger electrodermal responses to faces she could only have encountered since her illness than to unfamiliar faces, which implies that the face-processing system is able to continue to create representations of people even when they are not consciously recognized. A similar case was reported in Tranel and Damasio (1988, Case 2), with equivalent findings.

Covert recognition of the faces of people who have only been met since the patient's illness has also been found in patients with anterograde and retrograde face recognition defects, both with GSR (Tranel & Damasio, 1988, Cases 3 & 4) and learning tasks (de Haan et al., 1987a; Sergent & Poncet, 1990). Again, it is clear that some form of representation of newly encountered faces is still being created despite the absence of normal, conscious identification.

Prosopagnosia Without Covert Recognition

Although covert recognition of familiar faces can be demonstrated with a range of behavioral and electrophysiological indices, not all prosopagnosic patients show covert recognition effects.

For example, Table 12.3 contains data from the associative priming task for patient MS (Newcombe, Young, & de Haan, 1989) as well as PH (Young et al., 1988). Notice that MS showed associative priming from name primes (which he can recognize overtly), but that there was no difference between his reaction times in the related, neutral, and unrelated conditions when face primes were used. The priming effect was only found with name primes for MS, not faces.

Comparable findings of lack of covert recognition by some patients have been reported with GSR (Bauer, 1986; Etcoff, Freeman, & Cave, 1991) and learning tasks (Etcoff et al., 1991; Humphreys et al., 1992; McNeil & Warrington, 1991; Newcombe et al., 1989; Sergent & Villemure, 1989; Young & Ellis, 1989).

The finding that some prosopagnosic patients show covert recognition and some do not makes it clear that, as clinicians have long suspected (e.g., De Renzi, 1986a; Meadows, 1974), there is more than one form of prosopagnosia. Presence or absence of covert recognition may thus provide an important pointer to the nature of the functional impairment in each case.

Relation of Covert Recognition in Prosopagnosia to Other Forms of Neuropsychological Impairment

We have seen that prosopagnosic patients can show quite a wide range of phenomena indicating covert recognition of faces they do not recognize overtly. But are covert effects unique to prosopagnosia?

The answer is clearly "no." It is better to consider prosopagnosia to be one of a group of neuropsychological impairments in which covert effects can be found (Schacter, McAndrews, & Moscovitch, 1988; Young & de Haan, 1990). For example, there are reports of preserved ability to give the location of visual stimuli presented to perimetrically blind areas of the visual field (Pöppel, Held, & Frost, 1973; Weiskrantz, 1986; Weiskrantz, Warrington, Sanders, & Marshall, 1974), covert processing of "neglected" or "extinguished" stimuli (Marshall & Halligan, 1988; Volpe, Ledoux, & Gazzaniga, 1979), responses to words that cannot be overtly read in alexia (Coslett & Saffran, 1989; Shallice & Saffran, 1986), priming effects in patients with semantic memory impairments (Nebes, Martin, & Horn, 1984; Young, Newcombe, Hellawell, & de Haan, 1989), and priming of fragment completion tasks in amnesia (Warrington & Weiskrantz, 1968, 1970).

Schacter et al. (1988) characterized these impairments as involving failures of "access to consciousness." In each case there is no general alteration of consciousness, but specific types of information seem to be no longer able to enter awareness.

Summary and Implications

Before turning to consider issues, accounts, and more recent findings, I try now to summarize the key points that emerge from this tutorial review, and their implications.

The main point is that patients who do not recognize familiar faces when they are asked directly who the person is can nonetheless show evidence of recognition on a variety of measures including GSR, evoked potentials, eye movement scanpaths, learning of true and untrue information, and reaction times in matching, interference, and associative priming tasks. Covert recognition effects can be found not only to faces of people who had long been familiar to the patient, but also for faces of people who have only been encountered since the patient's illness.

In many of these tasks the information that is accessed covertly is nonetheless dependent on precise visual discriminations, and must reflect the operation of sophisticated visual recognition mechanisms. For example, interference on name classification from the semantic category of an "unrecognized" face is found even when the faces used are matched for overall appearance (de Haan et al., 1987a; see Fig. 12.1). Even more strikingly, the results from associative priming tasks indicate covert processing of the identity of a face that has been presented quite briefly. Bauer's (1984) and Bauer and Verfaillie's (1988) GSR results also involved covert processing of identity, and so did Sergent and Poncet's (1990) finding of preserved ability to match photographs of the same person's face across a 30-year age difference (using photographs of the people taken in 1955 and 1985). By "processing of identity" I mean that the visual system can narrow down the possibilities to the face of a specific person from all the thousands it has encountered in the past, and that it is still capable of using this information in certain ways (as reflected in associative priming, interference, etc.). I do not seek to claim that this means there is also covert retrieval of any very detailed semantic information about the individual.

For prosopagnosic patients with covert recognition, we can consider their impairment as involving a loss of awareness of recognition. This changes our conception of prosopagnosia, which had previously been considered an absolute recognition defect, with no distinction between conscious and nonconscious forms of recognition.

However, not all patients show covert recognition. There are also cases where there does seem to be a loss of both overt and covert recognition ability. It is thus useful to use tests of covert recognition to distinguish different forms of prosopagnosia due to varying underlying causes.

This would be interesting even if it were thought that these measures simply pick up the residual abilities of a recognition system that has suffered widespread general damage. But the fact that covert recognition effects involve the face's identity suggests that thinking in terms of a generally damaged recognition system is inadequate. What we find fits more easily with the idea is that a substantial part of the face recognition system is intact, but its *outputs* have been damaged or disconnected (Young & de Haan, 1988), and this allows us to see covert recognition as one of a group of neuropsychological impairments characterized by selective failures of access to consciousness for certain types of information (Schacter et al., 1988).

ISSUES, ACCOUNTS AND RECENT FINDINGS

Having examined the background of findings on covert recognition, I now turn to consider in more depth some of the issues that arise, accounts that have been given, and recent findings.

Extent of the Loss of Overt Recognition in Prosopagnosia

It is worth considering more carefully the extent of the loss of overt recognition in prosopagnosia, because this is obviously central to any claims of covert recognition. Reports of nonconscious recognition by neurologically normal people have been greeted with considerable skepticism, and great care is needed in conducting and interpreting such studies. Some of the same considerations apply to studies of covert recognition after brain injury.

The first possibility that needs to be considered is response bias. When looking at a face, prosopagnosic patients typically state that it does not seem familiar, and they have no idea who it is. However, it might be thought that they are simply very uncertain as to who it might be, and thus unwilling to venture any hypothesis about the face's identity or its familiarity to them. For example, if prosopagnosic patients are shown a series of faces and asked to pick out those that are familiar, it is usual to find chance-level performance because all of the faces are considered unfamiliar. It is thus desirable to eliminate the effects of what might be merely a very pronounced response bias. This can be done by means of forced-choice tasks (McNicol, 1972).

Table 12.4 shows results for forced-choice familiarity decision to faces and names by patients MS (Newcombe et al., 1989) and PH (Young & de Haan, 1988). On each trial, they were presented with a familiar face and an unfamiliar face, or with a familiar name and an unfamiliar name, and asked to choose the familiar member of each pair. The rationale behind this task is that the sense of familiarity is considered the most basic evidence of overt recognition (e.g., a common everyday error is to know that a face is familiar, but not who it is; Young, Hay, & Ellis, 1985).

TABLE 12.4
Forced-Choice Familiarity Decision to Faces
and Names by PH (Young, & de Haan,
1988), MS (Newcombe, Young, & de Haan,
1989), and Age-Matched Controls

	Faces	Names
PH	65/128	118/128
MS	67/128	116/128
Controls		
Mean	125.50	127.50
SD	3.33	0.84

As Table 12.4 indicates, both MS and PH show chance-level performance of forced-choice familiarity decisions to faces, but are well above chance with names (though still impaired in comparison to age-matched controls). The chance-level forced-choice performance to faces makes it clear that their inability to respond to face familiarity is not just a response bias; yet as we have seen, PH has been found to show a variety of covert recognition effects. In fact, de Haan et al. (1987a, Task 1) had shown that PH matched photographs of familiar faces more quickly than he matched photographs of unfamiliar faces using exactly the same photographs as were employed in this forced-choice familiarity decision task by Young and de Haan (1988).

So far, so good. We also need, though, to know that patients who are thought to show covert recognition are not gaining some degree of overt access to the specific information required by the test used to demonstrate covert recognition.

Again, there are grounds for being reasonably confident. For example, notice that in Bauer's (1984) study (Table 12.1) he included a condition in which his patient, LF, was asked to select the correct name for each face from the five alternatives used in the GSR test. LF performed very poorly in this task (choice of correct name for Famous faces = 20% correct, Family faces = 25% correct; chance = 20% correct), yet his GSR presented quite a different picture (maximum GSR to correct name for Famous faces = 60%, Family faces = 63%; chance = 20%). Hence LF could not perform successfully on an exactly equivalent test of his overt knowledge of the information he accessed covertly.

We have also examined the same point in our interference tasks with PH (de Haan et al., 1987a, 1987b). In these tasks, PH was asked to classify familiar names as those of politicians or nonpoliticians, and the names could be accompanied by a distractor face belonging to same or opposite semantic category (see Fig. 12.1). Like normal subjects, PH showed interference from the face distractors if they belonged to the opposite category to the name.

Although PH could not give any indication that he recognized the specific, personal identity of the faces we used in these tasks, it is obviously important to know how reliably he could assign them to "politician" or "nonpolitician" categories, because it was interference at this semantic category level that was investigated. In each of the three interference experiments we have reported for PH, he was therefore also given a test that required him to assign the faces (presented without accompanying names) to politician or nonpolitician categories.

In one experiment (de Haan et al., 1987a, Task 3) we used pop stars as the nonpoliticians, partly because we could then conveniently compare PH's performance to that of normal subjects (Young, Ellis, Flude, McWeeny, & Hay, 1986), but also because we were curious as to whether the possibility of arriving at the politician versus nonpolitician discrimination using relatively superficial features would prove important (age and hairstyle will distinguish most politicians from most pop stars). As expected, PH could achieve quite accurate classification of these faces as politicians or pop stars (only 4.2% errors), but he was very slow at doing this, with a mean reaction time for face categorization that was more than 200 ms longer than his slowest mean reaction time for any of the name categorization conditions used in the interference task. In another experiment (de Haan et al., 1987b), the nonpoliticians (television and film personalities) were chosen to be of comparable age to the politicians. This considerably reduced PH's ability to classify the faces overtly (30 of 48 correct), though he tried to deploy strategies such as thinking that the politicians would probably be less likely to be smiling. These may have been partially successful, because as Farah (1990) pointed out, his overt classification ability fell in a range that was close to being above chance level (62.5% correct; score 30/48, $z = 1.59$, $p = .06$). Finally, in the third experiment we have reported (de Haan et al., 1987a, Task 4) faces from the politician and nonpolitician categories were matched to each other on the appearance of the specific photographs used (with television personalities as the nonpoliticians; see Fig. 12.1), so that a purely visually based classification could not be successful. PH then performed at chance level (55.5% correct; score 40/72, $z = 0.83$, $p = .20$). However, in all three tasks he showed interference from the face distractors, regardless of the ease with which he could or could not assign them to the appropriate category when asked directly to do this. Hence the possibility of successfully achieving overt classification is not necessary in the production of the interference effects. There is interference even when overt classification of the faces is at chance level.

This impairment of PH's overt ability to assign faces to semantic categories was stable and consistent. De Haan et al. (1991) tested him on 20 repetitions of a politician versus nonpolitician decision task, using a set of five politicians and five nonpoliticians (all repeated 20 times). Across the 200 trials involved, PH made 104 correct choices (52% correct; chance = 50% correct), with no indication of any improvement in his performance. This contrasts markedly with cases involving semantic access impairment, where continuous exposure to the same stimuli with the same task requirement can "warm up" previously inaccessible representations (Shallice, 1987, 1988).

Also striking is the extent to which covert recognition effects can be task-specific. A good example comes from one of our learning tasks in which we taught PH to pair true and untrue names to photographs of our own faces (de Haan et al., 1987a, Task 8; untrue names were our own names, but paired to the wrong faces). Despite the fact that PH had never met any of us before his accident, he was 99% accurate (79 of 80 correct) with true pairings, but only 61% correct overall with untrue pairings (49 of 80). Yet when we took the very same photographs and mixed them with an equal number of unfamiliar faces, PH was at chance in deciding whether or not each person was one of the members of our research group (8 of 16 and 9 of 16 correct in two separate runs). He had not achieved any overt benefit from the substantial degree of covert recognition that he showed during the learning task.

The Parallel with "Automatic" Aspects of Normal Recognition

A number of different ways of thinking about covert recognition have been proposed. These are not necessarily incompatible with each other, but they are often given at different levels of description. I start with the most general, and end up with the more specific.

Let us begin by examining the relation of covert recognition to "automatic" aspects of normal recognition. For all neurologically normal people, recognition is mandatory (Fodor, 1983). We cannot look at a familiar face and decide whether or not to recognize it, no matter how hard we try. The operation of the recognition system proceeds automatically, outside conscious control. This is not to say that errors in recognizing people do not occur in normal people; they certainly do (Hay, Young, & Ellis, 1991; Young et al., 1985). But only a small proportion of these everyday errors reflect the operation of conscious decision mechanisms.

One way of thinking about covert recognition in prosopagnosia is therefore that it continues to reflect the automatic operation of part of the recognition system (Young, 1988). There are some grounds for this.

Consider, for example, the associative priming results for PH, shown in Table 12.3. Recall that in this experiment, PH was shown target names to classify as familiar or unfamiliar, and that each of the familiar target names was immediately preceded by a prime that was associatively related to the target, neutral (an unfamiliar person), or unrelated to the target.

In an influential article on associative priming effects in normal people, Posner and Snyder (1975) pointed out that priming could be mediated intentionally, by subjects trying to predict to themselves which target would follow the prime, or automatically, without conscious prediction. If the intentional effect applied, we would expect some cost in the form of slowed responses if the target was not as had been predicted from the prime. Hence, with an intentionally based priming effect, responses to targets preceded by related primes would be facilitated in comparison to responses to targets preceded by neutral primes, but there would also be a characteristic inhibition (i.e., slowing) of responses to targets preceded by unrelated primes, again in comparison to the neutral condition. For a purely automatic effect, we would only expect facilitation from related primes, with no inhibition from unrelated primes.

The form of the associative priming effect found for PH (see Table 12.3) fits Posner and Snyder's (1975) characterization of an automatic effect, because there was facilitation of responses to related targets (related < neutral) without inhibition of responses to unrelated targets (neutral = unrelated).

It is also known that neurologically normal people can show associative priming effects from stimuli whose presentation times are sufficient to allow them to be seen, but too brief for conscious identification (Carr, McCauley, Sperber, & Parmelee, 1982; McCauley, Parmelee, Sperber, & Carr, 1980). In some ways these form a good analogue of PH's problem, because he knows when he is looking at a face, but lacks any overt sense of whose face it is.

A particularly interesting example of the parallel between findings for normal subjects and prosopagnosic patients comes from Greve and Bauer's (1990) work with LF, the patient investigated in Bauer's (1984) GSR study. Greve and Bauer showed faces to LF for 500 ms each, and then paired each of these faces with a completely novel face. They found that LF showed a preference for the faces shown to him for only 500 ms as being "more likeable" than the faces he had not seen before, whereas when told he had seen one of the faces before and asked which it was he performed at chance level. An equivalent phenomenon of preference for briefly presented stimuli without overt recognition can be demonstrated in normal subjects (Zajonc, 1980).

One very general characterization of covert recognition, then, is that it reflects the continued automatic operation of part of the recognition system. For cases like PH (de Haan et al., 1987a) or LF (Bauer, 1984), what seem to be preserved are those aspects of recognition whose operation is relatively automatic, and does not require conscious initiation (Young, 1988).

Implicit Versus Explicit, and Related Distinctions

It is also possible to draw parallels between covert recognition and phenomena involving implicit memory, which were reviewed by Schacter (1987). This is useful in that it sets findings of covert recognition in a wider theoretical context, and Greve and Bauer's (1990) work shows neatly the benefits of this. But it needs to be done with care, because there are important underlying distinctions to be kept in mind.

A key distinction is between *tasks* and patients' *insight* into their abilities.

Here, I use the terms *direct* and *indirect* to refer to tasks designed to test recognition in different ways (see also Humphreys, 1981; Reingold & Merikle, 1988, 1990). A direct test will immediately inquire about the ability of interest ("Whose face is this?"; "Which is familiar?"; etc.), whereas in an indirect test the ability in question is introduced as an incidental feature of a task that ostensibly measures something else (effects of familiarity on face matching, effects of different types of face prime on name recognition, etc.). Conversely, I use *overt* and *covert* to refer to patients' insight into their recognition abilities. Overt abilities are ones that the patient knows she or he possesses, whereas covert abilities are found in the absence of acknowledged awareness.

In terms of the findings we have discussed so far, covert recognition of familiar faces is found with indirect tests, whereas the patients fail all direct tests. However, there are important exceptions to this tidy pattern, which make it unsatisfactory simply to equate covert recognition with the use of indirect tests.

The first exception is that not all indirect tests produce evidence of covert recognition. For example, whether PH shows better learning of true than untrue pairings in learning tasks is critically dependent on the type of material to be learned to each face. Young and de Haan (1988) found that he showed better learning of true than untrue names to faces when given the person's full name, but did not show this effect when only first names were used. This shows that covert effects arise at a level of recognition that does not encompass name retrieval, and implies more generally that using an indirect task is not in itself sufficient to produce evidence of covert recognition.

The second exception is that not all direct tests are performed at chance level. This was first noted by Sergent and Poncet (1990). They asked their prosopagnosic patient, PV, to choose which of two names (one correct, the other a distractor belonging to a person of the same gender and occupation) went with a particular face. Her performance (40 of 48 correct) was well above chance, though below that of control subjects (who made no errors). PV herself insisted she was guessing. We have replicated this finding with PH, who also performs this task at an overall level that is well above chance, though obviously impaired (30 of 40, 27 of 40, 26 of 40, and 27 of 40 correct in four separate runs; de Haan et al., 1991). Like PV, PH maintains that he is guessing.

Forced-choice decision between two alternative names for a face is a direct test, because it asks about identity ("Which name is correct for the face?"). It is therefore surprising to find above-chance performance, because all other direct tests have been failed by prosopagnosic patients. An important issue, however, concerns whether this forced-choice task elicits covert or overt face recognition abilities. Sergent and Poncet (1990) argued that overt recognition is not involved, because PV insisted she was guessing, she did not know when she had chosen correctly or incorrectly, and was usually just as ready to make a choice between two names even when these were both incorrect for the face shown.

Our findings with PH are the same (de Haan et al., 1991). Like Sergent and

Poncet (1990), we showed that PH was unaware of the information that allowed him to perform above chance level. When the original task with one correct and one incorrect name alternative was changed to one where both names were incorrect, PH continued to choose a name, oblivious to the fact that no correct answer was possible. In addition, his confidence ratings were the same whether the task included a correct name alternative or not. Therefore, we concluded (like Sergent & Poncet) that forced-choice name decision tasks can show covert recognition effects, even though a direct test is involved, and that PH and PV are comparable in that they both show covert face recognition on this type of task.

It seems that even though forced-choice name decision is a direct test, it allows the patients to utilize covert recognition abilities in some way. Note that this task depends on some form of preserved interaction between input recognition systems for faces and names, as do several of the tasks used to demonstrate covert recognition (see Young & de Haan, 1988). Examples include Bauer's (1984) application of the "guilty knowledge" test (Table 12.1), and our semantic priming, interference, and learning paradigms (de Haan et al., 1987a, 1987b; Young et al., 1988). Because forced-choice name decision involves both face and name inputs, it may tap into this interaction.

It is clear that although contrasts between direct versus indirect tests and overt versus covert abilities can play an important role in helping us initially to characterize patterns of intact and deficient performance, they are not in themselves an adequate explanation. However, neurological, psychological, and computational models have been proposed.

Neurological, Psychological, and Computational Models

Bauer (1984) argued that there are two separate cortico-limbic pathways involved in overt recognition and in orienting responses to emotionally salient stimuli; the ventral route (damaged in prosopagnosia) provides overt recognition, whereas the dorsal route (spared in prosopagnosia) gives the face its emotional significance. This proposal is elegant, and useful in that it can potentially be extended to provide an account of Capgras' syndrome (in which people claim that their relatives have been replaced by impostors) as a kind of "mirror image" of prosopagnosia (the face is recognized, but loses appropriate emotional significance: Ellis & Young, 1990), but the nature of the damage to the ventral route needs to be elaborated, in terms of the stage at which overt recognition breaks down.

Tranel and Damasio (1985) suggested that covert recognition arises when "facial templates" are intact, but the processes required for the "activation of multimodal associations" from the face are defective. This view was further developed by Tranel and Damasio (1988), who argued that the creation of face records holding information about the physical structure of known faces is intact, and that this is dependent on cortical areas 17, 18, and 19, which were largely preserved for their patients. However, in Tranel and Damasio's (1988) view the face records do not themselves contain any information about the identity of faces. Conscious recognition of identity requires activation of verbal and nonverbal nonface records, which would normally be achieved via the creation of an *amodal convergence zone* linking the face records to nonface records, and capable of "locking in" to signs of co-occurrent activity in the different sites, and even reconstituting such activity. Disruption of this network of linkages is, in Tranel and Damasio's (1988) model, responsible for the lack of overt recognition and presence of covert recognition effects (mediated via the intact face records) found in prosopagnosia.

This certainly seems to be along the right lines, though I think there are two areas where clarification or slight modification is needed. First, I have argued here that evidence from matching, learning, interference, and associative priming tasks shows that there is covert processing of identity in prosopagnosia. Second, the findings of Bruyer et al. (1983), de Haan et al. (1987a, 1987b, 1991), Young et al. (1988), Young and de Haan (1988), and Sergent and Poncet (1990) all imply that some multimodal associations are implicated in covert recognition, because in all these reports a salient characteristic of covert face recognition was its ability to interact with name processing. We therefore need to clarify which multimodal associations can and cannot be activated, and why.

Young and de Haan (1988) suggested that in covert recognition the face recognition system may have become disconnected from the cognitive system, but remain able to interact in limited ways with other input recognition systems. This is not inconsistent with Bauer's (1984) or Tranel and Damasio's (1985, 1988) proposals, but in its original formulation it suffered from the problem that Young and de Haan were not able to achieve a precise specification of the nature of the preserved interaction between input recognition systems.

This problem was eliminated in a computer simulation developed by Burton, Young, Bruce, Johnston, and Ellis (1991). The simulation is based on Burton, Bruce, and Johnston's (1990) implementation of Bruce and Young's (1986) model of face recognition. The Burton et al. (1990) implementation uses a simple interactive activation architecture (cf. McClelland & Rumelhart, 1981, 1988). Such models involve a number of distinct pools of units. All the units within a pool are connected to each other with inhibitory links. Units may be connected across pools by excitatory links.

Figure 12.2 shows the overall structure of the Burton et al. (1990) model. Following Bruce and Young (1986), Burton et al. proposed a number of pools of units corresponding to the following functional distinctions. Face Recognition Units (FRUs) are representations of the visual characteristics of a known person's face. These units receive input that is assumed to represent the output of visual processing by the perceptual system (structural encoding). Person Identity Nodes (PINs) are domain and modality-free gateways into semantic information. They

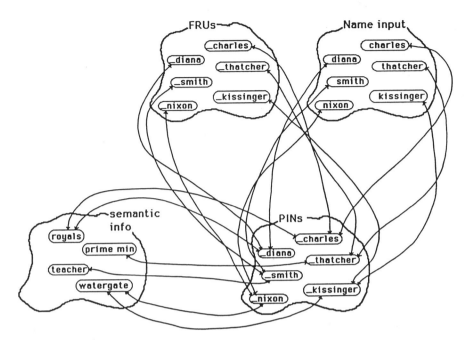

FIG. 12.2. Basic architecture of Burton, Bruce, and Johnston's (1990) interactive activation model of face recognition. From Burton et al. Copyright 1990 by British Psychological Society. Reprinted by permission.

may be accessed through any input domain (face, name, voice, etc.), and provide access to information about that person coded on Semantic Information Units (SIUs). Name Input Units (NIUs) represent the same level of abstraction as FRUs, providing a route into the system for the names of known individuals.

Input to the model is made by increasing the activation of an FRU or NIU. The effect of this is that activation is passed along excitatory links into different pools, thus increasing the activation levels of associated units. In all such models there is also a global decay function that forces units toward a resting activation. Hence, after input to the system, units tend to stabilize when the effect of input activation is balanced by the effect of decay.

In the Burton et al. (1990) model, familiarity decisions are taken at the PINs. An arbitrary threshold is set for the pool of PINs, and any unit that reaches the threshold level is taken to be recognized as familiar. Burton et al. showed that this conceptualization can simulate the properties of a number of effects in the literature on normal face recognition, including associative priming, repetition priming, and distinctiveness effects.

The mechanism by which associative priming takes place in the Burton et al. (1990) model is that after input to a particular FRU (say Prince Charles), the

"Prince Charles" PIN becomes active. As activation at this PIN rises, it in turn passes activation to the relevant SIUs (in this case, "royal"). Now, as this semantic unit rises in activation, excitatory activation is passed back into the PIN pool, to the "Princess Diana" PIN, which is connected to some of the same SIUs as the Charles PIN. The consequence of all this is that when the Charles FRU is made more active the Charles PIN will quickly rise above the threshold for a positive familiarity decision, and the Diana PIN will also rise, but stabilize below this threshold. However, on subsequent activation of the Diana FRU, the Diana PIN will quickly rise to threshold, because it is now above its resting level of activation. Hence associative priming effects are found.

It is important to note that in this model associative priming will take place across input domains. Because its mechanism likes in increased activation at the PIN level from the interaction of PINs and SIUs, subsequent input may come from any system that feeds into these PINs. So, for example, if a PIN has previously become active through presentation of a face, then subsequent presentation of a name will also be facilitated, because the appropriate PIN is already above resting activation.

To simulate the associative priming effects observed in PH, Burton et al. (1991) followed Young and de Haan (1988) in suggesting that PH's problem must affect the outputs of the FRUs. The functional impairment therefore seems to lie in the connection strengths between the pool of FRUs and the pool of PINs. Although some excitation is passed from an active FRU to its associated PIN, weak connection strengths mean that this activation is small compared to an intact system. The result of this is that the appropriate PIN is active, but below threshold. This activation at the PIN can be passed to the connected SIUs in the normal way, and hence to any associated PIN, though the levels of activation will be smaller. By halving the connection strengths between FRUs and corresponding PINs, Burton et al. were able to show that the system can still pass sufficient activation for associative priming from faces, even though these no longer raise the PINs above the recognition threshold.

This simulation shows that, if approached in the right way, covert recognition may be a more tractable problem than it at first appeared. Of course, there is no claim that a simple simulation of this type solves any of the more fundamental philosophical issues to do with the nature of awareness, but it does allow us to understand how a system that has lost one form of recognition ability can still show preserved priming and other effects.

Breakdown at Different Levels

One of the points I have already emphasized is that recognition can break down at different levels. This is also demonstrated by work we recently reported with patient NR (de Haan, Young, & Newcombe, 1992).

NR was unable to recognize familiar people by their faces in most tasks directly demanding recognition, whereas he remained able to recognize the same people by their names. Because of his severe impairment of overt face recognition, the forced-choice familiarity decision task was used as a stringent test for rudimentary overt face recognition abilities that might be missed by more conventional face recognition tasks. Unexpectedly, NR performed well above chance on this task (96 of 128 correct, $z = 5.57$, $p < .001$). His performance at choosing the familiar face was much better than the chance-level performance of PH or MS (see Table 12.4).

Exploration of covert recognition for NR mostly produced negative results. However, it was thought that the failure of most of the experiments involving indirect tests to reveal evidence of preserved recognition might be due to the fact that they did not include enough faces for which NR could show recognition in forced choice. This was confirmed in an experiment in which NR demonstrated priming from familiar faces that he had consistently chosen as familiar in all eight trials of a repeated forced-choice test (de Haan et al., 1992, Experiment 7). A cross-domain self priming task was used, in which a face prime was presented before a target name. The face could be that of the target (Same Person condition), a Neutral (unfamiliar) prime, or an Unrelated familiar person. NR's task was to classify the target name as familiar or unfamiliar. His reaction times to familiar target names are shown in Table 12.5, where it can be seen that there was facilitation of responses to the targets when they were preceded by the same person's face, provided it was one of the faces that NR consistently recognized as familiar in the forced-choice task. In contrast, no priming was observed from familiar faces that NR could not reliably discriminate from unfamiliar ones in forced choice (faces that were chosen as familiar 4 of 8 times in the repeated forced-choice test).

NR showed some conscious realization that he chose certain faces consistently as familiar. As the forced-choice familiarity decision test was repeated more

TABLE 12.5
Mean Reaction Times of NR's Correct Responses to Target Names
(in Milliseconds) Preceded by Same Person, Neutral, and Unrelated
Face Primes. (de Haan, Young & Newcombe, 1992).
Reaction times are subdivided according to whether
the face primes were consistently recognised
as familiar or not recognised in pre-test sessions.

	Same Person	Neutral	Unrelated
Face primes consistently recognized as familiar in pretest	1852	2224	2190
Face primes not recognized in pretest	2273	2101	2250

often, he became more sure of himself and commented on the fact that there "was something with that face," but he was unable to elaborate on this. Although this was not true for all of the faces he recognized in forced-choice familiarity decision tests, and NR certainly did not seem to get any strong feeling of familiarity as such, it is sufficient to lead us to reject the idea that he was relying entirely on covert recognition abilities.

It may thus be better to think of NR's performance on forced-choice face familiarity decision tests as reflecting a very weak degree of overt recognition. Cheesman and Merikle (1985) pointed out with reference to the psychophysical literature that under near-threshold conditions there is a certain region where subjects still perform above chance level, although subjectively they feel they are doing little more than guessing. This may well be analogous to what happened for NR. There were some faces that yielded some form of rudimentary recognition in forced-choice conditions, and could support a degree of facilitation in priming tasks. However, these often remained below or barely above the threshold for overt recognition, leaving NR unable to comment adequately the choices he was making.

In contrast to PH, NR was above chance at forced-choice recognition of face familiarity (though he was obviously still severely impaired at the task), and only showed priming from faces he could consistently recognize as familiar in forced choice. His consistent performance to certain items on the forced-choice familiarity decision test indicated that NR's deficit might well be better conceptualized as a storage than as an access problem (Shallice, 1987, 1988).

De Haan et al. (1992) suggested that NR had suffered degradation of face recognition units. Some of the stored face representations had been completely wiped out at this (face recognition unit) level, and there would be no preserved recognition of these faces. Other representations were sufficiently preserved that they could be recognized as familiar when the choice was between that face and an unfamiliar face, and they could support priming effects.

Clearly, this functional explanation is different from those we have offered for other patients with prosopagnosia we have investigated. We proposed that PH's consistent pattern of preserved recognition of familiar faces on most indirect tests reflected damage to the outputs of otherwise intact face recognition units (Young & de Haan, 1988). For MS, we proposed that the consistent absence of preserved recognition of familiar faces reflected higher order perceptual impairment (Newcombe et al., 1989), which would mean that there could be no effective input to face recognition units.

The implication is that there is an underlying hierarchy of possible loci of impairment. In terms of this hierarchy, MS's impairment was centered on a relatively early stage in the system, PH's was relatively late, and NR's lay between. Patterns of preserved and impaired abilities found in cases of prosopagnosia may be complex, but they are not random, and the use of functional models and appropriate experimental techniques has the potential to reveal the underlying order.

Other authors have also advanced similar proposals on the basis of recent work. Etcoff et al. (1991) and McNeil and Warrington (1991) both noted that the full range of findings on presence or absence of covert recognition cannot be accounted for simply by proposing that patients who do not show covert recognition have impaired perception; Etcoff et al.'s patient did not show covert recognition despite having many well-preserved perceptual abilities, and McNeil and Warrington found evidence of less intact perception for their cases with covert recognition. Both Etcoff et al. and McNeil and Warrington concluded that brain injury can selectively eliminate stored information about the appearance of familiar faces; in Bruce and Young's (1986) terms this would be equivalent to loss of the face recognition units.

Impairments affecting awareness can also be found at other levels of recognition. One example comes from our work with BD, a postencephalitic patient who was poor at recognizing people from face, name, or voice. This is a pattern quite unlike prosopagnosia, pointing to a much more "central" impairment. Yet BD showed evidence of preserved recognition abilities in learning tasks (Hanley, Young, & Pearson, 1989).

Even more striking are findings of unawareness of impaired recognition. Young, de Haan, and Newcombe (1990) reported the case of a woman with severe and stable face-processing impairments, SP, who showed complete lack of insight into her face recognition difficulties. SP was very poor at recognizing familiar faces, yet she was not distressed by this, and maintained that she recognized faces "as well as before." She said that she had no problems in recognizing faces in everyday life, in paintings, on the television, in newspapers or magazines, whereas formal testing showed that all of these must have been highly problematic. Even when directly confronted with her failure to recognize photographs of familiar faces, SP could only offer the suggestion that the photograph was a "poor likeness," or that she had "no recollection of having seen that person before."

In contrast to her lack of insight into her face recognition impairment, SP showed adequate insight into other physical and cognitive impairments produced by her illness, including poor memory, hemiplegia, and hemianopia. Her lack of insight into her face recognition impairment involved a *deficit-specific anosognosia*. We think that such deficit-specific anosognosias reflect impairment to mechanisms we need in order to monitor our own performance in everyday life (Young et al., 1990).

Provoking Overt Recognition

When we first began working with PH, he seemed to us to be completely unable to achieve overt recognition of familiar faces. De Haan et al. (1987a) noted that of the hundreds of famous faces they had shown him, only one (Mrs. Thatcher) had been spontaneously recognized, and that on only one occasion.

Since then, we have also noted other occasions on which PH has overtly recognized a face during the last few years. There are about a dozen faces he has recognized occasionally, but the only face we have noticed is beginning to be fairly consistently recognized is Mrs. Thatcher's (Young & de Haan, 1992). It will be interesting to see whether or not her fall from power reverses this trend.

The fact that some faces have been overtly recognized on rare occasions is important, because it indicates that PH's problem cannot be an absolute deficit. If we think of it in terms of impaired links between FRUs and PINs, it makes more sense to see the problem as involving weakened connection strengths (Burton et al., 1991) than as a complete disconnection.

The importance of this becomes clear in an extraordinary finding of Sergent and Poncet's (1990) study. They observed that PV could achieve overt recognition of some faces if several members of the same semantic category were presented together. This only happened when PV could determine the category herself. For the categories PV could not determine, she continued to fail to recognize the faces overtly even when the occupational category was pointed out to her. When the same faces were later presented one at a time in random order, PV was again unable to recognize any of them, including those she had recognized when they were placed in appropriate category groupings.

We have been able to replicate this phenomenon of overt recognition provoked by presentation of multiple exemplars of a semantic category with PH (de Haan et al., 1991). Table 12.6 shows data from a task in which PH was asked to recognize faces from three broadly defined semantic categories (politicians, television presenters, and comedians) and three narrowly defined categories (the

TABLE 12.6
Number (Max = 8) of Correct (+) and Incorrect (−) Overt
Identifications by PH in the Different Conditions of a Category
Presentation Task (de Haan, Young, & Newcombe, 1991) Involving a
Pretest with the Faces in Pseudorandom Order, Simultaneous
Presentation of All Eight Faces from a Particular Category,
and an Immediate Posttest and Delayed Posttest
(After a 2-Month Interval) with Pseudorandom Ordering

| | Pretest | | Category Presentation | | Posttest | | | |
| | | | | | Immediate | | Delayed | |
	+	−	+	−	+	−	+	−
Broad Categories								
Politicians	0	0	0	0	0	0	0	0
TV presenters	0	0	0	0	0	4	0	1
Comedians	2	2	1	0	2	2	1	0
Narrow Categories								
"Neighbours"	0	0	1	0	1	0	0	0
"Eastenders"	1	0	6	0	5	0	1	0
"Coronation St."	0	0	1	0	1	1	0	0

television soap operas "Neighbours," "Eastenders," and "Coronation Street"). There were eight faces from each category. It can be seen that there was a marked improvement in his ability to recognize the "Eastenders" faces when these were all presented simultaneously (the Category Presentation condition). There is no reason to think PH was guessing these or deducing them from cues such as age and hairstyle, because there were no misidentifications of the faces in this category. Note also that (in contrast to Sergent & Poncet's 1990 findings) the improvement in overt recognition of these faces transferred to an Immediate Posttest with the faces presented one at a time in pseudorandom order. The improvement did, though, dissipate across a 2-month interval (Delayed Posttest).

Sergent and Poncet (1990) offered a very similar account to the Burton et al. (1991) simulation, suggesting that their demonstration shows that "neither the facial representations nor the semantic information were critically disturbed in PV, and her prosopagnosia may thus reflect faulty connections between faces and their memories" (p. 1000). They hypothesized that the simultaneous presentation of several members of the same category may have temporarily raised the activation level above the appropriate threshold.

The disruption of overt face recognition in prosopagnosia is usually so complete that findings of covert recognition have been a considerable surprise. One cannot fail to be even more impressed by the finding that overt recognition can be provoked under certain conditions, at least for some patients (and some faces). This offers the hope that, given sufficient ingenuity, we may be able to find ways to help at least some of the people who suffer these very disabling conditions. Of course, any effective remedial technique based on such procedures is still a long way off, and will depend on knowing much more about the conditions under which overt recognition can be provoked and, above all, maintained. But the initial finding is more promising than anything that has emerged from conventional training procedures (e.g., Ellis & Young, 1988).

Overview

Work on covert recognition has come a long way in the last few years, from studies that simply demonstrated the existence of these phenomena after brain injury, to investigations intended to probe much more analytically into their nature. It has become clear that awareness of recognition can break down in a number of different ways after brain injury, but that there is an underlying order to these forms of impairment. The challenge for the future is to achieve well-specified models that can bring together these observations into a unified theory, and to explore their implications for remediation.

The phenomena of covert recognition present an intriguing challenge to our conceptions of awareness. In particular, they make it hard to accept the commonly held view that the same processes underlie visual analysis and awareness. Were this so, impairments involving the loss of awareness of a particular perceptual quality would always involve the loss of all ability to respond to that quality, regardless of the test used. Studies of covert processing show that this is far from the case.

Pressing this point further, we can see that the existence of covert processing of visual stimuli after brain injury forces us to stop thinking of visual experience as epiphenomenal. Instead, it highlights questions about the purpose of awareness, and what it allows us to do that we could not otherwise achieve. A promising idea is that we need to be aware of something in order to form a judgment or belief about it, and that awareness is indispensable to creatures capable of genuine judgment and belief (Lowe, 1992). Certainly, people like PH find that their inability to achieve overt recognition of most familiar faces is socially disabling; in everyday life they act as if they do not recognize people from their faces, despite the extensive covert recognition effects we have demonstrated.

Teuber (1968) likened the concept of agnosia to that of a "normal percept stripped of its meaning." However, as Bauer (1984) pointed out, findings of covert recognition show that in some cases the percept has only lost certain aspects of its meaning. These missing aspects are those that are crucial to intentional action.

What are preserved in brain-injured people who show covert recognition are automatic aspects of recognition whose functions include preparing the recognition system for what it is likely to encounter next (Young & de Haan, 1988), orientation to stimuli with motivational significance, and arousal responses that set a background emotional tone for any social interaction (Bauer, 1984). Thus covert recognition may well exert subtle influences on behavior, but at the level of intentional actions the consequences of the failure of overt recognition are overwhelmingly evident. Awareness of recognition is no pointless luxury.

ACKNOWLEDGMENTS

Much of the work described here has been carried out in collaboration with Freda Newcombe and Edward de Haan. We have also received a lot of help and advice from Vicki Bruce, Mike Burton, Andy Ellis, Hadyn Ellis, Rick Hanley, and Dennis Hay. Our work on recognition impairments has been supported by MRC grant G890469N to Edward de Haan and Andy Young, MRC grant G8804850 to Freda Newcombe and Andy Young, and ESRC grant R000231922 to Andy Young, Rick Hanley, and Freda Newcombe. I am grateful to the Press Association and the Lancashire Evening Post for help in finding suitable photographs for use as stimuli, to the Press Association for permission to reproduce Fig. 12.1, and to the British Psychological Society for permission to reproduce Fig. 12.2 (from Burton, Bruce, & Johnston, 1990).

REFERENCES

Bauer, R. M. (1984). Autonomic recognition of names and faces in prosopagnosia: A neuropsychological application of the guilty knowledge test. *Neuropsychologia, 22,* 457–469.

Bauer, R. M. (1986). The cognitive psychophysiology of prosopagnosia. In H. D. Ellis, M. A. Jeeves, F. Newcombe, & A. Young (Eds.), *Aspects of face processing* (pp. 253–267). Dordrecht, Netherlands: Martinus Nijhoff.

Bauer, R. M., & Verfaellie, M. (1988). Electrodermal discrimination of familiar but not unfamiliar faces in prosopagnosia. *Brain and Cognition, 8,* 240–252.

Benton, A. L. (1990). Facial recognition 1990. *Cortex, 26,* 491–499.

Bodamer, J. (1947). Die Prosop-Agnosie. *Archiv für Psychiatrie und Nervenkrankheiten, 179,* 6–53.

Bruce, V., & Valentine, T. (1986). Semantic priming of familiar faces. *Quarterly Journal of Experimental Psychology, 38A,* 125–150.

Bruce, V., & Young, A. (1986). Understanding face recognition. *British Journal of Psychology, 77,* 305–327.

Bruyer, R., Laterre, C., Seron, X., Feyereisen, P., Strypstein, E., Pierrard, E., & Rectem, D. (1983). A case of prosopagnosia with some preserved covert remembrance of familiar faces. *Brain and Cognition, 2,* 257–284.

Burton, A. M., Bruce, V., & Johnston, R. A. (1990). Understanding face recognition with an interactive activation model. *British Journal of Psychology, 81,* 361–380.

Burton, A. M., Young, A. W., Bruce, V., Johnston, R. A., & Ellis, A. W. (1991). Understanding covert recognition. *Cognition, 39,* 129–166.

Carr, T. H., McCauley, C., Sperber, R. D., & Parmelee, C. M. (1982). Words, pictures, and priming: On semantic activation, conscious identification, and the automaticity of information processing. *Journal of Experimental Psychology: Human Perception and Performance, 8,* 757–777.

Cheesman, J., & Merikle, P. M. (1985). Word recognition and consciousness. In D. Besner, T. G. Waller, & G. E. Mackinnon (Eds.), *Reading research: Advances in theory and practice* (Vol. 5, pp. 311–352). New York: Academic.

Coslett, H. B., & Saffran, E. M. (1989). Evidence for preserved reading in "pure alexia." *Brain, 112,* 327–359.

Damasio, A. R., Damasio, H., & Van Hoesen, G. W. (1982). Prosopagnosia: Anatomic basis and behavioral mechanisms. *Neurology, 32,* 331–341.

Damasio, A. R., Tranel, D., & Damasio, H. (1990). Face agnosia and the neural substrates of memory. *Annual Review of Neuroscience, 13,* 89–109.

de Haan, E. H. F., Young, A., & Newcombe, F. (1987a). Face recognition without awareness. *Cognitive Neuropsychology, 4,* 385–415.

de Haan, E. H. F., Young, A., & Newcombe, F. (1987b). Faces interfere with name classification in a prosopagnosic patient. *Cortex, 23,* 309–316.

de Haan, E. H. F., Young, A. W., & Newcombe, F. (1991). Covert and overt recognition in prosopagnosia. *Brain, 114,* 2575–2591.

de Haan, E. H. F., Young, A. W., & Newcombe, F. (1992). Neuropsychological impairment of face recognition units. *Quarterly Journal of Experimental Psychology, 44A,* 141–175.

De Renzi, E. (1986a). Current issues in prosopagnosia. In H. D. Ellis, M. A. Jeeves, F. Newcombe, & A. Young (Eds.), *Aspects of face processing* (pp. 243–252). Dordrecht, Netherlands: Martinus Nijhoff.

De Renzi, E. (1986b). Prosopagnosia in two patients with CT scan evidence of damage confined to the right hemisphere. *Neuropsychologia, 24,* 385–389.

Ellis, H. D., & Young, A. W. (1988). Training in face-processing skills for a child with acquired prosopagnosia. *Developmental Neuropsychology, 4,* 283–294.

Ellis, H. D., & Young, A. W. (1990). Accounting for delusional misidentifications. *British Journal of Psychiatry, 157,* 239–248.

Etcoff, N. L., Freeman, R., & Cave, K. R. (1991). Can we lose memories of faces? Content specificity and awareness in a prosopagnosic. *Journal of Cognitive Neuroscience, 3,* 25–41.

Farah, M. J. (1990). *Visual agnosia: Disorders of object recognition and what they tell us about normal vision.* Cambridge, MA: MIT Press.

Fodor, J. (1983). *The modularity of mind.* Cambridge, MA: MIT Press.

Greve, K. W., & Bauer, R. M. (1990). Implicit learning of new faces in prosopagnosia: An application of the mere-exposure paradigm. *Neuropsychologia, 28,* 1035–1041.

Hanley, J. R., Pearson, N., & Young, A. W. (1990). Impaired memory for new visual forms. *Brain, 113,* 1131–1148.

Hanley, J. R., Young, A. W., & Pearson, N. (1989). Defective recognition of familiar people. *Cognitive Neuropsychology, 6,* 179–210.

Hay, D. C., Young, A. W., & Ellis, A. W. (1991). Routes through the face recognition system. *Quarterly Journal of Experimental Psychology, 43A,* 761–791.

Hécaen, H., & Angelergues, R. (1962). Agnosia for faces (prosopagnosia). *Archives of Neurology, 7,* 92–100.

Humphreys, G. W. (1981). Direct vs. indirect tests of the information available from masked displays: What visual masking does and does not prevent. *British Journal of Psychology, 72,* 323–330.

Humphreys, G. W., Troscianko, T., Riddoch, M. J., Boucart, M., Donnelly, N., & Harding, G. F. A. (1992). Covert processing in different visual recognition systems. In A. D. Milner & M. D. Rugg (Eds.), *The neuropsychology of consciousness and cognition* (pp. 39–68). London: Academic.

Landis, T., Cummings, J. L., Christen, L., Bogen, J. E., & Imhof, H.-G. (1986). Are unilateral right posterior cerebral lesions sufficient to cause prosopagnosia? Clinical and radiological findings in six additional patients. *Cortex, 22,* 243–252.

Lowe, E. J. (1992). Experience and its objects. In T. Crane (Ed.), *The contents of experience.* Cambridge: Cambridge University Press.

Marshall, J. C., & Halligan, P. W. (1988). Blindsight and insight in visuo-spatial neglect. *Nature, 336,* 766–767.

McCauley, C., Parmelee, C., Sperber, R., & Carr, T. (1980). Early extraction of meaning from pictures and its relation to conscious identification. *Journal of Experimental Psychology: Human Perception and Performance, 6,* 265–276.

McClelland, J. L., & Rumelhart, D. E. (1981). An interactive activation model of the effect of context in perception, Part 1. An account of basic findings. *Psychological Review, 88,* 375–406.

McClelland, J. L., & Rumelhart, D. E. (1988). *Explorations in parallel distributed processing.* Cambridge, MA: Bradford.

McNeil, J. E., & Warrington, E. K. (1991). Prosopagnosia: A reclassification. *Quarterly Journal of Experimental Psychology, 43A,* 267–287.

McNicol, D. (1972). *A primer of signal detection theory.* London: George Allen & Unwin.

Meadows, J. C. (1974). The anatomical basis of prosopagnosia. *Journal of Neurology, Neurosurgery, and Psychiatry, 37,* 489–501.

Nebes, R. D., Martin, D. C., & Horn, L. C. (1984). Sparing of semantic memory in Alzheimer's disease. *Journal of Abnormal Psychology, 93,* 321–330.

Newcombe, F., Young, A. W., & de Haan, E. H. F. (1989). Prosopagnosia and object agnosia without covert recognition. *Neuropsychologia, 27,* 179–191.

Pöppel, E., Held, R., & Frost, D. (1973). Residual visual function after brain wounds involving the central visual pathways in man. *Nature, 243,* 295–296.

Posner, M. I., & Snyder, C. R. R. (1975). Facilitation and inhibition in the processing of signals. In

P. M. A. Rabbitt & S. Dornic (Eds.), *Attention and performance* (pp. 669–682). London: Academic.

Reingold, E. M., & Merikle, P. M. (1988). Using direct and indirect measures to study perception without awareness. *Perception and Psychophysics, 44,* 563–575.

Reingold, E. M., & Merikle, P. M. (1990). On the inter-relatedness of theory and measurement in the study of unconscious processes. *Mind and Language, 5,* 9–28.

Renault, B., Signoret, J. L., Debruille, B., Breton, F., & Bolgert, F. (1989). Brain potentials reveal covert facial recognition in prosopagnosia. *Neuropsychologia, 27,* 905–912.

Rizzo, M., Hurtig, R., & Damasio, A. R. (1987). The role of scanpaths in facial recognition and learning. *Annals of Neurology, 22,* 41–45.

Ross, E. D. (1980). Sensory-specific and fractional disorders of recent memory in man, 1. Isolated loss of visual recent memory. *Archives of Neurology, 37,* 193–200.

Schacter, D. L. (1987). Implicit memory: History and current status. *Journal of Experimental Psychology: Learning, Memory and Cognition, 13,* 501–518.

Schacter, D. L., McAndrews, M. P., & Moscovitch, M. (1988). Access to consciousness: Dissociations between implicit and explicit knowledge in neuropsychological syndromes. In L. Weiskrantz (Ed.), *Thought without language* (pp. 242–278). Oxford, England: Oxford University Press.

Sergent, J., & Poncet, M. (1990). From covert to overt recognition of faces in a prosopagnosic patient. *Brain, 113,* 989–1004.

Sergent, J., & Villemure, J.-G. (1989). Prosopagnosia in a right hemispherectomized patient. *Brain, 112,* 975–995.

Shallice, T. (1987). Impairments of semantic processing: Multiple dissociations. In M. Coltheart, G. Sartori, & R. Job (Eds.), *The cognitive neuropsychology of language* (pp. 111–127). London: Lawrence Erlbaum Associates.

Shallice, T. (1988). Specialisation within the semantic system. *Cognitive Neuropsychology, 5,* 133–142.

Shallice, T., & Saffran, E. (1986). Lexical processing in the absence of explicit word identification: Evidence from a letter-by-letter reader. *Cognitive Neuropsychology, 3,* 429–458.

Teuber, H.-L. (1968). Alteration of perception and memory in man. In L. Weiskrantz (Ed.), *Analysis of behavioral change.* New York: Harper & Row.

Tranel, D., & Damasio, A. R. (1985). Knowledge without awareness: An autonomic index of facial recognition by prosopagnosics. *Science, 228,* 1453–1454.

Tranel, D., & Damasio, A. R. (1988). Non-conscious face recognition in patients with face agnosia. *Behavioural Brain Research, 30,* 235–249.

van Zomeren, A. H., & Deelman, B. G. (1978). Long-term recovery of visual reaction time after closed head injury. *Journal of Neurology, Neurosurgery, and Psychiatry, 41,* 452–457.

Volpe, B. T., Ledoux, J. E., & Gazzaniga, M. S. (1979). Information processing of visual stimuli in an "extinguished" field. *Nature, 282,* 722–724.

Warrington, E. K., & Weiskrantz, L. (1968). New method of testing long-term retention with special reference to amnesic patients. *Nature, 217,* 972–974.

Warrington, E. K., & Weiskrantz, L. (1970). Amnesia: Consolidation or retrieval? *Nature, 228,* 628–630.

Weiskrantz, L. (1986). *Blindsight: A case study and implications.* Oxford, England: Oxford University Press.

Weiskrantz, L., Warrington, E. K., Sanders, M. D., & Marshall, J. (1974). Visual capacity in the hemianopic field following a restricted occipital ablation. *Brain, 97,* 709–728.

Young, A. W. (1988). Functional organization of visual recognition. In L. Weiskrantz (Ed.), *Thought without language* (pp. 78–107). Oxford, England: Oxford University Press.

Young, A. W., & de Haan, E. H. F. (1988). Boundaries of covert recognition in prosopagnosia. *Cognitive Neuropsychology, 5,* 317–336.

Young, A. W., & de Haan, E. H. F. (1990). Impairments of visual awareness. *Mind and Language,*
   5, 29–48.
Young, A. W., & de Haan, E. H. F. (1992). Face recognition and awareness after brain injury. In A.
   D. Milner & M. D. Rugg (Eds.), *The neuropsychology of consciousness* (pp. 69–90). London:
   Academic.
Young, A. W., de Haan, E. H. F., & Newcombe, F. (1990). Unawareness of impaired face recogni-
   tion. *Brain and Cognition, 14,* 1–18.
Young, A. W., & Ellis, H. D. (1989). Childhood prosopagnosia. *Brain and Cognition, 9,* 16–47.
Young, A. W., Ellis, A. W., Flude, B. M., McWeeny, K. H., & Hay, D. C. (1986). Face-name
   interference. *Journal of Experimental Psychology: Human Perception and Performance, 12,*
   466–475.
Young, A. W., Hay, D. C., & Ellis, A. W. (1985). The faces that launched a thousand slips:
   Everyday difficulties and errors in recognizing people. *British Journal of Psychology, 76,* 495–
   523.
Young, A. W., Hellawell, D., & de Haan, E. H. F. (1988). Cross-domain semantic priming in
   normal subjects and a prosopagnosic patient. *Quarterly Journal of Experimental Psychology,*
   40A, 561–580.
Young, A. W., Newcombe, F., Hellawell, D., & de Haan, E. H. F. (1989). Implicit access to
   semantic information. *Brain and Cognition, 11,* 186–209.
Zajonc, R. B. (1980). Feeling and thinking: Preferences need no inferences. *American Psychologist, 35,* 151–175.

13

Implicit Perception in Visual Neglect: Implications for Theories of Attention

Marcie A. Wallace
Carnegie Mellon University

The topic of this chapter is implicit perception in patients with parietal lobe lesions and the implications of this phenomenon for theories of attention. The dissociation between *implicit* and *explicit* cognitive processes has received much attention in neuropsychology lately. People who have apparently lost certain cognitive functions, such as the ability to learn new information, following a brain injury, are often able to demonstrate these same abilities when tested in specific ways (see Schacter, McAndrews, & Moscovitch, 1988, for a review). For instance, patients with amnesia might not explicitly remember having been shown a list of words and will not be able to recall the words on this list, but when asked to complete a three-letter stem with any word that comes to mind they will more often use a word that they saw on the list. Cowey, Young, and Coslett and Saffran (chapters 1, 11, & 12 of this volume) review the literature on implicit perception in cortical blindness, prosopagnosia (inability to recognize faces) and alexia (inability to recognize printed words).

Even though the dissociations between performance on these direct and indirect tests are empirically well established in many syndromes, there is still little consensus on the mechanism that permits these dissociations. In the present chapter, I examine implicit perception in patients with parietal damage who have visual neglect and extinction and focus on two related issues: What are the mechanisms by which parietal-damaged patients process unattended stimuli in the contralesional hemifield, and what are the implications of implicit perception in parietal-damaged patients for theories of visual attention?

THE SYNDROME OF VISUAL NEGLECT
AND EXTINCTION

Damage to the posterior parietal lobe of one hemisphere of the brain often results in the inability to notice stimuli occurring on one side of space. Because of the crossed organization of the visual system (see Cowey, chapter 1 of this volume) the effects of parietal damage are manifest primarily with stimuli in the side of space opposite the side of the lesion. This is known as the contralesional side. In addition, there is an asymmetry in parietal lobe attentional function such that left neglect following right parietal damage is more common than right neglect following left parietal damage, so many of the studies reviewed here included only right-parietal-damaged subjects. The tendency of parietal-damaged patients to not notice, or to neglect, contralesional stimuli is not due to the hemifield blindness that often co-occurs with parietal lesions. Patients who are blind in one visual field will compensate by turning their eyes and head to get a stimulus of interest into their preserved visual field. In contrast, patients with neglect do not seem to be aware that there is anything of interest on their contralesional side. This is true even of neglect patients with intact visual fields.

Patients with extinction to double simultaneous stimulation are similar to neglect patients, except that their deficit is not as severe. Acute visual neglect often resolves into chronic visual extinction (Karnath, 1988). Such patients can function fairly well on a daily basis, but their deficit appears when there is a competing stimulus on the ipsilesional side of the target. For example, the wife of one of the right-parietal-damaged patients whom I tested reports that when he rides in the front seat of a car, he keeps his head turned to look out the side window. The movement in the patient's right visual field attracts his attention so strongly that nothing else can compete for it.

A common method of testing for visual extinction involves asking the patient to detect movement of fingers held in his left and right peripheral visual fields. The patient is asked to decide whether one or both of the fingers is being wiggled. Patients with extinction can accurately perceive a single object or event at one time, but when two occur simultaneously the patients will only detect the one to the ipselesional (usually, right) side. Thus the patient is said to "extinguish" the stimulus in the contralesional visual field when there is simultaneous stimulation to both visual fields. Posner, Walker, Friedrich, and Rafal (1984) characterized the deficit as a difficulty in disengaging attention from an object in order to move it to another object in the contralesional direction (see chapter 8 of this volume).

But what is it that is lacking when the subject is unable to "pay attention" to stimuli in the left visual field? It is not clear whether information coming from the left is processed only minimally because basic perceptual processing does not proceed without attention or whether it is fully processed but cannot reach conscious awareness without attention.

HYPOTHESES CONCERNING ATTENTION

One common interpretation of the role of attention is that it functions to select a subset of the incoming information for further processing (e.g., Posner, 1978). This reduces the computational load on the brain by allowing it to fully process only selected stimuli. There has been an ongoing debate in the attention literature, however, as to the stage of information processing at which attention pares the amount of information for further processing. The early-selection theorists claim that attention must select a stimulus for further processing when only low-level features have been analyzed. One example of this is Triesman's (1988) hypothesis that attention is necessary for feature conjunction. Unless attention is paid to an object, the features (e.g., color, line orientation, and location) of that object will not be conjoined and it cannot be recognized as a complex object or reach awareness. This would suggest that attention acts on the information represented in the "feature maps" within the occipital lobes (see Cowey, chapter 1 of this volume). The late-selection theorists, in contrast, claim that an object can be processed at least as far as category extraction (e.g., deciding whether a character is a letter or a number) or specific identity before attention is necessary (e.g., Duncan, 1983). This would suggest that attention operates at a level of the visual system where objects are explicitly represented as objects, presumably the temporal lobes (see chapters 1 & 2 of this volume). On this late-selection view, the purpose of attention is to select the results of identification or categorization for use by response systems and awareness.

The implicit perception abilities of parietal-injured patients with neglect and extinction are relevant to the issue of early versus late selection in normal visual attention. If attention normally selects early, and the parietal damage alters the selection process, then the most straightforward prediction is that little information about neglected or extinguished stimuli should be available, either explicitly or implicitly. If attention normally selects late, after stimulus identity has been represented, and neglect or extinction only affects processing beyond this point, then we would expect much information about neglected and extinguished stimuli to be available, at least implicitly.

Implicit perception in parietal-damaged patients has been studied using a variety of experimental approaches. In the following review, I organize these studies into three general groups: those involving bilateral tachistoscopic presentation of pairs of stimuli (i.e., the classical situation for eliciting extinction), those involving free viewing of a single stimulus, and those involving single-word reading.

BILATERAL TACHISTOSCOPIC PRESENTATION

Volpe, LeDoux, and Gazzaniga (1979) were the first to look for implicit effects of visual stimuli occurring in the extinguished hemifield of parietal-damaged patients. Using a tachistoscope, they presented right parietal-damaged patients with stimuli in each hemifield, singly and in pairs. As expected with extinction patients, performance was good for naming objects or words presented individually to either visual field, but extremely poor for identifying the item on the left side when it occurred simultaneously with one appearing on the right side. Two of the four patients never named the item on the left correctly when it was paired with a right hemifield stimulus. Surprisingly, Volpe et al. found that the patients were good at making same/different judgments about two objects or words, one in each visual field, even though they were unable to identify the item on the left. Volpe et al. concluded that extinguished stimuli are fully perceived and that the deficit involves "a breakdown in the flow of information between conscious and nonconscious mental systems" (p. 724).

This surprising dissociation between identification and same/different matching was replicated by Karnath and Hartje (1987) in a patient with more severe neglect than the four reported in the previous experiment. Karnath and Hartje concluded that the information that the subjects are using to make correct same/different judgments is available "preattentionally."

The authors of these two articles were not explicit about the mechanisms that allows the results of the same/different comparison to enter consciousness whereas the identity of the object on the left is *un*able to enter. Volpe et al. (1979) said that the comparison process takes place "at a post-perceptual, pre-verbal level, with only the resultant comparison entering consciousness" (p. 724).

Farah, Monheit, and Wallace (1991) questioned the Volpe et al. (1979) conclusion that attention was a postperceptual process and that extinguished stimuli were fully perceived albeit unconsciously. We asked whether the same/different task might simply require less information about the stimulus on the left than an identification task and therefore appear to be relatively preserved. Consider an example from Volpe et al.'s article: a picture of a comb on the left and an apple on the right. If one sees only that the comb is long and narrow, one will correctly answer "different" on the same/different matching task because the apple is round. However, there are many objects that are long and narrow; so on the basis of this one feature the subjects would fail the identification task. We replicated the Volpe et al. experiment using eight simple geometric shapes as stimuli, and also extended their experiment by adding a condition in which the subject was asked to make a two-alternative forced-choice judgment about the identity of one of the items present in the display rather than generating the name for the item. In this way, the amount of visual information needed to perform the identification task is equated with that needed for the same/different task. For example, if a circle and a triangle were represented in a same/different trial there would also be an identification trial with the same stimuli and the subject would be asked "Did you see a circle or a cross?" to probe the identity of the object on the left.

In the condition that was a direct replication of the Volpe et al. (1979) experiment, with free identification rather than forced choice, our results were similar to theirs. The patients showed poor identification performance for the stimuli in the left hemifield and almost perfect performance for stimuli on the right. The patients performed well above chance on the same/different task, as did the Volpe et al. subjects.

The critical test, though, is how the patients performed on the forced-choice identification task. If it is the case that their performance appears preserved on the same/different task simply because it requires less information than the identification task, we would expect patients to perform well on the forced-choice task because it is equated for difficulty with the same/different task. The patients did perform similarly on the forced-choice and same/different tasks and this performance was significantly better than their performance on the free identification task. Therefore, we concluded that some information from the left visual field does get processed but the quality of this information is very minimal or degraded. The apparent preservation of perception when assessed by same/different matching is attributable to the relative ease of the task.

In order to gather converging evidence for our account of the Volpe et al. (1979) results, we ran the same experiment on college students, degrading the information coming into the subjects' left visual field by taping two layers of mylar on the left half of the computer screen. The results for the students were similar to the patients'. The students were poor at making a free identification of the left stimulus, but performed much better when asked to make a forced-choice or same/different judgment about the two items. It does not make sense that two sheets of mylar allowed the visual stimulus to be fully analyzed, but stopped the results of that analysis from reaching consciousness. Thus, this finding further supports the idea that the lack of attention in parietal patients reduces the quality of information the brain receives from the neglected hemifield, rather than preventing the fully processed information from reaching consciousness.

Further evidence for at least some processing of extinguished stimuli comes from Audet, Bub, and Lecours (1991). They adapted an experimental paradigm developed by Taylor (1977), who found that normal subjects were faster to identify a target letter as a *T* or a *K* if the neighboring letters matched the target letter, relative to a neutral condition in which the flanking letters were different.

Audet et al. (1991) used this task with parietal-damaged patients as an indirect measure of the processing that occurs in an unattended region of the subject's visual field. They modified Taylor's (1977) procedure so the flanking letter occurred on only one side of the target. In the control condition, the flanker was located above the target letter where its processing should not be affected by the patient's neglect. In the experimental condition, the flanker was located to the left of the target where it should be neglected. The task requires the subject to attend to a location in which a target letter will appear and name it as quickly as possible when it appears. The target appears for a brief period of time and is flanked by another letter. The flanking letter can be the same letter as the target, the other possible target letter, or a neutral letter.

Both of the patients tested showed the inhibiting effects of the flanker letter when it appeared above the target. However, only one of them showed effects in the horizontal flanker condition when the flanker was to the left of the target. Audet et al. (1991) concluded that the patient who showed effects of the flanking letter on the neglected side "[must be] capable of obtaining the perceptual description of a letter on the left . . . without generally being able to consciously use the information for decision and response purposes" (p. 26). They cited Cheesman and Merikle's (1986) possible explanations for these phenomena: "[1] either the stimulus information is too weak for the activation of any perceptual codes, or [2] the information is sufficient to activate a limited number of records, in which case tacit identification will occur without the perceptual integration necessary for a conscious experience" (p. 26). Note that the authors did not claim that perception is completed normally but the results of that perception are unable to enter consciousness. Instead they stated that the information from the contralesional stimulus is processed weakly, and although the limited processing is too weak for the object to gain access to consciousness, it is sufficient to influence processing of the ipsilesional stimulus.

Berti et al. (1992) asked whether the information from the extinguished hemifield was sufficient to access semantics, in other words, postvisual categorical representation. Their experiment was based on Volpe et al.'s (1979) experiment. They showed an extinction patient a picture in each hemifield and asked her whether the two objects shown had the same name. After making the same/different name judgment they asked the subject to name the items. What makes this study interesting is that the stimulus materials were broken down into three types of *same* pairs and two types of *different* pairs. Pairs to which the subject should respond "same" included: identical views of the same object, different views of the same object (one rotated 45° from the other), and two different exemplars of the same category (e.g., two different styles of camera). Pairs to which the subject should respond "different" are: objects from different categories that look dissimilar (e.g., a spoon and a camera), and objects from different categories that have the same basic shape (e.g., a spoon and a key). With this experimental design, the authors could assess whether extinguished stimuli were processed only within the visual system, or whether higher order categorical representations were also activated.

Looking at the data divided by the type of stimuli, the patient's performance was above chance on all same/different judgments, although she performed significantly better at making *same* judgments on trials where the two stimuli were identical than when they were the same object viewed from a different angle or when they were different exemplars of the same category. There was no significant difference between the two types of *different* trials in her ability to correctly classify them as different except on the last block. On this block, with a 10-ms duration, she performed better when the two objects were dissimilar in appearance than when the objects were similar in appearance. Her performance on the similar-appearance objects was still above chance.

Berti et al. (1992) explained that their results support the hypothesis that the subject is accessing categorical information in order to make the same/different judgments. If she were not accessing categorical information, but was simply using low-level visual information for her decisions, then she should incorrectly say "same" for different objects with similar shape and should incorrectly choose *different* for the same object viewed from different angles, because the outline and relative positions of the features would be different. Although the authors explained their data by saying that the patient has nonconscious access to categorical information, they did not take the strong position that this entails complete tacit knowledge with failure only to enter consciousness. They offered an alternative explanation that involves collateral priming or facilitation on *same* trials, similar to the phenomenon demonstrated by Audet et al. (1991).

Berti et al.'s (1992) patient's performance on the same/different task could be explained by her ability to obtain categorical information on only one of the two types of trial (e.g., the *same* trials), and to use the other response ("different") as a default when she did not have any information available. Generalizing from experiments with normal subjects, who are faster to recognize an object if they have just seen an object of the same type because of the shared representation between the two, the authors reasoned that it is possible for the representation of the object in the ipsilesional visual field to facilitate the representation of the object in the contralesional visual field sufficiently to obtain the category when the two items belong to the same category. This theory predicts that when asked to name both items (without doing the same/different task), parietal-damaged patients should name the items on the contralesional side with higher accuracy when the two items are the same than when the two items are different. Intermediate performance would be expected when the two items are from the same category, but are different in appearance.

SINGLE OBJECTS IN CENTRAL VISION

Marshall and Halligan (1988) asked whether implicit perception could affect a parietal-damaged patient's judgment of single items presented in central vision. They showed a patient with neglect a line drawing of a house with bright red flames on the left side of the picture. The patient described the drawing as being of a house. She did not mention the flames or mention that there was anything unusual about the house. When shown two line drawings of the house, one that contained flames and one that did not, the patient said she could see no difference. Thus the flames were being consistently neglected by the patient. However, when asked to choose which of the two houses she would rather live in, the patient chose the nonburning house on 14 of 17 trials. The authors stated that these "rational nonrandom preferences" (p. 766) seem to show that "the so-called neglected stimulus can exert an influence upon cognitive functioning, albeit at some pre-attentional, pre-conscious level" (p. 767).

Bisiach and Rusconi (1990) attempted to replicate Marshall and Halligan's (1988) findings using four right-parietal-damaged patients and four pairs of stimulus pictures. They used line drawings of a house with and without bright red flames on the left, a vase with and without flowers, an intact and broken wine glass, and a banknote with and without the left corner torn off. The first patient, who was tested using only the burning/nonburning house stimuli, showed no preference for either picture of the pair. The fourth patient refused to be tested on the houses, and noticed the critical difference on the glasses and vases during pretesting. She was, however, tested on the banknotes and also showed no consistent preference.

Two patients did show consistent preferences on some of the stimuli pairs. Unlike Marshall and Halligan's (1988) patient, both showed a preference for the burning house. These same two patients, however, also showed a preference for at least one of the "positive" stimuli (both preferred the unbroken glass and one patient preferred the vase with flowers). It would appear that these patients are noticing some difference between the pictures of the pair and are able to make consistent choices on the basis of this difference without any effect, conscious or unconscious, of the content of the picture. In any case, the patients do not meet Marshall and Halligan's criterion of rational nonrandom preferences. Two of the patients show nonrandom preferences, but each patient shows a preference that is not "rational" unless it is possible to rationalize their preference for living in the burning house.

Bisiach and Rusconi (1990) concluded that the patients choose the preferred picture on the basis of "insignificant, or 'confabulated' differences found in the non-neglected portions of the drawings" (p. 646). Based on the new evidence, they did not find implausible Marshall and Halligan's (1988) conclusion that neglected stimuli are processed to a high cognitive level.

SINGLE-WORD READING

Some right-parietal-damaged patients neglect the left halves of words, or the words on the left half of the page, when reading. This symptom has been called neglect dyslexia. Sieroff, Pollatsek, and Posner (1988) tested the ability of neglect patients to report the contralesional sides of word and nonword letter strings. Their task required subjects to look at a letter string or strings presented either in free vision or tachistoscopically and to report the letters present. They found that neglect patients reported the contralesional side of words more reliably than nonwords. They also found that the patients neglected the word on the contralesional side of a bilaterally presented pair more often than they neglected the ipsilesional, or "good," half of a longer word that spanned the same visual angle. This was true whether the stimuli were centered on fixation or lateralized so they extended from fixation into the ipsilesional visual field.

Although these two results might seem to imply late attentional selection, occurring after the stage of processing at which words are recognized as distinct from nonwords, Sieroff et al. (1988) favored an early-selection hypothesis. They suggested that attention "modulates the efficiency of registration of letters but is not absolutely necessary (p. 447). Using McClelland and Rumelhart's (e.g., 1986) model of interactive activation, Sieroff et al. proposed that patients show better performance for words than for nonwords because words are preexisting units and their letters can receive top-down support from word representations to overcome the lack of perceptual detail that results from the inability to attend to the contralesional half of a string. Because the nonwords do not have an existing representation in memory, the lack of detail cannot be overcome through top-down processes, thus the patient's performance is worse on these stimuli.

Behrmann, Moscovitch, Black, and Mozer (1990) tested two neglect dyslexics to determine whether the attentional deficit in neglect affects early or late processing. The two patients differed in the severity of their neglect. The authors found evidence suggesting both early and late selection of attention, but the effects found were contingent upon the severity of the neglect. In general, the performance of the patient with the more severe neglect suggested that the deficit affected early processing. He was mainly influenced by low-level features of the lexical items (e.g., the visual angle of the letter string). In contrast, the patient with less severe neglect was affected by the lexicality of the letter string, a higher level effect. When the patient with the more severe deficit was put into a situation that reduced the effects of neglect (e.g., moving the stimulus to the right in the patient's visual field, or cueing the subject to the left) he showed fewer low-level effects and more high-level effects. They concluded that only one attentional mechanism is involved, but that the severity of the deficit interacts with the ability to use top-down mechanisms, producing seemingly dissociable effects. If the neglect is too severe, however, it will prevent sufficient visual information from activating word-level representations at all. So we would not expect to find any implicit perception in extremely severe patients.

Brunn and Farah (1991) presented another possible explanation for the word superiority found in the reading performance of neglect dyslexics. Instead of a completion-like process whereby higher level representations fill in missing lower level information, it is possible that the distribution of attention is different in the word and nonword cases. Perhaps words cause a redistribution of attention over the whole string, because the word makes a perceptual unit. This would then permit better performance on the left side for words than for nonwords because the whole string would then be attended and be perceived more clearly.

Brunn and Farah (1991) added an additional test to the free-reading version of the Sieroff et al. (1988) experiment in order to measure the distribution of attention over the letter strings. The distribution of attention was tested in two ways. In one experiment, the letters were printed in different colors. The subjects' task was to report the color of each letter in the word or nonword string in addition to reading the letters. In the other experiment, the subjects were to bisect a line under the letter string that spans the same horizontal distance as the letter string. If the *wordness* of a letter string causes a contralesional reallocation of attention, then the attentional measures should show better performance on the left for the words than for the nonwords. Alternatively, if word reading is accomplished only by using feedback from higher level representations, without a redistribution of attention, then the subjects' performance on the attention measures should not be different for words than for nonwords because attention is applied similarly to each.

Brunn and Farah (1991) found that reading performance and performance on the attentional measures was better on the left for words than for nonwords. The authors interpreted their data as showing that better performance on the left side of words relative to nonwords is accompanied by a reallocation of attention toward the contralesional side of words but not nonwords. The authors explained the results using an interactive activation framework similar to the McClelland and Rumelhart (1986) model cited by Sieroff et al. (1988) and Behrmann et al. (1990), and proposing that attention can be attracted by activation of representations either by outside stimulation or by top-down support from high-level, lexical representations. When a patient with left neglect looks at a word in central vision the allocation of attention is initially deficient for the left half of the word. Featural information from the right is nevertheless well represented and starts activating letter and word representations. Information is also coming in from the left although, due to the attentional deficit, it is much weaker and more degraded than the information coming in from the right. If the stimulus is a word, it will start to activate word representations. Those representations will feed back activation to lower levels, including letter and feature processors that are analyzing the information from the left visual field. This top-down input to the left visual field is presumably what attracts attention. In contrast, with nonwords there is no high-level representation of the stimulus, and thus no top-down input to the left side of the letter string with concomitant attentional reallocation.

SUMMARY AND CONCLUSIONS

There are many findings of neglected or extinguished stimuli reaching relatively high levels of stimulus coding—shape, category, and even lexicality information seems to be available from stimuli that subjects may deny seeing or be unable to identify explicitly. At first, this evidence seems to support late selection. Late-selection theories claim that perceptual processing proceeds normally through category extraction or identification and that attention is only applied at this point in order to bring the resulting stimulus identity into awareness. An attentional deficit, then, would only affect the ability to become aware of the stimulus and its identity, but would not affect one's ability to perceive it and activate its representation.

However, several of the researchers whose work is reviewed here have proposed alternatives to this view. Their hypotheses are based on the idea that information representation is not all-or-none, but that representations can be partially activated. It may be that the parietal attentional mechanism affects early stages in the visual processing of stimuli, consistent with early-selection theories of attention, but that the reduced and degraded visual information that is extracted from the neglected stimulus is still sufficient to partially activate high-level representations.

So what can we conclude? Are both alternatives equally plausible? Neither is definitely ruled in or out by the available data, but evidence for low-level visual impairments (Behrmann et al., 1990; Farah et al., 1991) suggests that the early-selection hypothesis, with partial activation of higher level representations, is probably correct.

There is also the possibility that attention operates at more than one level and that neglect could occur due to damage at one or more of these levels. In this case, there could be differences in the abilities of neglect patients depending on the attentional level at which the deficit occurred. If there is only one attentional system that governs the full range of processing, then the only factor that should determine the performance of a patient with neglect on any of these tasks is the severity of the attentional deficit. We would therefore expect that if we gave these patients a number of these "indirect" tests of their attentional abilities that their scores on all of the tests should be correlated and should reflect the severity of their deficit. If, on the other hand, there are different types of attention and neglect then it should be possible to find patients who perform well on one task although performing poorly on another. Because of the sequential nature of the processing stream, however, a complete double dissociation may not be possible.

Future research, then, should be aimed at developing tests that could differentiate patients with deficits of late selection from patients with deficits of early selection so we can determine whether there is one attentional mechanism and damage to it would result in a continuum of severity or whether there are qualitatively different types of attention that would produce qualitatively different types of neglect when damaged. The results so far suggest that there is one type of neglect and that it is a deficit of early processing. These tests must be designed carefully in order to prevent misinterpretation of the resulting data. Behrmann et al. (1990) demonstrated that data that seem to show two types of attentional deficit can be misleading. Their initial data appeared to support the hypothesis that their two patients had deficits of different attentional mechanisms—one patient's deficit being in the early-selection mechanism, the other patient's in the late-selection mechanism. However, when they tested the more severe neglect patient in a manner that taxed his attention less, he performed more like the patient with the less severe deficit. They concluded that both patients had the same deficit, but that the severity of the deficit interacted with the ability to benefit from top-down processing, thereby producing what seemed to be qualitatively different behaviors. Future research must be equally careful in its methods and conclusions.

REFERENCES

Audet, T., Bub, D., & Lecours, A. R. (1991). Visual neglect and left-sided context effects. *Brain and Cognition, 16,* 11–28.

Behrmann, M., Moscovitch, M., Black, S., & Mozer, M. (1990). Perceptual and conceptual factors in neglect dyslexia: Two contrasting case studies. *Brain, 113,* 1163–1183.

Berti, A., Allport, A., Driver, J., Dienes, Z., Oxbury, J., & Oxbury, S. (1992). Levels of processing for visual stimuli in an "extinguished" field. *Neuropsychologia, 30,* 403–415.

Bisiach, E., & Rusconi, M. L. (1990). Breakdown of perceptual awareness in unilateral neglect. *Cortex, 26,* 643–649.

Brunn, J. L., & Farah, M. J. (1991). The relation between spatial attention and reading: Evidence from the neglect syndrome. *Cognitive Neuropsychology, 8,* 59–75.

Cheesman, J., & Merikle, P. M. (1986). Word recognition and consciousness. In D. Besner, T. G. Waller, & G. E. McKinnon (Eds.), *Reading research: Advances in theory and practice* (pp. 311–352). New York: Academic.

Duncan, J. (1983). Perceptual selection based on alphanumeric class: Evidence from partial reports. *Perception and Psychophysics, 33,* 533–547.

Farah, M. J., Monheit, M. A., & Wallace, M. A. (1991). Unconscious perception of "extinguished" visual stimuli: Reassessing the evidence. *Neuropsychologia, 29,* 949–958.

Karnath, H.-O. (1988). Deficits of attention in acute and recovered visual hemineglect. *Neuropsychologia, 26,* 27–43.

Karnath, H.-O., & Hartje, W. (1987). Residual information processing in the neglected visual half-field. *Journal of Neurology, 234,* 180–184.

Marshall, J. C., & Halligan, P. W. (1988). Blindsight and insight in visuo-spatial neglect. *Nature, 336,* 766–777.

McClelland, J. L., & Rumelhart, D. E. (1986). *Parallel distributed processing: Explorations in the microstructure of cognition.* Cambridge, MA: MIT Press.

Perrett, D., Rolls, E. T., & Caan, W. (1982). Visual neurons responsive to faces in the monkey temporal cortex. *Experimental Brain Research, 47,* 329–342.

Posner, M. I. (1978). *Chronometric explorations of the mind.* Englewood Cliffs, NJ: Lawrence Erlbaum Associates.

Posner, M. I., Walker, J. A., Friedrich, F. J., & Rafal, R. D. (1984). Effects of parietal lobe injury on covert orienting of visual attention. *Journal of Neuroscience, 4,* 1863–1874.

Schacter, D. L., McAndrews, M. P., & Moscovitch, M. (1988). Access to consciousness: Dissociations between implicit and explicit knowledge in neuropsychological syndromes. In L. Weiskrantz (Ed.), *Thought without language* (pp. 242–278). Oxford, England: Oxford University Press.

Sieroff, E., Pollatsek, A., & Posner, M. I. (1988). Recognition of visual letter strings following injury to the posterior visual spatial attention system. *Cognitive Neuropsychology, 5,* 427–449.

Taylor, D. A. (1977). Time course of context effects. *Journal of Experimental Psychology: General, 106,* 404–426.

Triesman, A. (1988). Features and objects: The fourteenth Bartlett memorial lecture. *The Quarterly Journal of Experimental Psychology, 40A*(2), 201–237.

Volpe, B. T., LeDoux, J. E., & Gazzaniga, M. S. (1979). Information processing of visual stimuli in an "extinguished" field. *Nature, 282,* 722–724.

Author Index

A

Adams, M. J., 166, *168*
Adams, R. J., 186, *209*
Adelson, E. H., 11, *30*
Ahern, G. L., 173, 178, *210*
Aine, C. J., 223, *236*
Albert, M. L., 112, *131,* 300, *328*
Albright, T. D., 11, 17, *28, 30,* 50, 53, 55,
    58, 104, 110, *128,* 248, *267*
Alexander, M. P., 150, 151, 153, *169*
Alklman, J. M., 219, 220, *236*
Allman, J., 11, *27*
Allman, J. M., 25, *30,* 273, *293*
Allport, A., 104, *127,* 183, 208, *209,* 364,
    365, *370*
Allport, D. A., 124, *127,* 217, *235,* 318, *328*
Alpert, N. M., 271, 273, 275, 276, 283, 287,
    289, *294*
Amsterdam, J. B., 270, 279, 280, 283, 286,
    294
Andersen, R. A., 283, *292*
Anderson, C., 307, *329*
Angelergues, R., 332, *356*
Anker, S., 243, *265*
Arehart, D. M., 253, *265*

B

Arguin, M., 155, 158, *168,* 184, *209*
Armstrong, D. L., 249, *265*
Aslin, R. M., 246, 247, 252, *265*
Atkinson, J., 243, 260, *265, 266*
Atwater, J. D., 255, *265*
Audet, T., 363, 364, *370*

B

Baddeley, A. D., 46, *58*
Badgio, P. C., 155, 158, *170*
Baldwin, B. A., 12, *29,* 55, *59,* 110, *129*
Banks, M. S., 241, *265*
Barbieri, C., 178, 184, 187, *209, 210*
Barlow, H. B., 55, *58,* 106, *130*
Baron, J., 220, *235*
Baron, R. J., 34, *58*
Barton, M., 290, *293*
Bartrip, J., 263, *266*
Bateman, A., 70, *100*
Bauer, R. M., 79, *98,* 113, *127,* 320, *328,*
    332, 333, 337, 338, 340, 343, 345, 354,
    355, 356
Baxter, D., 178, 182, *209*
Bay, E., 19, *27,* 105, *127*

Baylis, G. C., 50, 52, 55, *58, 59,* 109, *131,* 138, *146*
Baynes, K., 324, *328*
Beaumont, J. G., 24, *27*
Becker, C. A., 116, *127*
Becker, L. E., 249, *265*
Behrman, M., 302, *328*
Behrmann, M., 176, 180, 182, 184–186, 192, 198, 202, *209, 212,* 224–226, *235, 237,* 367–379, *370*
Bender, D. B., 104, 110, *129*
Bender, M. B., *98,* 105, *127*
Benson, D. F., 67, *98,* 105, *131*
Benson, P. J., 35, 50–52, 55, 57, *59, 60,* 91, *100*
Benton, A. L., 117, *127, 355*
Benzing, L., 184, *213*
Bergen, J. R., 155, *168*
Bernardo, K. L., 249, *265*
Berti, A., 106, *127,* 178, *209,* 364, 365, *370*
Besner, D., 167, *169,* 305, *329*
Bettucci, D., 35, *59,* 91, *100, 127*
Bevan, R., 50–52, 55, 57, *60*
Biederman, I., 35, 41, *58,* 72, *98,* 133, *146,* 279, *292*
Bienfang, D. C., 21, *31*
Bisiach, E., 106, *127,* 173–175, 178, 182, *209,* 272, *293,* 366, *370*
Black, S., 149, 150, 152, 167, *168,* 367–369, *370*
Black, S. E., 173, 174, 176, 178, 180, 182, 184–186, *209,* 301, 302, *328*
Blume, H. W., 175, *213*
Blumstein, S. E., 231, *237*
Bodamer, J., 55, *58,* 106, *127,* 332, *355*
Bogen, J. E., 109, *129, 356*
Bogyo, L. C., 317, *330*
Bolgert, F., 333, *357*
Bolozky, S., 224, *238*
Bonforte, S., 231, *239*
Bonito, V., 178, *210*
Bonnet, C., 75, *99*
Borkowski, J. G., 117, *127*
Bornstein, B., 111, *127*
Bötzel, L., 24, *27*
Boucart, M., 73, 75, 76, *99, 100,* 337, *356*
Bourbon, W. T., 291, *293*
Bourke, P. A., 217, *235*
Bower, G. H., 290, *293*
Bowers, D., 175, *211*
Boyes-Braem, P., 106, *131*
Boylan, A., 229, *238,* 250, *267*

Brandt, J. P., *128*
Brennan, C., 229, *238*
Breton, F., 333, *357*
Briand, K. A., 157, *168*
Brigell, M. G., 17, *27*
Britten, K. H., 252, *267, 268*
Broadbent, D. E., 183, *209,* 217, *235*
Broadbent, W. H., 103, *127*
Brody, B. A., 290, *293*
Broennimann, R., 53, *60*
Bronson, G. W., 242, 243, 246, *265*
Brown, W. P., 118, *127*
Bruce, C., 11, *28,* 50, 53, 55, *58,* 104, 110, *128*
Bruce, V., 46, *58,* 335, 346, 347, 348, 351–354, *355*
Brunn, J. L., 149–151, 153, 167, 168, *170, 209,* 225, *235,* 367, 368, *370*
Bruyer, R., 63, *99,* 105, *127,* 333, 334, 346, *355*
Bub, D., 70, *99,* 184, 189, *209,* 220, *235,* 301, 302, *328,* 363, 364, *370*
Bub, D. N., 149, 150, 152, 167, *168*
Buchanon, D., 150, *170*
Buchsbaum, M. S., 219, 221, *237,* 288, *295*
Buchtel, H. A., 178, *109*
Budin, C., 112, *129*
Bullier, J., 18, *28*
Bundesen, C., 277, *295*
Buonanno, F. S., 271, 273, 275, 276, 283, 287, 289, *294*
Burkhalter, A., 249, *265*
Burton, A. M., 346–348, 353–354, *355*
Bushnell, D., 17, 18, *27*
Bushnell, I. W. R., 243, *265*
Bushnell, M. C., 219, *239*
Butter, C. M., 174, 178, *209*
Butters, N., 290, *293*

C

Caan, W., 35, *60,* 138, *146, 370*
Calabresi, P., 229, *238*
Callahan, J., 37, *58*
Calvanio, R., 119, *129,* 135, *146,* 150, 151, *169,* 282, *293,* 321, *329*
Campbell, R., 15, *27,* 108, *128*
Campion, J., 16, 19, *27,* 105, *127*
Canfield, R. L., 253, *265*
Cantwell, D., 231, *239*
Capitani, E., 174, *209*

Caplan, B., 176, *209*
Caplan, D., 70, *99*
Caplan, L. R., 150, *168,* 300, *328*
Caramazza, A., 149, 150, 155, 156, 159, 165, *169, 170,* 181, 184, *210, 213*
Carey, D. P., 19, *29,* 112, *129*
Carman, G. J., 25, *30*
Carr. T. H., 166, *168,* 220, 226, *238,* 343, *355, 356*
Carson, R. E., 180, *211*
Casey, B. J., 261, *267*
Cavanagh, P., 155, 158, *168,* 279, *293*
Cave, C. B., 272, 276, 287, *294*
Cave, K. R., 153, 157, *168, 171,* 277, *293,* 337, 351, *356*
Celesia, C. G., 17, 18, *27*
Chabris, C. F., 271, 273, 275, 276, 283, 287, 289, *294*
Chain, F., 111, *129*
Chakravarty, I., 36, *58*
Chambers, D., 284, *293*
Chan, F., 249, *265*
Charcot, J. M., 119, *128*
Charles, E. R., 7, 8, *29, 30*
Chase, P., 39, 40, 41, 46, 47, *60,* 123, *130*
Cheesman, J., 321, *328,* 350, *355,* 364, *370*
Chertkow, H., 70, *99,* 220, *235*
Chitty, A. J., 50–53, 55, 57, *60*
Choi, A. Y., 21, *31*
Christen, L., 109, *129, 356*
Clark, C. R., 233, *236*
Clarkson, M. G., 246, *267*
Cleton, P., 176, 180, 182, *213*
Clifton, R. K., 246, *267*
Clohessy, A. B., 229, *236,* 260, *265*
Clowes, M., 78, *99*
Cohen, A., 182, 203, *212,* 222, 229, *236, 238,* 289, *295*
Cohen, J., 176, *210, 265*
Cohen, L. B., 242, 262, *265*
Cohen, Y., 260, *267*
Colby, C. L., 4, 6, 21, *28*
Coldren, J. T., 255, *265*
Cole, M., 107, *128*
Collins, A. M., 124, *128*
Collins, R. C., 232, *236*
Colombo, A., 175, *210*
Colombo, J., 255, *265*
Coltheart, M., 124, *128,* 150, 167, *168, 169,* 305, 317, *328, 329*
Compton, P., 226–228, *236*
Condry, H., 252, *267*

Conel, J. L., 245, 248, 249, *266*
Cooper, L. A., 269, *296*
Cope, P., *29*
Corbett, J., 8, *28*
Corbett, J. J., 105, *131*
Corbetta, M., 175, *210,* 218, 219, 232, *236*
Cornacchia, L., 175, *209*
Coslett, H. B., 149, 150, 152, 168, *169,* 175, *211,* 299, 302, 303, 314, 318, 321, 323–325, 337, *329, 355*
Costello, A. D., 178, 180, *210*
Covey, E., 11, *28*
Cowey, A., 4, 7–9, 11, 15–23, *27, 28, 29, 31,* 113, *129,* 248, 250, *266*
Coyette, F., 63, *99*
Crinella, F., 231, *239*
Crook, J. M., 8, *28*
Cubelli, R., 178, *210*
Cummings, J. L., 109, *129, 356*
Cunningham, V. J., *29*
Cutting, J. E., 279, *293*

D

Daffner, K. R., 173, 178, *210*
Damasio, A., 8, *28,* 135, *146*
Damasio, A. R., 104, 105, 109, 125, *128, 131,* 135, *146,* 320, 325, *329, 330,* 332–334, 336, 345, 346, *355, 357*
Damasio, H., 8, *28,* 104, 109, 125, *128, 329,* 332, *355*
Daniel, P. M., 4, *28*
Danta, G., 21, *28*
Dasheiff, R. M., 272, *293*
Davelaar, E., 167, *169,* 305, *329*
Davidson, D. L. W., 35, *60,* 91, *100*
Davis, D. N., 46, *61*
Dawson, R. J. M., 78, *100*
Dean, P., 19, *27*
Debruille, B., 333, *357*
Deelman, B. G., 336, *357*
DeFalco, F. A., 150, *169*
Degos, J. D., 178, *212*
De Haan, E., 19, *28,* 106, 108, 113, 115–117, 121, *128, 130, 132,* 178, *214,* 320, *330,* 334–346, 348–352, 354, *355, 356, 357, 358*
Dehaene, S., 182, *210*
Deiber, M. P., *29*
Dejerine, J., 149, 150, *169,* 299, 323, *329*
Del Pesce, M., 175, *211*

DeMonasterio, F. M., *30*
Denny-Brown, D., 174, *210*
De Renzi, E., 111, *128*, 134, 135, *146*, 175, 178, 184, 187, *209, 210*, 283, *293*, 337, *355*
Derrington, A. M., 8, *28*
Derryberry, D., 230, *236*
de Schonen, S., 111, *128*
Desimone, R., 13, 22, *28, 30*, 50, 53, 55, *58*, 95, 96, *100*, 104, 110, *128*, 180, *210*, 222, *237*
De Tanti, A., 178, *210*
Deutsch, D., 183, *210*
Deutsch, G., 291, *293*
Deutsch, J. A., 183, *210*
de Yoe, E. A., *26*, 243, 279, *293*
Dhawan, M., 226, 227, *238*
Dienes, Z., 364, 365, *370*
Dittrich, W. H., 50, *59*
di Vita, J., 48, *61*
Dobmeyer, S., 175, *210*, 218, 232, *236*
Dobson, V., 242, *268*
Done, J., 262, *266*
Donnelly, N., 73–75, 77, 78, 90, 95, 96, *99, 100*, 337, *356*
Dore, J., 230, *236*
Downing, C. J., 95, *99*, 223, *236*
Driver, J., 183, *213*, 364, 365, *370*
Ducarne, B., 111, *129*
Duell, R. M., 232, *236*
Duensing, F., 124, *128*
Duncan, G. H., 219, *239*
Duncan, J., 78, *99*, 361, *370*
Dywan, C., 174, *209*
Dziurawiec, S., 251, 263, *266*

E

Early, T. S., 231, *236*
Eddy, J. K., 119, *128*
Edelman, S., 36, *60*
Edelstyn, N., 19, *28*
Efron, R., 67, *99*
Eisenberg, H. M., 291, *293*
Ellis, A. W., 178, 181, 183, 208, *213, 210, 214*, 225, *236*, 307, *329*, 339, 341, 342, 345–348, 352, 353, *355, 356, 358*
Ellis, H. D., 55, *59*, 109, *132*, 251, 263, *266*
Emde, R., 250, *268*
Enns, J., 79, *99*

Eriksen, C. W., 165, *169, 203, 210*
Escourolle, R., 111, *129*
Etcoff, N. L., 337, 351, *356*
Ettlinger, G., 19, *28*, 105, *128*
Evans, A., 220, *235*
Evans, A. C., 219, *239*

F

Faglioni, P., 175, 184, 187, *210*
Farah, M. J., 66, 67, 69, 72, *99*, 106, 110, 119, 123, *128, 129, 131*, 135, 139, 141, 145, *146*, 150, 151, *169*, 176, 178, 182, *209, 210*, 225, *235*, 269–272, 279, 280, 282, 287, *293, 294, 295*, 321, 326, *329*, 341, *356*, 362, 367–369, *370*
Faust, C., 111, *129*
Feinberg, T. E., 174, *210*
Feldman, M., *98*, 105, *127*
Felleman, D. J., 4, 7, 9, *28*, 273, *293*
Fendrich, R., 17, *28*
Fery, P., 176, 180, 182, *213*
Feyereisen, P., 105, *127*, 333, 334, 346, *355*
Finke, R. A., 269, 279, 289, *293, 294*
Fiore, C., 231, *239*
Fischler, I. S., 226, *236*
Florence, M., 55, *59*
Flude, B., 178, 180, 181, 183, *210*
Flude, B. M., 225, *236*, 341, *358*
Flynn, R. A., 270, 279, 280, 283, 286, *294*
Fodor, J., 342, *356*
Foote, S. L., 231, *237*
Fox, P. T., 24, *30*, 175, *213*, 218–221, 228, *236, 237, 238*, 273, 289, *293, 295*
Frackowiak, R. S. J., 25, *29, 31*, 218, 219, *236, 239*
Fragassi, N. A., 150, *169*
Francis, W. N., 202, *210*, 305, 318, *329*
Franklin, M. B., 230, *236*
Franzel, S. L., 157, *171*
Frederix, M., 63, *99*
Freeman, H., 36, *58*
Freeman, R., 337, 356, *356*
Freeman, T., 84, *99*
Freund, D. C., 303, *329*
Freyd, J. J., 280, *294*
Friberg, L., 270, *296*
Friedland, R. P., 173, 176, 190, *210*
Friedman, R. B., 150, 151, 153, *169*
Friedrich, F. J., 174–176, *213*, 222, 225, 229, *236, 238*, 289, *295*, 360, *370*

Friedrich, T. J., 187, *210*
Fries, W., 17, *28*
Frisby, J. P., 48, *59*
Friston, K. J., 25, *29, 31*, 218, 219, *236, 239*
Frith, C. D., 262, *266*
Frith, D. C., 218, 219, *236*
Frost, D., 337, *356*
Fujii, T., 178, *210*
Fukada, Y., 53, *61*
Fukatsu, R., 178, *210*
Funnell, E., 124, *127*, 318, *328*
Fusillo, M., 299, 300, *329*

G

Gabrieli, J. D. E., 272, *294*
Gadotti, A., 15, 22, *29*
Gaffan, D., 20, *28*
Gainotti, G., 71, *101*
Gardiner, M. M., 115, *129*
Gardner, H., 98, *101*, 112, *131*, 300, *328*
Gattass, R., 11, *28*
Gazzaniga, M., 287, *294*
Gazzaniga, M. S., 17, *28*, 287, *293*, 337, *357*, 361–363, *370*
Geffen, G. M., 233, *236*
Geffen, L. B., 233, *236*
Gelade, G., 77, 78, *101*, 157, *170, 171*, 183, *213*, 277, *296*
Geminiani, G., 178, *209*
Gentile, D. A., 252, *266*
Gentilini, M., 178, 184, 187, *210*
Gentilucci, M., 188, *213*
Gernsbacher, M. A., 225, *236*
Geschwind, N., 299, 300, *329*
Giard, M. H., 271, *293*
Gil de Diaz, M., 111, *128*
Gilmore, G. C., 165, *169*
Girard, P., 18, *28*
Givón, T., 225, *236*
Gizzi, M. S., 11, *30*
Glass, A. L., 119, *128*
Goldberg, M. E., 4, 6, 13, 21, *28*, 96, *101*
Goldenberg, G., 271, *294*
Goldman-Rakic, P. S., 173, *210*, 219, *236*, 284, *294*
Goldstein, K., 123, *129*
Gomori, A. J., 138, *146*
Gono, S., 174, *211*
Gonon, M. A., 271, *293*

Goodale, M. A., 19, *29*
Goodglass, H., 112, *129*
Goodman, G. S., 253, *266*
Gormican, S., 77, *101*, 222, *239*
Gould, J. L., 110, *129*
Gould, S. J., 274, *294*
Grady, C. L., 180, *211*, 232, *237*
Graf, P., 281, *294*, 320, *330*
Grailet, J. M., 63, *99*
Grainger, J., 167, *170*
Gray, M., 34, 36, 37, 43, 48, *59*
Gray, W., 106, *131*
Greenberg, J. P., 67, *98*
Greenwood, P. M., 232, *237*
Greve, K. W., 343, *356*
Griffin, J., 165, *169*
Gross, C. D., 104, 109, *128*
Gross, C. G., 11–13, 17, *28, 29, 30*, 50, 53, 55, *58*, 110, *129*, 248, *267*
Grossberg, S., 98, *99*
Grossenbacher, P., 226–228, *236*
Grossi, D., 150, *169*
Grüsser, O. -J., 24, *27*
Gum, T., 189, *209*
Gurnsey, R., 19, *29*

H

Haber, L. D., 174, *210*
Haith, M. M., 253, *265, 266*
Halgren, E., 55, *59*
Halligan, P. W., 174, *211*, 337, *356*, 365, 366, *370*
Hamilton, S. E., 271, 273, 275, 276, 283, 287–289, *294*
Hammond, K. H., 119, *128*
Hammond, K. M., 280, 282, *293*
Hampton, J. A., 115, *129*
Hanley, R., 149, 150, 152, 153, *169*
Hanley, J. R., 351, *356*
Harding, G., 73, *100*
Harding, G. F., 337, *356*
Hari, R., 9, *30*
Harries, M. H., 37, 38, 41, 43, 45–48, 50–53, 55, 57, *59, 60*
Harter, M. R., 223, 226, 227, *236*
Hartje, W., 362, *370*
Hasselmo, M. E., 50, 52, *59*
Hawkins, H. L., 223, *236*
Hawryluk, G. A., 138, *146*

Haxby, J. V., 180, *211*, 232, *237*
Hay, D. C., 106, 109, *129*, *132*, 178, *214*, 339, 342, *356*, *358*
Hazan, C., 253, *266*
Head, A. S., 34, 50, 53, 55, *60*, 110, *130*
Hécaen, H., 117, *130*, 332, *356*
Hedley-White, T., 150, *168*
Hedley-Whyte, T., 300, *328*
Heeley, D. W., 35, *59*, 91, *100*
Heilman, K. M., 173, 175, *211*, 232, 233, 237
Heit, G., 55, *59*
Held, R., 250, *266*, 337, *356*
Hellawell, D., 113, 115–117, *132*, 335, 337, 345, 346, *358*
Hellawell, D. J., 179, *214*
Henderson, L., 149, *169*
Henik, A., 225, *236*, 263, *267*
Hercovitch, P., 180, *211*
Hersh, H., 165, *169*
Heywood, C. A., 7–9, 11, 15, 19, 20, 22, *27*, *28*, *29*, 113, *129*
Hietanen, J. K., 50–52, 55, *59*, *60*
Hillis, A. E., 176, 181, *210*
Hillyard, S. A., 223, 226, *237*
Hilton, R. C., 21, *28*
Hinton, D., 48, *59*
Hinton, G. E., 82, *99*, 184, *211*, *212*, 324, *329*
Hirsch, H. V. B., 251, *266*
Hobson, J. A., 234, *237*
Hoffman, J. E., 158, *169*, 203, *210*
Hofstader, D. R., 55, *59*
Holmes, G., 88, *99*, 121, *129*
Holtzman, J. D., 287, *293*
Holtzman, P., 287, *294*
Hood, B., 243, 260, *265*, *266*
Hood, R., 253, *268*
Horenstein, S., 174, *210*
Horn, L. C., 337, *356*
Horowitz, B., 180, *211*
Horwitz, G., 287, 288, *294*
Houck, M. R., 158, *169*
Howard, D., 71, *99*, 301, 321, 322, *329*
Howell, J., 149, 150, 152, 167, *168*, 301, *328*
Howes, D., 300, *328*
Hubel, D. H., 8, *29*, *31*, 97, *100*, 228, *237*
Hudson, P. T. W., 226, *238*
Humphrey, G. K., 19, 48, *29*, *59*
Humphreys, G. W., 41, 48, 49, 57, *59*, 64–67, 69, 70, 72–79, 82, 84–86, 90, 91, 95, 96, *99*, *100*, *101*, 105, *129*, 135,

146, 157, *170*, 174, 176, 178, 180, 182, *211*, *213*, 303, 337, *330*, 344, *356*
Hurlbert, A. C., *29*
Hurtig, R., 334, *357*
Huttenlocher, P. R., 249, *266*
Hyvarinen, J., 283, *294*
Hyvarinen, L., 9, *30*

I

Ikeuchi, K., 36, *59*
Imhof, H. -G., 109, *129*, *356*
Inhoff, A. W., 229, *238*, 289, *295*
Inzhagi, M., 178, *210*
Ionasescu, Y., 300, *329*
Ishiai, S., 174, *211*
Isono, H., 8, *30*

J

Jackson, J. H., 263, *266*
Jackson, M., 124, 125, *131*
Jakobson, L. S., 19, *29*
James, M., 41, *61*, 67, 72, *101*
James, W., 217, *237*
Janer, K. W., 219, *237*
Jeeves, M. A., 34, 50, 53, 55, *60*, 110, *130*
Jeffreys, D. A., 24, *29*
Joanette, Y., 158, *168*
Job, R., 71, *101*
Johnsen, J. A., 284, *295*
Johnson, D., *131*
Johnson, M. H., 228, 229, *237*, 242–259, 263, *266*, *267*
Johnson, R. S., 91, *100*
Johnston, J. C., 142, *146*
Johnston, R. A., 35, *59*, 346, 347, 348, 352–354, *355*
Jolicoeur, P., 48, *59*, 281, *294*
Jonasson, J. T., 167, *169*, 305, *329*
Jones, K., 112, *129*
Jones-Gotman, M., 117, *129*
Jordan, T. R., 35, *59*, 91, *100*
Judd, T., 98, *101*
Julesz, B., 155, *168*

K

Kaji, S., 55, *61*
Kamaya, T., 174, *211*

Kaplan, E., 8, *30*
Karmiloff-Smith, A., 249, *266*
Karnath, H. -O., 360, 362, *370*
Karnath, O. H., 174, *211*
Kartsounis, L., 66, 72, 97, *100*
Kawano, K., 55, *61*
Kay, J., 149, 150, 152, 153, *169, 170,* 302, 321, 323, *329*
Keele, S. W., 75, *100*
Keil, F. C., 124, *129*
Kendrick, K. M., 12, *29,* 55, *59,* 110, *129*
Kenealy, P., 24, *27*
Kennard, C., 25, *29, 31,* 218, *239*
Keyes, A. L., 226, 227, *236*
Kimura, I., 178, *210*
Kinsbourne, M., 141, *146,* 150, 151, *169,* 175, 176, 180, 188, *211,* 321, *329*
Kirsch, N. L., 174, *209*
Kisley, A., 250, *268*
Kisvarday, A. F., 17, *29*
Kleefield, J., 175, *213*
Kleffner, D., 252, *268*
Klein, B., 112, *129*
Klein, K. L., 135, *146*
Klein, R. M., 157, *168*
Koenderink, J. J., 34, 37, *59*
Koenig, O., 270, 278, 279, 282–284, 290, *294, 295*
Kogure, K., 178, *210*
Kolb, B., 173, *211*
Konorski, J., 55, *59,* 125, *129, 146*
Koriat, A., 151, *169*
Kosslyn, S. M., 269–291, *293, 294, 295*
Kozlowski, L. T., 279, *293*
Krauskopf, J., 8, *28*
Kreindler, A., 300, *329*
Kroll, J. F., 123, *129*
Kucera, H., 202, *210,* 305, 318, *329*
Kurtzberg, D., 243, *268*

Lange, J., 118, *129*
Lange-Malecki, B., 8, *28*
Lappin, J., 150, *170*
Larsen, A., 277, *295*
Larson, W. L., 21, *30*
Laterre, C., 105, *127,* 333, 334, 346, *355*
Latto, R. M., 17, *27*
Latz, E., 250, *268*
Lavender, A., 43, 45, *59*
Lawler, K. A., 23, *29*
Lecours, A. R., 363–365, *370*
LeDoux, J. E., 337, *357,* 361–363, *370*
Lee, B. B., 8, *28, 29*
Lee, K., 222, *238*
LeMay, M., 21, *31*
Lennie, P., 8, *28*
Leonard, C. M., 55, *58,* 138, *146*
LePlane, D., 178, *212*
Levine, D. N., 105, 119, *129,* 135, *146,* 150, 151, *169, 293, 295,* 321, *329*
Lewis, T. L., 243, *267*
Lewontin, R. C., 274, *294*
Lhermitte, F., 111, *129*
Liddle, P. F., 218, 219, *236*
Lissauer, H., 64, 66, 67, 71, *100*
Livingstone, M. S., 8, *29,* 97, *100,* 104, *129*
Logan, G. D., 217, *237*
Logothetis, N. K., 7, 8, 15, *29, 30*
Looker, S., 43, 47, 48, *60*
Loomis, J. M., 165, *169*
Lowe, D. G., 33, 38, 39, 41, 50, *59,* 77, *100,* 275, 279, 280, *295*
Lowe, E. J., 354, *356*
Luck, S. A., 223, *236*
Lueck, C. J., 25, *29, 31,* 218, *239*
Lund, J., 248, *266*
Luria, A. R., 289, *295*
Luzzatti, C., 174, *209,* 272, *293*

L

LaBerge, D., 96, *100,* 162–164, *169,* 218, 219, 221, 226, 227, *237,* 288, *295*
Ladavas, E., 175, 176, 184, *211,* 232, *237*
Laguna, J. F., 323, *329*
LaLonde, M. E., 226, 227, *236*
Lamertsma, A. A., *29*
Landis, T., 15, *27,* 109, *129,* 150, *169,* 299, 300, *329, 356*
Langdon, P. M., 48, *59*

M

Macdonald, B., 25, *30*
Macko, K. A., 279, *295*
MacRae, D., 107, *129*
Maddison, S., 35, *61*
Madigan, S. A., 318, *329*
Mai, N., 21, *31*
Malhas, M. S. M., *171*
Maljkovic, V., 271, 273, 275, 276, 283, 287–289, *294*

Mangun, G. R., 223, 226, *237*
Marcar, V. L., 21, *28, 29*
Marcel, A. J., 16, *29,* 321, *329*
Marin, O. S. M., 317, *330*
Marin-Padilla, 249
Marr, D., 33–35, 38, 39, 41, 48, 50, *59,* 72, *100,* 133, *146,* 284, *295*
Marrett, A., 219, *239*
Marrett, S., 220, *235*
Marrocco, R. T., *30*
Marshall, J., 174, *211,* 337, *357*
Marshall, J. C., 124, *128, 356,* 365, 366, *370*
Marshall, W. H., 4, *31*
Marsolek, C. J., 281, 283, *294, 295*
Martin, A., 123, *129*
Martin, D., 173, 174, 176, 178, *209*
Martin, D. C., 337, *356*
Martin, K. A. C., 8, *29*
Martin, P. R., 8, *29*
Matelli, M., 188, *213*
Mathivet, E., 111, *128*
Maunsell, J. H. R., 7, 25, *29, 31,* 245, *266,* 279, 280, 282, *295*
Maurer, D., 242, 243, *267*
Mayhew, J. E. W., 48, *59*
Maylor, E. A., 257, 260, *267*
McAndrews, M. P., 337, 339, *357, 370*
McCarthy, R., 124, *131*
McCarthy, R. A., 20, *31,* 137, *146*
McCauley, C., 343, *355, 356*
McClelland, J. L., 84, *100,* 123, *130,* 142, *146,* 166, 167, *169,* 184, 185, *212, 213,* 275, 285, *295,* 346, *356,* 367, 368, *370*
McConachie, H. R., 108, *130*
McDonald, J. E., 167, *170*
McGlynn, S. M., 106, *130*
McGuinness, E., 11, *27*
McKee, J., 8, *28*
McMullen, P. A., 145, *146*
McNeil, J. E., 22, *29,* 337, *356*
McNicol, D., 339, *356*
McWeeny, K. H., 341, *358*
Meador, K. J., 186, *209*
Meadows, J. C., 332, 337, *356*
Medin, D. L., 124, *131*
Mehta, Z., 119, 121, *128, 130*
Meizen, F. M., 273, *293*
Meizin, F. M., 175, *210,* 218, 219, *236*
Merigan, W. H., 7, *29*

Merikle, P. M., 321, *328,* 344, 350, *355, 357,* 364, *370*
Mervis, C. B., 106, *131*
Mesulam, M. M., 173, 175, 178, *210, 212, 213,* 232, *237*
Metcalf, D., 250, *268*
Meyer, E., 219, *239*
Meyer, E. I., 220, *235*
Meyer, J. S., 174, *210*
Meyer, M. M., 145, *146*
Michel, F., 18, *29, 30,* 176, 198, *213*
Miezin, F., 11, *27,* 218–220, 232, *236*
Mikami, A., 8, *30*
Milberg, W., 231, *237*
Miller, R. T., 230, *236*
Miller, S. L., 226, 227, *236*
Milner, A. D., 9, 19, *29,* 34, 35, 50, 53, 55, *59, 60,* 91, *100,* 110, 117, *130*
Milner, B., 104, *129, 130,* 281, *295*
Mingolla, E., 98, *99*
Mintun, M., 219, 220, *237*
Mintun, M. A., 274, *293*
Mishkin, M., 96, *101,* 104, *131,* 180, *211, 213,* 221, *239,* 279, 280, 282, *295, 296*
Mistlin, A. J., 34, 50–53, 55, 57, *60,* 110, *130*
Mitchell, D. W., 255, *265*
Miyashita, Y., 53, *60*
Mohler, C. W., 17, *30*
Monheit, M. A., 178, *210* 362, 369, *370*
Mora, B. M., 25, *30*
Moran, J., 13, *30,* 95, *100,* 104, *128,* 180, *210,* 222, *237*
Morison, V., 243, *268*
Moriya, M., 53, *61*
Morrison, J. H., 231, *237*
Morrow, L. A., 176, 178, *210, 212,* 232, *237*
Mortara, F., 35, *60*
Mortara, R., 91, *100*
Morton, J., 166, *169,* 242, 251, 263, *266, 267*
Moscovitch, M., 176, 178, 180, 182, 184–186, 198, 202, 208, *212,* 225, *235,* 337, 339, *357,* 367–369, *370*
Movshon, J. A., 11, *30,* 252, *267*
Mozer, M. C., 167, *170,* 176, 180, 182, 183–186, 192, 195, 198, 202, 208, *209,* 225, 226, *235, 237,* 367–369, *370*
Muir, D. W., 246, *267*
Mulder, J. A., 78, *100*
Muller, H. M., 82, 84, 85, 95, *99,* 180, *211*

Mullin, J. T., 243, *265*
Mustapha, M., 223, *236*
Mutani, R., 35, *60,* 91, *100*

N

Näätänen, R., 218, *237*
Nakayama, K., 21, *31*
Nalwa, V., 50, 52, *59*
Navon, D., 90, *100,* 277, *295*
Nebes, R. D., 337, *356*
Neisser, U., 217, *237*
Newcombe, F., 8, 15, 19, *28, 29,* 63, *100,*
    104–106, 111, 113–117, 121, 124,
    125, *129, 130, 131, 132,* 178, 180,
    181, 208, *214,* 334–346, 348–352,
    355, 356, 358
Newsome, W. T., 20, 11, *30, 31,* 167, *170,*
    252, *267, 268,* 279, 280, 282, *295*
Nichelli, P., 178, *210*
Nielsen, J. M., 107, 113, 119, *130*
Nishihara, H. K., 33, 34, 38, 39, 41, 48, 50,
    59
Nissen, M. J., 233, *238*
Norman, D., 183, *212*
Norman, J., 151, *169*

O

O'Boyle, D. J., 21, *28*
O'Reilly, G., 175, *213*
Odajima, N., 174, *211*
Ogden, J. A., 175, *212*
Ogden, W. C., 233, *238*
Ohta, S., 25, *30*
Oldfield, R. C., 114, *130*
Oram, M. W., 50–52, 55, *59, 60*
Orchard-Lisle, V., 71, *99*
Orsini, A. L., 150, *169*
Ortega, J. E., 50–52, 55, *60*
Osborne-Shaefer, P., 175, *213*
Oxbury, J., 364, 365, *370*
Oxbury, S., 364, 365, *370*

P

Paap, K. R., 167, *170*
Paillard, J., 18, *30*

Paivio, A., 269, 290, *295,* 318, *329*
Pallis, C. A., 107, 111, *130, 146*
Palmer, S. E., 39, 40, 41, 46, 47, *60,* 123,
    130, 284, *295*
Pandya, D. N., 245, 249, *267,* 325, *329*
Papagno, C., 106, *127*
Papanicolaou, A. C., 291, *293*
Parasuraman, R., 232, *237*
Pardo, J. V., 219, *237*
Pardo, P. J., 219, *237*
Pare, E. B., 20, *30,* 252, *267*
Parmelee, C. M., 343, *355, 356*
Parsons, L. M., 48, *59, 60*
Pashler, H., 155, 158, *170*
Pattacini, F., 178, *210*
Paterson, R., 157, *170*
Patterson, K. E., 84, *100,* 124, *128,* 149,
    150, 152, *170,* 182, 184, *212,* 302, 321,
    323, *329*
Pearson, N., 336, 351, *356*
Pélissier, A., 149, *169*
Penfield, W., 125, *130*
Perani, D., 106, *127,* 173, 174, *209, 214*
Perez-Cruet, J., 107, *128*
Perkins, D. N., 78, *100*
Peronnet, F., 271, *293*
Perrett, D. I., 34, 35, 37, 38, 41, 43, 45–48,
    50–53, 55, 57, *59, 60, 61,* 91, *100,* 110,
    130, 138, *146, 370*
Perry, V. H., 17, *28*
Pesce, M. D., 232, *237*
Peterhans, E., 11, *31*
Peters, A. M., 319, *330*
Petersen, S. E., 24, *30,* 175, *210, 213,* 218–
    221, 228, 232, *236, 237, 238,* 256, *267,*
    289, *295*
Petronio, A., 175, *211*
Phaf, R. H., 226, *238*
Phillips, C. G., 106, *130*
Pierrard, E., 105, *127,* 333, 334, 346, *355*
Pillon, B., 111, *129*
Pinker, S., 279, *293*
Plaut, D., 184, *212*
Podgorney, P., 275, 276, 288, 289, *295*
Podreka, I., 271, *294*
Poeck, K., 150, *170*
Poggio, T., 36, *60*
Polkey, C. F., *329*
Pollatsek, A., 166, *168,* 182, *213,* 224, 225,
    238, 239, 366–368, *370*
Pomerantz, J. R., 87, *100*

Ponceau, M., 18, *30*
Poncet, M., 334, 336, 338, 344–346, 352, 353, *357*
Pöppel, E., 337, *356*
Porter, J., 21, *27*
Posner, M. I., 24, *30*, 75, *100, 130,* 175, *213,* 216, 174–176, 178, 182, 188, 203, *210, 212, 213,* 217–229, 231–233, *236, 237, 238, 239,* 243, 250, 253–260, *265, 266, 267,* 289, *295,* 342, 343, *356,* 360, 361, 366–368, *370*
Potkin, S., 231, *239*
Potter, D. D., 34, 50, 53, 55, *60,* 110, *130*
Potter, M. C., 123, *129*
Premack, D. G., 264, *267*
Presti, D., 222, *238*
Price, C. J., 74, *100*
Price, N. J., 226, 227, *236*
Prinzmetal, W., 157, *170,* 222, *238*
Proffitt, D. R., 279, *293*
Provinciali, L., 175, *211,* 232, *237*
Provost, D., 276, 287, *294*
Ptito, A., 21, *30*
Puerto, A., 35, *61*
Purpura, D. P., 245, *267*
Purpura, K., 8, *30*
Pylyshyn, Z. W., 276, 287, *295*

Q

Quillian, M. R., 124, *128*
Quinlan, P. T., 74, 78, 79, *99, 100,* 157, *170,* 184, *213*

R

Rabin, P., 151, *171*
Rabinowicz, T., 245, *267*
Rafal, R. D., 174–176, 203, *212, 213,* 222, 229, 231, *236, 238,* 263, *267,* 360, *370*
Raichle, M. E., 24, *30,* 175, *213,* 218–221, 228, 231, *236, 237, 238,* 273, 289, *293, 295*
Ramachandran, V. S., 94, *100*
Ramer, A. L. H., 230, *236*
Ramier, A. -M., 117, *130*
Rapcsak, S. Z., 323, *329*
Rapopart, S. I., 180, *211*

Rapp, B. C., 149, 150, 155, 156, 159, *170,* 184, *213*
Raskin, S. A., 110, *131*
Ratcliff, G., 63, *100,* 105, 113, 114, 119, 124, *128, 130, 131,* 176, *212, 237,* 290, *295*
Rauch, S. L., 271, 273, 275, 276, 283, 287, 289, *294*
Rayner, K., 224, *238*
Rectem, D., 105, *127,* 333, 334, 346, *355*
Reed, S. K., 284, *295*
Reeves, G., 174, *209*
Regard, M., 15, *27,* 150, *169,* 299, 300, *329*
Reiman, E., 231, *236*
Reingold, E. M., 344, *357*
Reisberg, D., 284, *293*
Renault, B., 333, *357*
Rensink, R. A., 79, *99*
Reuter-Lorenz, P. A., 149, 150–153, 167, 168, *170*
Richards, J. E., 260, 261, *267*
Richardson, A., 283, *296*
Riddoch, M. J., 41, 48, 49, *59,* 63, 64, 67, 69, 70, 72–75, 77, 78, 79, 86, 90, 91, 95, 96, *99, 100, 101,* 105, *129,* 135, *146,* 176, 180, 182, *211, 213,* 303, *330,* 337, *356*
Rizzo, M., 105, *131,* 334, *357*
Rizzolatti, G., 188, *213*
Roberts, L., 125, *130*
Robinson, D. L., 96, *101*
Rocha-Miranda, C. E., 104, 110, *129*
Rock, I., 48, *61,* 281, 284, *296*
Rockland, K. S., 245, 249, *267*
Rodman, H. R., 17, *30,* 248, *267*
Roland, P. E., 270, *296*
Rolls, E. T., 35, 50, 52, 55, *58, 59, 60, 61,* 110, *131,* 138, *146, 370*
Romero, R. D., 176, *210*
Roper-Hall, A., 35, *61*
Rosch, E., 39, 40, 46, 47, *60,* 106, 123, *130, 131*
Ross, E. D., 336, *357*
Rothbart, M. K., 228, 229, 230, *236, 237, 238,* 243, 250, 253–260, *265, 266, 267*
Rovamo, J., 9, *30*
Rubens, A. B., 105, 113, *127, 131,* 323, *329*
Rugg, M. D., 227, 228, *238*

Rumelhart, D. E., 166, *169,* 184, 185, *212,*
    213, 285, *295,* 346, *356,* 367, 368,
    370
Rusconi, M. L., 178, *209,* 366, *370* -
Russell, W., 104, *130*

S

Saffran, E. M., 149, 150, 152, 168, *169, 170,*
    299, 301–303, 307, 310, 314, 321–325,
    337, *329, 330, 355, 357*
Sai, F., 243, *265*
Saito, H., 8, *30*
Saito, H. -A., 53, *61*
Sakata, H., 35
Salapatek, P., 241,*265*
Salin, P. A., 18, *28*
Salzman, C. D., 252, *268*
Samuels, S. J., 162, *169*
Sanders, M. D., 337, *357*
Sandson, J., 226, 227, *238*
Sandstrom, D. J., 242, *268*
Santucci, R., 178, *209*
Sartori, G., 71, *101*
Saso, S., 178, *210*
Sato, S., 157, *170*
Scandolara, C., 188, *213*
Scapinello, K. E., 110, *131*
Schacter, D. L., 106, *130,* 281, *294,* 320,
    330, 337, 339, 343, *357*
Schapiro, M. B., 180, *211*
Scheerer, E., 167, *170*
Schein, S. J., 22, *30,* 104, *128,* 180, *210*
Schiepers, C., 149, *170*
Schiller, P. H., 7, 15, *29, 30,* 222, *238,* 243,
    244, *268*
Schmidt, H., 157, *171*
Schneider, W., *238*
Schomer, D. L., 175, *213*
Schultz, R. W., 117, *131*
Schvaneveldt, R. W., 167, *170*
Schwartz, M. F., 317, *330*
Schwartz, T. L., 242, *268*
Scioloto, T., 229, *238*
Segui, J., 167, *170*
Seibert, M., 36, *61*
Seidenberg, M. S., 84, *100,* 184, *212, 213*
Sejnowski, T. J., 82, *99*
Selemon, L. D., 173, *210*

Seltzer, B., 325, 326, *329*
Semenza, C., 104, *131*
Sepe, O., 150, *169*
Sergent, J., 18, 25, *30, 31,* 287, *296,* 324,
    330, 332, 334, 336, 337, 338, 344–346,
    352, 353, *357*
Seron, X., 63, *99,* 105, *127,* 333, 334, 346,
    355
Serrant, A., 150, *169*
Serrat, A., 299, 300, *329*
Servan-Schreiber, D., 262, *265*
Sethi, K., 186, *209*
Shafer, S., 36, *61*
Shallice, T., 63, *101,* 112, 119, 124, 125,
    131, 149, 150, 152, 154, 168, *170, 171,*
    184, *211, 212,* 220, *238,* 299, 301, 302,
    305, 307, 310, 314, 322–325, 337, 342,
    350, *330, 367*
Shapley, R. M., 8, *30*
Shepard, R. N., 269, 275, 276, 288–290,
    293, 295
Shields, C., 11, 15, *29*
Shiffrar, M. M., 279, *292*
Shipp, S., 14, *31*
Shoben, E. J., 115, *131*
Shulman, G. L., 175, *210,* 218, 219, 226,
    227, 232, *236, 238,* 277, *296*
Sieroff, E., 176, 182, 198, 201, *213,* 224,
    225, *239,* 366–368, *370*
Signer, M., 150, *170*
Signoret, J. -L., *31,* 333, *357*
Silveri, M. C., 71, *101*
Simpson, J. I., 6, *31*
Slater, A., 243, *268*
Smith, E. E., 124, *131*
Smith, J., 263, *267*
Smith, M. E., 55, *59*
Smith, P. A. J., 34, 50, 53, *60,* 110, *130*
Smith, Y. M., 17, *27*
Snodgrass, J. G., 112, 120, *131,* 155, 157,
    170
Snyder, A. Z., 218, 228, *238,* 289, *295*
Snyder, C. R. R., 116, *130,* 341, 343, *356*
Somers, M., 243, *268*
Somogyi, P., 17, *29*
Soso, M. J., 272, *293*
Sousa, A. P. B., 11, *28*
Souther, J., 90, *101*
Sperber, R. D., 343, *355, 356*
Sperling, G., 159, *170,* 223, *239,* 277, *296*

Spiers, P. A., 175, *213*
Spitz, R. V., 252, *268*
Spreen, O., 117, *127, 131*
Squire, L. R., 281, *295*
Stacey, C. B., 174, *210*
Stachowiak, F. J., 150, *170*
Staller, J., 150, *170*
Stanley Thompson, H., 105, *131*
Stechler, G., 250, *268*
Steiner, M., 271, *294*
Stelmach, G., 18, *30*
Sternberg, S., 191, *213*, 219, *239*, 276, *296*
Sterzi, R., 175, *209*
Stevens, K. A., 98, *101*
Stoerig, P., 16–18, *27, 28, 29, 31*, 248, *266*
Strawson, C., 212, *235*
Strypstein, E., 105, *127*, 333, 334, 346, *355*
Sugushita, M., 174, *211*
Swanson, J. M., 231, *239*
Sykes, M., 157, *171*
Szalai, J. P., 173, 176, 178, *209*

T

Talbot, J. D., 219, *239*
Talbot, S. A., 4, *31*
Tanaka, J. W., 141, *146*
Tanaka, K., 8, *30*, 53, *61*
Taylor, *330*
Taylor, A. M., 39, 40, *61*, 63, 67, *101*, 105, *131*
Taylor, D. A., 165, *170*, 363, *370*
Temple, C. M., 112, *131*
Tennes, K., 250, *268*
Terazzi, E., 35, *60*, 91, *100*
Teuber, H. -L., 123, *130*, 354, *357*
Thomas, S., 46, 50–52, 55, 57, *60, 61*
Thompson, W. L., 271, 273, 275, 276, 283, 287–289, *294*
Thorpe, S. J., 35, 36, *61*
Thurstone, L. L., *131*
Tieman, D. G., 251, *266*
Tieman, S. B., 251, *266*
Timosa, N., 251, *266*
Tipper, S. P., 181, 183, *209, 213*
Toleikis, S. C., 16–18, *27*
Tosoni, C., 21, *30*
Townsend, J., 83, 86, *101*

Townsend, J. T., 155, 157, *170*
Tranel, D., 125, *128*, 320, *330*, 332, 336, 345, 346, *355, 357*
Treisman, A. M., 77, 78, 90, *101*, 155, 157, *170, 171*, 183, *213*, 222, *239*, 277, *296*, 361, *370*
Tricklebank, J., 243, *265,*
Trolle, E., 107, *129*
Troscianko, T., 73, *100*, 337, *356*
Tucker, D., 226–228, *236*
Tumosa, N., 251, *266*
Tweedy, J., 110, *131*
Tzelgov, J., 225, *236*

U

Ullman, S., 36, *61*, 279, *296*
Umilta, C., 175, 178, *211, 212*
Ungerleider, L. G., 11, *28*, 96, *101*, 104, *128, 131*, 180, *210, 211, 213*, 221, *239*, 279, 280, 282, *295, 296*

V

Vaina, L. M., 21, *31*
Valberg, A., 8, *28*
Valburg, A., 8, *29*
Valenstein, E., 173, 175, *211*
Valentine, T., 46, *58*, 335, *355*
Vallar, G., 106, *127*, 173, 175, *209, 214*
Van Den Abell, T., 232, 233, *237*
Van Den Roovaart, B. P., *171*
Van der Heijden, A. H. C., *171*, 226, *238*
Vanderwart, M., 112, 120, *131*
van doorn, A. J., 37, *59*
Van Essen, D. C., 4, 7, 9, 25, *28, 31*, 219, 220, *236*, 243, 245, *266, 268*, 273, 279, *293*
van Hoesen, G. W., 109, *128*, 135,*146*, 332, *355*
van Hof-van Duin, J., 242, *268*
van Zomeren, A. H., 336, *357*
Vargha-Khadem, F., *329*
Vaughan, H. G., 243, *268*
Vecera, S., 260, *265*
Verfaillie, M., 333, 338, *355*
Villemure, J. -G., 332, 337, *357*
Volpe, B. T., 337, *357*, 361–364, *370*

von Cramon, D., 21, *31*
von der Heydt, R., 11, *31*
Von Gierke, S., 272, 287, *294*
Vu, B., 173, 176, 178, *209*

W

Walker, J. A., 174, 175, 176, 187, *210, 213,*
    222, *236,* 360, *370*
Wallace, M. A., 149, 150, 153, *169,* 321,
    326, *329,* 362, 369, *370*
Wang, G., 270, 279, 280, 283, 286, *294*
Wapner, W., 98, *101,* 112, *131*
Warach, J., 282, *295*
Warrington, E. K., 20, 22, *29, 31,* 39, 40, 41,
    61, 63, 67, 72, 97, *100, 101,* 105, 112,
    119, 124, *131,* 137, 138, *146,* 149–152,
    154, *169, 171,* 176, 178, 180, 182, *209,*
    210, 211, 214, 302, 305, 321, 322, *329,*
    330, 337, 351, *356, 357*
Watson, J. D. G., 25, *31,* 218, *239*
Watson, R. T., 173, 175, *211*
Wattam-Bell, J., 243, *265*
Waxman, A. M., 36, *61*
Webb, W., 150, *170*
Weinstein, E. A., 173, 176, 190, *210*
Weintraub, S., 173, 175, 178, *210, 213*
Weise, S. B., 271, 273, 275, 276, 283, 287,
    289, *294*
Weiskrantz, L., 16, 19, *27, 31,* 320, *330,*
    337, *357*
Weiss, R., 37, *58*
Welch, J., 179, *214*
Well, A. D., 224, *238*
Wentworth, N., 253, *268*
Wessinger, M., 17, *28*
Whelan, H., 175, *211*
Whishaw, I. Q., 173, *211*
Whitehead, R., 223, *239*
Whitteridge, D., 4, *28*
Wiesel, T. N., 8, *31*
Wilbrand, H., 54, *61,* 119, *131*
Wilkinson, F., 15, 21, *28*

Willmes, K., 271, *294*
Wilson, B., 182, *212*
Wilson, J., 277, *296*
Wingfield, A., 114, *130*
Wolfe, J. M., 153, 157, *171*
Wong, A. B., 178, *210*
Wood, M. M., 249, *265*
Woodruff, G., 264, *267*
Woodward, D. P., 223, *236*
Wurst, S. A., 223, *239*
Wurtz, R. H., 13, 17, 20, *28, 30,* 96, 97,
    101, 252, *267*

Y

Yaginuma, M., 174, *211*
Yamada, T., 8, *28*
Yamadori, A., 112, *131,* 300, *328*
Yamane, S., 55, *61*
Yang, L., 225, *236*
Yarbus, A. L., 286, *296*
Yarmey, A. D., 110, *131*
Yasuda, M., 8, *30*
Yin, R. K., *131*
Yonas, A., 252, *266*
Young, A. W., 19, *28,* 106, 109, 113, 115–
    117, *129, 130, 132,* 178, 179, 181, 183,
    208, *210, 214,* 225, *236,* 307, 320, *329,*
    330, 334–354, *355, 356, 357, 358*
Youpa, D., 231, *239*
Yuille, J. C., 318, *329*

Z

Zaidel, E., 318, 319, *330*
Zajonc, R. B., 343, *358*
Zatorre, R. J., 21, *30*
Zeki, S., 8, 9, 11, 14, 15, 22, 25, *29, 31,*
    106, *130,* 218, *239*
Zeki, S. M., *296*
Zeltin, M., 104, *131*
Zihl, J., 21, *31*

Subject Index

A

achromotopsia 8–9, 11, 15, 22, 25
alexia, pure 138–141, 149–171
  as a low level perceptual deficit 150
  as a pattern recognition deficit 150–152
  as a word-specific deficit 152
  implicit reading in 152, 299–330, 337
anterior attention system 175, 219, 227, 235
apperceptive visual agnosia 19, 64, 66–69, 72
apraxia 35, 36
associative visual agnosia 64, 69–71, 72, 74,
  133–140

B

binding problem 283–284
blindsight 16–18, 235, 248, 337

C

category specific agnosia 20, 112–127, 133–
  145
characteristic views 34–36, 43, 48, 51
color perception 23, 47, 218, 226 *see also*
  color-selective cells, achromotopsia
color-selective cells 7, 9, 11, 13, 14
covert face recognition 16, 18, 320, 331–354

D

depth disparity-selective cells 7, 9, 14, 21
disconnection syndrome 15, 20, 103, 125,
  149, 303–304, 339, 346
dorsal visual system 12, 14, 23, 35, 96–97,
  221, 282, 283–284, 345
drawings by agnosic patients 64–66, 121–122,
  124

E

early versus late selection in visual attention
  183–186, 208, 217–239, 361–370
event related potentials (ERP) 18, 23–24, 26,
  226, 243, 271, 333, 338
extinction 174, 178, 337, 360, 361–365

F

face inversion effect 110, 142
face perception 24, 25 *see also* face cells, face
  inversion effect, prosopagnosia
face recognition, development of 263–264
face cells 11, 14, 15, 22, 47, 50–58, 110, 138
feature integration
  in normal reading 225
  in visual agnosia 75–88, 156–158

G

galvanic skin response (GSR) 332–333, 338
grandmother cell 12–13

I

implicit reading *see* alexia, pure
inside-out cortical development 244–245

L

letter recognition 149–171
letter-by-letter reading *see* alexia, pure
levels of processing in vision 3, 20, 54, *67,*
    71–72, 145, 181, 348–351, 368
living and nonliving things, agnosia for *see*
    category-specific agnosia

M

magnetic resonance imaging (MRI) 25, 26
magnetoencephalography (MEG) 26
magnocellular visual system 5–9, 12, 244
two and one-half (2.5)-dimensional sketch 50
mental imagery 18, 24, 39, 46, 118–122,
    269–296, 318
    image inspection 276–289
    image maintenance 289–290
    image segmentation 66–69, 183, 194
    image transformation 290–291
    relation to perception 270–274
modularity 9, 26, 27, 152, 217, 223
motion perception, disorders of 9, 20–21, 23,
    218, 251–252
motion-selective cells 7, 9, 17, 251–252

N

neglect 9, 14, 23, 217–239, 272, 337
    and reading 173–214, 366–368
    implicit perception in, 359–370
    neuropathology of 173, 175, 231–234, 360
neural network models 12, 13
    of category-specific knowledge 123
    of face recognition 346
    of reading and attention 184–186, 191–202

    of visual search 82–87
neuroimaging *see* event related potentials
    (ERP), magnetic resonance imaging
    (MRI), magnetoencephalography (MEG),
    and positron emission tomography (PET)
norepinephrine (NE) in visual attention 231–
    234

O

object agnosia *see* visual object agnosia
object-centered representation 12, 33–58, 181–
    182, 263
object-selective cells 53, 55
optic aphasia 69, 303–304, 323, 325
orientation-selective cells 7, 9, 53

P

parallelism in visual processing 5, 14, 243–
    244
parietal cortex *see* dorsal visual system
parvocellular visual system 5–9
positron emission tomography (PET) 23, 24–
    25, 26, 218–223, 226, 270, 271
posterior attention system 175, 219–235
preferential inspection paradigm 41–45, 47, 48
priming
    perceptual 164–166
    repetition 225–228
    semantic 116–117, 225–228, 335–336,
        338, 349, 365
principal axis 39, *40,* 41, 43, 47, *49*
prosopagnosia 8, 9, 12, 15, 16, 18, 19, 20,
    21, 22, 23, 54, 55, 58, 79, 106–107,
    109–112, 133–138, 143–144, 320, 332
    covert recognition *see* covert face recogni-
        tion
    developmental 108–109

R

retinotopic organization 4, 17
right hemisphere reading 310, 317–320, 324

S

SERR model 82–92, 95

simultanagnosia 151
  dorsal simultanagnosia 72, 73
  ventral simultanagnosia 72
striate cortex 16, 18, 25
structural description 34, 140–145

U

usual and unusual views 39, *40,* 41, 47, 48, *49,* 67

V

ventral visual system 14, 35, 96–97, 221, 282, 283–284, 345
viewer-centered description, 33–58, 263
viewpoint consistency constraint 38, 41
viewpoint independent description *see* viewer-centered representation

visual attention 13–14, 72, 217–239
  and mental imagery 288–289
  and reading 173–214
  development 228–231, 241–268
visual awareness
  in face recognition 331–354
  in visual attention 359–370
  in reading *see* alexia, implicit reading
visual imagery 18
visual object agnosia 9, 19, 35, 36, 63–98, 104–112, 133–140
visual search
  in pure alexia 155–162
  in visual agnosia 75–98, 155–162

W

word superiority effect 141, 168, 182, 185, 191, 225, 301